BVLGARI
Treasures of Rome

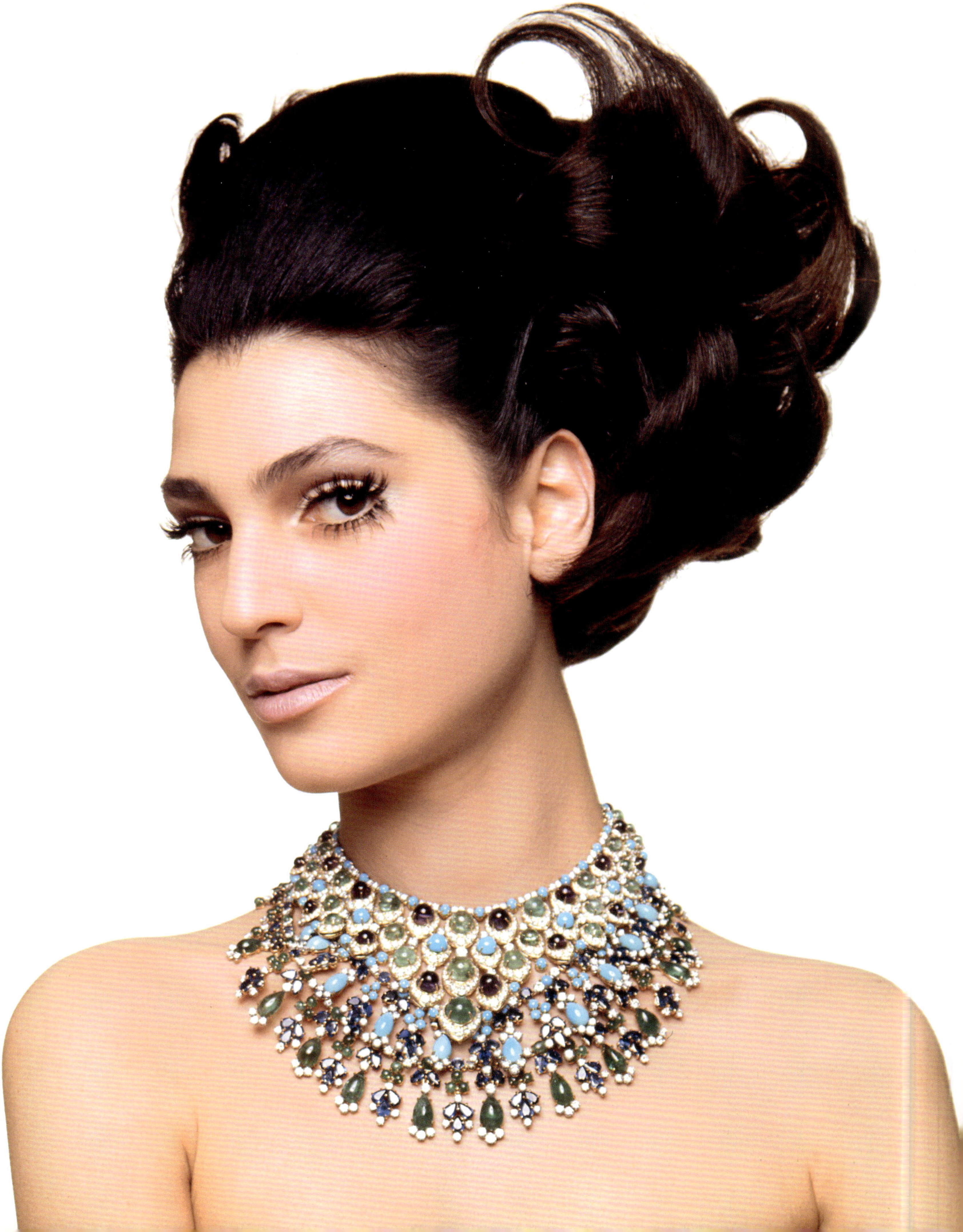

BVLGARI
Treasures of Rome

Vincent Meylan

ACC ART BOOKS

ISBN: 978 185149 879 6

British Library Cataloguing-in-Publication Data
A catalogue record for this book is available from the British Library

The author and publisher gratefully acknowledge the permission granted to reproduce the copyright material in this book. Every effort has been made to trace copyright holders and to obtain their permission for the use of copyright material. The publisher apologises for any errors or omissions in the text and would be grateful if notified of any corrections that should be incorporated in future reprints or editions of this book.

Every effort has been made to secure permission to reproduce the images contained within this book, and we are grateful to the individuals and institutions who have assisted in this task. Any errors or omissions are entirely unintentional, and the details should be addressed to the publisher.

Frontispiece: *Benedetta Barzini wearing a spectacular multi-gem Bulgari bib necklace, photograph © Gian Paolo Barbieri 1968.*
Page 5: *Bulgari cabochon emerald link bracelet with diamonds, rubies and emerald and ruby beads. Private collection.*
Page 6: *Bulgari multi-gem brooch and matching ear clips. FD Gallery Collection, New York.*
Page 296: *Bulgari diamond and Burmese ruby cluster ear clips, c.1950. FD Gallery Collection, New York.*

MIX
Paper from responsible sources
FSC® C013123

Printed in Italy
for ACC Art Books Ltd., Woodbridge, Suffolk, England

www.accartbooks.com

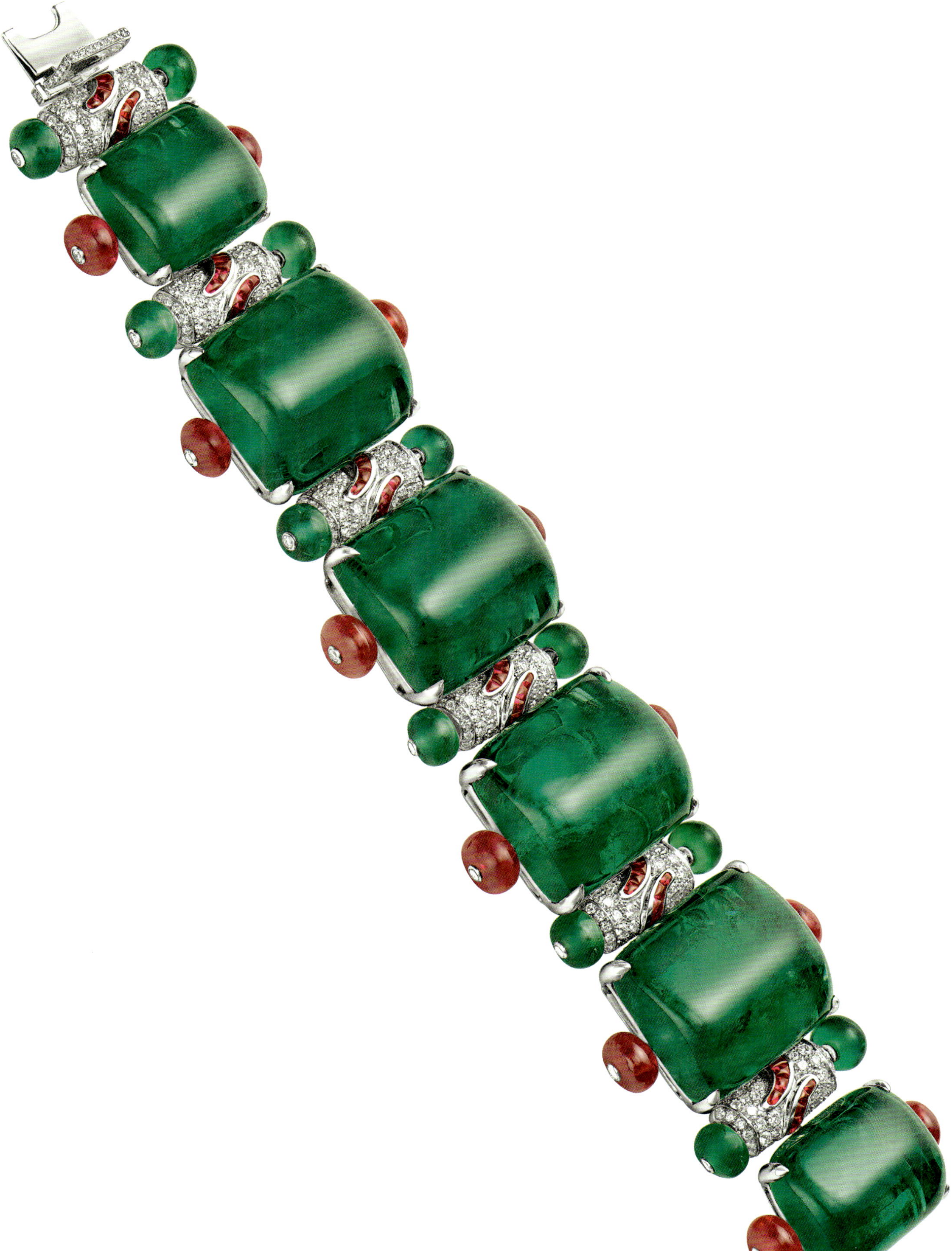

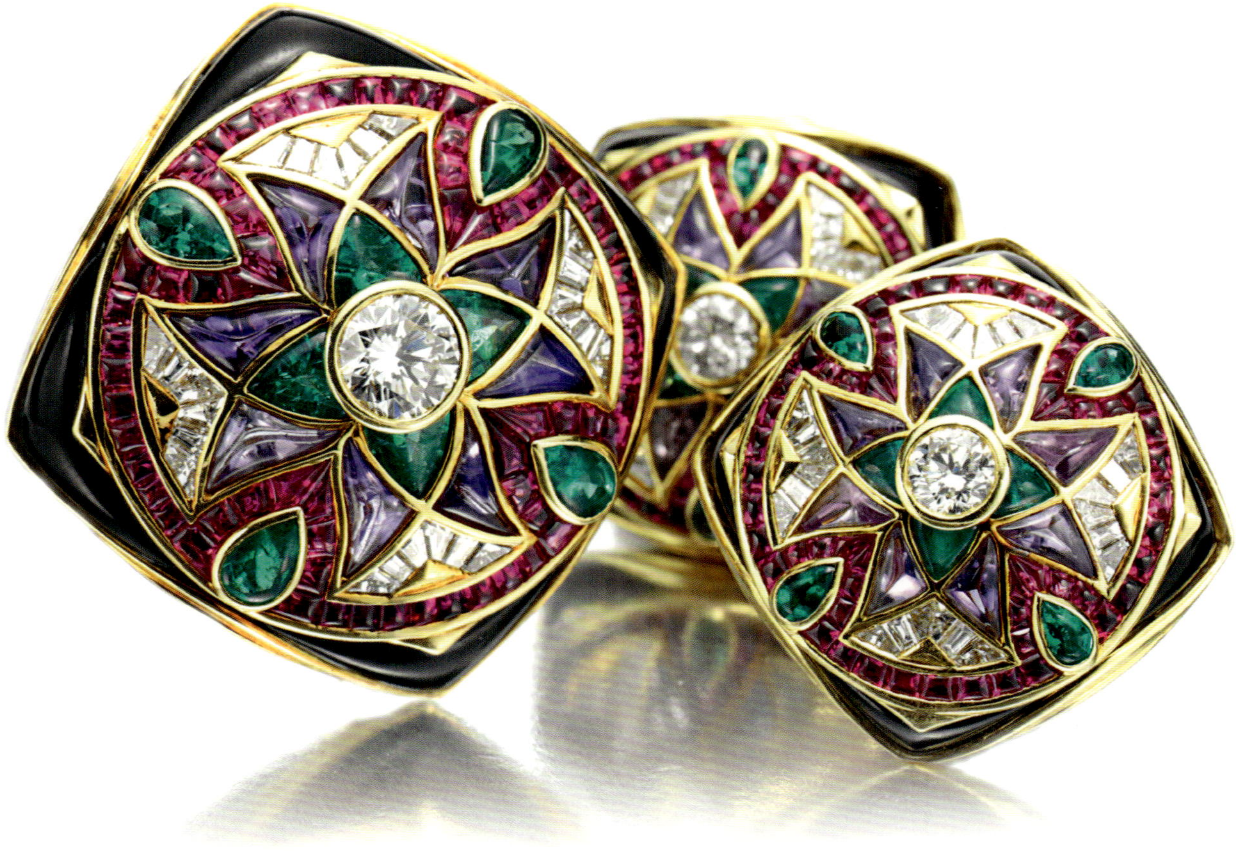

Contents

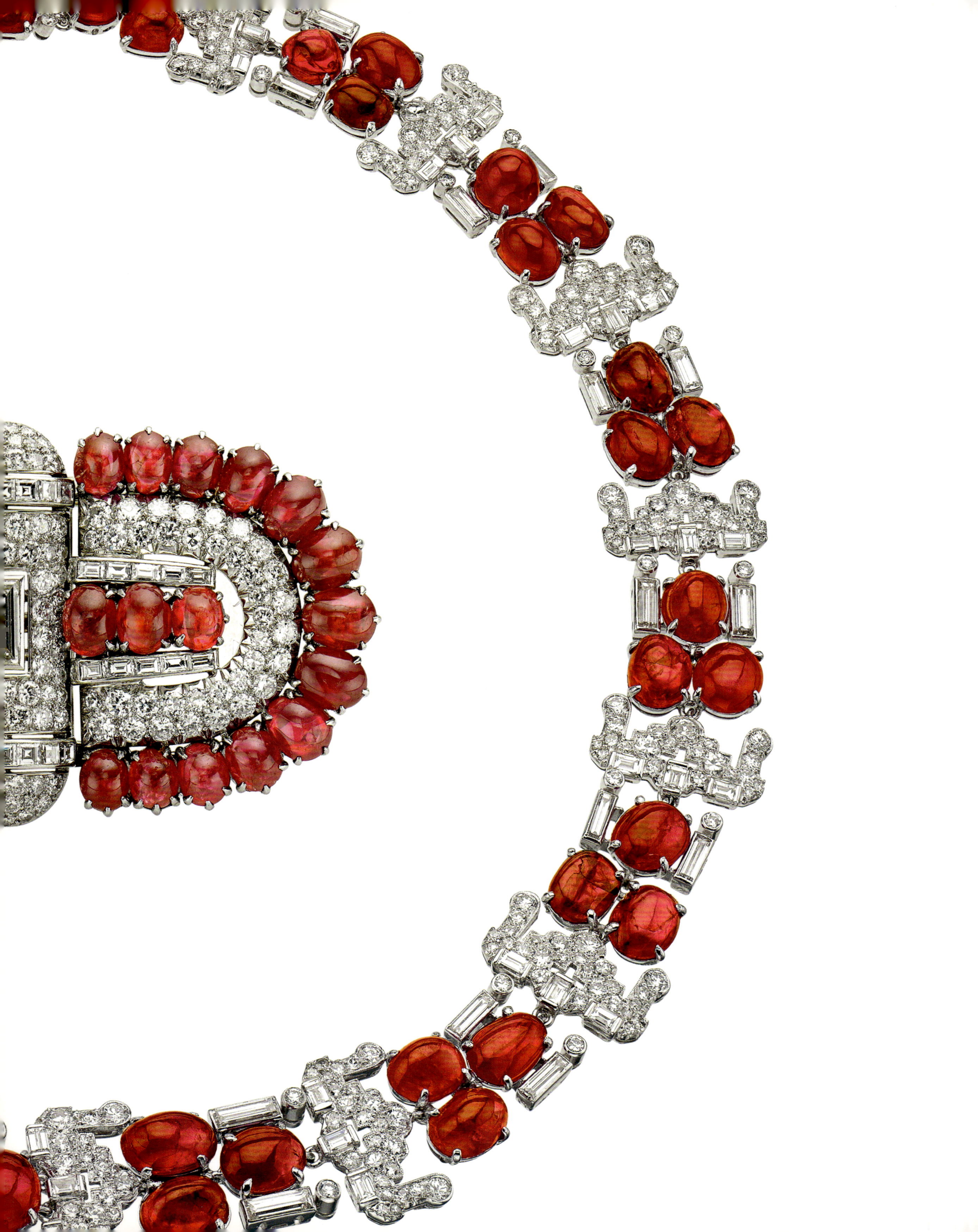

Chapter 1

THE WOMAN WHO WANTED TO KILL MUSSOLINI

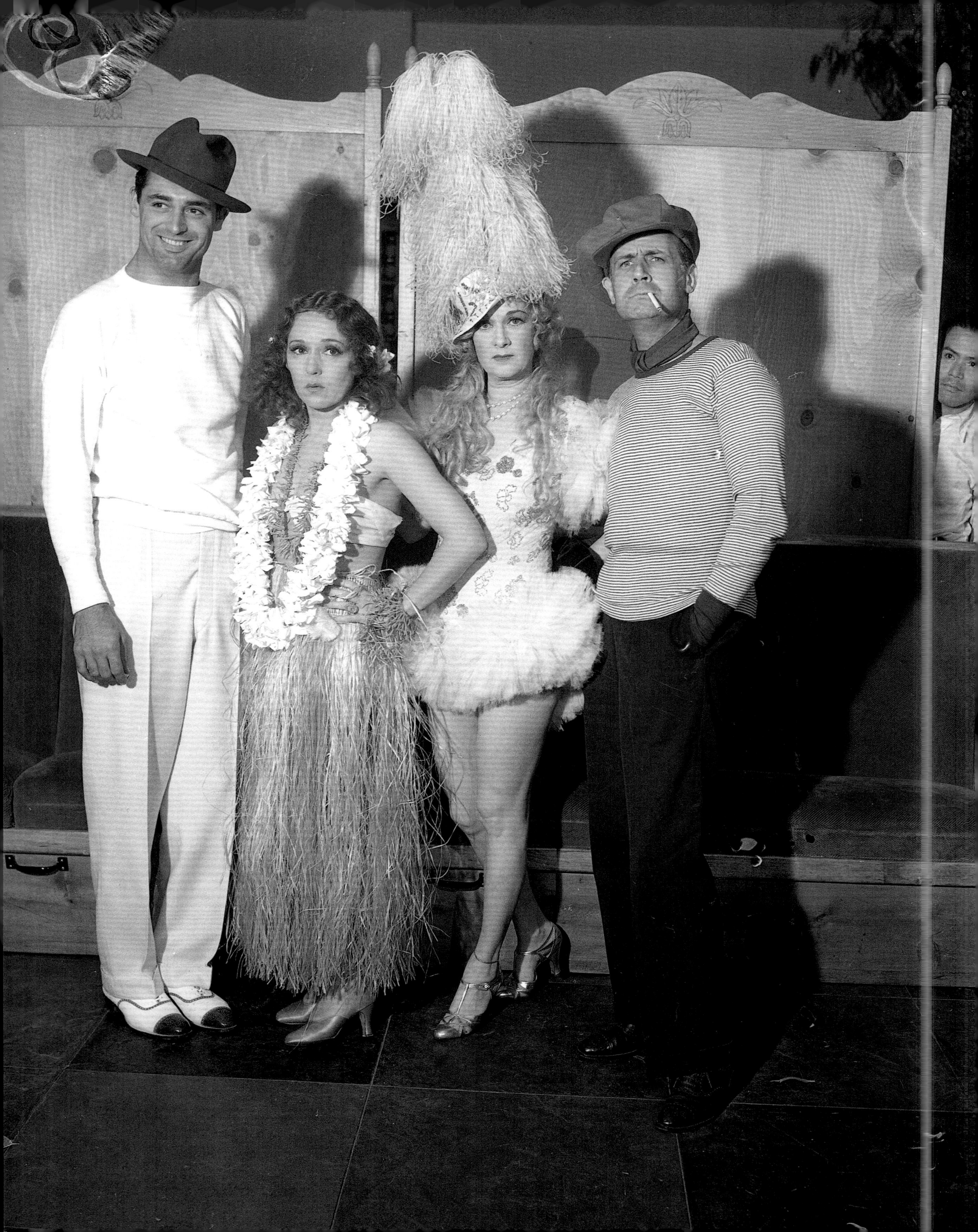

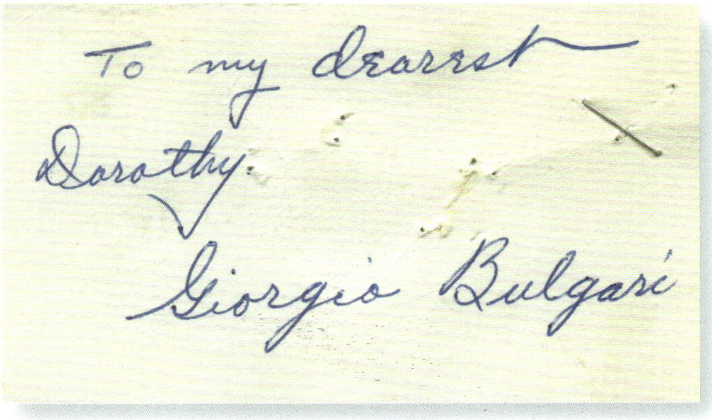

Dorothy di Frasso (1888-1954)

July 1939, the last party at Villa Madama...

Tonight, for the first time, she was wearing the fabulous diamond necklace that Giorgio Bulgari had delivered to her that same afternoon. Thirteen large cushion-cut diamonds were suspended from a series of diamond and platinum motifs in the form of papyrus flowers; the exotic foliage set with hundreds of baguette and brilliant diamonds. This piece of jewellery marked a clear break in the style of the jeweller. It was innovative, much closer to the neck than the long chains that had been the fashion during the last fifteen years. It was less solemn, also. This necklace was not a ceremonial piece, but an ornament intended to make the woman who wore it more beautiful. Aside from the sumptuous double-row necklace of fine pearls she had inherited from her mother, it was the most beautiful of all her jewels. She had paid 550,000 lire for it. Giorgio Bulgari had even confessed to her that it was the most important purchase made at his house during the whole of 1939. In any case, the price did not matter! Those flashes of light that sparkled around her neck were exactly what she needed to face the party she was hosting this evening, as it was, perhaps, the last one.

Since the beginning of spring, an atmosphere of war had been hanging over Rome. In April, Italy had invaded Albania. In one bite, the armies of Mussolini had consumed this little operetta kingdom. Its very recent sovereign, Zog I, had just married a charming, and very ruined, Hungarian countess, Geraldine Apponyi, during a sumptuous ceremony in Tirana. A royal palace had been built especially for the occasion. And Giorgio Bulgari had confided to her that some of the wedding gifts had been acquired in his shop in Via dei Condotti. Less than a year later, the palace was occupied by an Italian governor and the Albanian royal family had gone into exile with their jewels

Facing page: *Dorothy di Frasso at one of the legendary parties she organised during the 1930s, with two of her closest friends, Cary Grant and Mary Pickford.* **Previous page:** *1930s ruby and diamond Bulgari necklace and brooch. Bulgari Heritage Collection.*

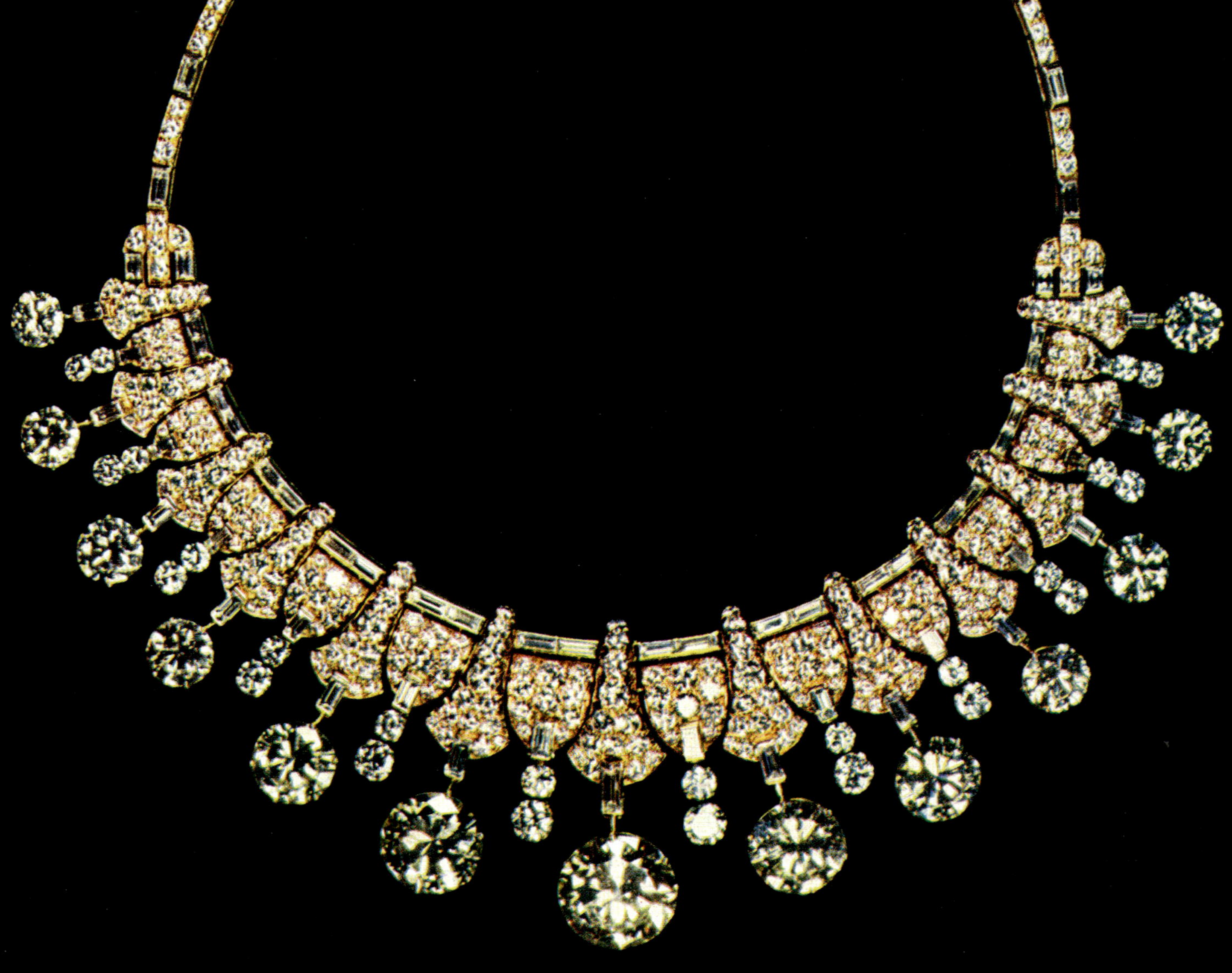

and wedding gifts. Although determined to imitate the exploits of its Italian ally, Hitler's Germany, which had already swallowed Austria and a part of Czechoslovakia, no longer concealed its lust for fragile Poland. There was no doubt that France and Great Britain would not accept this new aggression and would declare war on the invader. Mussolini was on the side of the Nazis, themselves allied with the Soviet Communists. And soon, Europe and the world would once again burst into flames.

Dorothy di Frasso was aware of all of this. She was undoubtedly one of the best informed women in the Italian capital. Not only was her sister-in-law a lady-in-waiting to Queen Elena, but for the last fifteen years she had received the whole court, a good part of the government, and the great majority of the diplomatic corps at her Roman home, Villa Madama. Moreover, from the United States, her brother, Bertrand Taylor, kept sending her cables asking her to leave Europe as soon as possible. He had even announced his intention to come and fetch her. The war was only a matter of weeks away.

She was not frightened by the chaos that was coming. It was during these moments of risk that she felt the most alive. And she had never baulked at adventure. Even if the last one, here in Rome, had ended in a resounding fiasco. One of her American friends had informed her of a new formula for explosives based on dynamite, and she had tried to sell the patent to Mussolini, Italy's dictator. Crown Prince Umberto, one of her friends, had acted as an intermediary. Seduced by the idea, "Il Duce" had agreed to fund up to $40,000 for the first experiments. Alas, they had proved inconclusive. In addition, she had made the mistake of embarking on an affair with Bugsy Siegel, an extremely seductive American mobster, whose violent nature she had underestimated. Of Jewish origin, Siegel had met Nazi dignitaries in Rome, notably Hermann Goering. He had threatened to liquidate him, according to the expeditious methods of the Mafia. She had had some difficulty in putting Siegel on a boat that was sailing back to the United States.

For thirty years, her life as an elegant and rich woman, travelling between Europe and the United States, had been punctuated by the Atlantic crossings of these luxurious steamers. The SS *Conte di Savoia,* with its suites opening out to private verandas looking out to sea, its hall whose baroque decoration was inspired by the gallery of the Palazzo Colonna in Rome, had been favoured by her since its launch in 1932. The transition between her two worlds was always pleasant on board this floating palace, which had been launched by none other than the Italian Crown Princess Marie-José. When she took a detour via Paris, she embarked at Cherbourg on the legendary liner *Normandie,* the maritime temple of Art Deco. And when she was in London, she chose the SS *Europa*, which sailed from Southampton.

From the beginning of spring to the end of summer, she was staying in Rome. Her husband, Count Carlo Dentice di Frasso, lived there permanently in the Villa Madama, the royal mansion they had bought and restored together after their marriage in 1923. During the autumn and winter she was on her own. This part of the year unfolded under the sun of California. In Hollywood, her best friend Marlene Dietrich, who frequently rented her Beverly Hills house at 925 North Bedford Drive, was always waiting for her. In these two houses Dorothy had created comfortable and sumptuous homes; the ideal settings for the extraordinary parties that had become part of her legend. In Rome, an extremely worldly capital, the rhythm of these parties was such that one of her friends, the heiress Barbara Hutton, had said: *"Nobody understood exactly if countess di Frasso was giving a party that lasted the whole summer or if her week-end parties lasted the whole week…"*.

Built on the slopes of Monte Mario, the villa was sumptuous in its classical elegance. In 1517, Cardinal Jules de Medici, who was not yet Pope Clement VII, had ordered Raphael to design the plans. Giulio Romano, scarcely 20 years old, had taken charge of the mural paintings. And Giovanni da Udine had created the stuccoes inspired by the Domus Aurea, the palace of Emperor Nero, which had recently been rediscovered. In Hollywood, her home was very different, having the appearance of a Mexican hacienda. But the common point of the two residences was the layout of the private apartments. Her friend, Elsie de Wolfe, the woman who had invented the trade of interior decorator, had supervised all the details. In Rome, she had imagined what was perhaps

Facing page: *Platinum and diamond necklace from the 1960s, very similar to the one created by Bulgari for Dorothy di Frasso in 1939.*

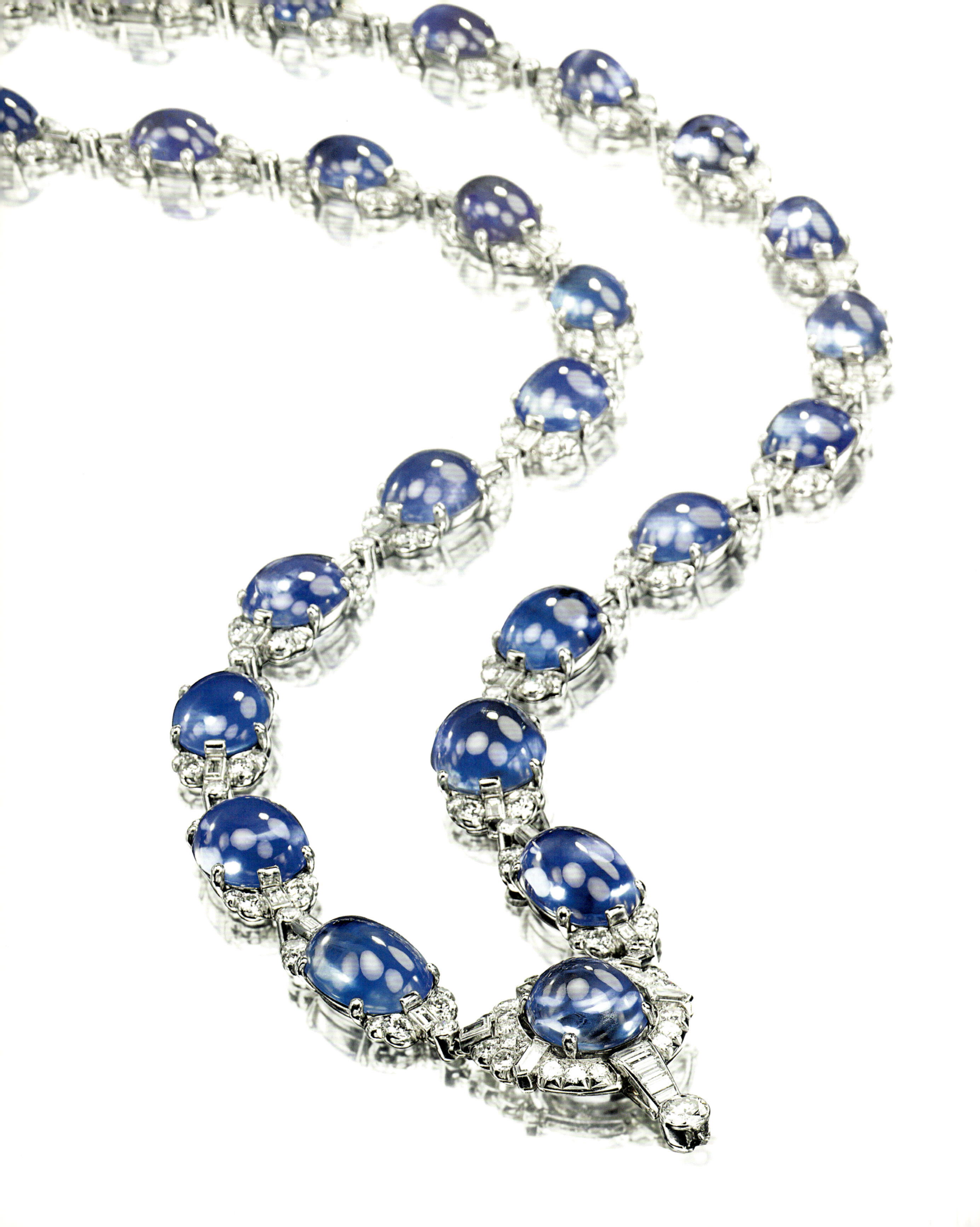

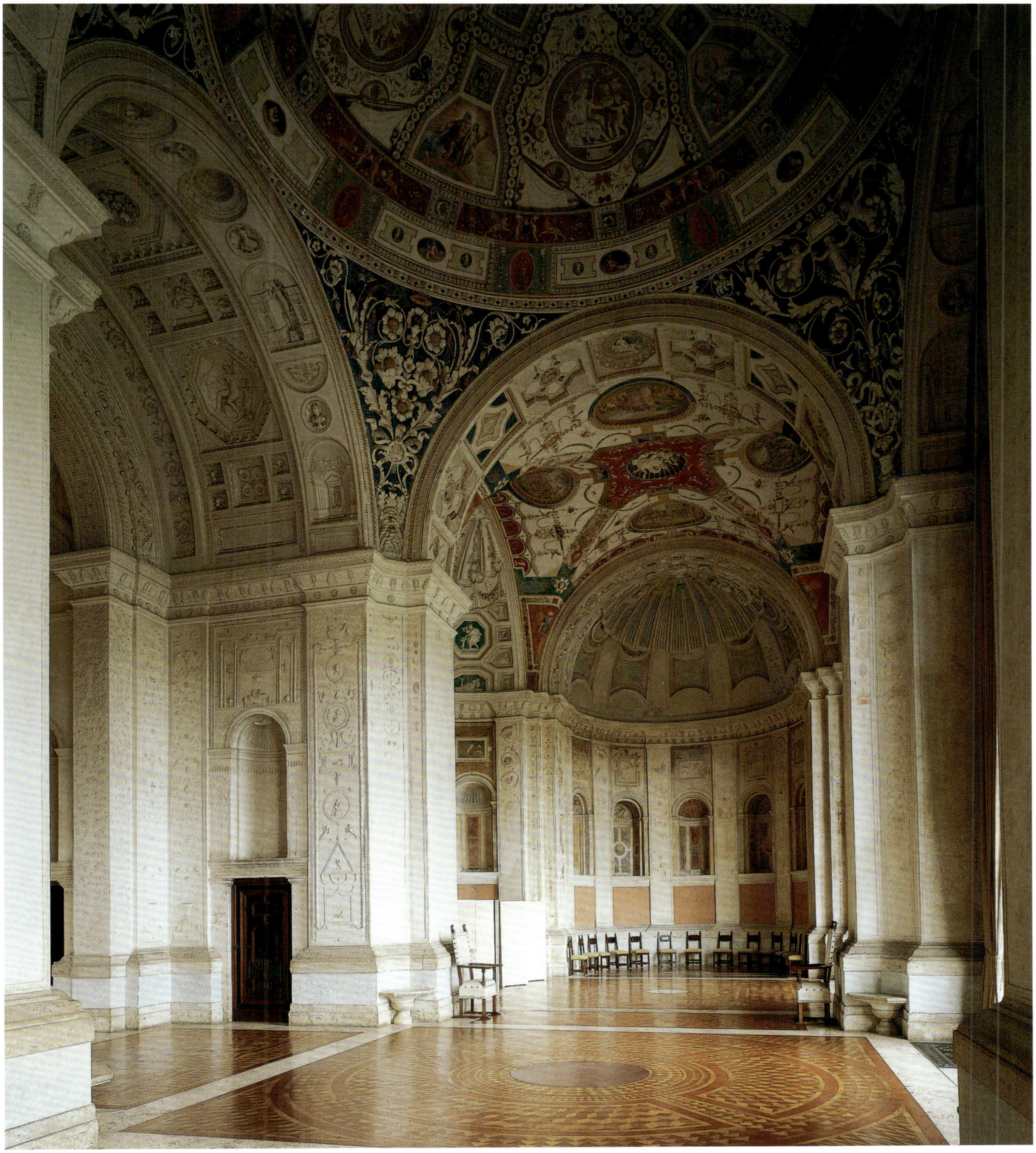

Above: *The Renaissance gallery on the ground floor of Villa Madama in Rome, where Dorothy di Frasso gave her fabulous parties in the 1930s.* **Facing page:** *Bulgari sapphire and diamond sautoir from the 1930s, which was sold by Christie's Geneva, 2012.*

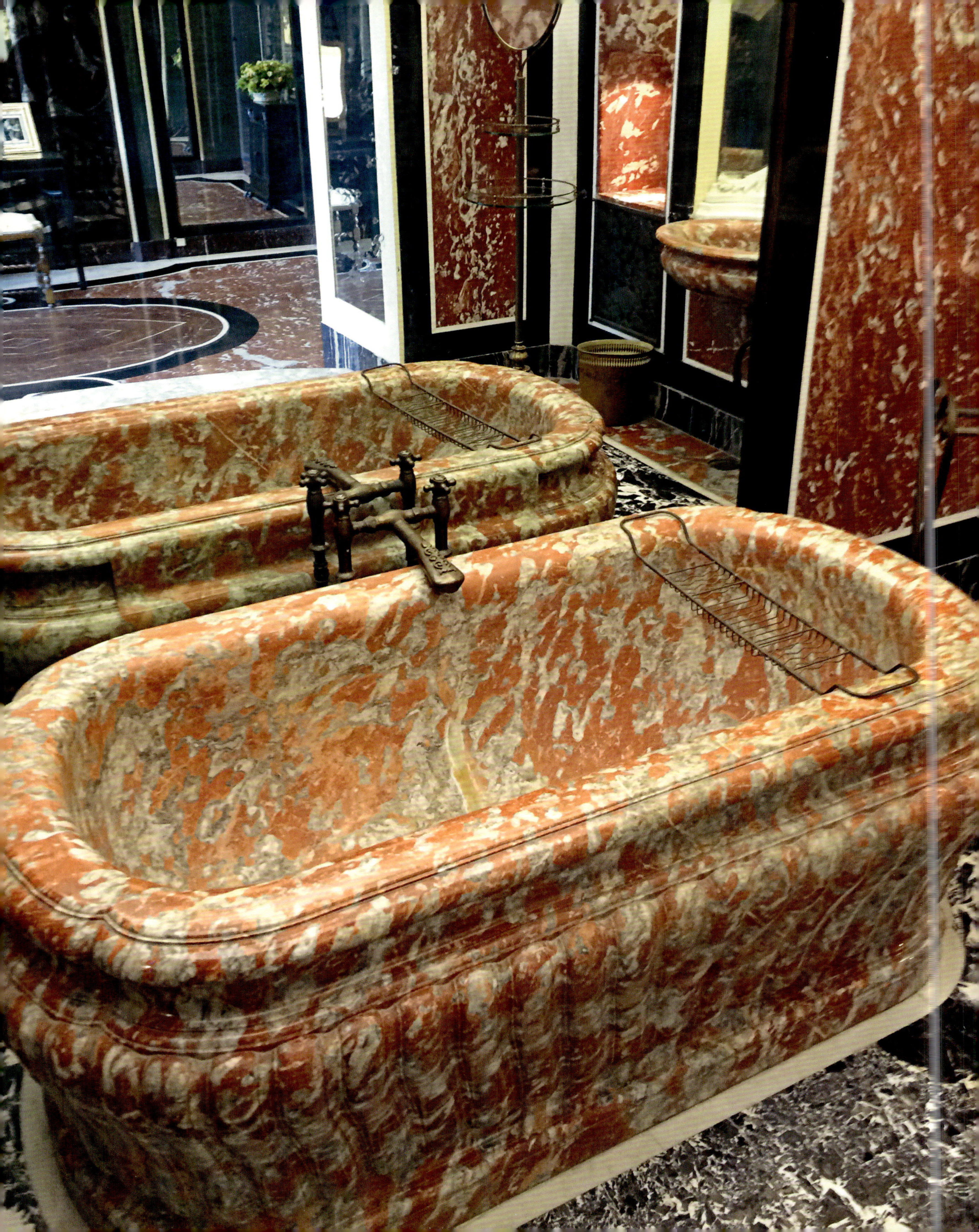

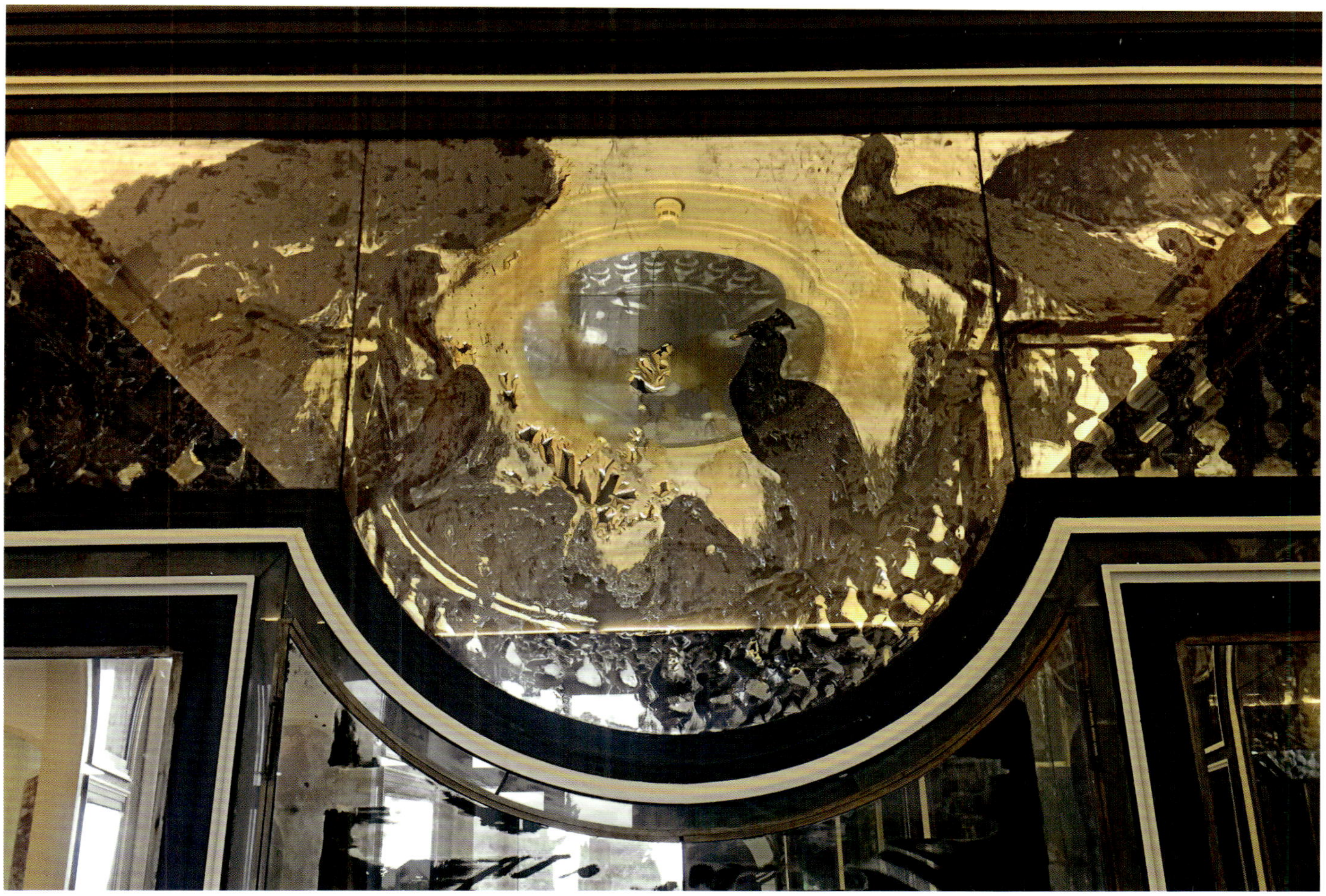

the most beautiful bathroom in the world: a double room in the antique style, one part of which was reserved for dressing, make-up and coiffure, the other dedicated to ablutions. A basin and a tub made of red marble with reflections of blood jasper furnished the bathroom part. The gilded bronze taps were in the shape of the golden fish that adorned the coat of arms of the Dentice di Frasso family. The walls were covered with red marble framed in black threads, as was the floor. In the dressing room, the decoration was repeated though with one detail altered: the red marble panels of the walls had been replaced by large mirrors, on which the oxidized silhouettes of monkeys and peacocks could be seen. Displayed on the dressing table was the 34-piece solid gold *nécessaire de toilette* that Bulgari had created for this unique client.

Facing page: *Dorothy di Frasso's marble bath tub in Villa Madama, which is still the same today.* **Above:** *The peacocks in Dorothy's bathroom in Villa Madama.*

It was here that she would put the last touches to her make-up and her jewels. And it was here that she was dreaming tonight, contemplating the reflection of her diamond necklace in the mirror. The air was hot. The city was stifling. But the Cardinal de Medici had foreseen these heavy summers. By choosing to build his country home on a hillside above the city, he had secured a slight breeze at night during the warmer months. The doors to the terrace that bordered the bedroom were open. And, following the ritual that she had established more than ten years ago, she would sit down for a moment by the stone balustrade to watch the arrival of the first guests. Philomena, her maid, had brought the cocktail tray and the cigarettes. *"From my terrace,"* she often declared, with the arrogance that characterised her, *"I see all Rome except the Vatican, which is hidden by the hill, and this suits me very well."* To make her entrance at the perfect moment was the first secret of a good hostess. It was necessary to allow the guests to enjoy a first drink, to chat a little, even to criticise. It was only when the party had begun and just

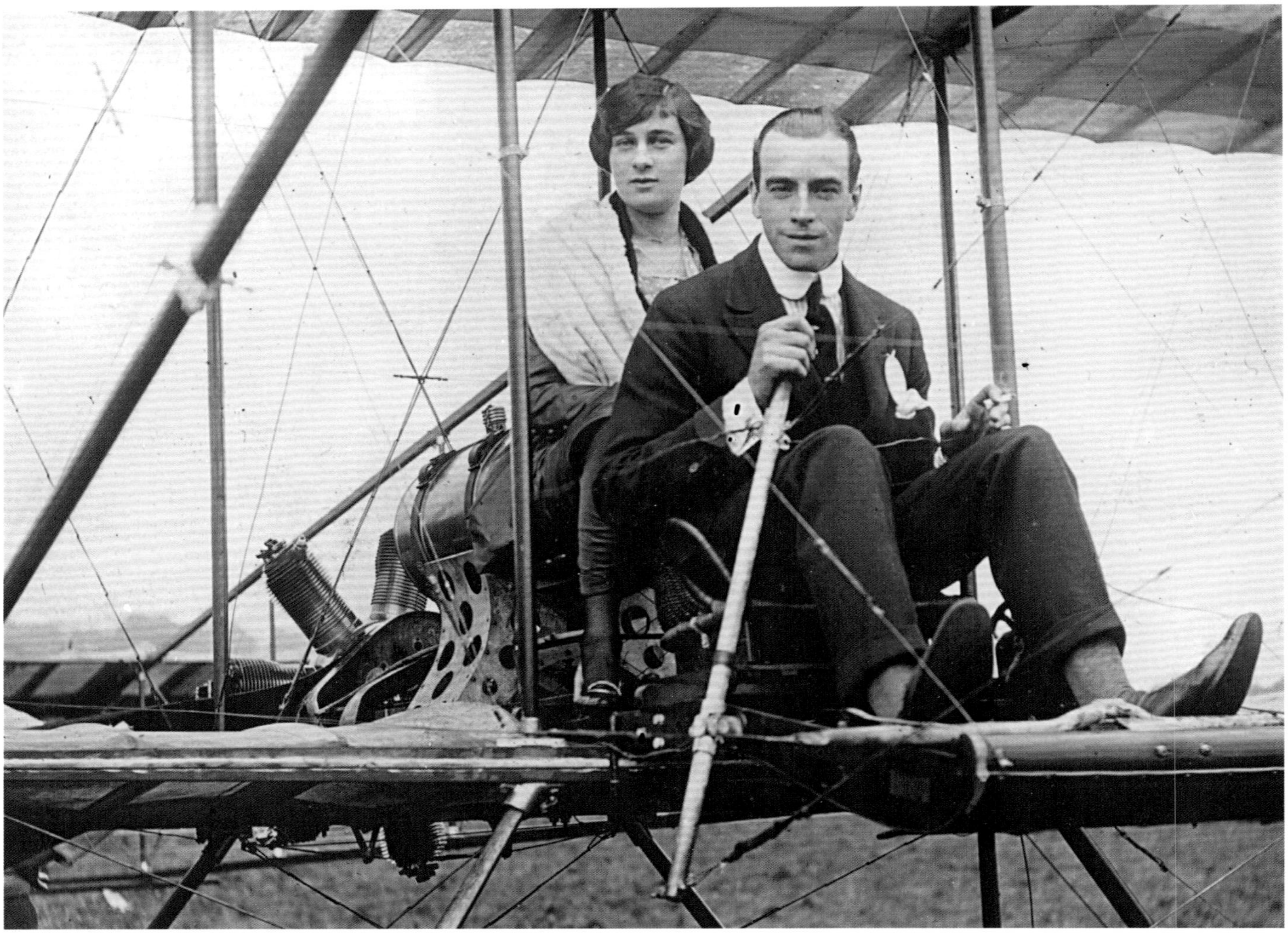

before the arrival of the most important guests, whose cars she could see from the terrace, that she would make a grand entrance, like a star, and announce: *"Ah, I think the crown prince's car is arriving!"*

Traditionally, the whole city attended the last party of the summer given by Countess di Frasso just before returning to the United States. Only a few very old-fashioned families of the Black Nobility, faithful to the Pope, still pretended to ignore her. The ambassadors, the fashionable aristocrats, the wealthy businessmen, the princes of the House of Savoy, the numerous Royal Highnesses exiled in the Eternal City, and the stars of international cinema, all crowded into her salons and gardens. Her party marked the end of the social season. This year, without doubt, there would be numerous guests. Yet, she had not organised any special attraction. There would be none of the eccentric ideas she had conceived over the last fifteen years: no costumed ball; no boxing rings set up in the parterres with bookmakers taking the bets; no birds flying under the vaults imagined by Raphael. Nor had she chosen to enter on a white horse, as she had done three years ago. Tonight, the two main attractions of the evening would be the imminent war and the diamonds that the Countess di Frasso was wearing around her neck. Tomorrow, all Rome would speak only of her necklace, of her new folly. Behind the walls of their immense palaces, the princesses would chat once more about "that scandalous American lady". The Queen would question her sister-in-law Emilia. And journalists would go to Bulgari on Via dei Condotti to try to find out the price of the jewel. Yet again, she was the talk of the town. And that was fine. "Anything but boredom!" was the motto she had chosen to live by a long time ago.

She had been born on 13 November, 1888. According to the American journalist Michael Stern, who was based in Rome and a neighbour of hers, as he lived in

Villa Spiga at the foot of Monte Mario: *"This little girl, who was to acquire a title and make a big splash in society was born in the very middle class town of Watertown, New York. Her brother, Bert, was born, four years later. Her father was Bertrand Leroy Taylor Senior, who had married the well-to-do Nelly Caldwell. Mr Taylor operated a leather goods business which prospered handsomely. At the turn of the century, the family moved to New York and Mr Taylor purchased a seat on the New York stock exchange on whose boards of governors he later served."* [1]

Indeed, her genealogical tree, although very suitable, included not the slightest hint of exoticism. No adventurer, no gold-digger or ambitious immigrant from Germany or Russia to earn his fortune in a generation. The Taylors, like the Caldwells, belonged to the oldest middle-class families to be found in the New World. Some of them had become famous at the time of the founding fathers of the American nation since they were born on the East Coast at the beginning of the 18th century. This generation of bourgeoisie, a little conformist, was perhaps the cause of the boredom that she had always fought against. Their wealth, built largely in the leather trade, was comfortable, but it had nothing to do with the legend that surrounded Dorothy. Elsa Maxwell, the celebrated journalist who had earned the reputation of knowing – she believed – all the secrets of the great men of this world, could repeat and write everywhere that her "friend Dorothy" had inherited twelve million dollars; it was not the truth. Admittedly, she had grown up in a very comfortable atmosphere, but she had not been one of those fabulous heiresses, the "Dollar Princesses", like Consuelo Vanderbilt or Anna Gould, whom penniless European aristocrats were eagerly chasing for their fabulous dowry in order to help them rebuild their more or less decrepit ancestral homes.

Facing page: *Dorothy and her first husband, Claude Grahame White.* **Below:** *Count and Countess di Frasso, c.1920.*

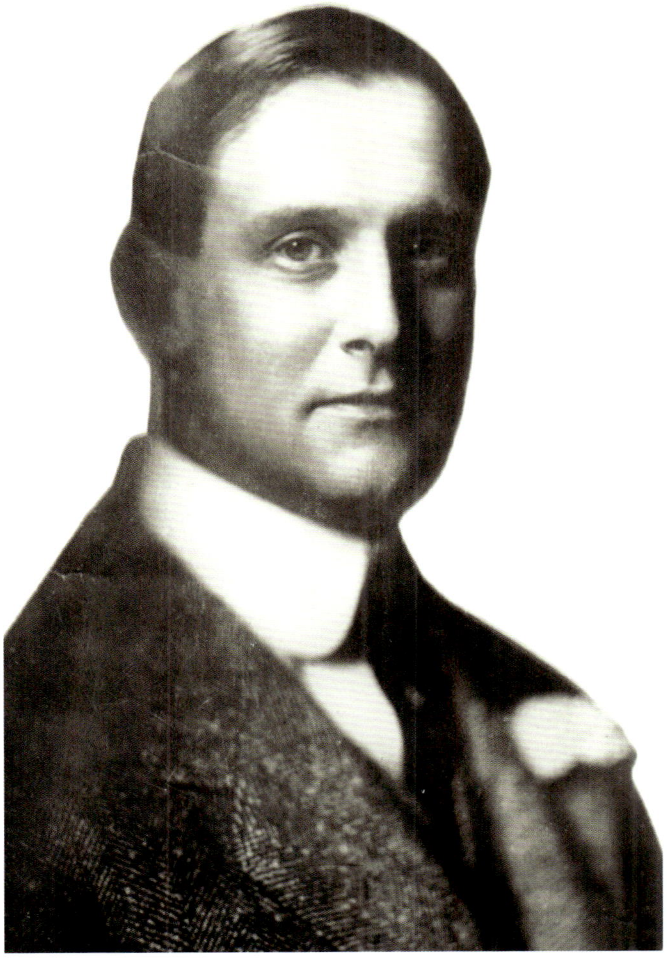

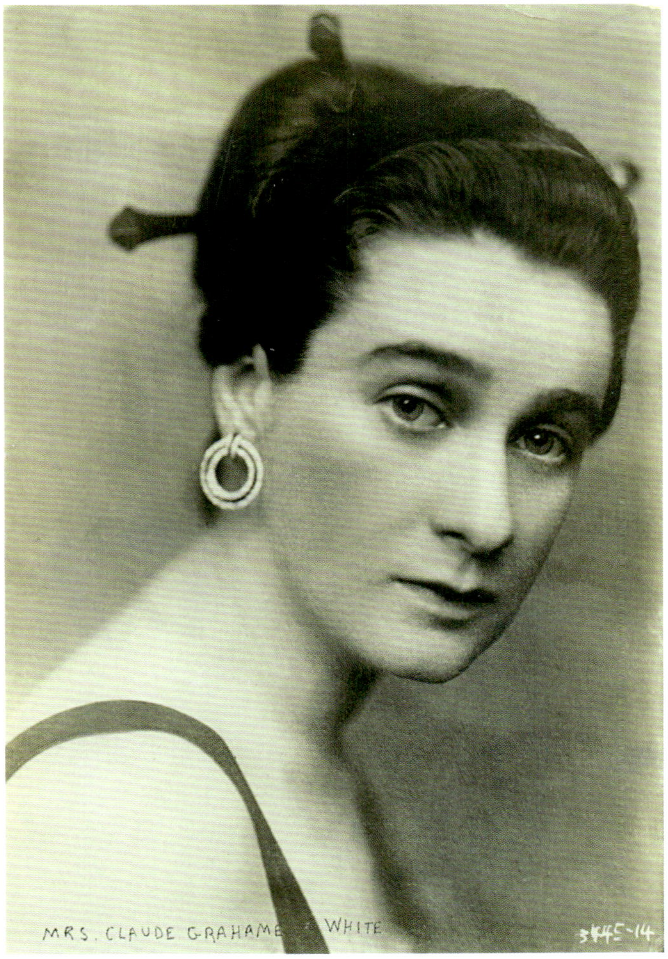

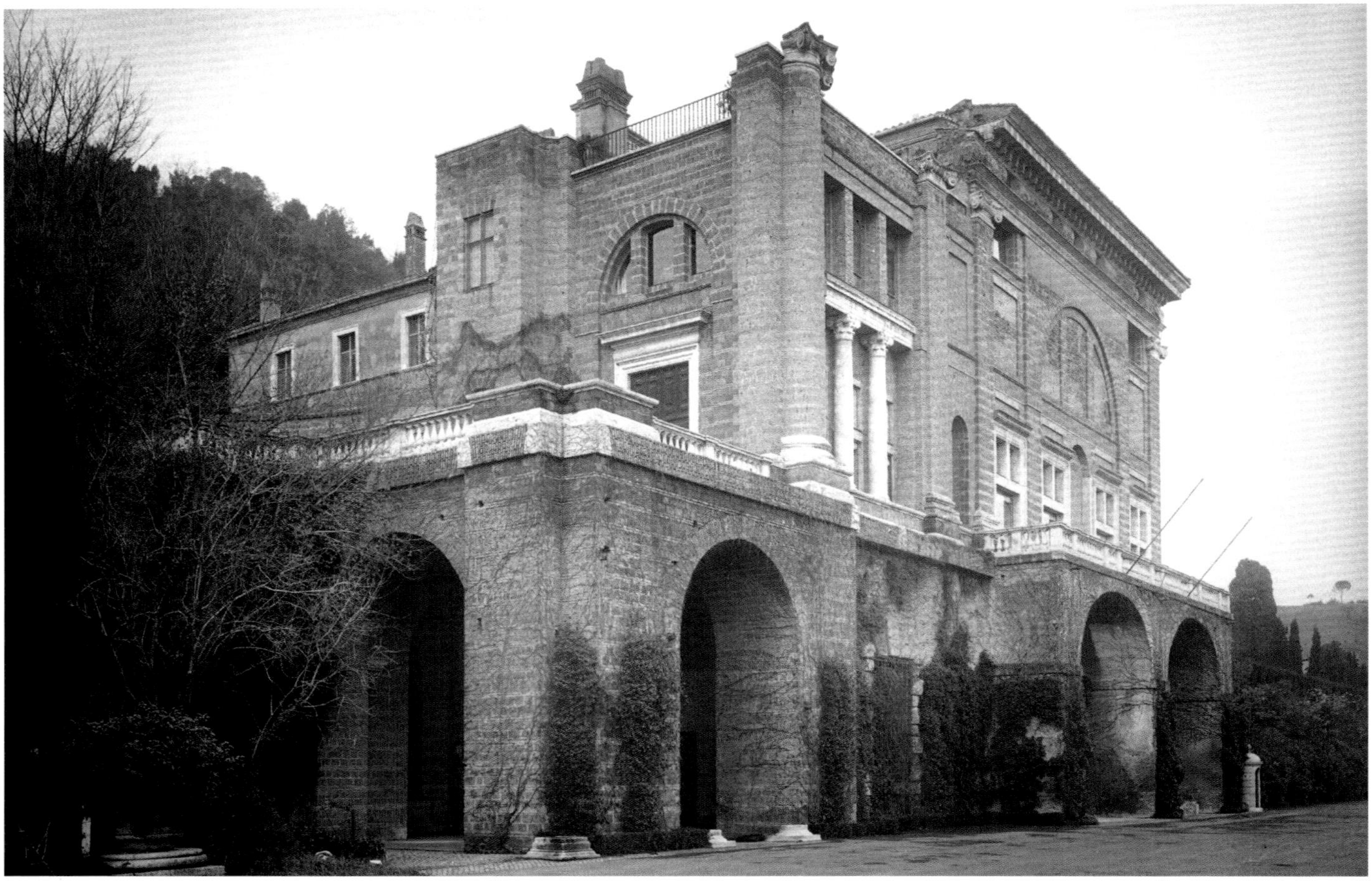

Her first marriage had been a thunderbolt. In 1910, after a failed engagement with James Ralph Bloomer, a Cincinnati stockbroker, she had left for Europe. The press at the time were constantly praising the courage of a new type of hero: the pioneers of aviation. In 1909, Louis Blériot had completed his first crossing of the Channel, becoming a celebrity worldwide. And it was at his school near Étampes that Claude Grahame White, a 30-year-old British man, had learnt to fly. Returning to England, he set out to conquer the air by participating in his first aerial race in April 1910. On this occasion he was pitted against the Frenchman, Louis Paulhan. Dorothy, like all England, followed the progress in the papers. Staged by the *Daily Mail*, the aim was to link London to Manchester by air, in less than 24 hours. The newspaper had put forward the colossal prize money of £10,000. Claude had lost. However, a few months later, he won his second race, with a lower prize of £1000. More importantly, he had made the headlines of American newspapers by flying over Washington. He had even landed – without permission – on Pennsylvania Avenue, a few blocks from the White House.

With his square and determined chin and blue eyes Claude Grahame White had a roguish charm no one could resist. And Dorothy fell for this English pilot with a violent passion. A photograph, taken at the time of their marriage, shows the two young lovers installed in Claude's plane. Of course, there is no cabin, nor even a chair. The pilot is perched on a small seat at the front of the engine; his wife is behind him. Claude sports a confident, winning smile. Dorothy still has the shy look of a young girl who is not a smashing beauty. Shrouded in heavy clothes probably intended to protect her from the cold air, she strikes a slightly awkward pose. The newlyweds are preparing to leave by plane for France, where they will spend their honeymoon. Dorothy confessed at the landing that she had spent the greater part of the journey with her eyes closed and her arms clasped around her husband's neck. Claude had succeeded in a

Above and facing page: *Villa Madama on the hill above Rome and Dorothy di Frasso's bedroom.*

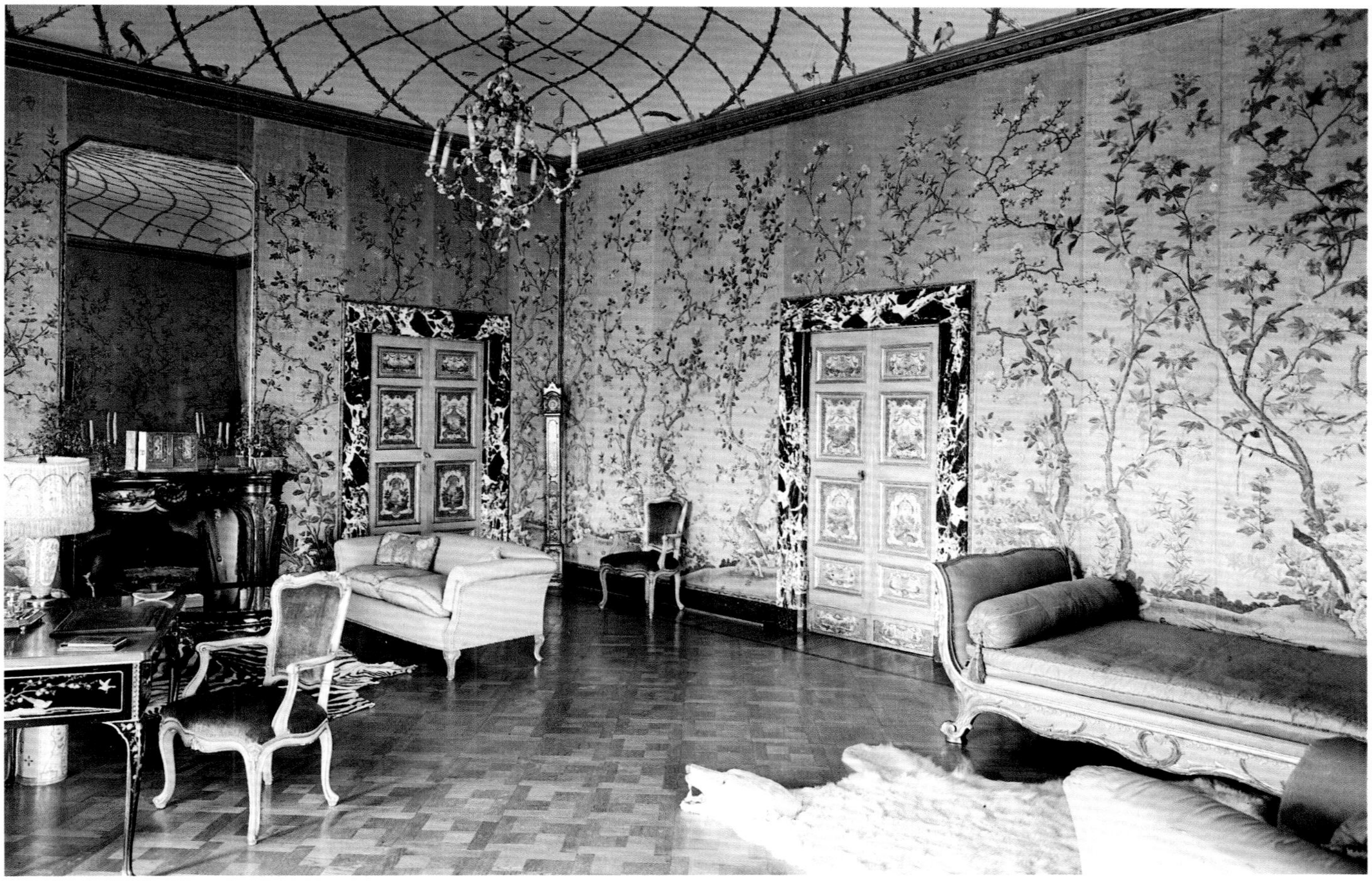

new exploit: to fly over the Channel whilst comforting Dorothy, panicked by her first flight.

Alas, Claude Grahame White was not a man of a single passion. His incessant travels and his many adventures exhausted his young wife's patience in less than four years. If one believes Elsa Maxwell: *"Dorothy always did have a peculiar sense of humor. She hired a detective to check on Grahame White, and startled the birds for miles around with her howls of laughter when a detailed report was submitted. The ceiling of the bedroom of Ethel Levey (her bosom pal) was painted skye-blue and depicted a plane coming through the clouds as though it was preparing to make a forced landing on the bed."* [2] In the January of 1916 she had, in accordance with the conventions of British justice, "summoned him to restitute her marital rights": *"Dear Whitie, just writing a few lines, to ask you, to make a home and restore my full rights as a wife. I am ready and willing to blot out the memory of what's happened in the past to mar our happiness during our short matrimonial life. I have done my best to break off your attachment from the woman who so far has made our lives unbearable and I do hope it's not too late for you to give her up and return to me."* [3]

It was in vain. The divorce was announced shortly afterwards. In the turmoil of the First World War, nobody noticed. In peacetime, the young woman returned to the United States. Five discreet years followed: between 1918 and 1923 there was no mention of Dorothy Taylor in the American press until, in May 1923, she lost a fabulous bracelet of sapphires with an estimated value of several thousand dollars in a New York taxi. It had an illustrious provenance: it used to belong to the Grand Duchess Milica Nikolaevna of Russia.

The coincidence is amusing. As well as being the wife of the Grand Duke Peter Nikolaevich, a cousin of Tsar Nicholas II, the Grand Duchess, who was born Princess Milica of Montenegro, was also the sister of Queen Elena of Italy, of whom Dorothy was just about to become a loyal subject. The Grand Duchess lived in exile in France and some of her jewellery was beginning to appear on the market. Perhaps the most extraordinary part of this story was that the taxi driver turned out to be an honest man: he returned the jewel to its rightful owner.

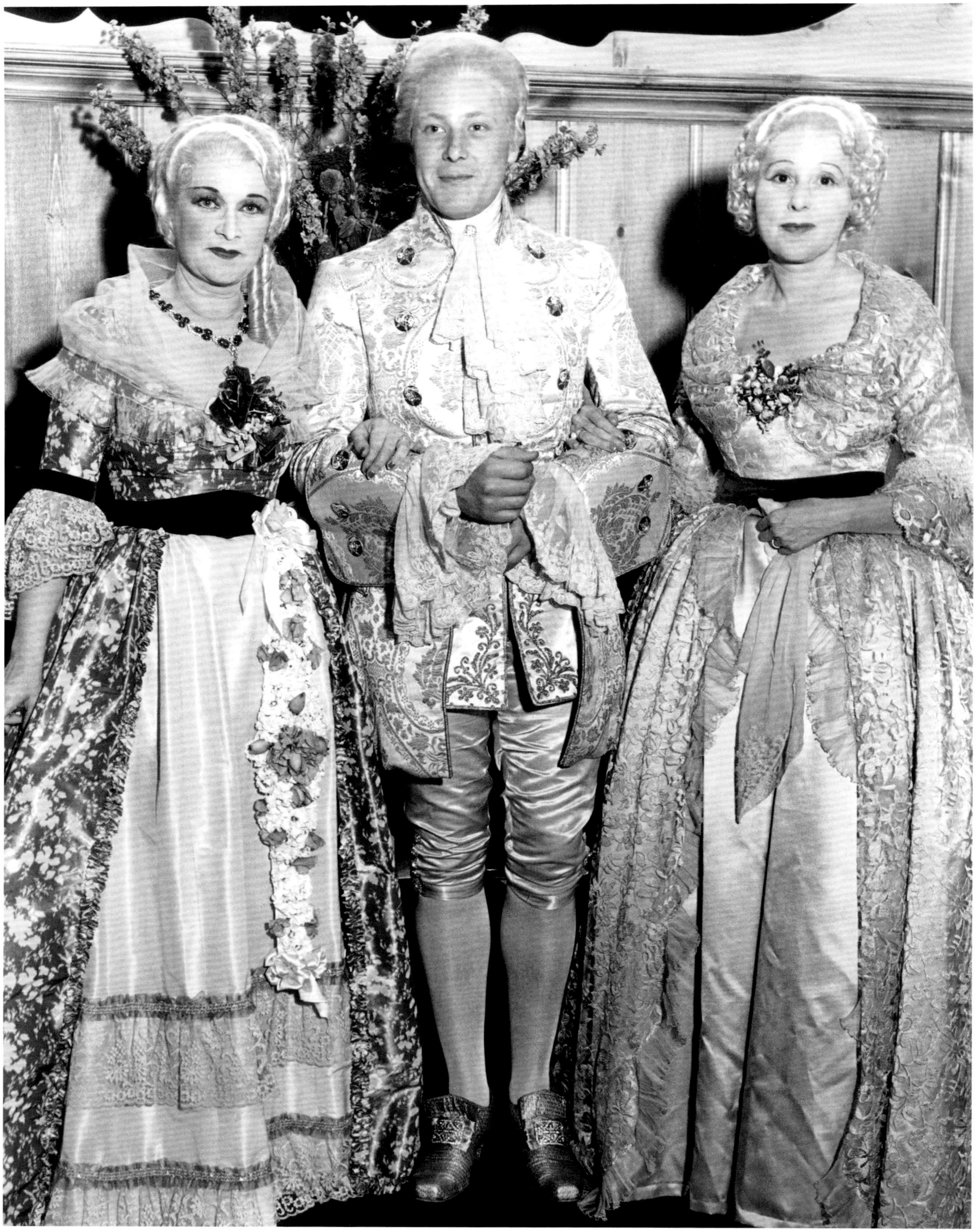

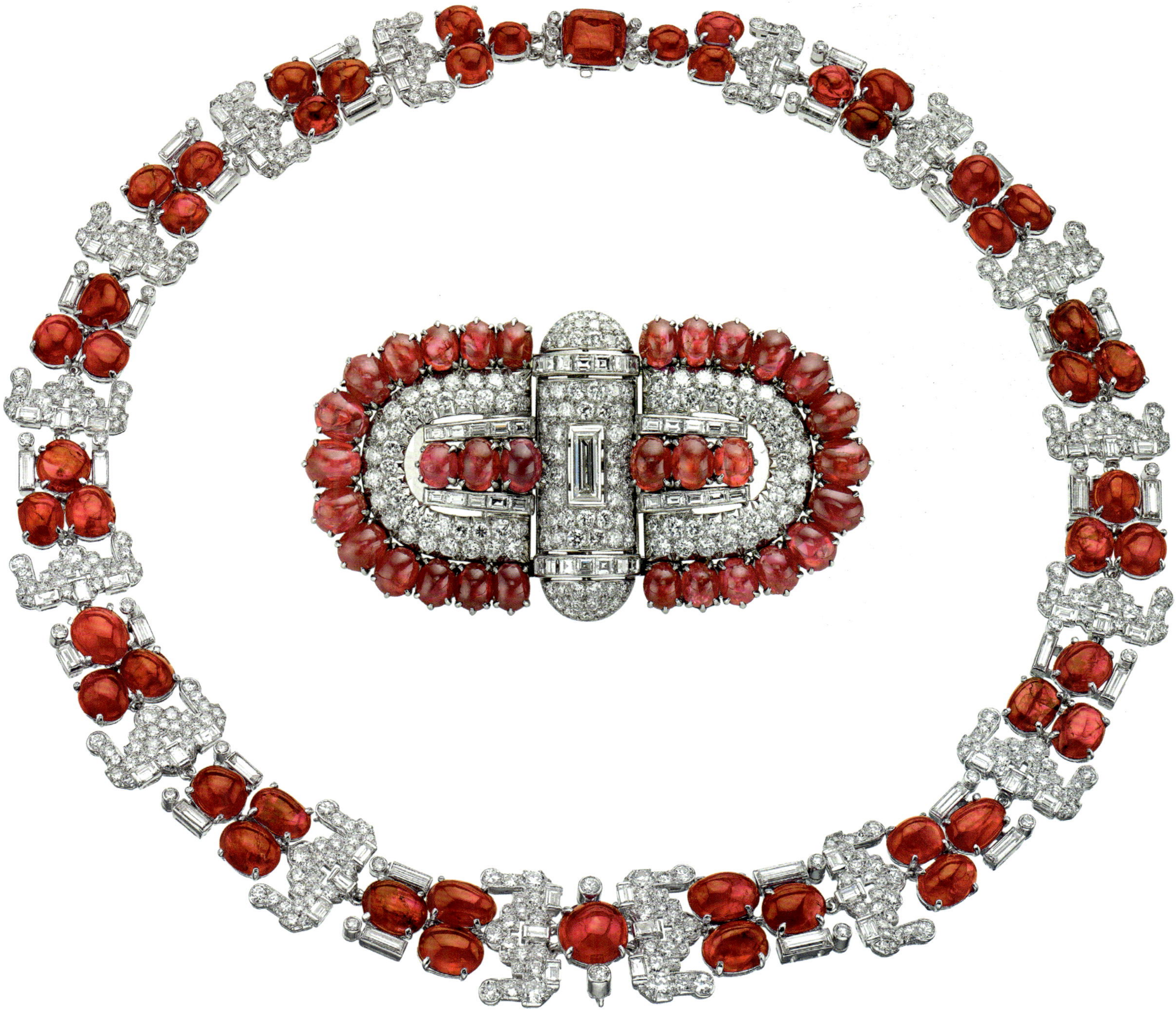

Above: *1930s ruby and diamond demi-parure signed by Bulgari. The necklace is very similar to that worn by Dorothy di Frasso in the photograph opposite. Bulgari Heritage Collection.*
Facing page: *Countess di Frasso with two of her guests at one of her famous costume parties at Villa Madama.*

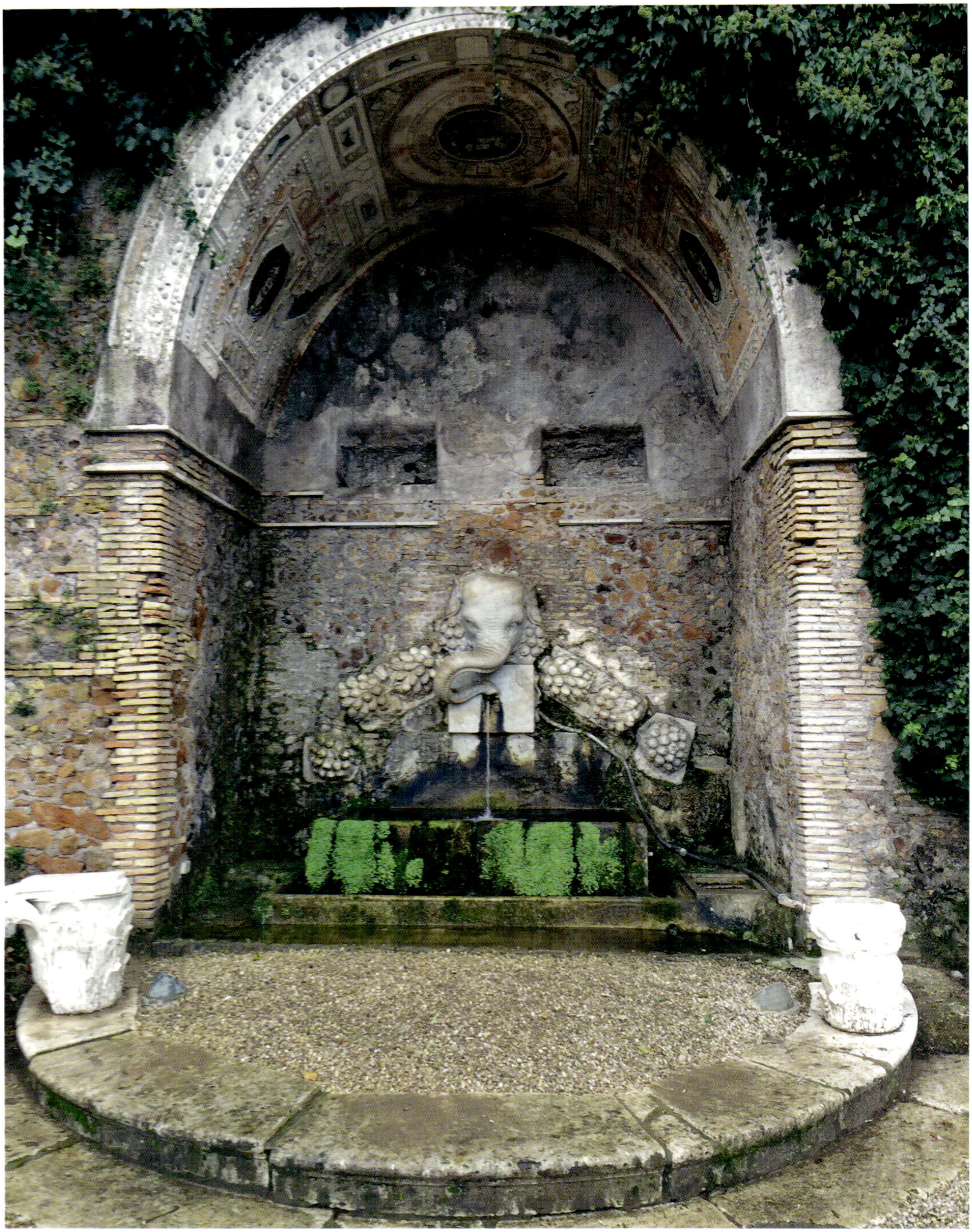

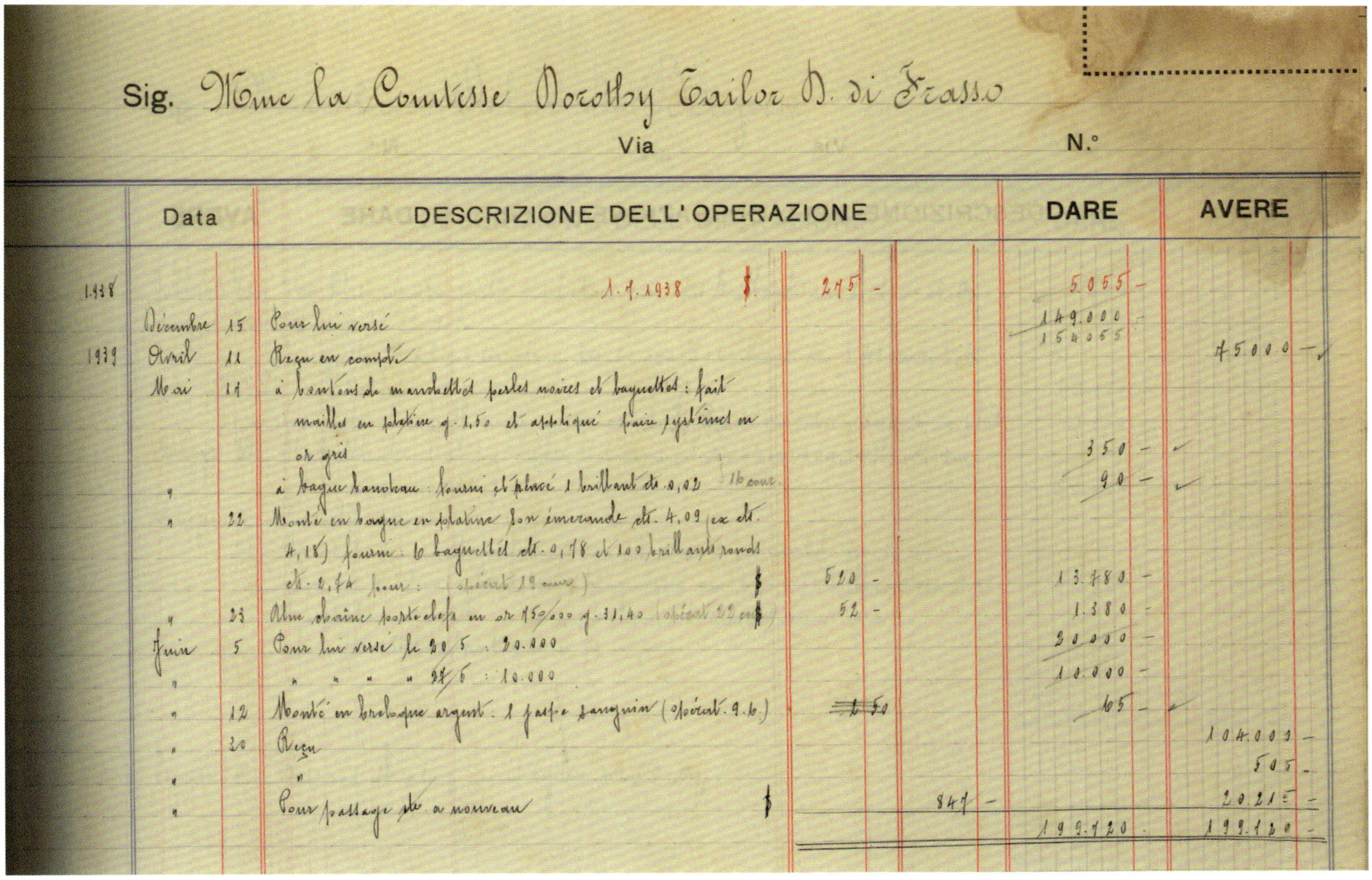

A few weeks later, on 9 June, 1923, American newspapers reported on the second marriage of Miss Dorothy Taylor to an Italian aristocrat, Count Carlo Dentice di Frasso. There was a discreet ceremony at a family friend's house in New York. The mother of the bride was very ill and could not attend. However, the Italian Ambassador, Prince Gelasio Caetani, was present. Count Dentice di Frasso was not an adventurer. He was a diplomat, and belonged to an excellent family of the Neapolitan nobility, whose estates are located in the north of Puglia, near Brindisi. In this region, the family had two castles: San Vito dei Normanni and Carovigno. Carlo was born in the first of these two residences, on 22 January, 1876. Allied with all the European aristocracy, the di Frassos experienced the First World War almost as a family affair. The Count's mother, Princess Dentice di Frasso (née Chotek) was a cousin to the Duchess of Hohenberg, wife of the Archduke Franz-Ferdinand, heir to the throne of Austria. The assassination of this couple in Sarajevo in 1914 was the spark that set fire to Europe.

Facing page: *The Elephant Fountain, one of the wonders of Villa Madama.* **Above:** *A page from the Bulgari archives, showing the name of "Comtesse Dorothy Taylor di Frasso"*

Previously married to American, Georgina Wilde, the elegant diplomat had his first union annulled in 1921. According to the testimonies of the Taylor family, he had known Dorothy and her family for years. The letters that the Countess di Frasso wrote for more than ten years to her father bore witness to their love for each other, even though they did not seem to be constantly faithful during the twenty-two years that their marriage would last. Of course, this union offered to this impoverished aristocrat some pecuniary advantages; he received an annuity paid by his father-in-law. Above all, he could fulfill his dream to settle in Rome, with a certain style, though under the affectionate control of the Taylor family, who seemed to protect Dorothy from the spending habits she and her husband had in common The Villa Madama was acquired following a very precise

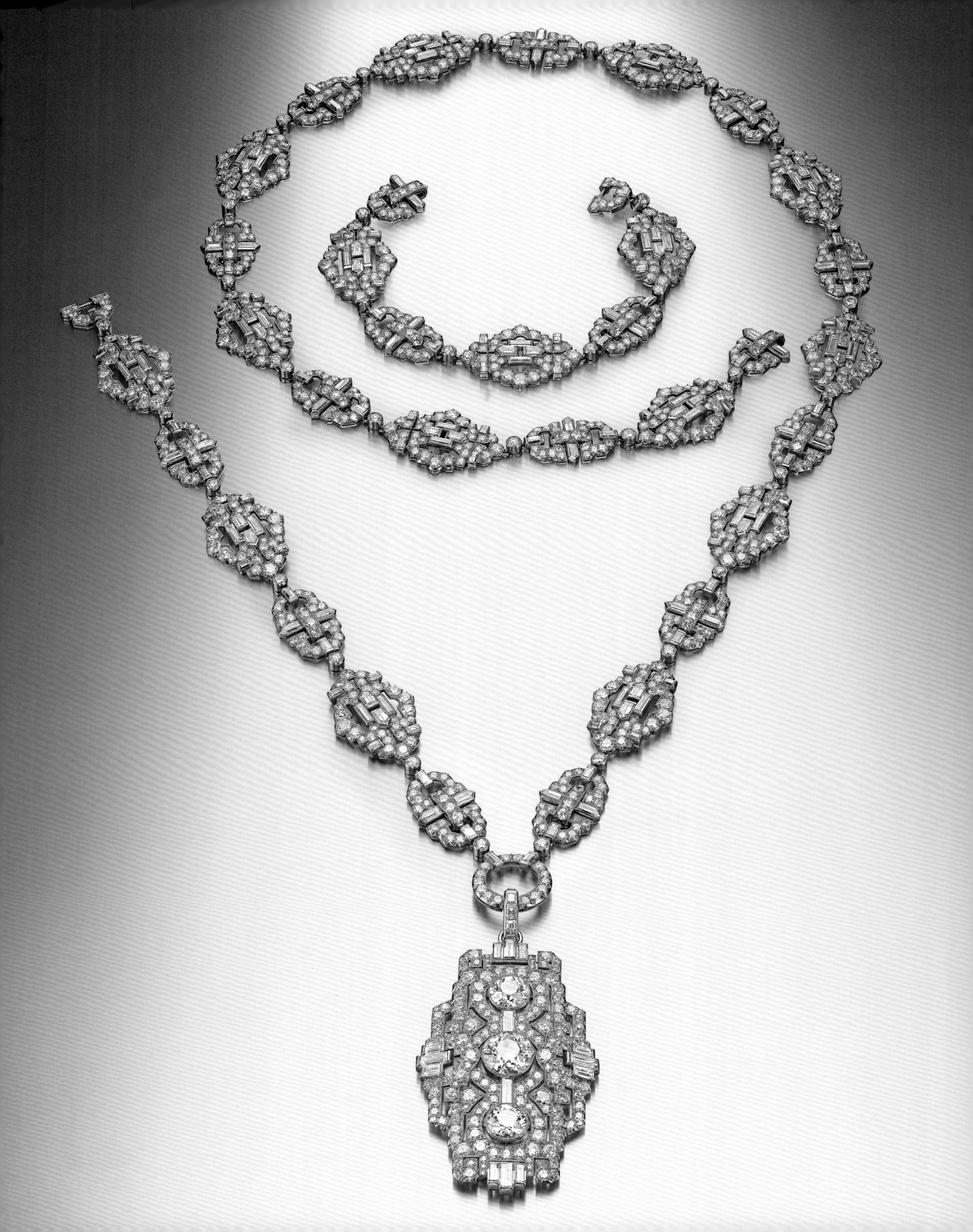

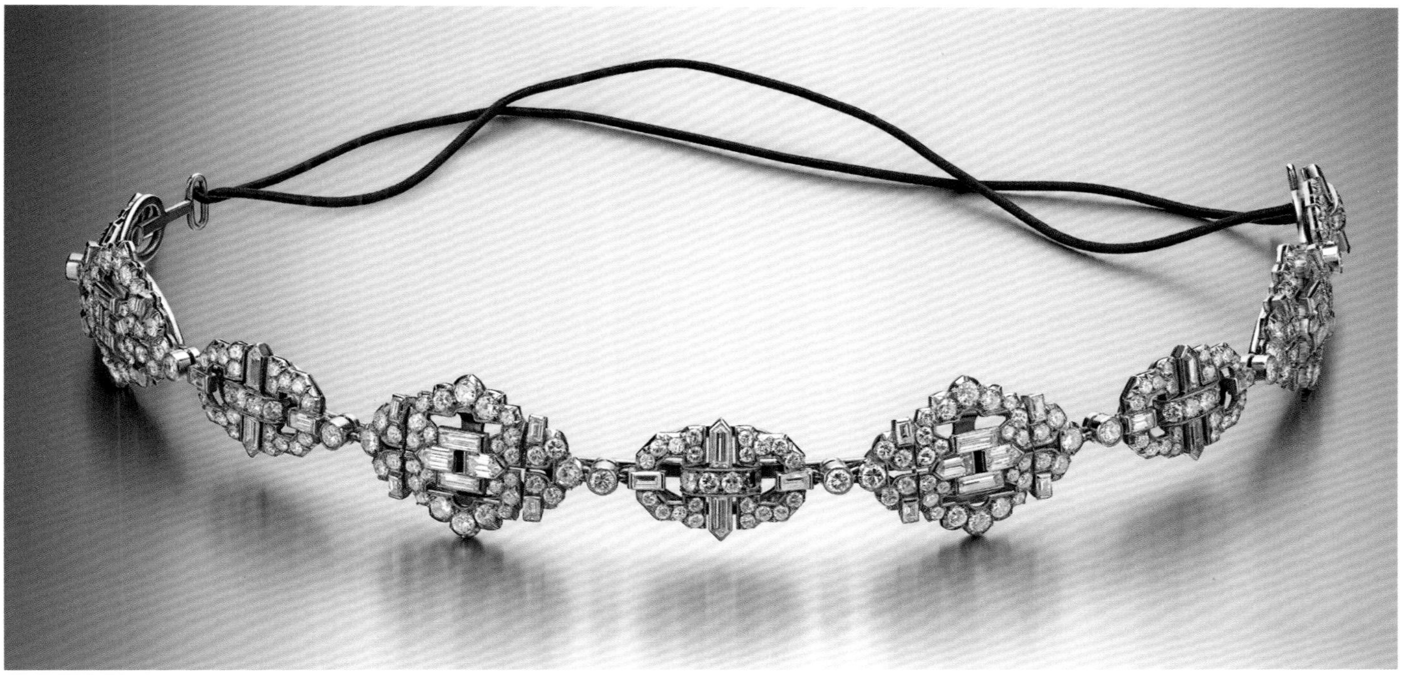

agreement: two thirds would belong to Dorothy and one third to Carlo; but if Carlo were to die first, his share would pass to Bertrand, Dorothy's brother.

According to Michael Stern, who is definitely very well informed: *"Dorothy's mother died three months after her daughter's wedding, leaving an inheritance of $1,533,204 38 cents."* [4] The young woman who had already received $100,000 on her marriage inherited nearly $500,000. This sum ensured her a comfortable income and probably facilitated the purchase of the villa. Eleven years later, in 1934, on the death of her father, who, also according to Stern, left a legacy of $1,250,000, she received nearly $600,000. Even if it was not as important as some would say, this fortune allowed for an extremely luxurious lifestyle. It would also enable her to conquer Rome.

By the start of the summer of 1923, the new Countess di Frasso was 35 years old. She was determined to shine after those morose years that had followed her disastrous first marriage. London had seen her defeated and abandoned. In New York, the city of her youth, she became bored. Paris had nothing more to teach her. Rome, on the other hand, was a beautiful sleepy city, full of promises. The previous year, a new political leader, Benito Mussolini had become the prime minister of the young kingdom of Italy. He had promised to return the city to its ancient glory. Villa Madama was the epitome of the city. It had been dormant for centuries, in neglectful laziness, while its fabulous decoration gradually disappeared. No one knows how the couple discovered this mansion, but their first visit was undoubtedly an archaeological exploration. In 1923 it was uninhabitable. The walls had only just been saved by a Toulouse patron, a dozen years before. The estate, which comprised several tens of hectares, was uncultivated. During the 19th century, it had even been transformed into a farm. Henry James, who visited it in 1873, testified to its decay: *"The place has become the shabbiest farmhouse, with muddy water in the old pièces d'eau and dunghills on the old parterres.... Margaret Farnese was the lady of the house, but where she trailed her cloth of gold the chickens now scamper between your legs over rotten straw."*

This disaster was the result of the hazards of history. At the death of Pope Clement VII, the villa entered the patrimony of the Medici. In 1537, the death of Alexander de Medici, assassinated by his cousin and perhaps lover, Lorenzaccio, marked the end of the elder branch of this family. His widow, Margaret of Austria, illegitimate daughter of Charles V, inherited the villa. Titled "Madame" in honour of

Facing page and above: *Bulgari diamond sautoir and pendant created for Countess Contini Bonacossi. It can be dismantled and worn as a tiara and three bracelets. Bulgari Heritage Collection.*

her Imperial birth, of which she was very proud, she lent her name to the house. She would bequeath it to the family of her second husband, Octave Farnese, Duke of Parma. The building remained the property of the princes of Parma until the extinction of this line at the beginning of the 18th century. It then passed, like the Palazzo Farnese of Rome, to the Bourbon kings of Naples who allowed it to fall into ruin. By the beginning of the 20th century, it had become a farm belonging to the Count of Caserta, successor of the kings of Naples, who lived in exile in Cannes. In 1913, he sold the villa to Maurice Bergès, a Toulouse entrepreneur, an Italophile, who saved the walls. Ten years later, the Count and the Countess di Frasso began its complete restoration.

Everything had to be done again. The first step was to reopen the colossal arcades that had once linked the state apartments to the gardens. They had been walled up. All the stucco and all the paintings had to be recreated. The Count and Countess di Frasso also decided to create a spiral stone staircase, which was a masterpiece of architecture. The restoration of the garden was entrusted to Norah Lindsay, an English friend of Dorothy. She conceived a labyrinth of topiaries whose paths strewn with gravel became an extension of the reception rooms on the ground floor. The extraordinary Fountain of the Elephant, named in memory of the pachyderm offered by the King of Portugal to Pope Leo X in 1514, was the main decorative feature. In 1928, once the work had been completed, Dorothy and Carlo even financed the publication of a book celebrating the rebirth of their home.

Today, as before, discovering the Villa Madama is a magical experience, even if only half the architectural project proposed by Raphael was ever built. The entrance, very discreet, is located on the side, in the centre of a semicircle, originally designed to include a green theatre on the hillside. The vestibule opens onto a series of enormous rooms, the ceilings of which are adorned with stuccoes by Giovanni da Udine and the antique motifs created by Giulio Romano. The ground floor of the wing overlooking the city of Rome is occupied by huge rooms, furnished with Renaissance antiques, Italian paintings and comfortable sofas and armchairs. In the mezzanine, a series of apartments was reserved for the servants. The first floor was added at the request of the Count and the Countess di Frasso. Facing the gardens, above the three salons, were the suites reserved for guests. The bedroom and bathroom of Count di Frasso were in the corner of the building. It was from the terrace off Dorothy's apartments that one got the best views of the city.

Within a few years, in her Renaissance palace overlooking the Eternal City, the Countess di Frasso had become the second Queen of Rome, after Queen Elena. Some of the princely families of the city may have had palaces more sumptuous and larger than her own, but none of the balls or dinners that they held came anywhere near the splendour and originality of Dorothy's. Her secret was the sense of freedom she offered, that and the mix of guests. In contrast to the great noble families of the courts – there were two in Rome, that of the Pope and that of the Kings of Italy – she cared neither for tradition nor for high birth. Anyone who provided a little fun would be invited. The director Alfred Hitchcock, who stayed with her in the 1930s, described Villa Madama as: *"An open house for celebrities, dignitaries and royalties on the loose as well as other congenial characters."* [5] Even "Il Duce" considered the restless life of this house with a certain indulgence. The café society with which Dorothy surrounded herself gave his authoritarian regime an appearance of tolerance and a certain worldly veneer, which was not to be dismissed. Unlike Berlin, where one was bored and worried in an atmosphere of surveillance and perpetual denunciation, Rome was still a capital where one could enjoy some of the most beautiful parties of the interwar period.

Dorothy di Frasso's guest list featured many names that are to be found in the rare Bulgari books that survived the Second World War. Jewellery, as well as elegance, played a fundamental role in this worldly life. And here too, Dorothy loved to innovate. There was no question of her wearing classical jewels, the flowery 19th-century tiaras and brooches that were still in vogue with her in-laws. Her meeting with Giorgio Bulgari was an important moment in both their destinies. They shared the same ambition, the same modern spirit. The letters and telegrams kept in the archives of the Taylor family testify to the real affection that united them.

Facing page: *Gary Cooper in 1930. At the time, he was considered one of the most handsome men in Hollywood.*

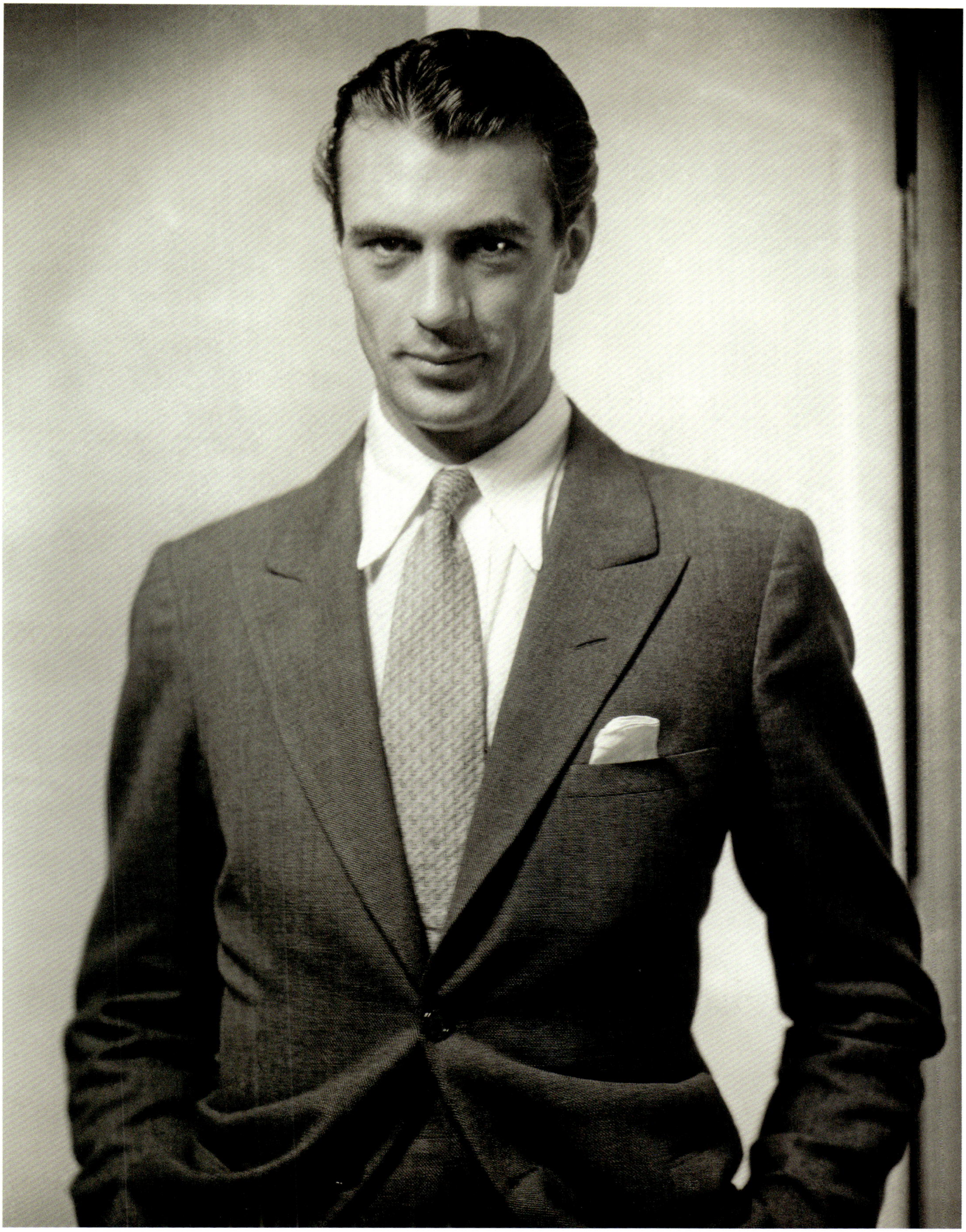

The second son of Sotirio Bulgari who created the house, Giorgio Bulgari began his career at the beginning of the 20th century. Sotirio was an exceptional craftsman. In the early mornings he would work the precious metals in his workshop, then he would spend the afternoons selling in his shop, often his own creations. His two sons, Giorgio and Costantino, had a far better education than he received. Costantino was a scholar who specialised in trading precious objects. At that time a good half of the shop on the Via dei Condotti was filled with a selection of rare objects in silver, vermeil, jade or enamelled gold. Giorgio, on the other hand, was a specialist in precious stones. According to family tradition, he had the idea to turn his father's goldsmith's trade into a successful jewellery business during a trip to Paris.

His grandson, Nicola Bulgari confirms this theory: *"At the time, all the jewellery and fashion world was centered around Paris and Paris only. If you were interested in those things, you had to go there. My father was 18 years old in 1908, and he was travelling to Paris for the first time. He went to Place Vendome and Rue de la Paix. Cartier, Boucheron, Mellerio, Van Cleef & Arpels, Chaumet ... Try to imagine what it looked like in 1908! It was the golden time of jewellery in Paris. Apparently it was not very easy to convince his father. Sotirio was a very conservative man. He had built his small empire around silverware and he did not want his son to ruin it. He was sure that Giorgio was mad. Fortunately my father got on very well with his brother Costantino. They were both very ambitious and they had a very international vision of their life in general. They were Greeks, living in Italy, travelling everywhere in Europe. They were very cosmopolitan in their way of life, not traditional Italians. Both were also dreamers, which is good for an entrepreneur."* [6]

And the dream had become reality. By the beginning of the 1930s, all the elegant people in Rome were regular customers of the boutique located on the Via dei Condotti. Princes Colonna, Orsini, Boccompagni Ludovisi, Torlonia, the Volpi family, Count Ciano (Mussolini's son-in-law) and his wife Edda, the Duke of Spoleto, Prince and Princess Christopher of Greece are all mentioned in the archives. They acquired jewellery but also pieces of silver. In 1939, the same day that Dorothy ordered her diamond necklace, another famous customer, the Countess Contini Bonacossi bought a pair of ruby and diamond earrings. She already owned a beautiful diamond necklace by Bulgari. It was one of those classical *"chaînes d'huissier"*, a long chain with a pendant. It could also be worn as three bracelets and a tiara. From 1925 to 1935, the house produced dozens of these parures set with diamonds and coloured gems, which were often cabochons. This shape of stone was a legacy of Byzantine jewellery. Rather than facets, invented in Belgium during the Renaissance, Greek and Russian jewellers always favoured the rounded polish of the cabochons.

Some prestigious foreigners who would play a key role in the history of Bulgari, also arrived around this time. Family tradition relays an anecdote about a necklace given as a present to Dorothy di Frasso by a particularly generous friend, the legendary American billionaire Barbara Hutton, one of the greatest collectors of diamonds of all time. According to Paolo Bulgari: *"Barbara Hutton resided for a month or two at Villa Madama when she first came to Rome in 1931. She had been invited by Countess Di Frasso. To thank her, she went to Bulgari to buy a necklace. She slipped it under the pillow of Countess Di Frasso just before leaving Rome. That's how my father got to know her."* [7]

Barbara Hutton was not the only guest to stay at Villa Madama during the summer of 1931. A gentleman stayed in one of the guest rooms. Dorothy, who had just reached the age of 43, was a little bored. Her marriage with Count di Frasso had brought her the emotional balance she was looking for. But sometimes she missed the storms of passion she experienced with Claude Grahame White. A phone call, in May, changed all that. One of her friends called her from Venice:

—Dorothy, darling! A friend of mine is staying in Venice. He's had a bad time in Los Angeles and he decided to come to Europe to relax. But he doesn't know anyone.

—No problem, tell him to come to Rome. I won't be there for another two weeks, but I'll warn Giuseppe, my cameriero. He'll take care of him. What's his name?

—Gary Cooper! By the way, he's an actor.

Facing page, top: *A page from the Bulgari accounts showing "Comte Contini".* **Bottom:** *Gouache sketches of diamond and ruby Bulgari jewellery from the 1930s. Bulgari Historical Archives.*

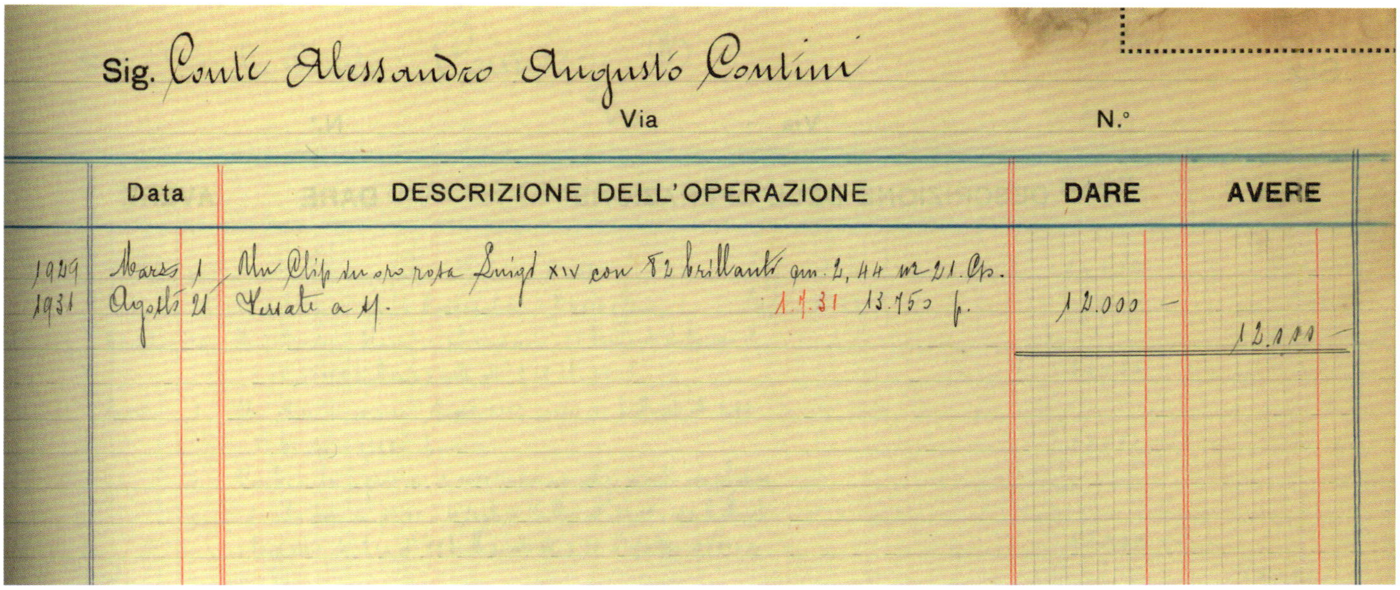

Sig. Conte Alessandro Augusto Contini

Via N.°

	Data		DESCRIZIONE DELL'OPERAZIONE	DARE	AVERE
1929	Marzo	1	Un Clip in oro rosa Luigi XIV con 82 brillanti gm. 2,44 cr 21. Cts.	12.000 —	
1931	Agosto	21	Versato a M. 1.7.31 13.750 f.		12.000 —

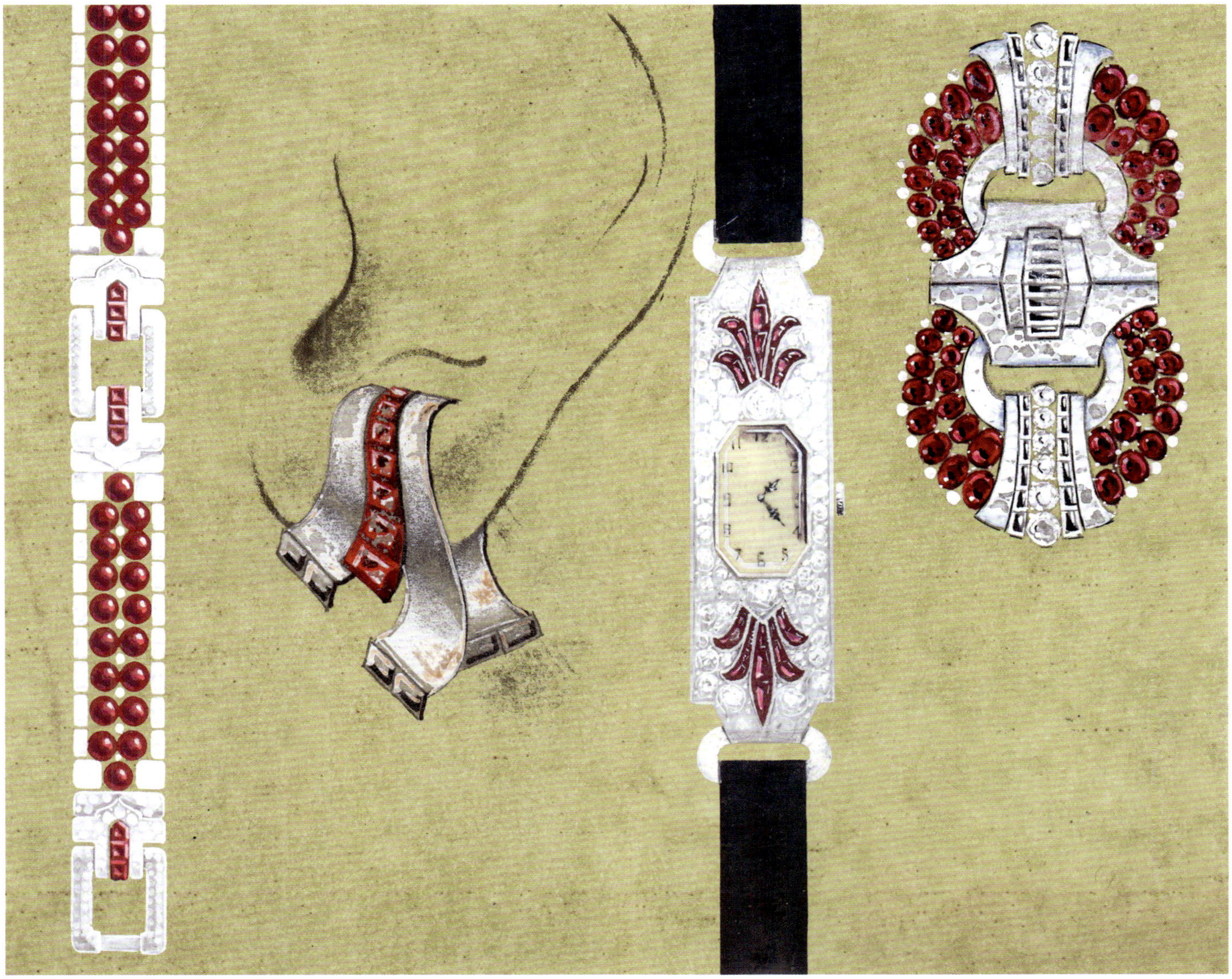

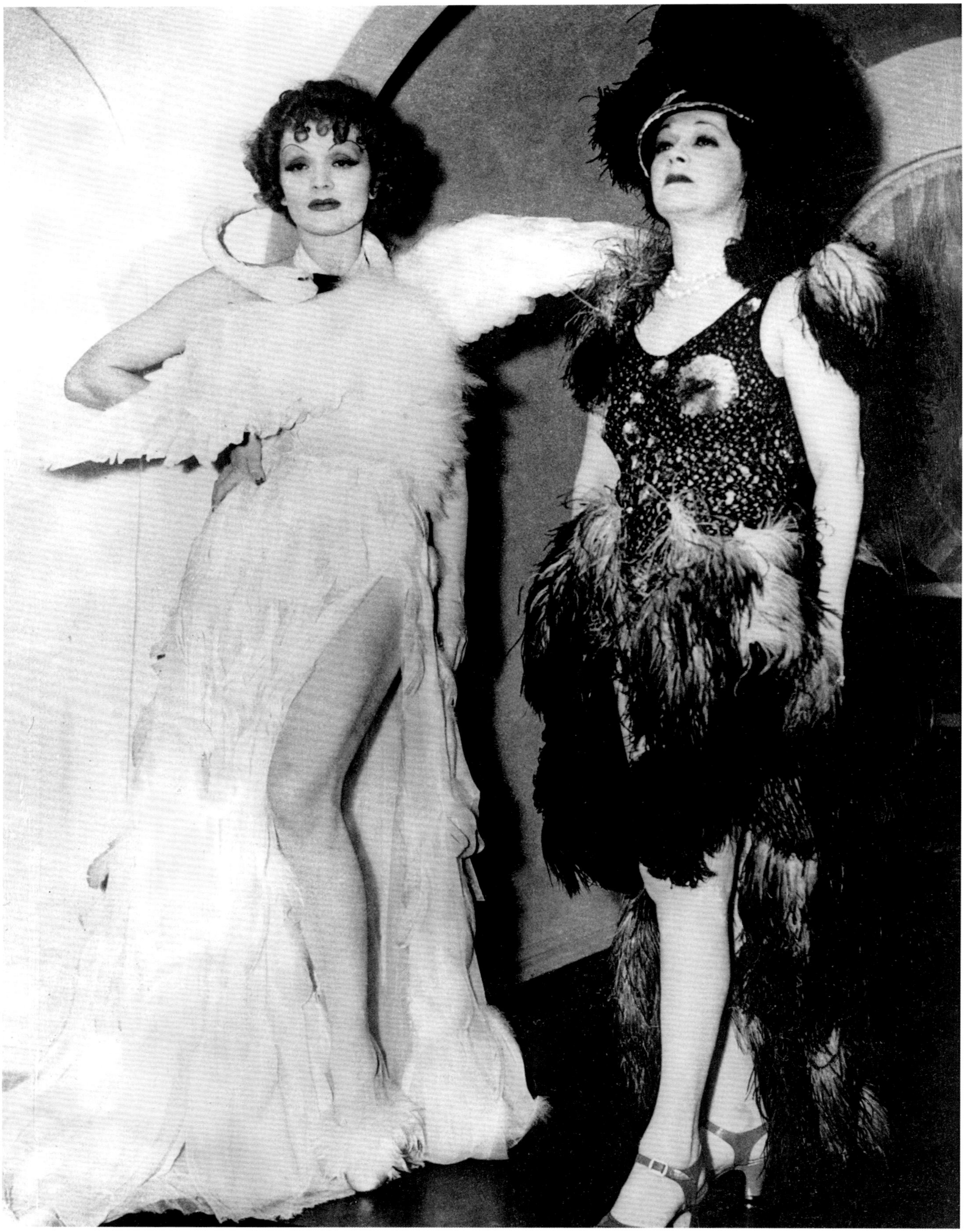

Two weeks later, the relationship that would become the envy of women all around the world began. At the time, Hollywood, the dream machine, was in full swing. And Gary Cooper was one of its gods. This blue-eyed cowboy, 6ft 3in tall, was going to shatter the boredom that surrounded Dorothy. Much silliness has been written about this love affair. At best, Gary Cooper is portrayed as a gigolo who was offered a wardrobe and a long vacation by a man-eating aristocrat. The truth is a little different. Born in 1901, to a family of British émigrés of very bourgeois origin, Gary Cooper was certainly younger than Dorothy, but in the jungle of the American cinema, he was definitely one of its gentlemen. His parents, Charles and Alice Cooper, were rather successful farmers in Montana. Gary and his brother grew up on horseback, with wide open spaces, helping to care for a herd of 500 head. They also received a good education, which culminated with two years of boarding school in England. In early 1924, the Cooper family moved to Los Angeles. Gary, who had studied drawing, had an artistic flair. His physique ensured that he was soon offered work as an extra in silent films. Very quickly, he climbed the ladder to celebrity. From $50 a week in 1926, his salary rose to $175 by 1927. He became a star in 1929, with *The Virginian*, one of the first classic Westerns. In that movie, he created the role of the romantic cowboy, handsome, a little taciturn and reserved, who lives according to the rules of a very strict code of honour.

This success earned him international fame and an avalanche of scripts, which Paramount urged him to shoot. In less than sixteen months, he completed ten films. While shooting, *Morocco,* the most famous of these, he met a young Prussian actress who had just arrived in Los Angeles. Basking in the worldwide success of her latest film, *The Blue Angel,* her name was Marlene Dietrich. She was accompanied by her favourite director, Josef von Sternberg, who had written a screenplay especially for her. The story told of the chaotic love affair of a cabaret singer and a French legionnaire in Morocco, with a desert setting. The film is a monument to kitsch but it works, even today, thanks to the charisma of its two stars. The final scene, during which Marlene, perfectly made-up, with huge false eyelashes, takes off her shoes to join a troop of Moroccan women who have decided to follow the legion in the desert is a piece of movie history. The atmosphere of the shooting was tense. Sternberg was madly in love with Dietrich, who naturally succumbed to Cooper's charms.

Facing page: *Dorothy di Frasso and Marlene Dietrich in the 1930s in their famous costumes: black and white swans.*

At the beginning of 1931, Hollywood's most famous cowboy found himself in bad shape. He had lost 14 pounds and was going through a form of depression. His romantic life, mainly adventures with his screen partners – Lupe Velez, Clara Bow and Marlene – was in chaos. It was at this point that he chose to stop everything and leave for Europe. On the day of his departure, Lupe Velez, who had a reputation as a flamboyant Mexican diva, went to the station to shoot him as he was getting on the train to New York. Hoping to find peace and anonymity in North Africa, he landed in Algiers to discover that he was as famous there as he was in Hollywood. Assaulted by the press, he left and travelled as discreetly as was possible to Italy, where he arrived in May 1931. In Venice, one of the capitals of European social life, a friend advised him to go and spend a few weeks in Rome, at the Countess di Frasso's. Her house was a safe place. No one would be able to spy on him or photograph him. What was more, the Countess had horses; she went hunting several times a week. And Villa Madama was the most comfortable house in Rome. During the first days of his stay at Villa Madama, Cooper was alone. He probably spent these days by the pool, at the side of the terrace garden.

It was the end of May when they met, Dorothy having arrived in Rome for her traditional stay. It was love at first sight! He had only one desire, which was to regain that carefree attitude he had lost in Hollywood. Dorothy's absolute love could restore his sense of confidence. With her, everything was simple. Her fortune, her social circle, her fantasy... made everyday life a perpetual holiday. Dorothy, of course, was crazy about her cowboy. A few years later, a journalist asked her to describe her idea of paradise. With great aplomb, she replied: *"The English writer Max Beerbohm said that paradise to him was a four-poster bed in a field of poppy and mandragora. I say it depends who is between the sheets."* Barbara Hutton, who was a witness to the idyll, was very impressed by

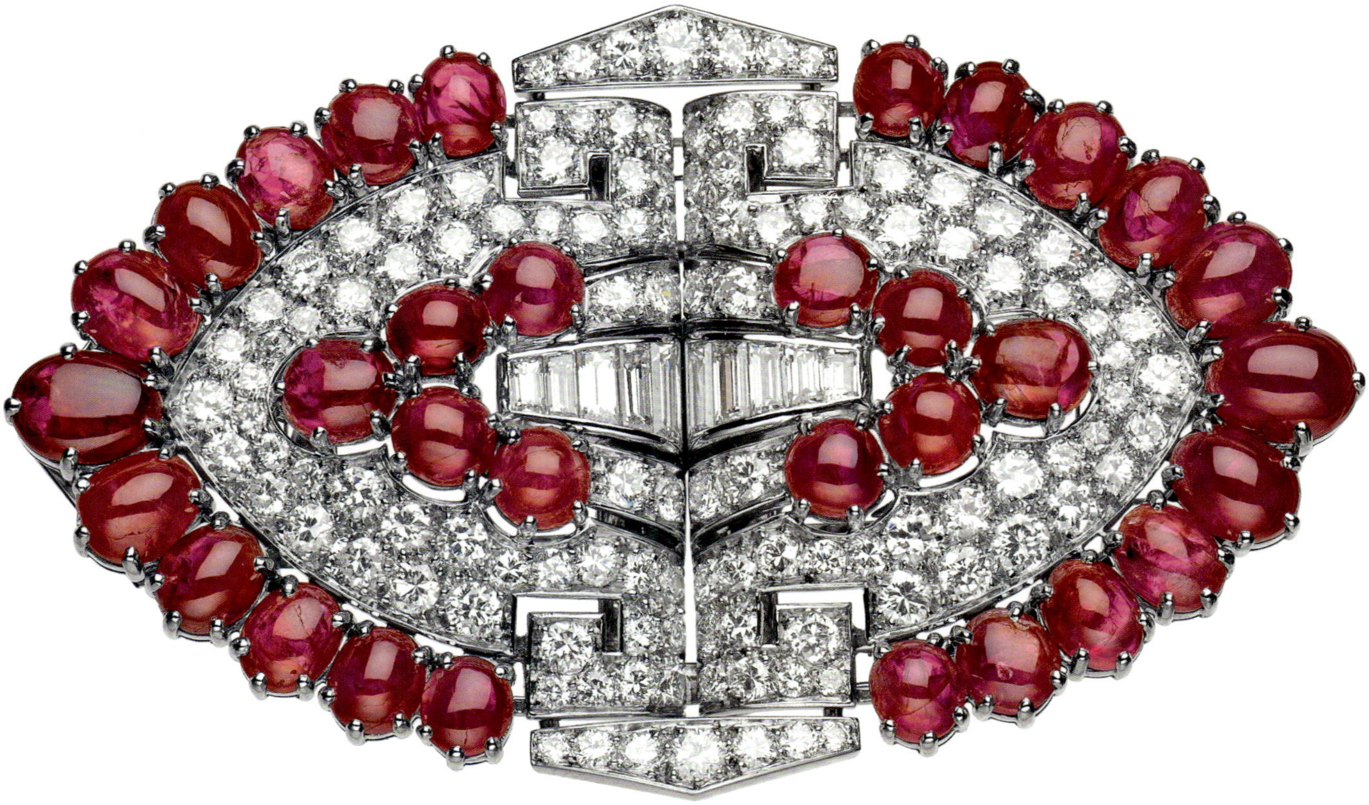

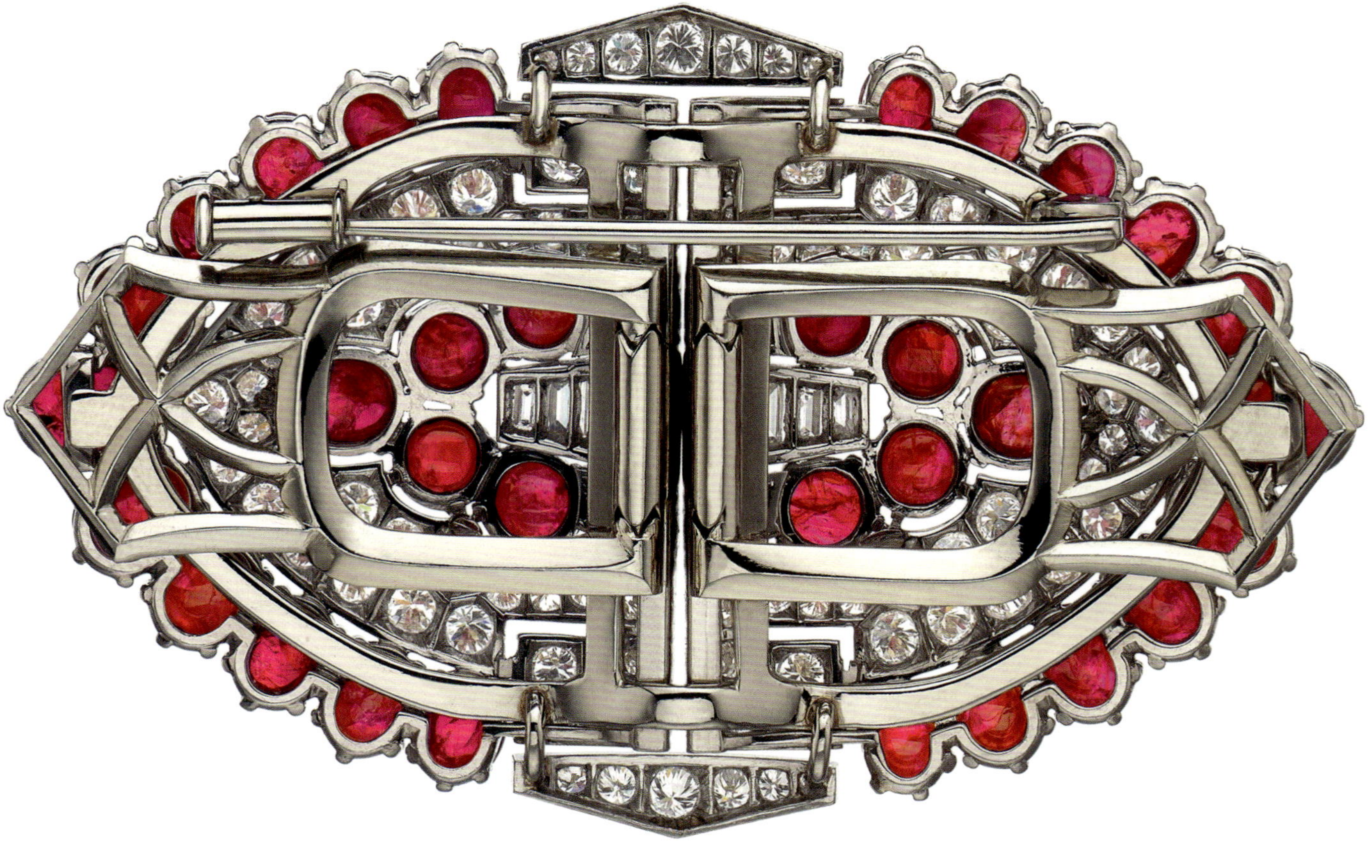

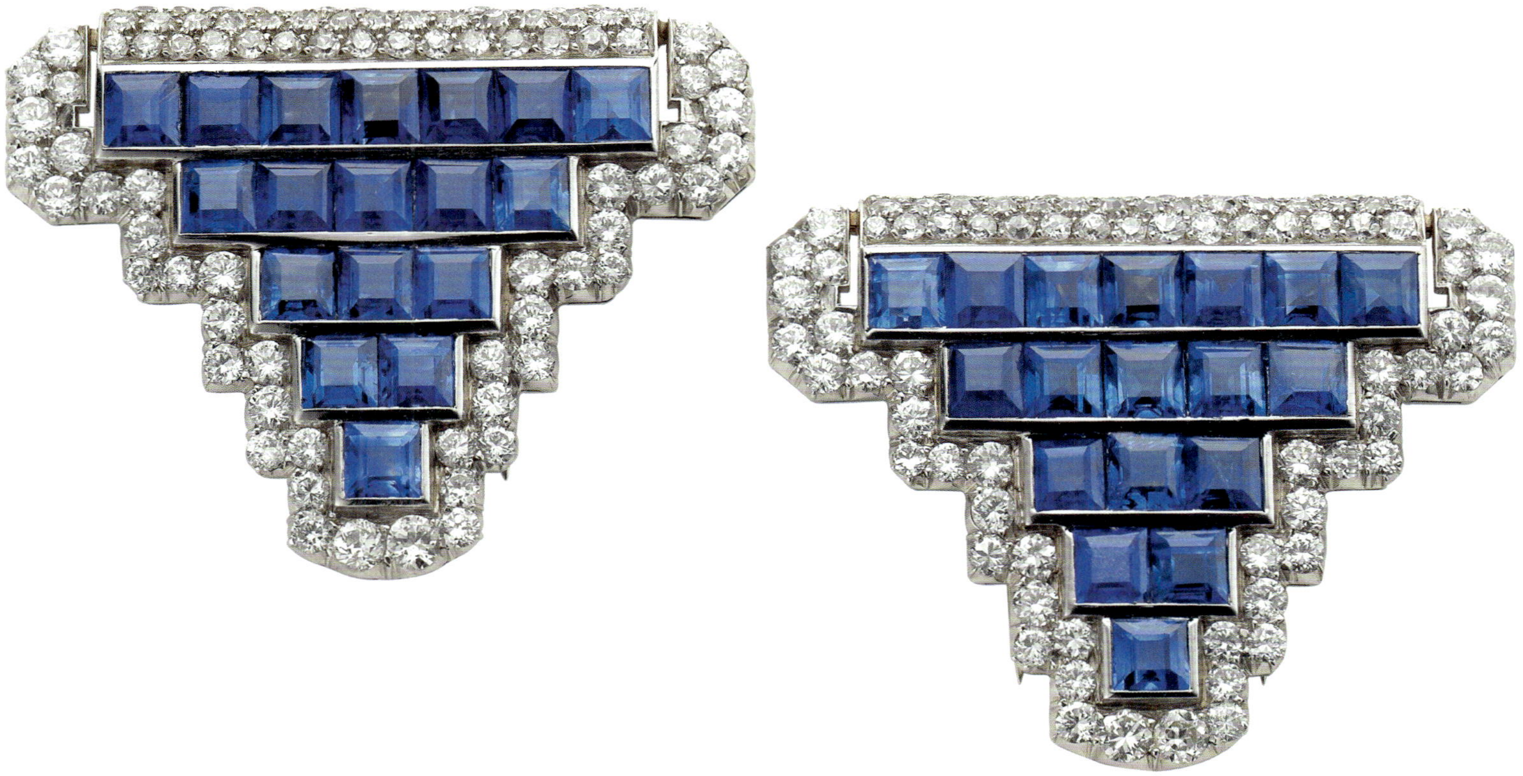

the graciousness of Count di Frasso, who didn't raise an eyebrow during the whole affair.

Together, Gary and Dorothy lived a fabulous year. Deciding that her boyfriend's wardrobe was insufficient for their worldly life together, she took him to 21 via Boncompagni to see Domenico Caraceni, a tailor from Abruzzo. Caraceni dressed the most elegant men of Rome. At Bulgari, Dorothy bought the inevitable men's accessories, cufflinks and cigarette case. From parties to soirées, the season continued and it was exceptional. The previous year, Crown Prince Umberto had married the ravishing Princess Marie José of Belgium. They made a dazzling couple, even though they did not seem very much in love. They were accompanied by the Duke and the Duchess of Aosta (a princess of France). Her sister, Princess Christopher of Greece, also resided in Rome. All, or almost all, were customers of Bulgari. The cinema, an activity favoured by Mussolini, was beginning to develop. The film studio Cinnecittà would not be created until 1937, but the production of films with large budgets had already begun.

The love story was too beautiful to stop in September, when Gary returned to the United States. In order to keep him, Dorothy invented an even crazier project than his Roman holiday: an African safari cruise that would last five months. The two lovers arranged to meet in Naples in October 1931 and embarked on a yacht chartered by Dorothy to cross the Mediterranean to Alexandria. From there, they sailed the Nile down to Cairo, where a plane was waiting for them. In three stages, across Upper Egypt and Sudan, they flew to Nairobi to begin the safari. At the time, this type of adventure was still very dangerous – the climate, the fevers, tribes were not always friendly… and, of course, the wild animals. The balance between nature and man was maintained; their chances were about equal. Cooper hunted elephant, buffalo, and lion. On his return, he could display 65 trophies. Dorothy shot film. Hours of film, on which she recorded all the activities of the man she loved. Sadly, these films have disappeared. Only the start of the rainy season at the beginning of 1932 forced them to return to Europe at last. They embarked at Mombasa, on a long cruise

Facing page: *Front and reverse of a double ruby and diamond clip, Bulgari, 1930. Bulgari Heritage Collection.* **Above:** *Double clip with square-cut sapphires framed by diamonds, signed Bulgari. Private collection.*

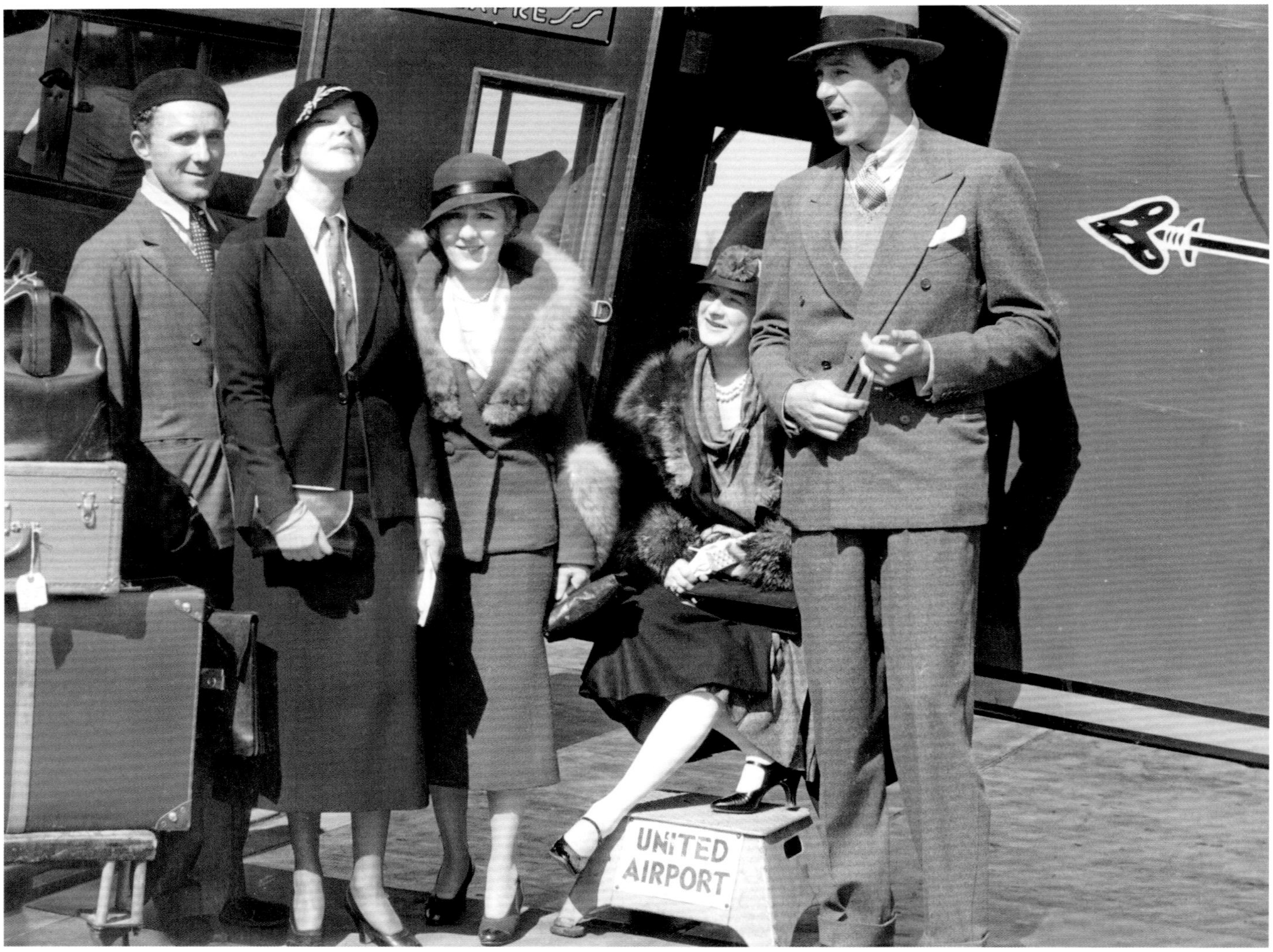

taking them back to Naples, via the Suez Canal and the Mediterranean.

It was a couple in love, radiant and determined to conquer the world that took the road to Hollywood in April 1932. Cooper had regained all the dynamism that he had lost in recent years. Dorothy, for her part, was living a love story with one of the most handsome and charming men in the world. She had offered him her world. Now, it was up to him to open his own. One of the first to welcome them was, of course, Marlene Dietrich. Her daughter, Maria Riva, remembers her first encounter with the extraordinary Countess: *"The first time I saw Dorothy di Frasso was in Hollywood with Gary Cooper. She was then quite plump, but so vivacious and attractive, and Gary was crazy about her, and she about him. When Dorothy saw the slim princesses from Hollywood, she started to diet."* [8] Marlene, for whom all other women were ugly, was clearly a harsher critic than her daughter, though she also understood that Dorothy was not simply a bored rich woman: *"She is more sympathetic and more intelligent than rich people usually are."* [9] Dorothy, as usual, bought a house: the famous mansion of 925 North Bedford Drive. She entrusted the decoration to Elsie de Wolfe. *"And what a house!"* explains Maria Riva in the book she dedicated to her mother, Marlene. *"When a wall was not lined with mirrors, it was covered with exotic birds perched in branches with silvery foliage. The tables were fitted with mirrors as well as the lamps and all the door frames. (...) The carpets that dotted the whole house had long white hairs in the 1830 style. The ground floor resembled the floor of a New Zealand sheepfold after shearing. The dining room could accommodate twenty people around a mirror table."* [10]

As soon as she was settled in her new home, the Countess di Frasso gave her first party. She had all

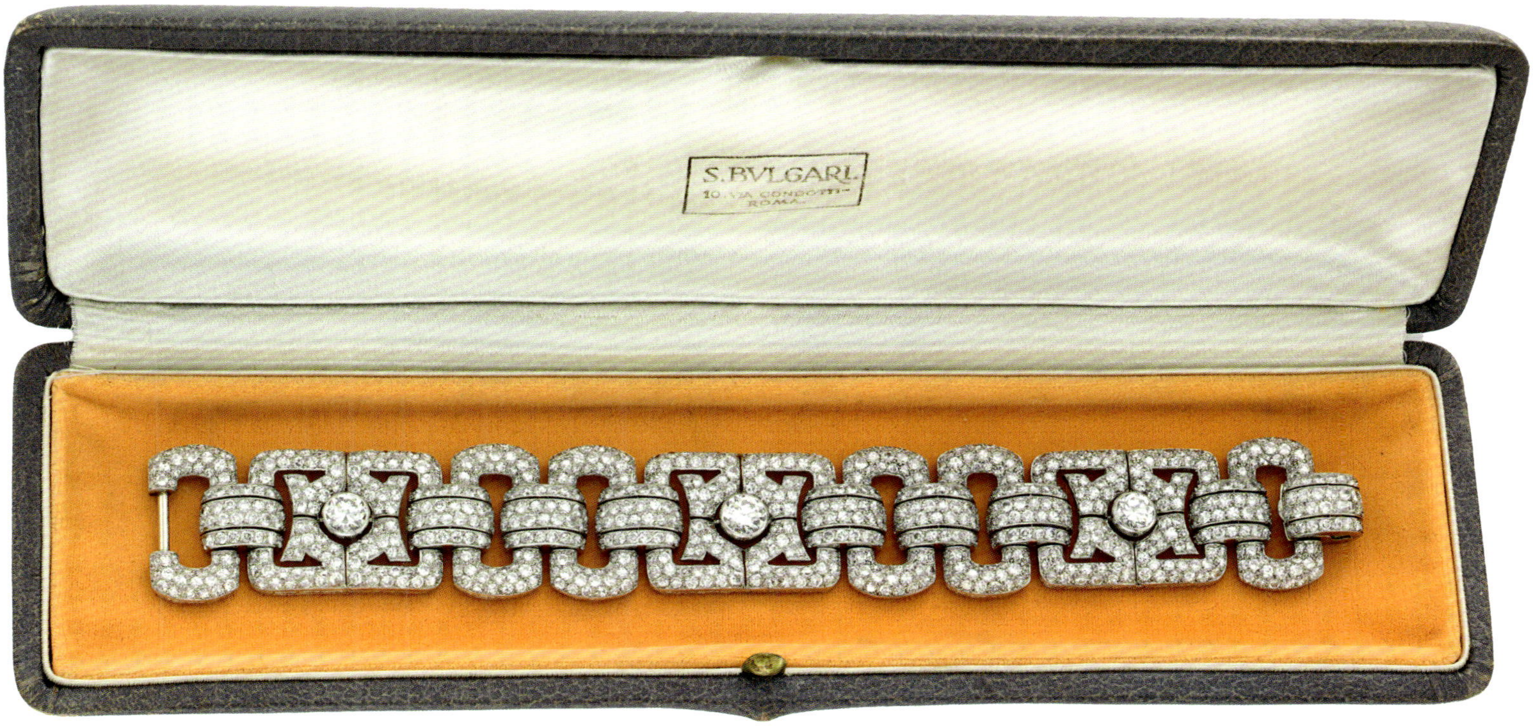

the ingredients for success! Her lover was a movie star. She was rich, inventive and had a noble title. A photograph of this time shows Gary Cooper dressed as an Native American, while Dorothy chose a rather daring nun costume. At another party, she dressed up as a Tyrolean man, with feathered hat and lederhosen. She sat next to none other than Louis B. Mayer, one of Hollywood's tycoons. At one ball, she dressed in black feathers. Her friend, Marlene appeared in an extraordinary costume as "Leda and the Swan". The star was dressed in just a few white swan feathers; the head of the animal wrapped around her neck in an extremely ambiguous pose. To complete her legendary status, the Countess di Frasso bought a Rolls Royce especially designed for her. A Phantom II model. The car has survived and according to experts, it is one of the most beautiful Rolls Royces in the world.

Elsa Maxwell confesses in her memoirs that the Hollywood evenings of Countess di Frasso far exceeded hers in extravagance. So much alcohol would be consumed that guests would sometimes let go of their inhibitions, leading to colourful behavior. At a Louis XIV costume ball one famous actress had become so intoxicated that she sat on the floor and launched into a loud lament. The lady was, it seems, well known for this behaviour. Her lover always carried very strong sedatives that he slipped into a glass in order to make her sleep to stop her cries. The head waiter was tasked with offering her the glass in question on a tray, which he skilfully presented. But ...

Facing page: *Dorothy di Frasso (seated), Gary Cooper, Mary Pickford and some of their friends, preparing for their flight to New York.* **Above:** *Diamond bracelet created by Bulgari in the 1930s. FD Gallery Collection, New York.*

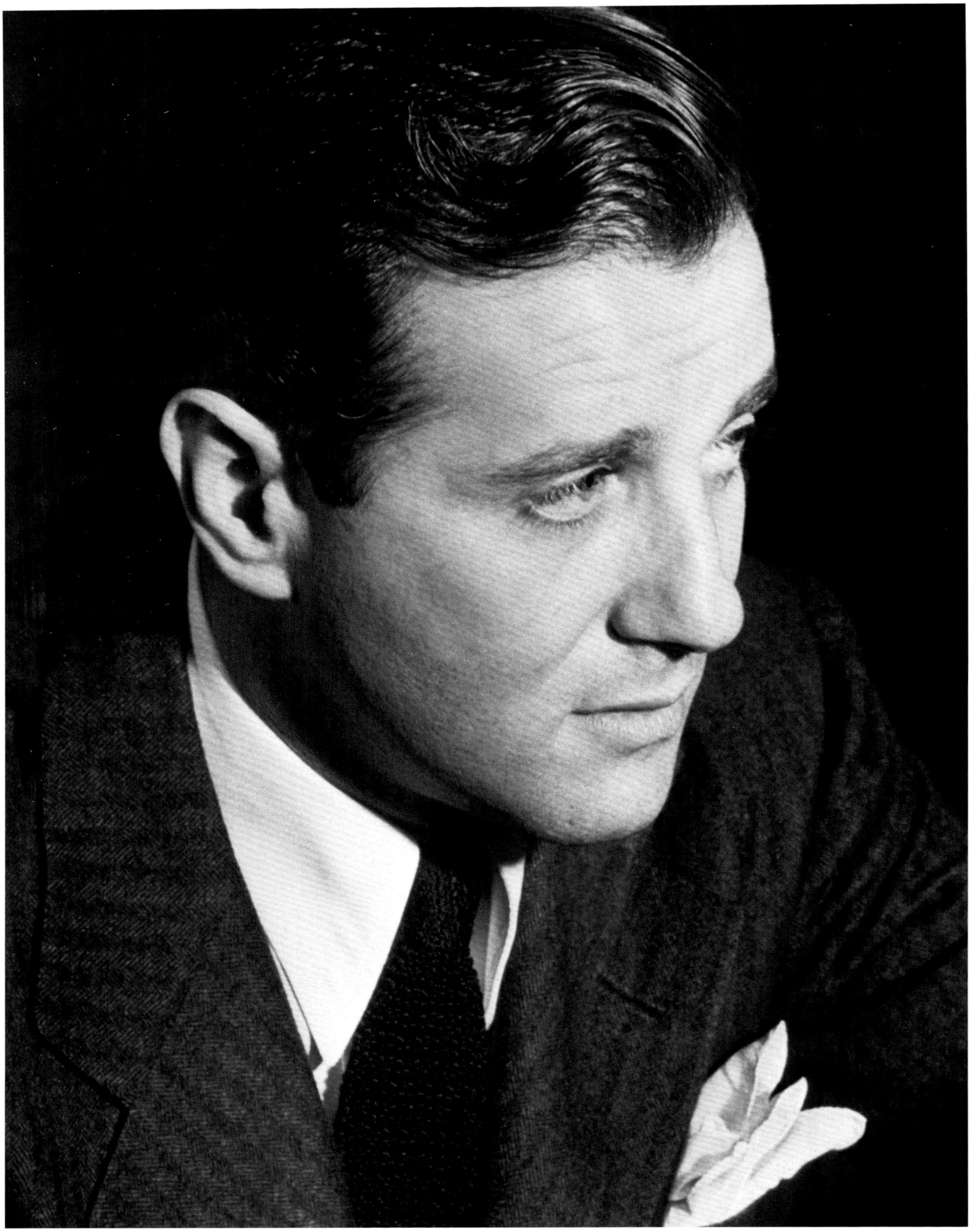

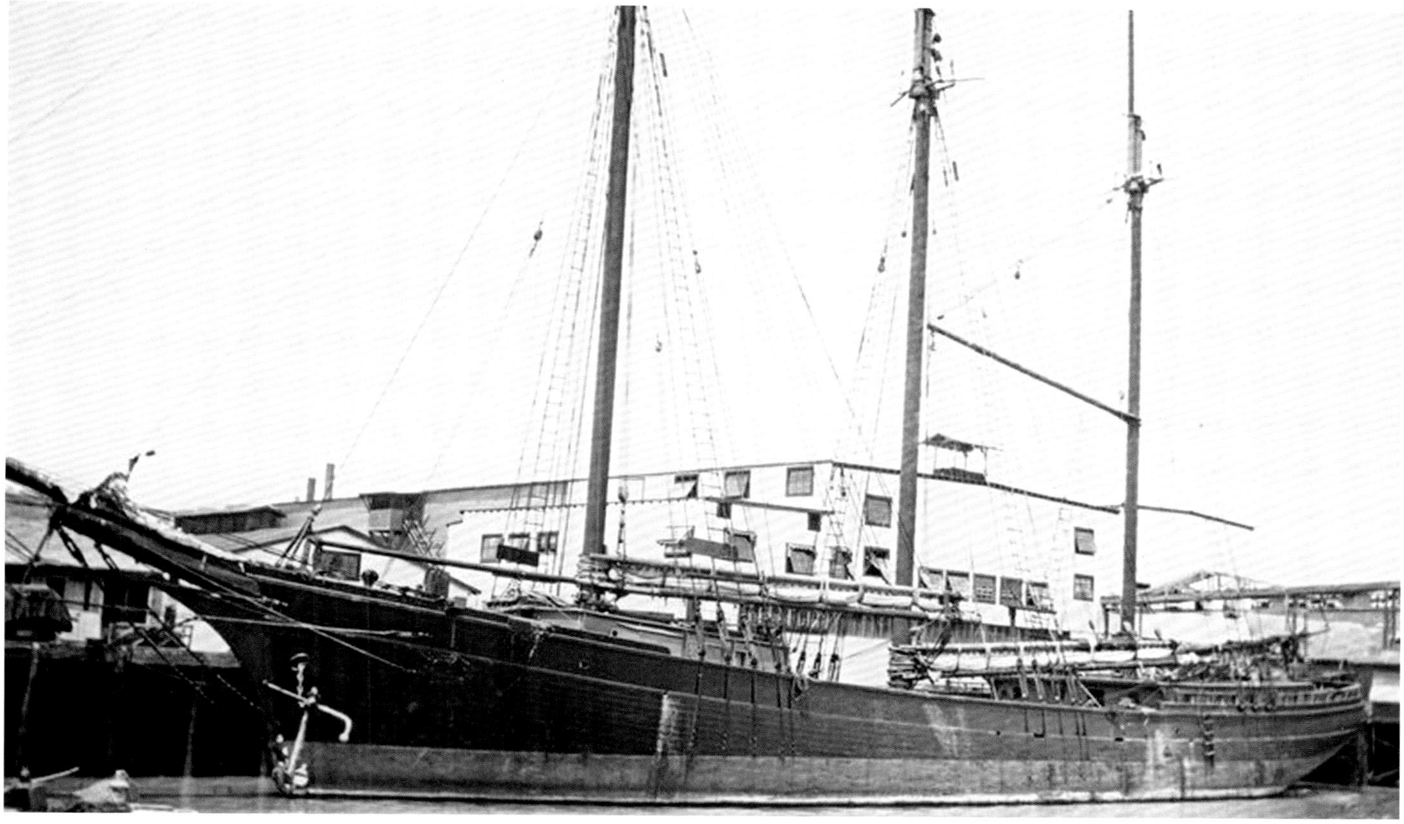

"While the butler was threading across the crowded dance floor, he passed Leslie Howard and Merle Oberon, who were madly infatuated with each other. Howard grabbed the glass intended for the victim and drained it before the horrified butler could stop him. It had an instantaneous effect on him. He collapsed to the floor in seconds with the glass at his lips. He was carried to an upstairs bedroom and another potion was whipped up for the actress. This time it was delivered to the right person and she was carried in the same bedroom which started looking like a funeral parlor with those two stiff bodies laid on the bed. At this point, contessa di Frasso thoughtfully observed: 'Anybody else who feels like getting drunk better make arrangements now to have his body taken to the next of kin'." [11]

A few months were enough to complete the conquest of Hollywood. Unfortunately, all this was no longer fun for Gary Cooper. At 35, he now aspired to more stability in his private life. He had just met a young actresss, Veronica Balfe whom he would marry the following year. Dorothy doesn't seem to have been very angry. This new Hollywood life had given a little spice to her existence. After Gary Cooper, she went on to be linked with several film stars, including Clark Gable, Cary Grant, Charles Boyer and Tyrone Power. In the spring of 1933, after having entrusted her new house to Marlene, she returned to Italy. Travelling with her was the biggest star of American silent film, Mary Pickford. Nicknamed "America's Sweetheart", Pickford was going through a difficult period. Her marriage to another Hollywood legend, Douglas Fairbanks, was in a bad way. He has cheated on her. Legend has it that it was in Rome, at Villa Madama, that their break-up was confirmed.

At the time, Dorothy's love for Rome, and especially for its dictator Mussolini, was beginning to turn sour. Dorothy had a personal motive for hating Mussolini. The Villa Madama was a burden to maintain, even for the Taylors' fortune. The extravagant lifestyle the house required was now even more difficult to finance with the added expense of the house in Los Angeles. Apparently, Count di Frasso had realised the situation sooner than his wife. It was becoming difficult to keep this extravagant house, especially as Mussolini wanted

Facing page: *Bugsy Siegel, Dorothy's love interest from 1937.*
Above: *The* Metha Nelson, *which Dorothy rented in 1938 for her legendary treasure hunt.*

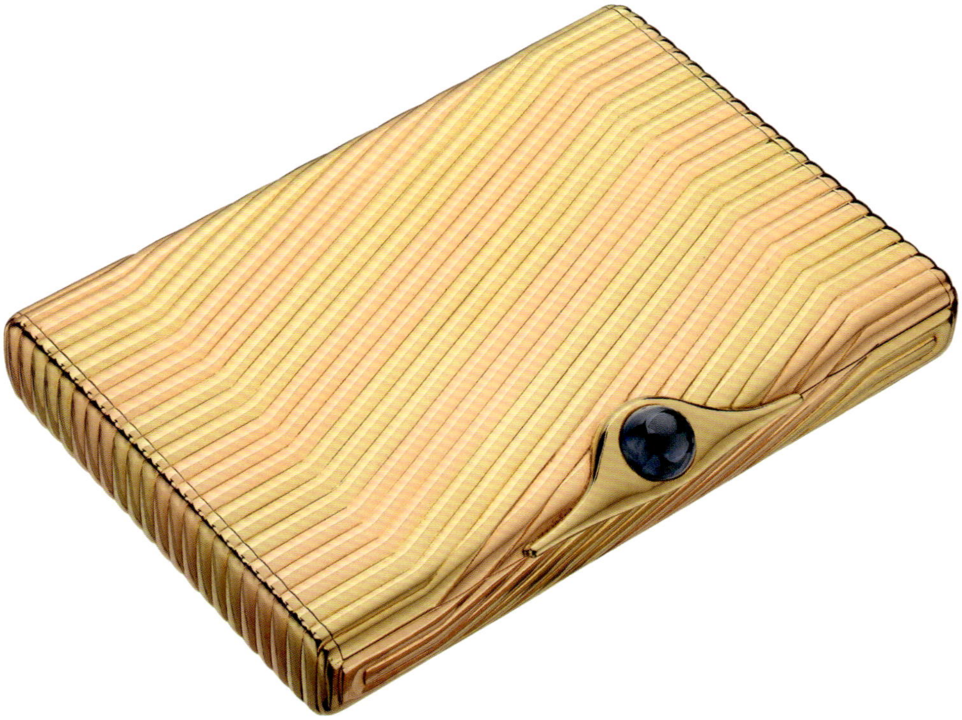

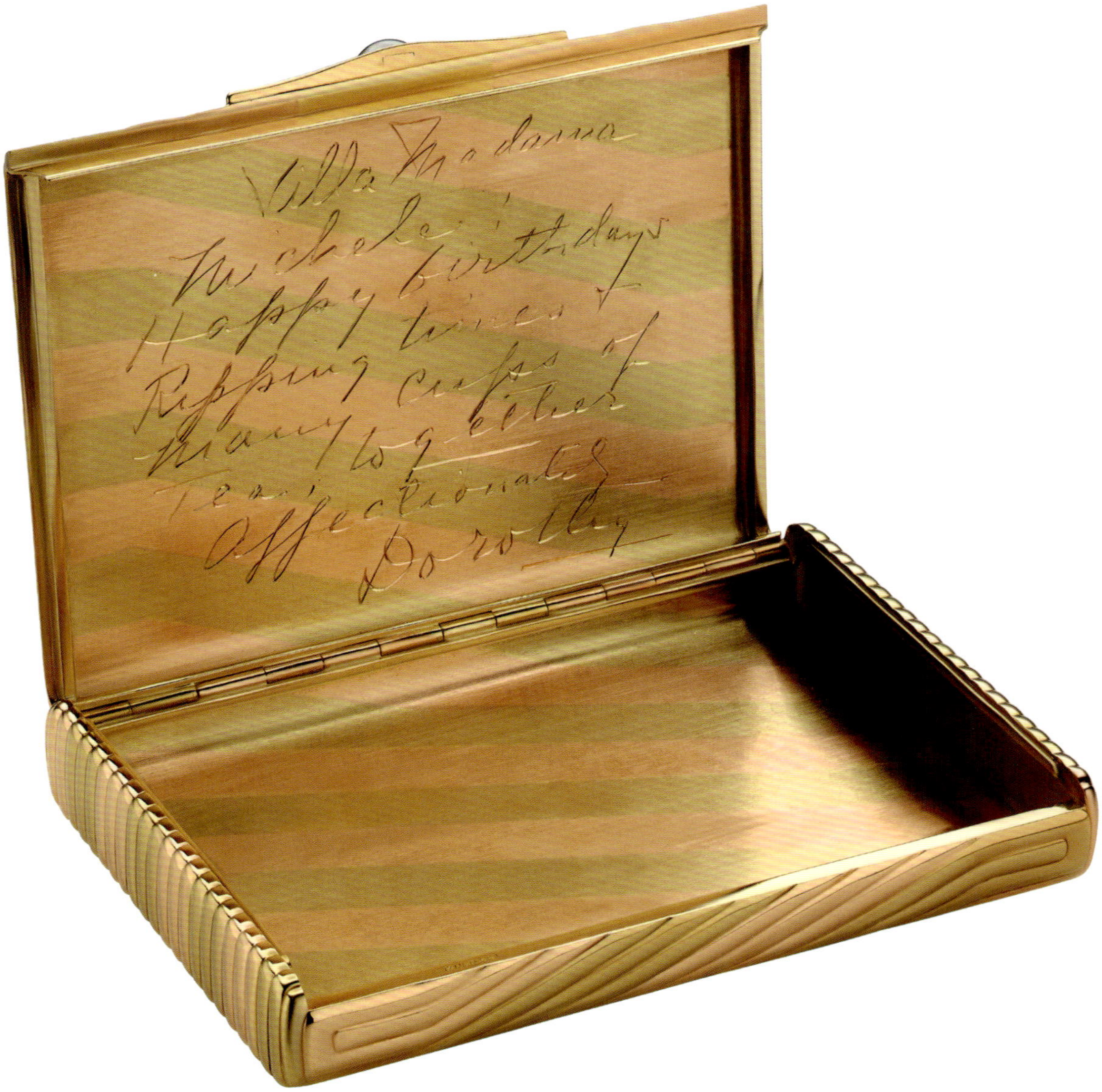
Villa Madama
Happy birthdays
Affectionately
Dorothy

to acquire a prestigious residence for the reception of foreign guests. A purchase price of 37 million lire was mentioned, though it shouldn't be ruled out that the sale might have been somewhat forced. Up until 1940, the di Frassos continued to live at the Villa for part of the year. The relationship between the dictator and the countess became so bad that at one point Dorothy considered the possibility of murder.

It was also during one of these meetings that the young Maria could not help wondering whether her mother, did not share "*…something more than just a rented house*" with the Countess di Frasso; she had after all had several liaisons with women. Of the Mussolini incident, Maria recalls: *"The Countess was on the point of leaving for Italy to kill Mussolini! She had an unstoppable plan! Planting another cigarette in her long ivory cigarette holder, she told us in detail: She had been told that tiger whiskers, once crushed and mixed with food, were capable of perforating human intestines like a thousand sharp needles … and would cause sudden death by peritonitis. (…) Since there were only two tigers left at the Rome zoo, she had to fly to get there before they died."* [12] Were the tigers of the Rome zoo too old? Did the whiskers not have the promised power? Or had Dorothy, having been made to see reason by her husband, renounced her plan? In any case, Mussolini survived. A few years later, it was Marlene Dietrich who would ultimately contribute to his fall. Having taken American citizenship, she would accompany the American army to the front and actively participate in the offensive of the American armies in Italy at the end of the Second World War.

Fortunately for the Countess di Frasso, another man came into her life. He was as handsome as her previous amours, though perhaps a little less distinguished. Above all, he represented the supreme thrill. A gangster of the great era, Benjamin Siegel was one of the heads of the Yiddish Connection, the Jewish branch of the American mafia. His nickname "Bugsy", which means "crazy", referred to his dangerous character and violent attitude, especially towards women. After a profitable career in New York, where he specialised in racketeering and gaming, he chose to up sticks and settle in California, where the climate seemed more profitable. Having briefly been linked to the "Blond Bombshell", Jean Harlow, he aspired to respectability, which the Countess di Frasso could offer in spades. They met on the racetrack, whereupon Bugsy deployed all his charm to seduce this "woman of the world".

The meeting gave rise to one of the most extraordinary experiences of their lives. In September 1938, Bugsy and Dorothy embarked on a treasure hunt together. The cruise on the schooner, *Metha Nelson* would turn out to be the most unlikely adventure in the Countess di Frasso's life. The expenses of Rome and Hollywood had dug holes in her fortune. And one evening, in a bar in Los Angeles, the couple met an old sailor, full of whisky, who told them the fabulous story of the treasure of Peru. In 1820, when the armies of the liberator San Martín approached Lima, the Viceroy had the Peruvian treasure put on board an English vessel, which sailed away just in time. On board were dozens of tons of gold, silver, thousands of precious stones, 36 pectoral crosses and two life-size gold statues of the Virgin Mary holding the infant Jesus in her arms. This booty, worth $300 million in the 1930s, had never been found. The ship's captain had apparently buried the treasure on Cocos Island, more than 500 kilometres off the coast of Costa Rica. The old drunken sailor claimed to have seen a map of Cocos Island marking the spot of the buried treasure, which he sketched for them.

Dorothy had asked Bugsy Siegel to round up a crew. The chosen sailing boat was the *Metha Nelson,* a late 19th century ship which was also a star in Hollywood. It appeared in numerous films, among them *Mutiny on the Bounty*, in which a friend of Dorothy's, Clark Gable, acted. The hastily assembled crew was in fact a gang of criminals who more or less needed to take off for a few weeks. Only three of them had sailed before. The position of captain was entrusted to Mario Bello, who was none other than the father-in-law of Jean Harlow, the former girlfriend of Bugsy. *"The first day out, the yacht became a meeting caldron of hatred over the division of the treasure and the attentions of the ship's nurse. Day after day the crew decided to drink more, especially after a few disappointing discoveries."* [13]

"Instead of millions of gold coins, we found millions of red ants," Dorothy later confided to reporter Louella Parsons on her return to California. The return trip was

Facing page: *Gold cigarette case, signed Bulgari. This was bought by Dorothy di Frasso as a gift for one of her friends. Bulgari Heritage Collection.*

a catalogue of disasters that would have been comical had the situation not become so dangerous. With the virtue of the nurse – who was 22 years old – coming more and more under threat, Mario Bello, 55, decided to marry her during a stopover. He celebrated his marriage with ten days of drunkenness, during which he disappeared having challenged a young officer who had shown a little too much interest in Bello's young wife, to a duel. The frustrated crew mutinied and two men were put in irons. Then, just a few hours after hearing a radio announcement of an incoming hurricane, all of the boat's machinery broke down! The expedition was only saved by a robust freighter escorting the *Metha Nelson* as far as Acapulco, at a cost of a few thousand dollars, of course.

Back in California on 15 January, Dorothy and Bugsy, weren't ready to admit defeat. It was at this point that they embarked on the adventure of the revolutionary process of making dynamite and trying to sell it to Mussolini. Though it sounds like a tall tale, the story was corroborated after the Second World War by Crown Prince Umberto, who went on to become the last King of Italy, and by Count Ciano, Mussolini's son-in-law, who records the events in his diary. Strangely, on her arrival in Rome, Dorothy seems to have rushed to her friend Giorgio Bulgari, where she bought a set of cufflinks and buttons in black pearls and diamonds. She also asked him to alter her beautiful ring that was set with an emerald of 4.09 carats. The adventure of dynamite also having turned sour, she chose to stay on in Rome, despite the growing dangers in Europe. She was not the only one to show a certain lack of worldly awareness. During the same summer of 1939, as the war clouds gathered, her friend Marlene Dietrich chose to stay on the Côte d'Azur at the Cap d'Antibes.

At the end of August, Bertrand Taylor, Dorothy's brother, took charge. *"A few days before WWII was declared, Dorothy's brother and my husband went to Italy to get her out,"* explains Fay Taylor, who married Dorothy's nephew. *"My husband said she was 'outspoken' and I assumed they were afraid that she would not leave. They were faced with a legal problem."* [14] Dorothy had been an Italian citizen for more than ten years, and she had never had her American passport renewed. She did not have a passport at that time, so they had to put her on a boat for Mexico. From Mexico, it seems she managed to reach New York. The official maritime register of arrivals records her name on 23 September, 1939. A priority on arrival was to deposit her gems at a jeweller's to value them and probably to have them cleaned. Having left Rome with minimum baggage, she probably had to pack them quickly in a travel bag. The inventory lists $315,000 worth of jewels. The double-row pearl necklace inherited from her mother was the most important piece, with a value of $70,000; after that, the Bulgari diamond necklace, which was estimated to be worth $40,000. The emerald, ruby, diamond and pearl necklace, possibly the one acquired at Bulgari by Barbara Hutton in 1931, was estimated at $30,000. A second diamond necklace was valued at $27,000. The emerald ring created by Bulgari just before her departure for Rome, was worth $7,500.

With Dorothy rescued, her nephew also had to return to the United States. In the nick of time, he found a place on the last plane that took off from Marseilles the day before the declaration of war. By amazing coincidence, there was another famous passenger on the same plane: the young actor, Tyrone Power. And it was with him that Dorothy would return to Rome, to Villa Madama and Bulgari in the aftermath of World War II…

Facing page: *This diamond, emerald, ruby and rock crystal necklace, is part of the Festa collection. It is set with a 29.35-carat Sri Lankan sapphire, a 13.95-carat spinel and a 3.55-carat emerald.*

1. *No Innocence Abroad* by Michael Stern, Random House, 1953. **2.** *RSVP, Elsa Maxwell's own story,* Little Brown Editions, 1954. **3.** *No Innocence Abroad, op. cit.* **4.** *Ibid.* **5.** *Poor Little Rich Girl* by David Heymann, Lyle Stuart, 1983. **6.** Interviews with the author: *Rome, Passion, Jewels* by Vincent Meylan, Electa, 2014. **7.** *Ibid.* **8.** Film Museum Berlin, Newsletter 66, August 2004. **9.** *Marlene Dietrich* by Maria Riva, Flammarion, 1993. **10.** *Ibid.* **11.** *RSVP, Elsa Maxwell's own story, op. cit.* **12.** *Marlene Dietrich, op. cit.* **13.** *RSVP, Elsa Maxwell's own story, op. cit.* **14.** Interview with the Taylor family

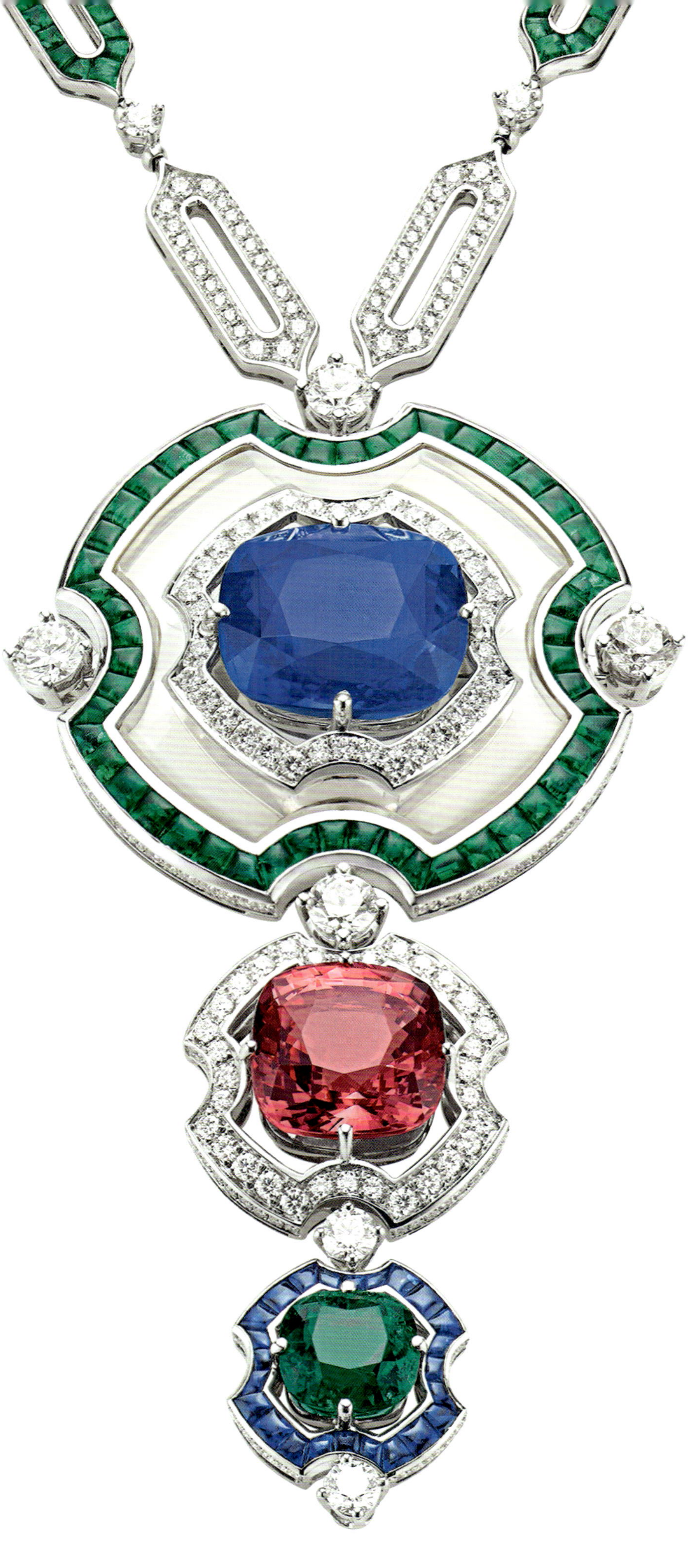

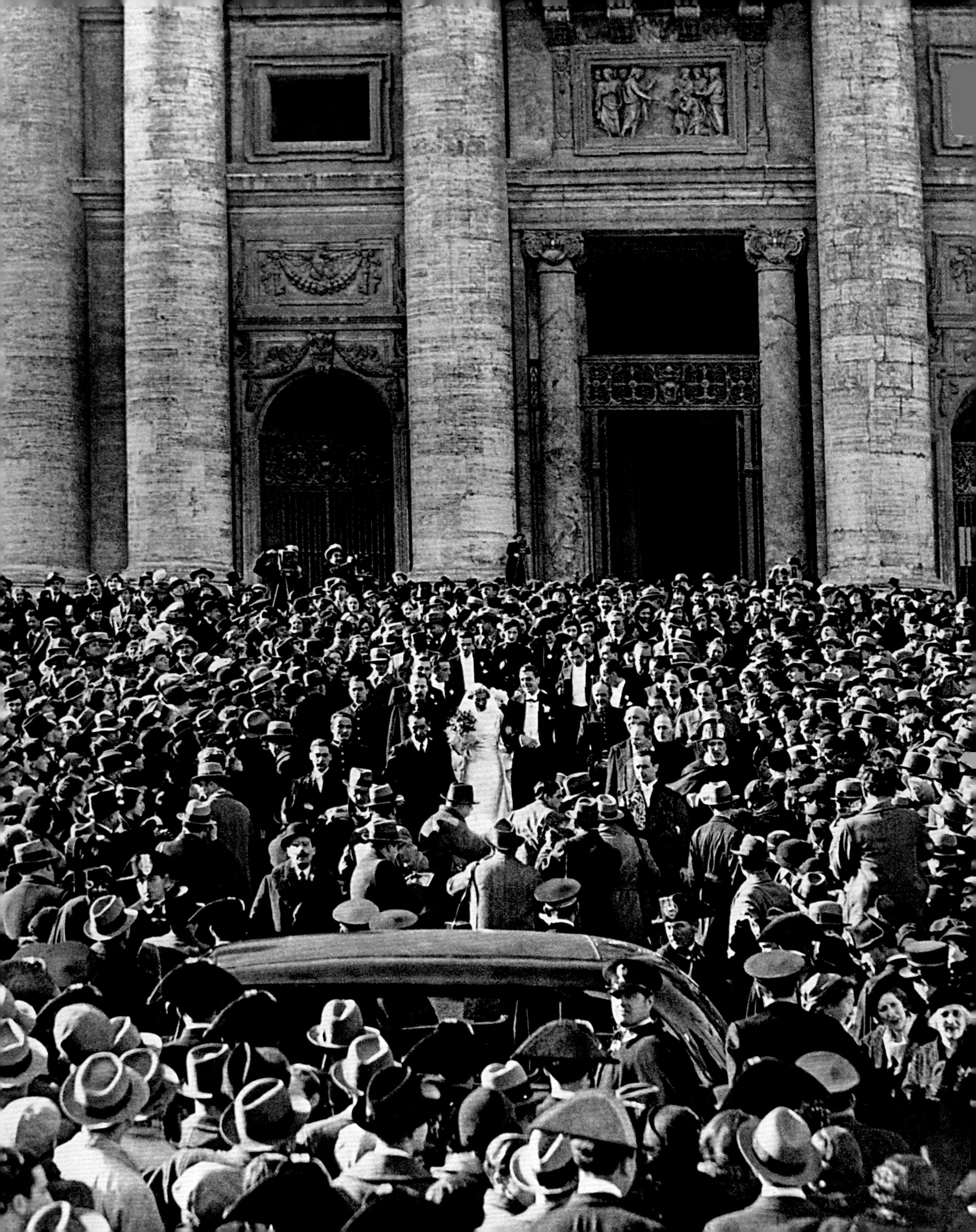

Chapter 2

THE WEDDING OF A SPANISH PRINCESS

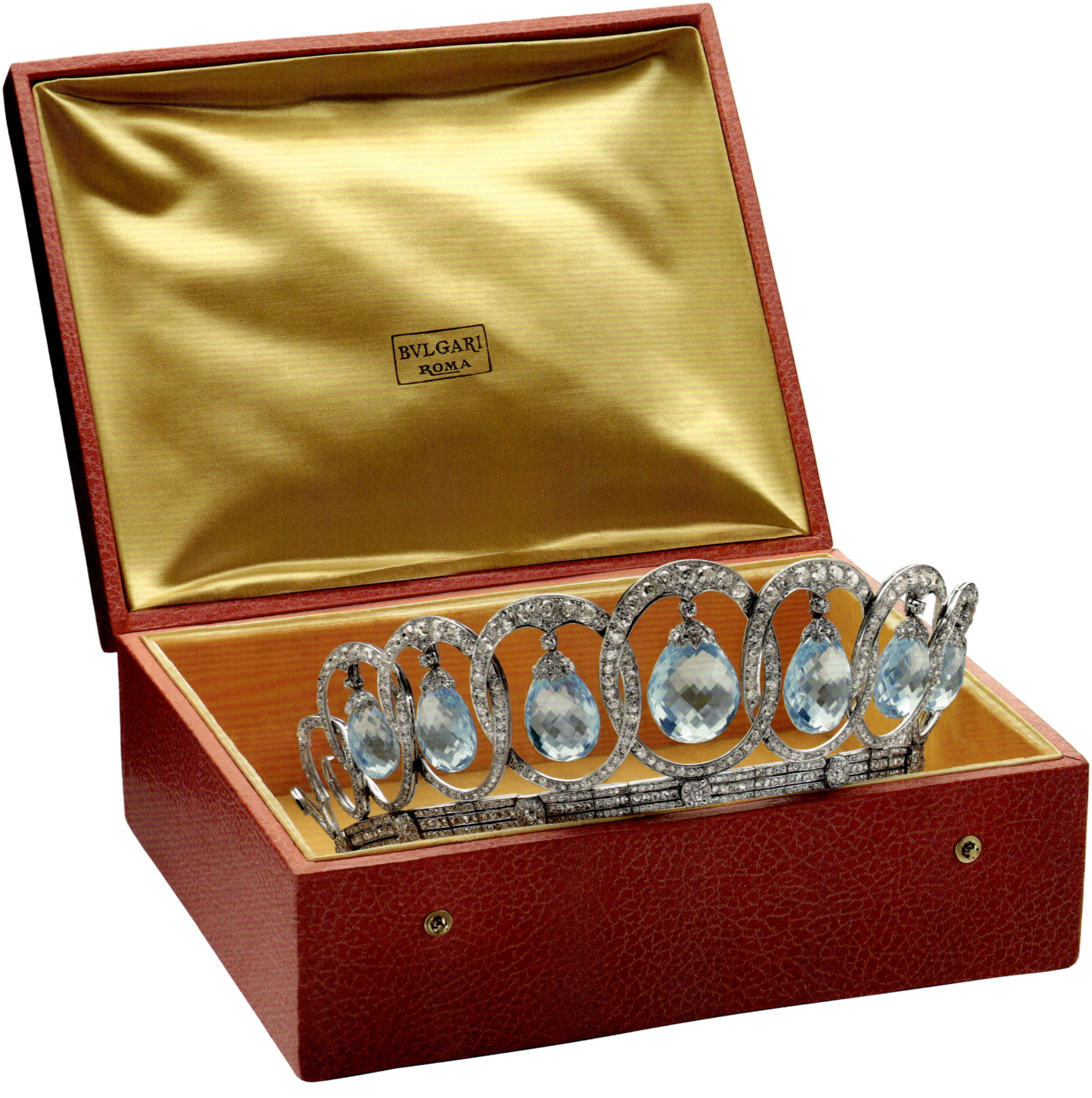
BVLGARI
ROMA

Beatriz de Bourbon, Princess of Civitella-Cesi (1909-2002)

Rome, Church of the Jesuits, 14 January 1935

Since the days of the Borgia Popes, natives of Valencia, Rome had never seen so many Spaniards staying within its walls. More than 5,000 had made the trip to cheer their royal family in exile. They were massed on the esplanade in front of the main Jesuit church, waiting patiently for the bride and groom. A hundred princes and princesses from all over Europe, the entire Roman aristocracy and, of course, the King and Queen of Italy, had taken their places in the heart of the church. His Majesty, King Alfonso XIII of Spain had been living in Rome for the last four years. Today, his eldest daughter, HRH Infanta Beatriz, would be getting married to Don Alessandro Torlonia, Prince of Civitella-Cesi, the heir of a great Roman noble family.

For the first time in its history, Bulgari was faced with the very special custom of royal weddings: the wedding presents. Indeed, tradition has it that a young royal or aristocratic bride would receive a suite of jewels, antique or modern, from her future husband, family and in-laws. This collection would reflect the luxury and elegance in which the young woman would live from now on. It would be exhibited in the days before the ceremony, either at the bride's house or at the jeweller's.

Obviously, wedding presents for a King's daughter would need to be particularly impressive. Especially since the Torlonia family was very rich. Originally from Auvergne, these Frenchmen, who used to be called Tourlounias, left their country during the mid-18th century. Having settled in Rome, within a single generation, they became the bankers for the Pope. This lucrative business enabled the family to amass a considerable fortune and a long list of honours, including several noble titles. During the 19th century, following an alliance with the Borghese, the Torlonia family divided into three branches: that of the Dukes of Poli and Guadagnolo; the Princes Torlonia; and the Princes Civitella-Cesi, of which Alessandro was heir.

Faithful to the tradition of Roman gigantism, the palace that the young Prince inherited was immense. The square edifice was built around two courtyards between Via Bocca di Leone, Via Borgognona, Via Mario dei Fiori and Via dei Condotti, standing fewer than 50 meters from the Bulgari shop. It was quite natural, therefore, that it was Giorgio and Costantino Bulgari who were approached to create the jewels to be presented to the Infanta on the occasion of her marriage. *"My father bought a lot of things for my mother at Bulgari when they married in 1935,"* recalls Princess Olimpia Torlonia. *"I think he had chosen this jeweler because Bulgari at that time represented novelty. In the 1930s, this house was not the traditional jeweler of the Roman aristocracy. It was an innovative, fashionable brand."* [1] The rare archives kept by the house and dating from before the Second World War indeed show that some members of the royal family of Spain who were exiled in Rome had been clients of Bulgari since 1934.

For his future wife, Prince Alessandro chose a large pavé-set diamond bracelet, the height of fashion in the 1930s. Art Deco white jewellery reigned.

Facing page: *The diamond and aquamarine tiara created by Bulgari in 1935 as wedding gift for Infanta Beatriz of Spain. Private collection.* **Previous page:** *The bride and groom in front of St Peter's Basilica in Vatican City.* **Overleaf:** *HRH Infanta Beatriz of Spain and Don Alessandro Torlonia, Prince of Civitella-Cesi at the Vatican for their audience with His Holiness Pope Pius XI after their wedding ceremony on 14 January, 1935.*

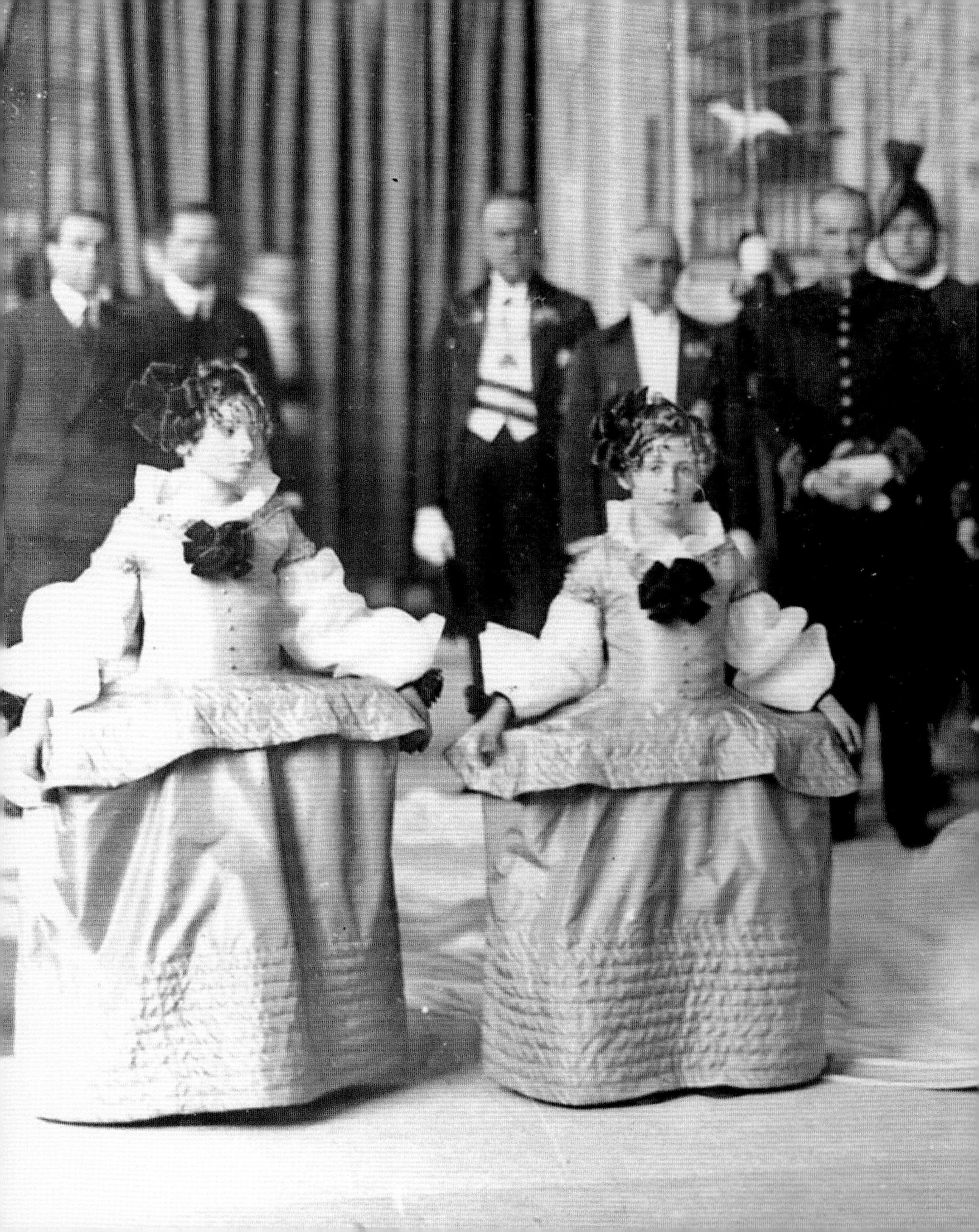

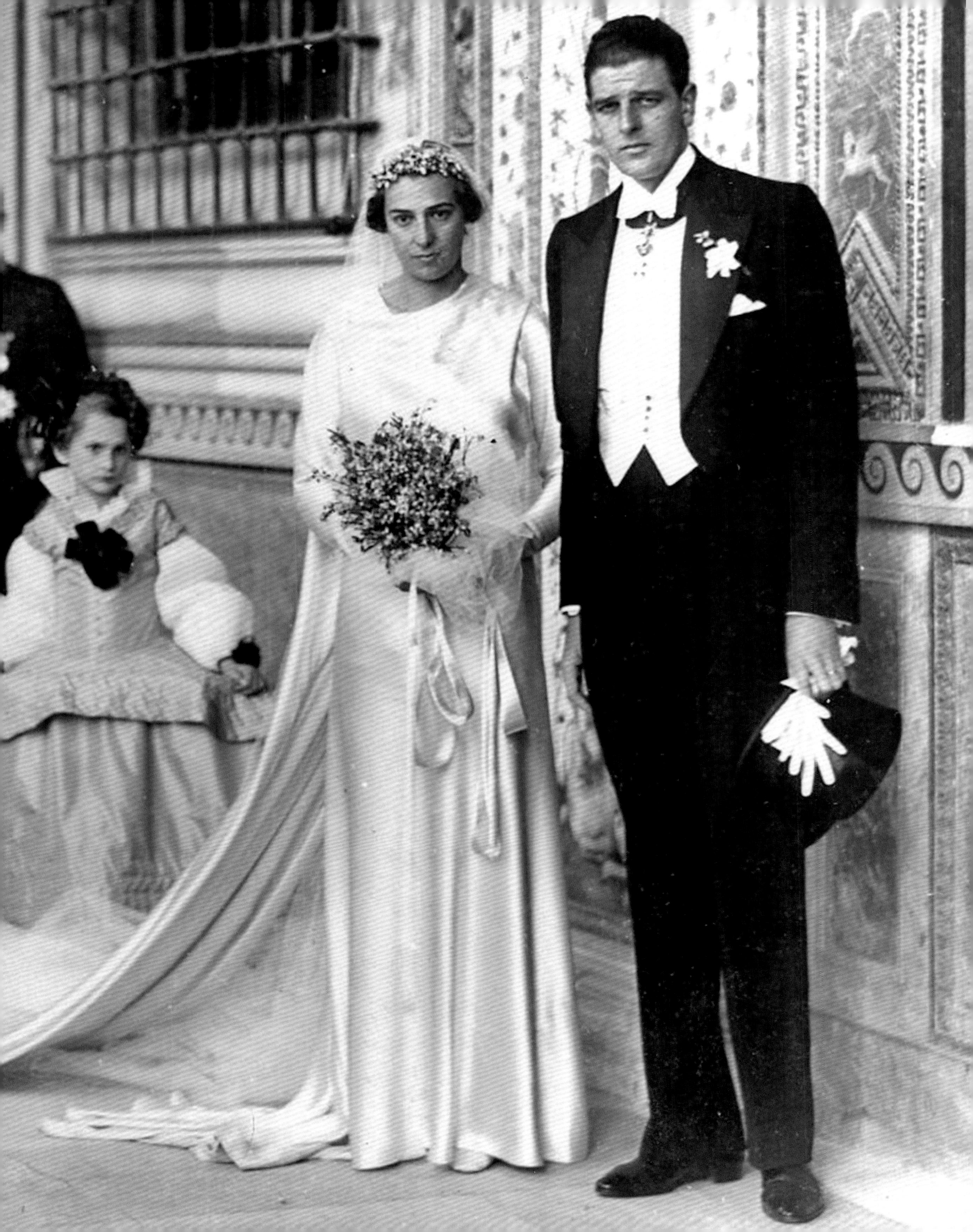

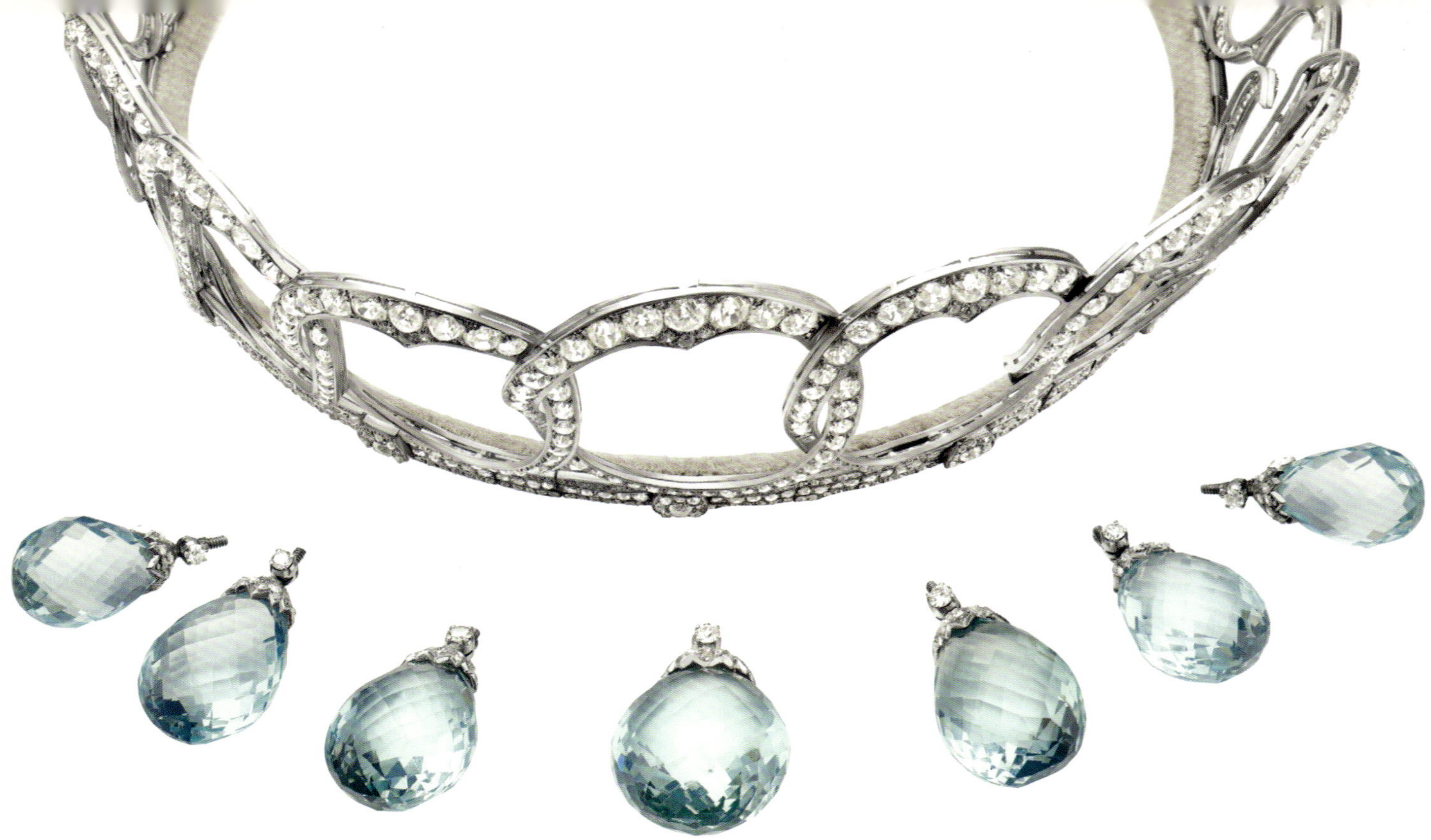

The aquamarine and diamond tiara created by Bulgari in 1935 for Infanta Beatriz of Spain, with and without its aquamarine pendants. Private collection.

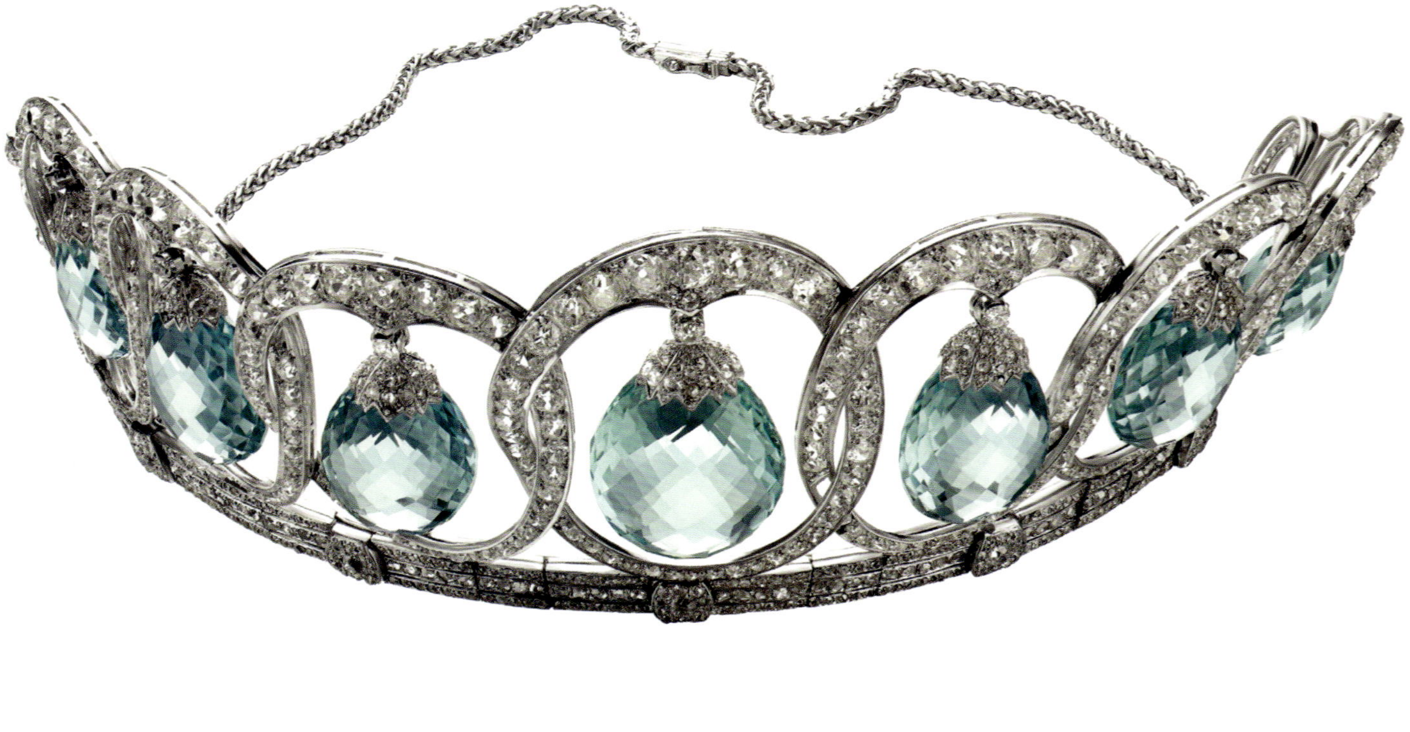

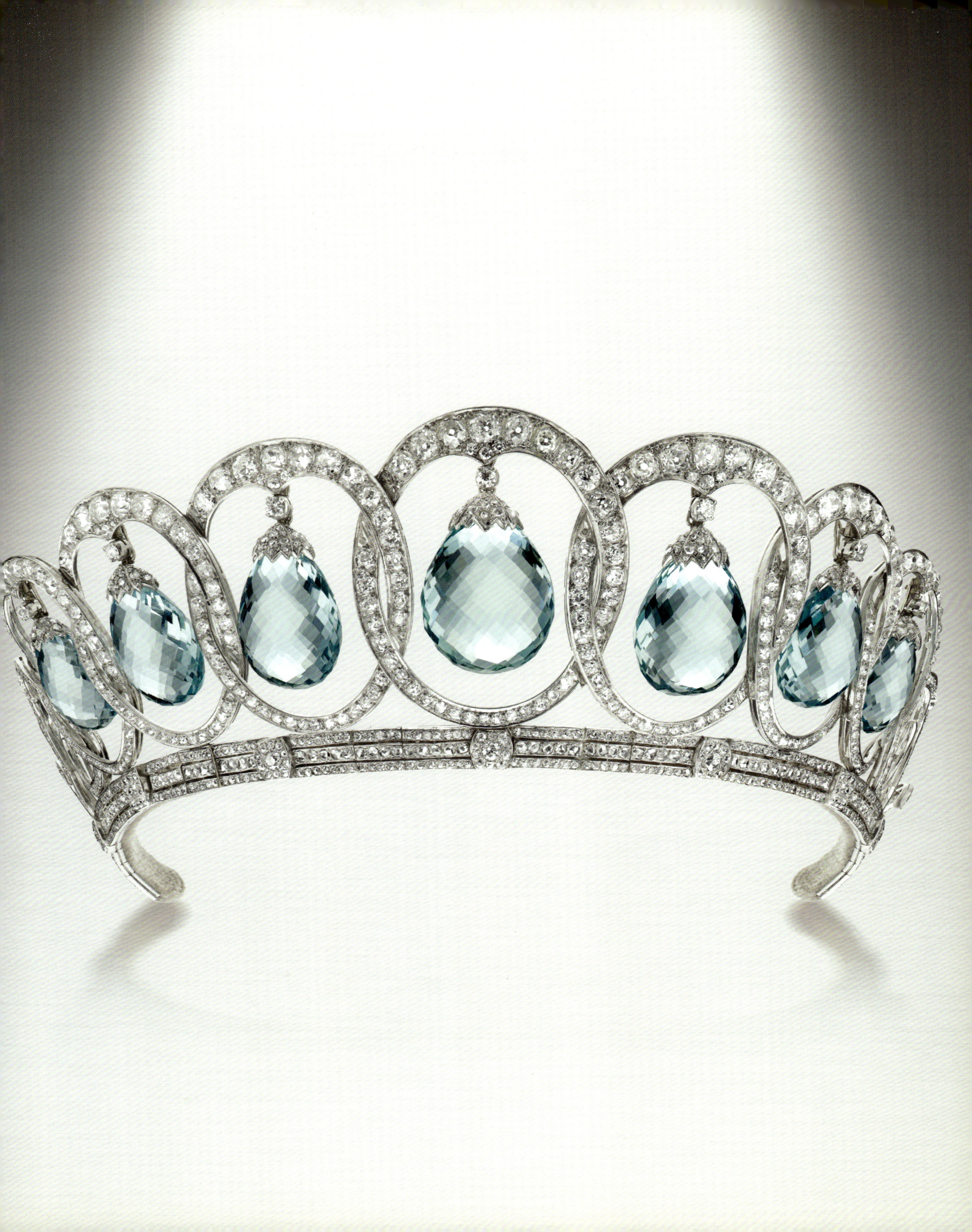

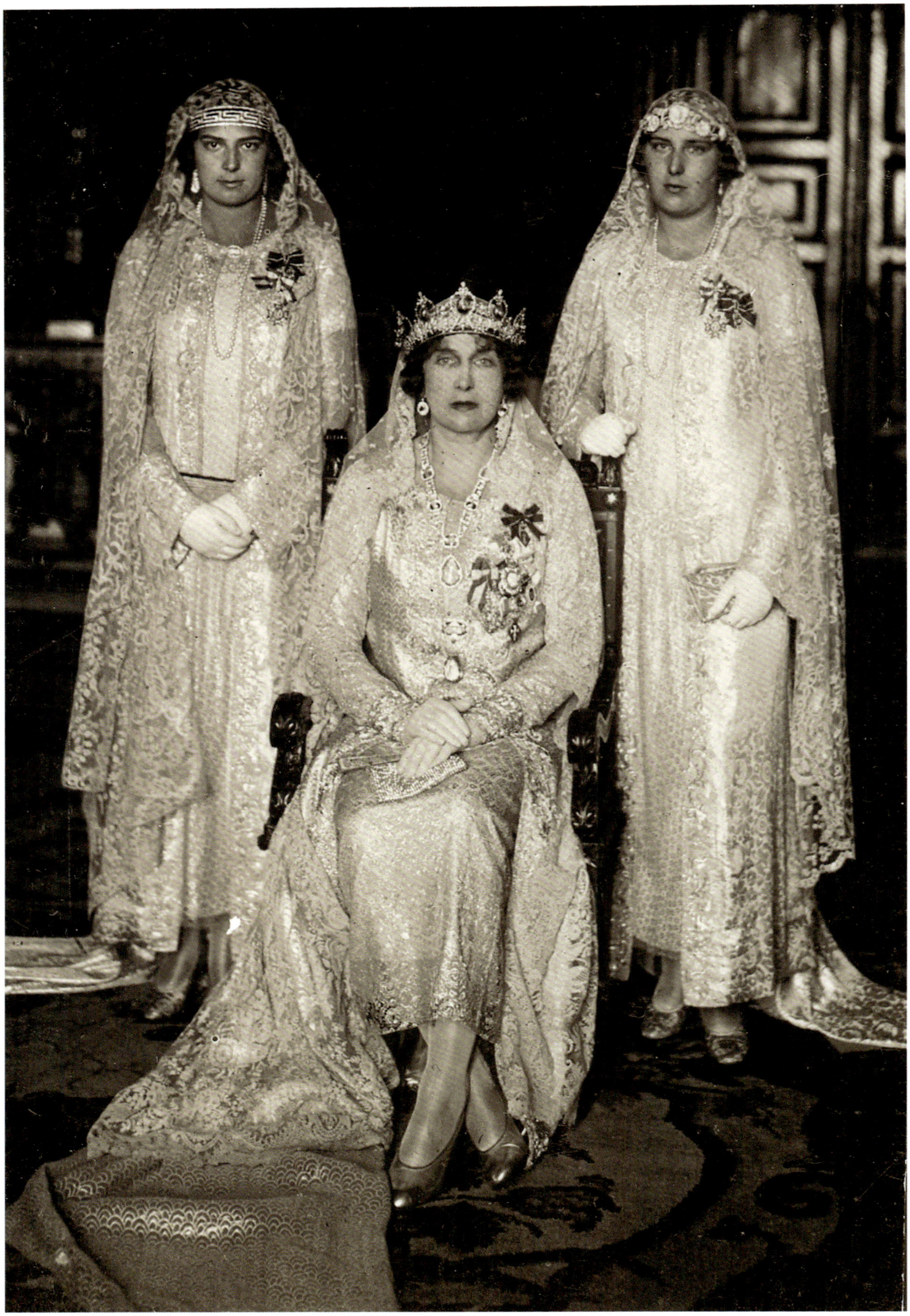

It flourished on evening dresses, with impressive décolletés. The arms, often naked from the shoulder to the wrist, left room for as many bracelets as could be accumulated. The one created by Bulgari for the Infanta was composed of three rectangular plaques pavé-set with brilliants on platinum linked by five diamond-set chains. Set in the centre of each of the three plaques was a much larger cushion-cut diamond. To accompany this jewel, other pieces presented by the Prince, his family and the sovereigns of Spain were also created by Bulgari.

For political reasons, the ceremony took on an extraordinary splendour. The King of Spain was in exile, but he had not abdicated and he had comfortable financial means. The wedding of his eldest daughter was, therefore, a fitting royal occasion. The church, built in the 16th century, was the basilica of the Jesuits. Saint Ignatius of Loyola, their founding father, is buried there. On 14 January, 1935, the square in front of the church was crowded. Monarchists, journalists and the simply curious are all there waiting for the royal show to begin.

The morning ended in a peal of bells announcing the departure of the bride and groom. The Infanta, a slim, elegant brunette, did not wear any jewellery. Around her were gathered her maids of honour, whose dresses had been inspired by the paintings of Velázquez, the influential painter of the Spanish Golden Age, at the court of Madrid. The gentle wind raised her veil. She gave her arm to her husband, who beside his petite wife looked like a giant. This union of pomp and circumstance was also a marriage of love: *"Alessandro Torlonia was very tall, very good looking,"* recalled the Infanta. *"We got engaged and my father accepted this marriage without any restrictions. I think he always got along well with my husband. As my fiancé was not of royal blood and I occupied a place in the succession to the throne of Spain, I had to renounce my rights. But it cost me no sacrifice."* [2] Before getting into their car Alessandro and Beatriz waved to the crowd. They were awaited at

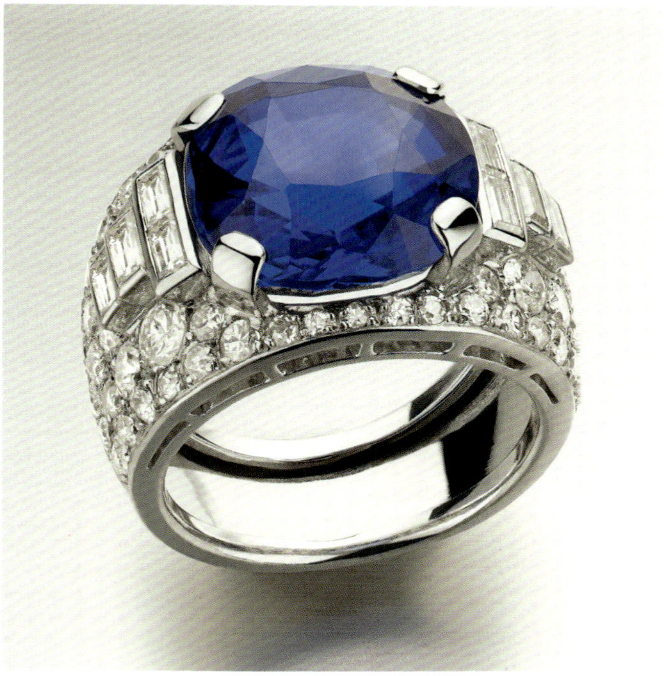

the Vatican, where they would receive the blessing of Pope Pius XI. In the early afternoon, they arrived at the Grand Hotel on Via del Corso, the Roman palace where the royal family of Spain resided. One hundred and twenty-five of the most prestigious guests had been invited to the wedding breakfast hosted by King Alfonso XIII in the palace ballroom.

The only sadness on the day was the absence of the mother of the bride, Queen Victoria Eugenie, who lived in London. Indeed, the Spanish King and Queen had not spoken to each other for nearly three years. Exile had only revealed their profound differences. Their marriage, which had, however, also been a love affair, was traversed by a series of dramas. Their wedding day in Madrid, on May 31, 1906, had been spattered with blood. A Catalan anarchist had thrown a bomb into the procession as they returned to the royal palace from the church ceremony. The Spanish court tradition stipulating that the royal carriage should be preceded by an empty Coach of Honour, was all that saved the newly-weds. The horses and bodyguards were not spared. On arriving at the royal palace, the shocked young Queen kept screaming: *"I saw a man who didn't have legs anymore ..."*

A year later, on May 10, 1907, a new disaster struck the couple on the birth of their first son, Alfonso, Prince of Asturias. In accordance with the tradition of the court of Madrid, the newborn prince was circumcised. He almost died. The doctors could

Facing page: *Queen Victoria Eugenie "Ena" of Spain with her two daughters, Maria Cristina (left) and Beatriz (right). The Queen wears her original diamond and aquamarine tiara, which would be transformed by Bulgari in 1935.* **Above:** *This diamond and sapphire trombino ring was created by Bulgari for the Infanta Beatriz of Spain, Princess of Civitella-Cesi. Private collection.*

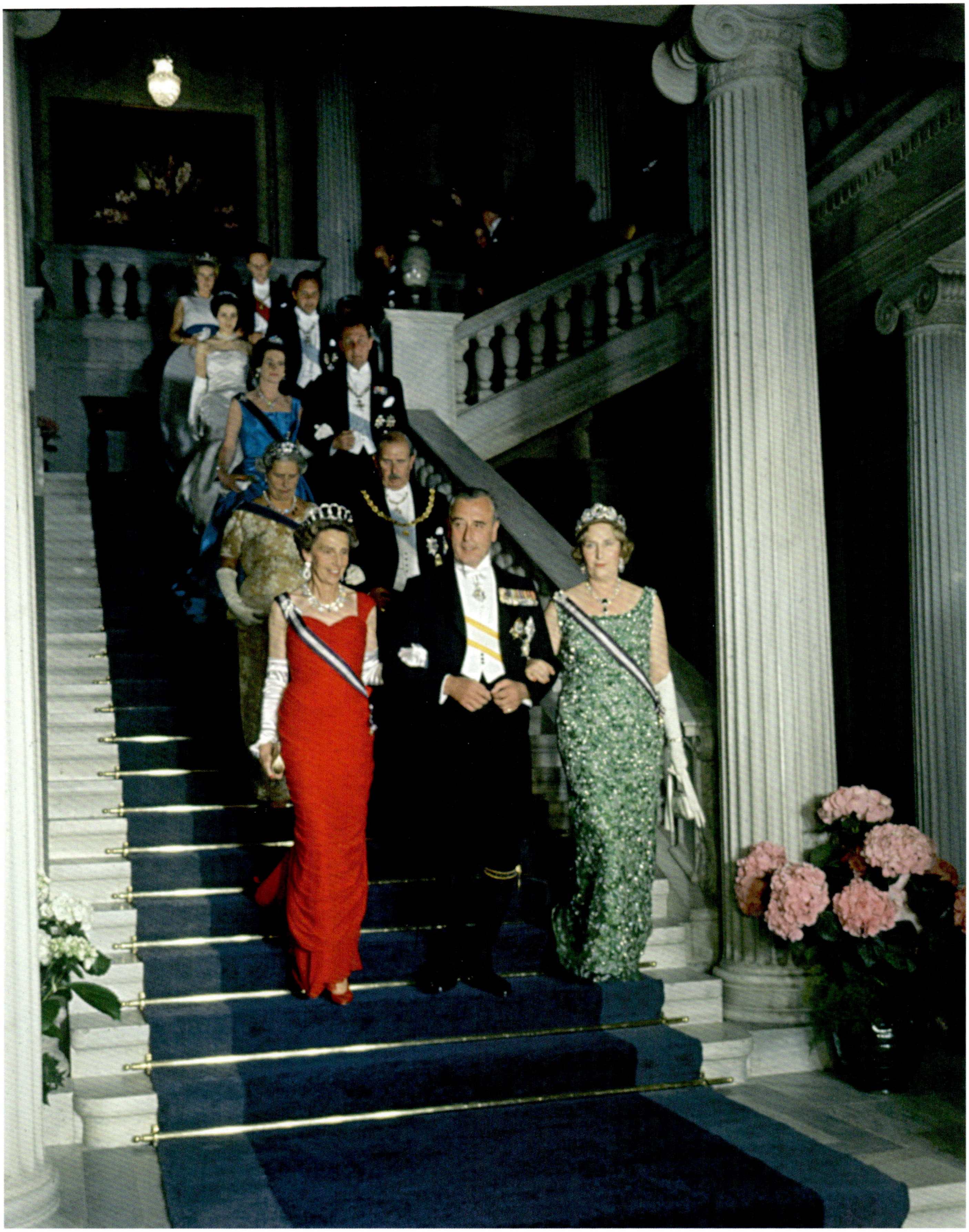

only state the terrible truth: the heir to the throne of Spain was a haemophiliac. Like many of her first cousins, including the Russian Tsarina, Alexandra Feodorovna, Victoria Eugenie of Battenberg, carried the terrible illness inherited from her grandmother, Queen Victoria. This disease, which affects only men but is carried and passed on by women, prevents blood from clotting in the event of an injury. Haemorrhage can therefore be fatal.

For the King, the shock was devastating. Since the birth he lived in fear of his eldest son's death. Five other children, however, would come into the world, with one drama after another. Jaime, the second son, was born perfectly healthy; unfortunately a mistreated childhood illness left him profoundly deaf. By 1914, the birth of their last child, Prince Gonzalo, marked the end of the love story of the royal couple. Little Gonzalo also turned out to be haemophiliac. Their third son, Juan, and the two Infantas – Beatriz and Maria Cristina – were spared this curse.

As long as they reigned, the King and the Queen had agreed to pretend that they were still a united couple. Exile had freed them of this constraint. Chased from Spain in 1931, they settled first in Paris. During a stay in Fontainebleau, there was a particularly memorable scene. At the end of a long argument, the Queen told her husband that she never wanted to see "his horrible face again". Alphonse XIII, who never was of a very faithful nature, settled in Rome in 1933, with his children. Victoria Eugenie returned to live in London, the city of her youth. Even so, the series of disasters did not stop. In August 1934, the Infante Gonzalo, barely twenty years old, died suddenly of a haemorrhage. During a trip to Austria, a driver hit the car in which he was a passenger and which his sister, Beatriz, was driving. This new ordeal did not bring the Spanish King and Queen any closer. And so, a year later, even the wedding of their daughter Beatriz, could not force them to appear together in public.

Though the Queen may have been absent, she still sent sumptuous wedding presents to her eldest daughter. Her most important gift was a parure of aquamarines and diamonds. Since her childhood, the Queen of Spain had always had a preference for these stones of beautiful azure blue, matching the colour of her eyes. She remembered admiring her first cousin, the Tsarina Alexandra of Russia, fifteen years older, clothed in court dress, adorned with enormous aquamarines. So, at the beginning of her marriage, when King Alfonso XIII had asked her what her favourite stones were, she replied, after some hesitation and almost timidly, that she was very fond of aquamarines.

The parure that her husband gave her exceeded all her hopes. The stones were enormous. They were set on a necklace, a pair of earrings, a brooch and a ring. Seven enormous pear-shaped aquamarines were mounted in the centre of seven diamond foliage motifs that made up a voluminous tiara in the form of aureole. The necklace, the bracelet, the brooch and the earrings were very easy to wear. On the other hand, this style of tiara was no longer considered fashionable by 1935, and it was also far too large in circumference for the flat modern hairstyle of the time.

"Originally it was created for my grandmother the Queen of Spain and for a much more voluminous hairstyle," recalled Princess Olimpia Torlonia, Infanta Beatriz's younger daughter. *"With the flat headdresses of the 1930s, it was impossible to wear, that's why Papa asked Bulgari to design a new, less imposing setting. The necklace, the earrings and the brooch are still as they were. The aquamarines of the tiara are removable. It can be worn with or without. Bulgari created two jewels with the stones of the original diadem. The new aquamarine tiara and a lily flower diamond necklace that my mother sold in the 1980s. I do not know why."*

The diamonds needed for the mounting of this necklace were completed with another present from Queen Victoria Eugenie: a series of large diamonds that came from one of her most beautiful jewels. *"Every year,"* said Princess Olimpia Torlonia, *"My grandfather offered my grandmother two diamonds. After twenty years, she ended up having a very long necklace that was not so fashionable in the 1930s. She transformed it into a double necklace and distributed to her children the diamonds that had been removed. Those that were offered to my mother were also mounted on the necklace created by Bulgari."* [3]

Bulgari's relations with the royal house of Spain did not stop with this marriage. A second Spanish

Facing page: *In Athens for the wedding of her nephew, Prince Juan Carlos of Spain, the Infanta Beatriz is dressed in red, and wearing her diamond jewels – necklace, tiara (without the aquamarines) and brooch – all created by Bulgari. She is accompanied by her cousin, Lord Mountbatten, on his left arm is Infanta Maria Cristina of Spain.*

royal union was held in Rome that year. Again, Giorgio and Costantino were responsible for creating jewellery for the bride. On March 4, Infante Jaime, deaf and mute since childhood, married a young Franco-Italian aristocrat Miss Emmanuelle de Dampierre, whose mother was a Ruspoli princess. Just before the ceremony, the Prince renounced his rights to the Spanish crown because of his disability. He was granted the title of Duke of Segovia by his father. Like her sister-in-law Beatriz, the new Duchess of Segovia received sumptuous jewels. Bulgari's order books show that the Infante Jaime ordered a pair of diamond and sapphire earrings to be turned into clips for this occasion. Another Spanish royal command is mentioned in Bulgari's archives. It dates from the month of March 1936 and concerns the current King Felipe VI of Spain's grandfather, the Infante Juan, Count of Barcelona, who is recorded as having bought a gold and sapphire cigarette case for 5,700 lire.

Prince Alessandro Torlonia and his wife the Infanta Beatriz were also regular visitors to the Maison on Via dei Condotti. Their purchases concerned jewels or precious objects, including jade, which the Infanta collected. Four children would be born from their marriage: Sandra, Marco, Marino and Olimpia. The first three took their first breath in Rome, at Torlonia Palace. On the occasion of the birth of their second son, Marino, on 13 December, 1939, Prince Alessandro ordered a gold and diamond ring from Bulgari for 6,900 lire.

It was with the birth of their grandchildren that the relationship between the exiled Spanish King and Queen began to improve. Queen Victoria Eugenie decided to attend the christening of her grandchildren, which took place in Rome. On 28 February 1941, she was even present at the Grand Hotel on the day of her husband's death. Europe was by now at war and her return to London after the funeral was tricky to organise. So she decided to settle for a time with her son-in-law and daughter at the Torlonia Palace, where she remained for a year. After four years of the fog and rain in London, she appreciated the light of the Eternal City. At Torlonia Palace, she occupied a series of rooms overlooking Via dei Condotti, the street on which Bulgari was situated.

"The palace is in the centre of Rome," her daughter, the Infanta Beatriz would explain many years later. *"It is not one of the oldest, such as the Borghese Palace or the Ruspoli Palace, but it was certainly the most pleasant palace in the city, mainly because of the warm character of my husband."* The Infanta recalls that though her mother had been brought up in the strict environment of her grandmother, Queen Victoria of England and her mother-in-law, Queen Marie Christine of Spain, Queen Victoria Eugenie agreed to a more relaxed etiquette in exile. To the astonishment of some neighbours, it seems that she appeared one morning, in a very relaxed outfit: from one of her windows on Via dei Condotti, she was seen in deep conversation with her neighbour opposite, Count Chigi. He was attired in a dressing gown. The Queen had curlers in her hair!

During her stay in Rome, Queen Victoria Eugenie ordered several jewels from Bulgari. The Queen of Spain was largely a woman of another time. She played constantly with precious stones, which were an important part of her life. Her children always worried that she travelled carrying real treasures. She had two maids and her jewellery always had to be watched over by one of them. She changed the settings often. *"My father had offered my mother a very beautiful brooch in the shape of a knot, all diamonds, created by Bulgari,"* remembers Princess Olimpia Torlonia. *"I still possess it. My grandmother, enjoyed it so much that she ordered exactly the same one."* [4]

Queen Victoria Eugenie's stay in Rome ended in January 1942. German pressure on Italy was becoming heavier and heavier. The Hotel d'Angleterre, a former guesthouse of the Torlonia Palace, had been requisitioned by the German army, which was now encamped in front of the palace where the Queen was living. As she was of English origin, she was increasingly perceived as a suspicious person in the eyes of the fascist government. With the help of the Italian royal family, particularly Queen Elena, with whom she was very close, Queen Victoria Eugenie discreetly left Rome for Switzerland. The Infanta Beatriz, her husband and their three children left a few months later. Like Prince Doria Pamphilj, Don Alessandro, who was greatly opposed to fascism, was threatened with arrest. It was for this reason that their last child, Olimpia, was born in Lausanne on 27 December 1943.

Facing page: *The diamond bow brooch created by Bulgari for Infanta Beatriz of Spain. Private collection.*

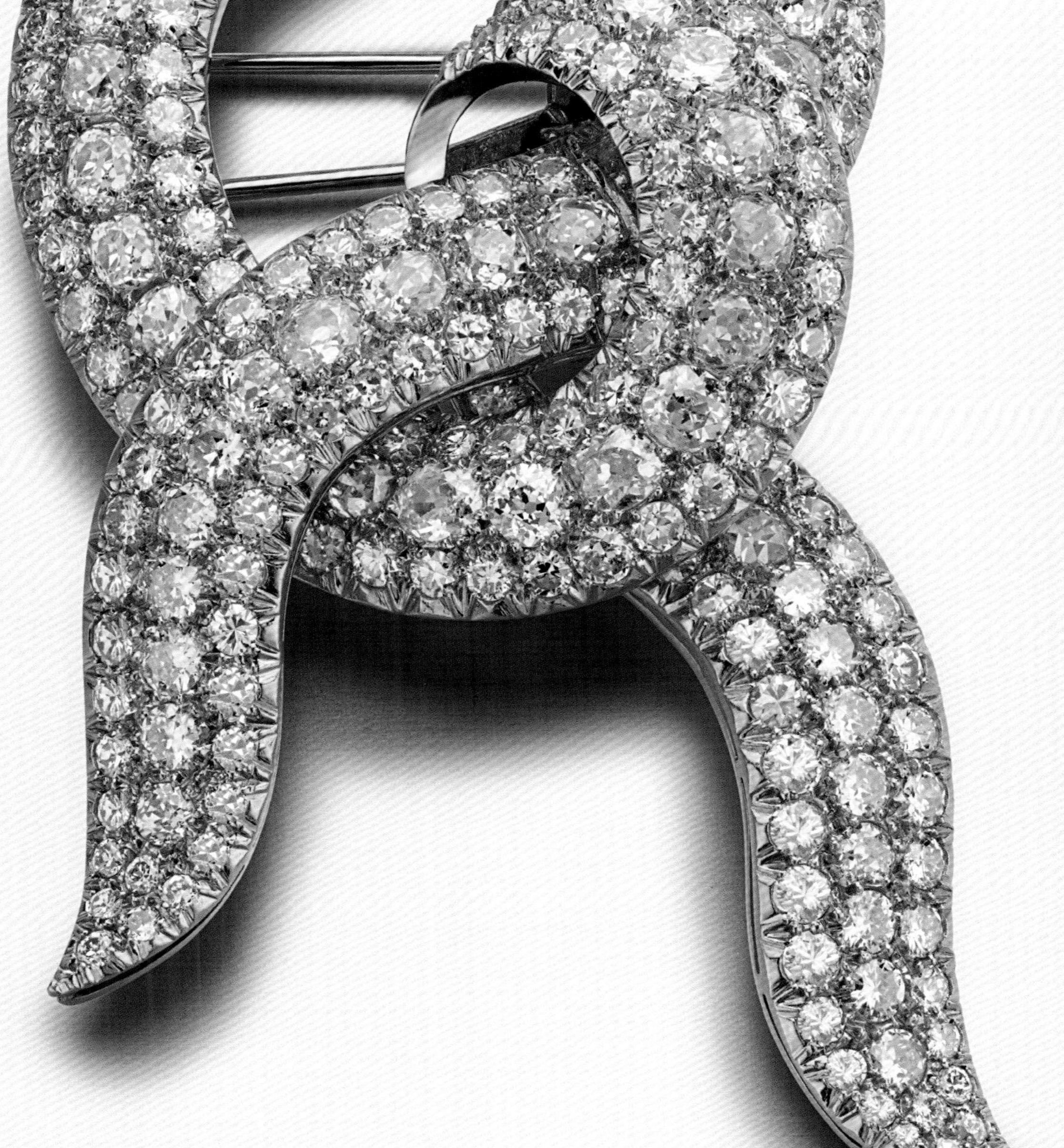

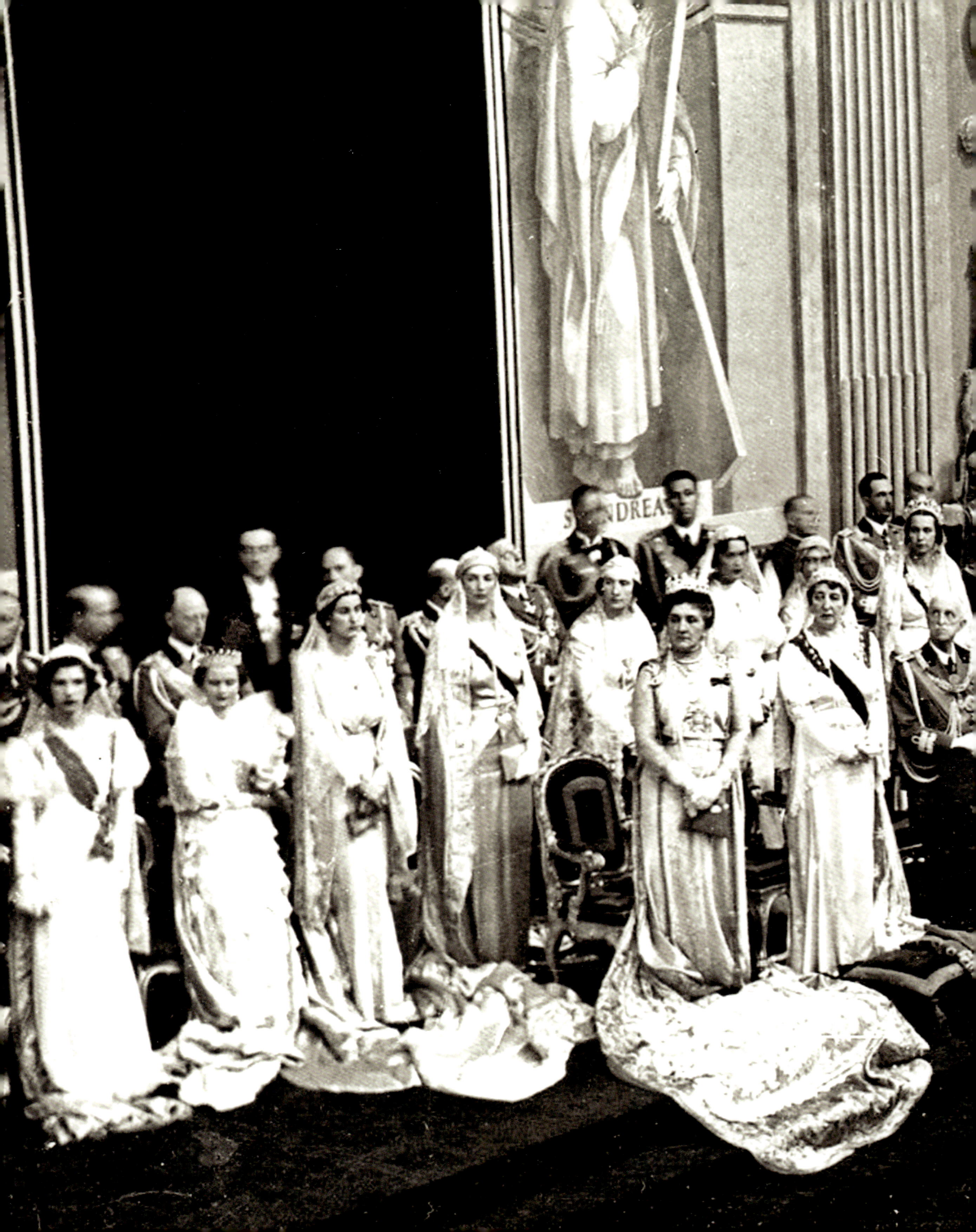

1930
The Royal Year

It was a very elegant jewel, of very small dimensions, and entirely set with diamonds. A simple bandeau composed of 19 motifs fixed on a line of brilliants. On each of the two sides, a flexible metal strip was arranged so as to fix the ornament in the coiffure of the wearer. Dated to the year 1930, it would have been created for the occasion of the marriage of the Crown Prince Umberto and the Princess Marie José of Belgium.

The ceremony took place on 8 January, in the vaults of the Pauline Chapel in the Quirinal Palace. The son and heir apparent of King Victor Emmanuel III and Queen Elena married the daughter of the King Albert I, and Queen Elisabeth of Belgium. The event was of considerable significance for the royal household, for the whole of Italy, and also for the prestige of the city of Rome. This royal wedding was the first to be celebrated in the Eternal City following the signing of the Lateran Pacts. Eleven months earlier, these treaties put an end to 60 years of dispute between the Holy See and the Kingdom of Italy. Throughout this period the Papal rulers, entrenched behind the walls of the Vatican Palace, shunned the new kingdom of Italy and its dynasty, which had stolen not only their states but also many of their Roman possessions, including the Quirinal Palace.

The signing of the treaties enabled the Italian monarchy to finally emerge from the ostracism in which the condemnation of the Holy See had kept it. When Victor Emmanuel III wished to marry at the end of the 19th century, he had been forced to marry an Orthodox princess belonging to the very discreet princely dynasty of Montenegro. The marriage of his son with a Belgian princess, related not only to all the Catholic dynasties but also to the Saxe-Coburgs of England, was a diplomatic victory. All Europe was invited to the nuptials. And Rome had never been so full of tourists, princes, and ambassadors.

The ceremony began at ten o'clock in the morning. The photographs from inside the Pauline Chapel show the diamond diadem created by Bulgari; with the bride and groom standing in front of the altar. Government representatives sat to their right. The royal families of Italy and Belgium were on the left. The congregation was divided into two groups, men on one side and women on the other. Protocol obliged each woman to wear a long white mantilla. On the right side of the chapel was a series of immaculate silhouettes: dozens of women in court dress draped in white mantillas restrained by diadems. It is possible that Bulgari created other jewels for this ceremony, but since the house has kept very few archives dating back to that period, it is difficult to trace any orders.

When the ceremony was finally over, the newlyweds drove to the Vatican to ask for the blessing of the Holy Father. Then came the wedding breakfast at the Quirinal Palace: crayfish in tartare sauce, pheasant with watercress, asparagus in mushroom sauce, ice cream in Palermo-style, wedding cake, Dutch waffles. There was no champagne served; instead, Italian wines were the stars: Capri white, Falerno red and Asti Spumante.

On the guest list for the royal wedding were many Bulgari customers. One of these was Princess

Facing page: *A ceremony at the Italian court in the 1930s. Queen Elena and the princesses all wear the mandatory court uniform: a long white veil held in place with a diamond diadem.* **Overleaf:** *A diamond tiara created by Bulgari in 1930, probably for the occasion of the marriage of the Crown Prince Umberto of Italy to Princess Marie José of Belgium. Qatar Museum – National Collection of Qatar.*

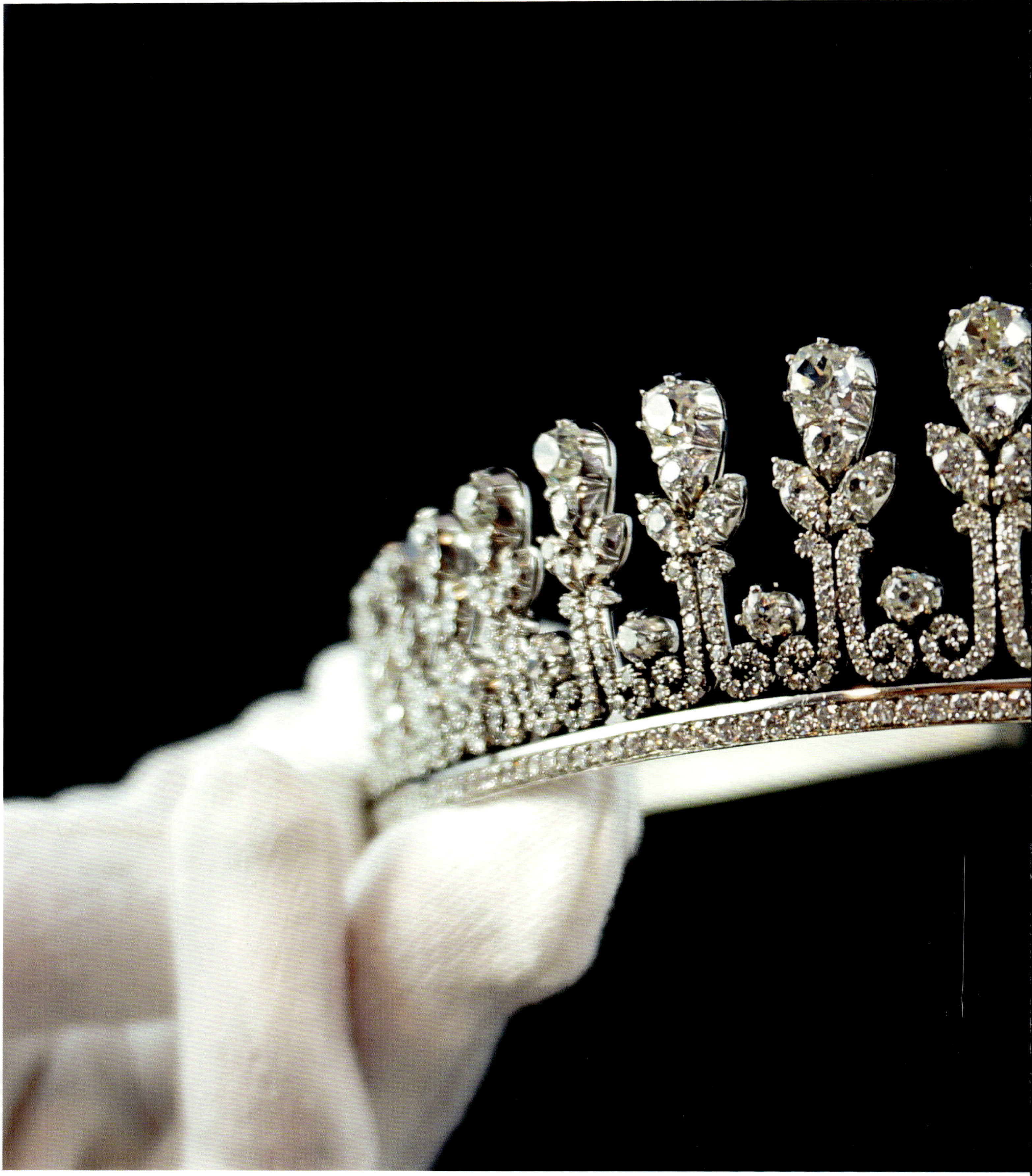

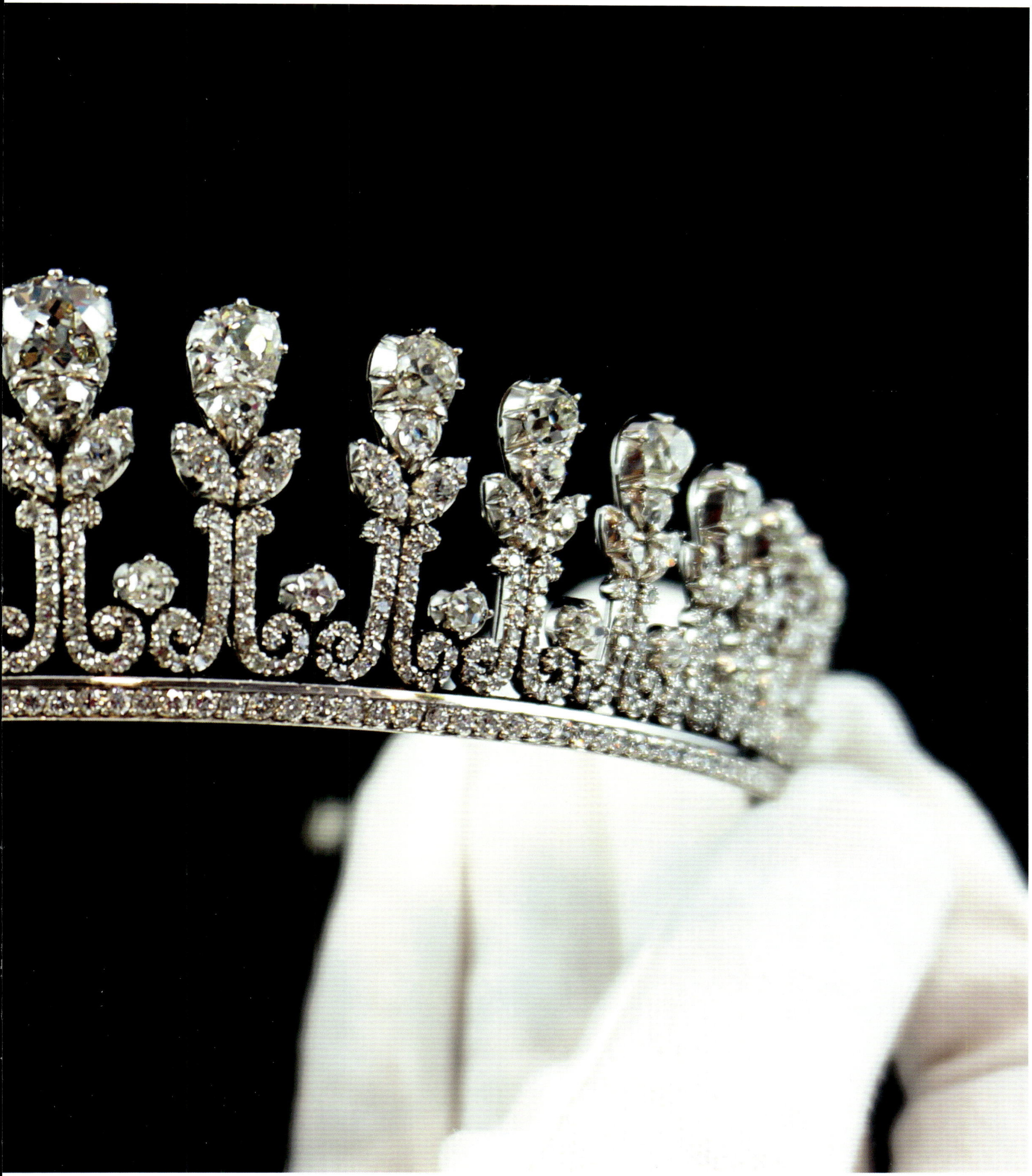

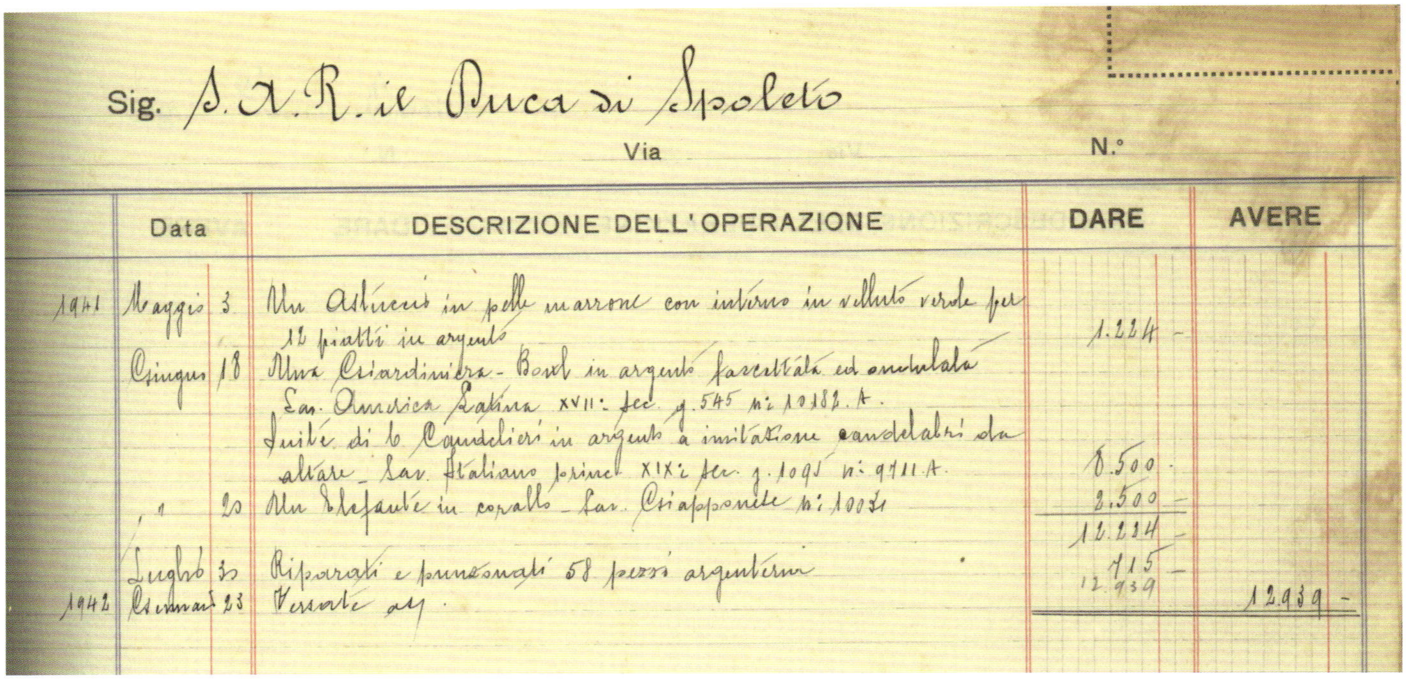

Sig. S.A.R. il Duca di Spoleto

Via N.°

Data			DESCRIZIONE DELL'OPERAZIONE	DARE	AVERE
1941	Maggio	3	Un Astuccio in pelle marrone con interno in velluto verde per 12 piatti in argento	1.224 –	
	Giugno	18	Una Giardiniera - Bowl in argento faccettata ed ondulata Lav. America Latina XVII sec. g. 545 n. 10182.A.		
			Suite di 6 Candelieri in argento a imitazione candelabri da altare _ Lav. Italiano princ. XIX sec. g. 1095 n. 9711.A.	8.500	
	"	20	Un Elefante in corallo _ Lav. Giapponese n. 10021	2.500 –	
				12.224 –	
	Luglio	30	Riparati e punzonati 58 pezzi argenteria	715 –	
				12.939	
1942	Gennaio	23	Versato ...		12.939 –

Françoise de France (1902-1953). The previous year, she had married Prince Christopher of Greece and they now lived in Rome at the Prince's property, the Villa Anastasia. Daughter of the Pretender to the Throne of France, the Duke of Guise, who was living in exile in Belgium, Princess Françoise was one of the most elegant women in the Italian capital. A portrait taken around that time, shows her dressed in a long sheath of satin glitter, a fur stole draped over her shoulders. Her head is adorned with a diamond headband diadem, very similar to that created by Bulgari in 1930 for the royal wedding.

In 1940, soon after the death of her husband, Princess Françoise left Italy with her son Prince Michael to settle in Morocco, before moving to Spain and, finally, France, where she died in 1953. By strange coincidence, her son would inherit her twin necklaces in gold and silver. The date of their creation is unknown, but they are both shaped in tubogas, a metalwork technique creating flexible interlocking links, which was very fashionable for jewellery from the 1930s to the '50s. Both are in the form of a snake, one of the most famous symbols of Bulgari. Strangely, it does not appear in the Maison's collections until the 1940 and 1950s.

Alas for the history of Bulgari, the names of the sovereigns and princes of the house of Savoy appear very rarely in the archives. The only ones to have made regular orders, and especially for pieces of ancient silverwork were the Duke and Duchess of Spoleto. Born in 1900, the Duke was a Prince of the Aosta branch of the Royal House of Italy. He was also the first cousin of Princess Françoise of France, since his mother, the Duchess of Aosta, was a Princess of France. In 1939, in Florence, the Duke of Spoleto had married Princess Irene of Greece, daughter of King Constantine I of Greece. She was a niece of Prince Christopher of Greece. And it was Bulgari who provided a very important part of the silver given on the occasion of this marriage.

Above: *A document in the Bulgari archives showing the name of the Duke of Spoleto who married Princess Irene of Greece in Florence, 1939. Both bride and groom were clients of Bulgari.* **Facing page:** *Princess Christopher of Greece (née Princess Françoise of France). She is wearing a diamond tiara very similar to those that were created by Bulgari during the 1930s.* **Overleaf:** *Necklace from the Festa collection set with fourteen aquamarines weighing 163.14 carats.*

1. Interview with the author. **2.** *Cinco dias con la infanta Beatriz de Borbón y Battenberg*, by Pilar Garcia Louapre, Vision Libros, 2007. **3.** Interview with the author, 2015. **4.** Interview with the author, 2015.

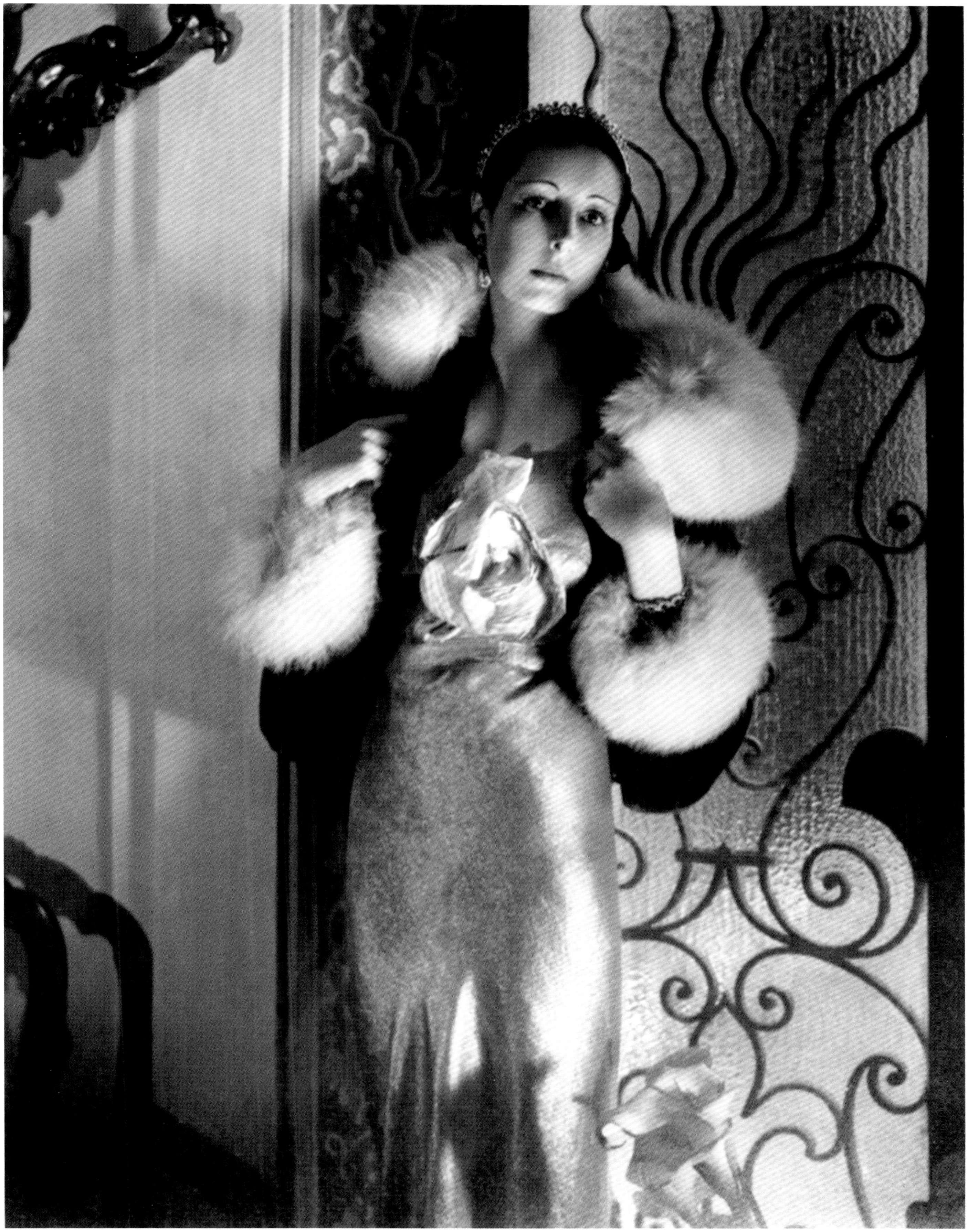

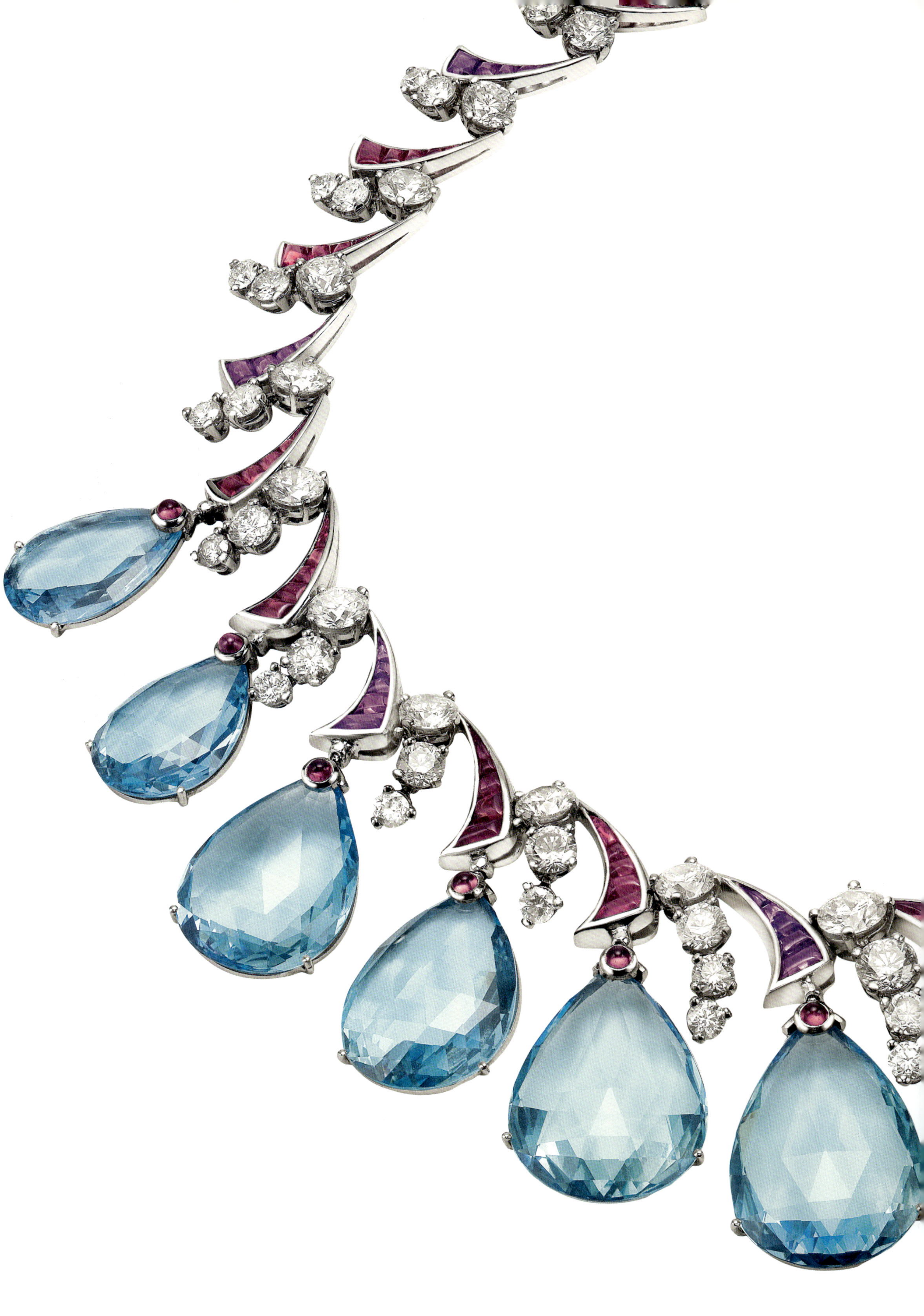

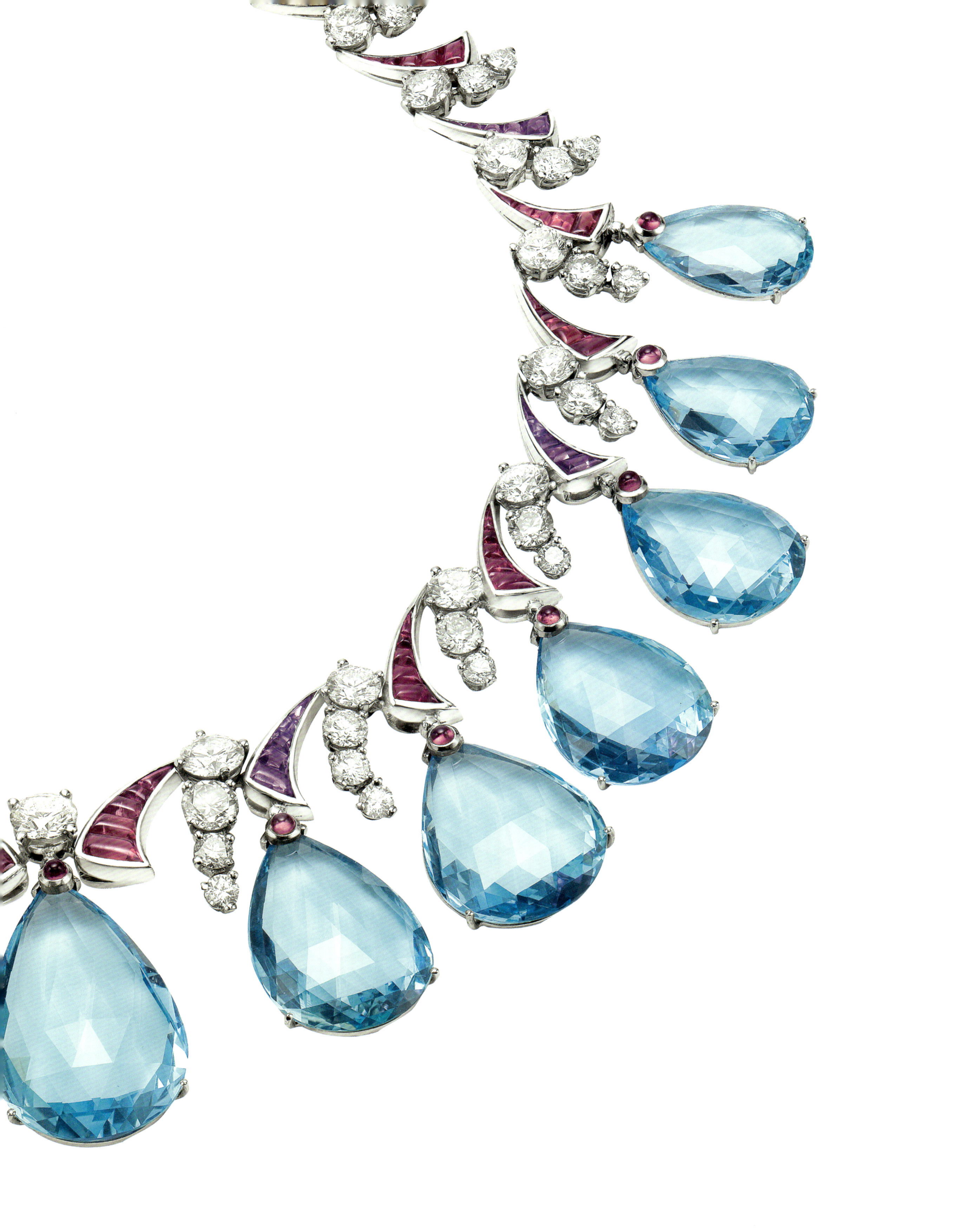

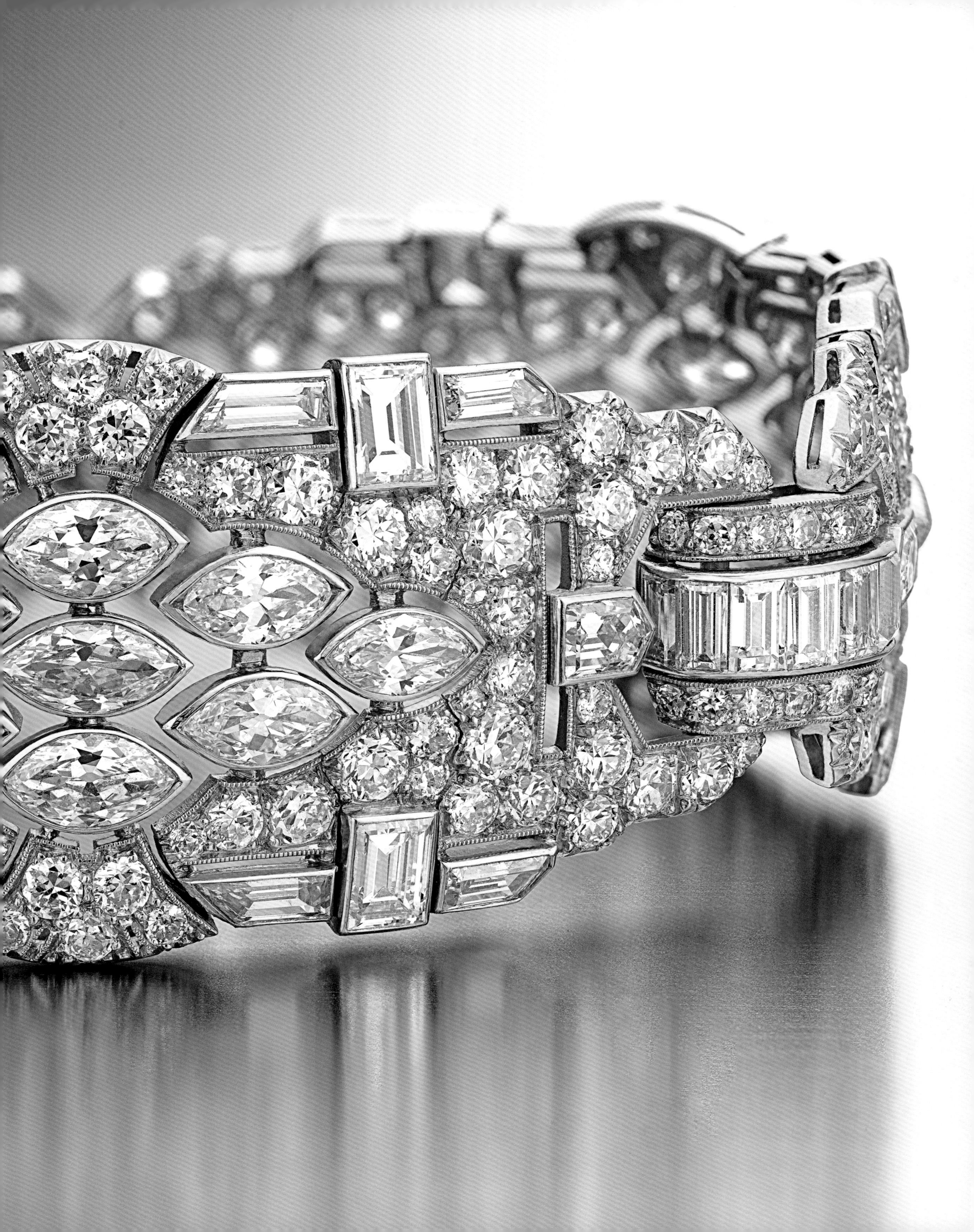

Chapter 3

COUNT CINI'S RANSOM

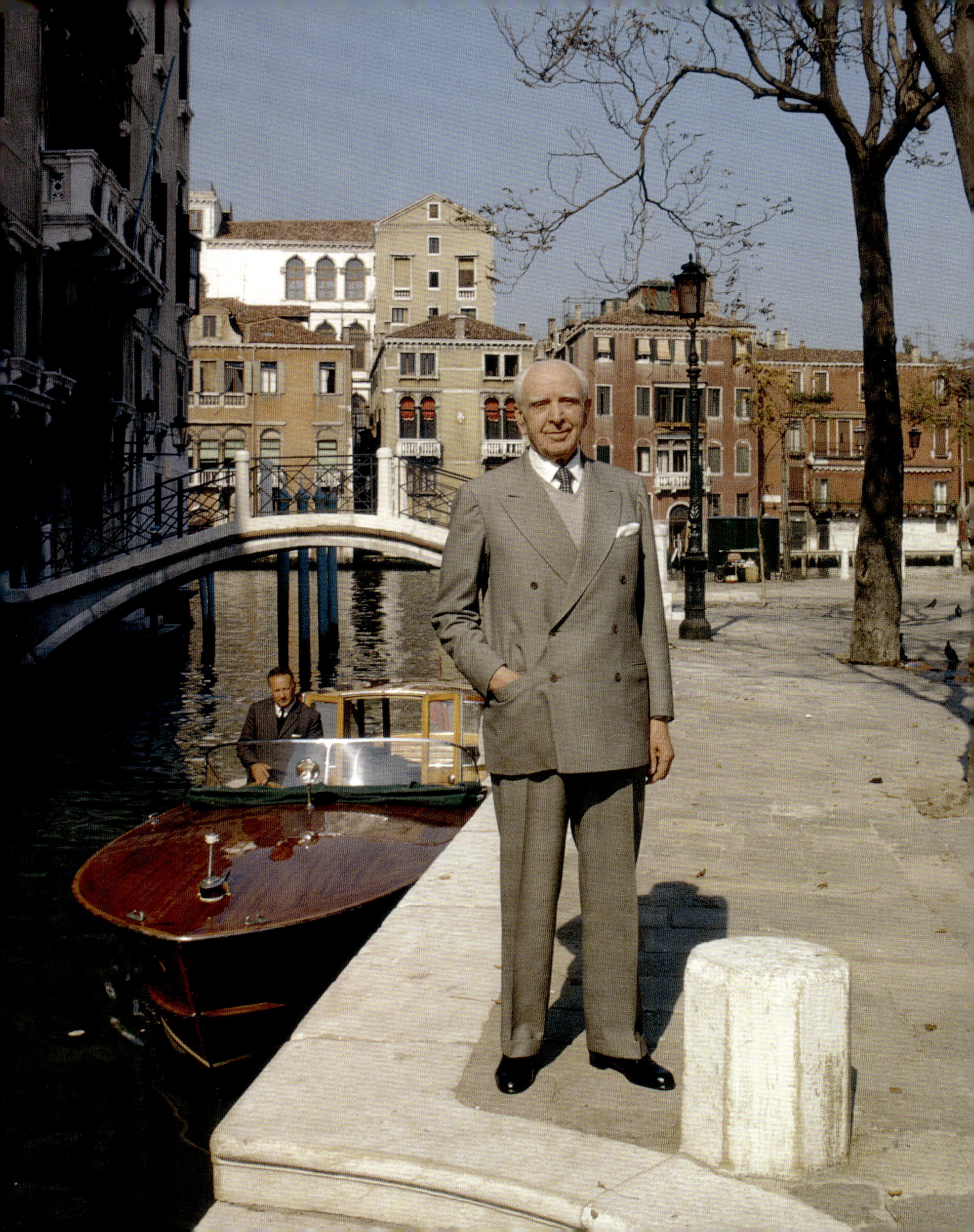

Vittorio Cini (1885-1977) and Giuseppe Volpi (1877-1947)

Berlin, Hotel Adlon, 29 June 1944

Giorgio Cini would not allow anyone but himself to carry his suitcase. Not only did it contain a fortune, but, moreover, the millions concealed in it represented the life of his father. Or rather his ransom. Millions of marks, dollars, pounds, all his mother's jewels, and even a few precious stones that Giorgio and Costantino Bulgari had entrusted to him during their secret meeting in Rome a few days earlier. The end of the war was coming. The allies had landed in Normandy. All Germans over the age of 15 were at the Front – East and West. And Giorgio Cini was in Berlin. In desperation, he had come to buy his father's life.

On 8 September, 1943, Count Cini of Monselice had been arrested in Rome by the SS. Since then, he had disappeared without trace. Minister of Communications during the last Mussolini government, he had broken with the Fascist dictatorship during the summer. He had been one of the influential men in the secret process that had led to the deposition of Mussolini on 24 July. The consequences of this political shift were violent and immediate. Hitler's Germany decided to intervene directly in the government of Italy. Anti-Semitic measures worsened and the pace of arrests of opponents increased.

For months, Giorgio Cini had conducted investigations to find out where his father was being held. Thanks to his bribes and some courageous friends, he had finally learned that Vittorio was incarcerated in Dachau, Bavaria. So, he had launched a brave scheme: to save his father's life by "buying" as many Nazi dignitaries as he could. The Cinis' fortune was colossal. Still, it was necessary to transform some of it into bargaining chips. And as quickly as possible. It was with this that Giorgio and Costantino Bulgari had been able to give him invaluable help. *"In Rome, the Cinis lived very close to us,"* recalls Paolo Bulgari. *"I was seven or eight years old and I remember very well that one afternoon my father took us to the Cini home, one of my brothers and I. Giorgio, the son of Count Cini, had asked him for advice on what to do after the arrest of his father."* [1]

The two families had known each other for more than twenty years. During the years before the Second World War, Count Cini was Bulgari's most important client. He owned two exceptional diamonds weighing 24 carats each. The first was a cushion-cut in a beautiful deep blue. The second, an emerald-cut, was a perfect bright pink. They had been bought by Giorgio Bulgari in the United States in the early 1930s. The few archives from this period kept by the house list some of Count Cini's purchases; and they are very impressive. According to Paolo Bulgari, the Count bought *"not one piece of jewellery but a whole showcase. And not one showcase at a time, but two or three. He bought everything and left everything in my father's safe."* [2] The archives confirm his words. On 7 November, 1939, the purchase of 39 gold and silver objects for 325,000 lire is recorded. Two weeks previously he had bought two antique goblets in gold, for 62,000 lire. Then came jade for 175,000 lire, three diamond bracelets for 20,000, 24,000 and 39,000 lire; two pins for 103,000 lire; two clips and a collar for 34,000 lire... Count Cini's total purchases for the year of 1939 amounted to nearly 800,000 lire.

Facing page: *Count Cini, one of Bulgari's regular clients during the 1930s. He is photographed in front of his palace in Venice.* **Previous page:** *Art Deco diamond bracelet. Bulgari Heritage Collection.*

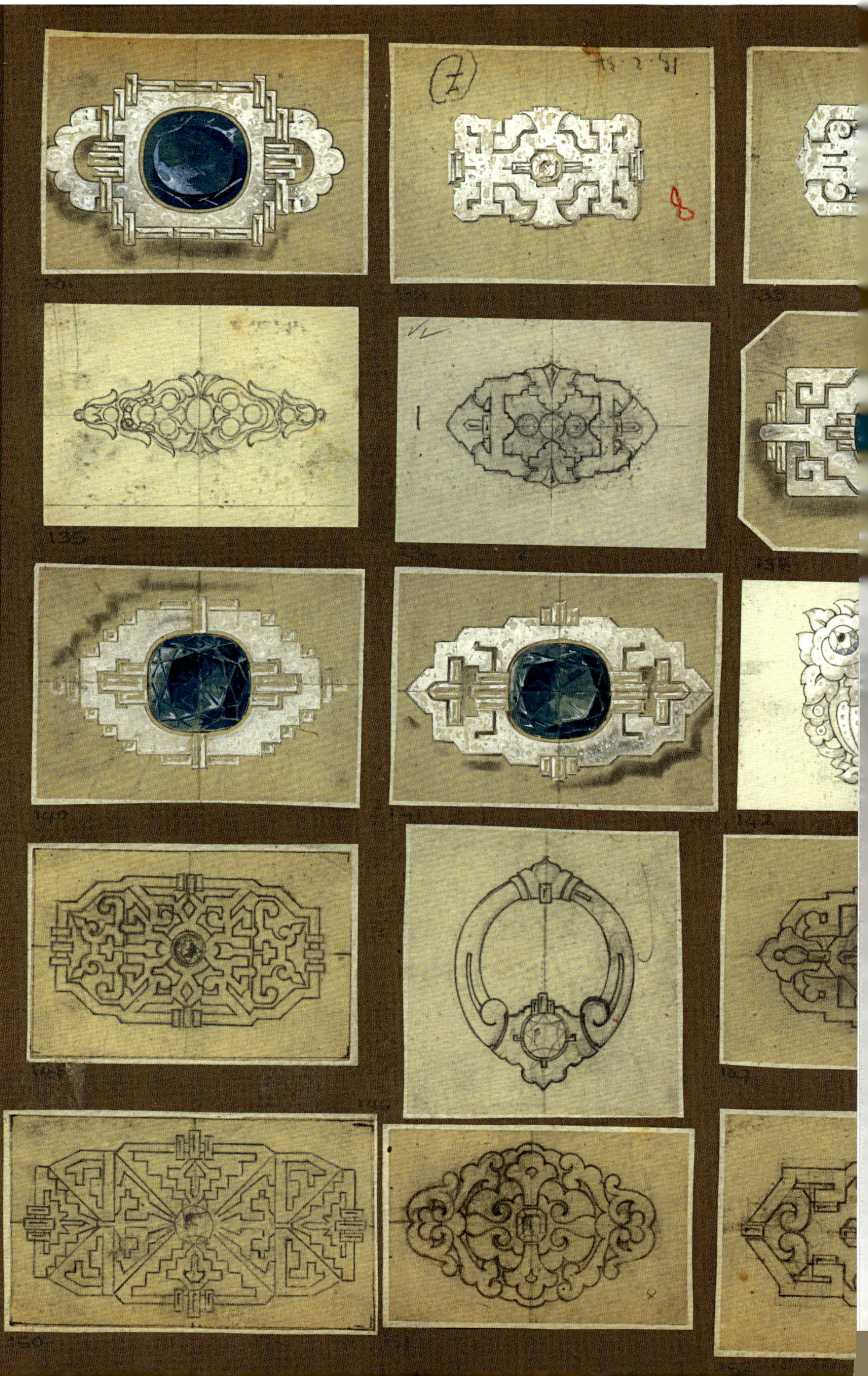
135
140
142

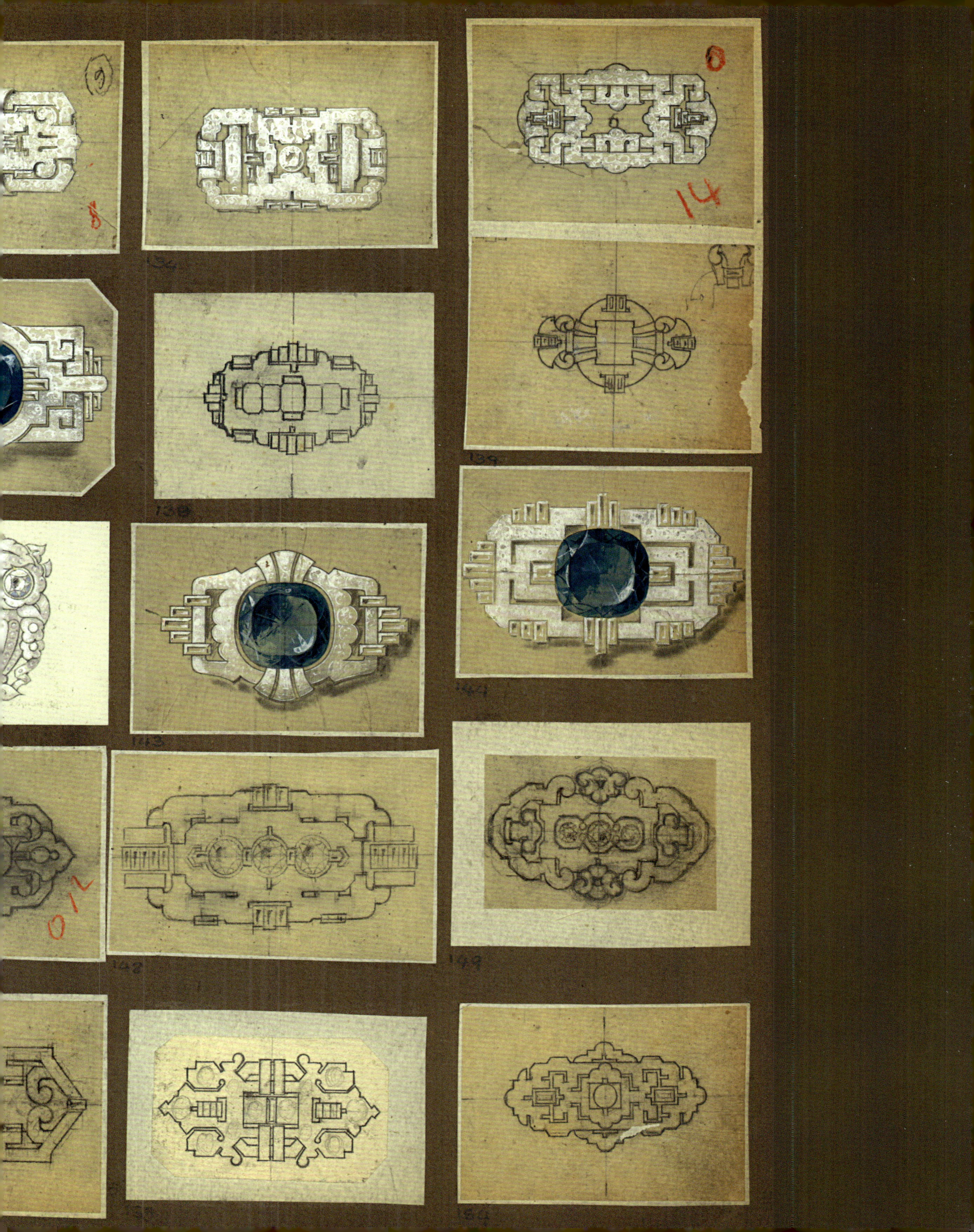

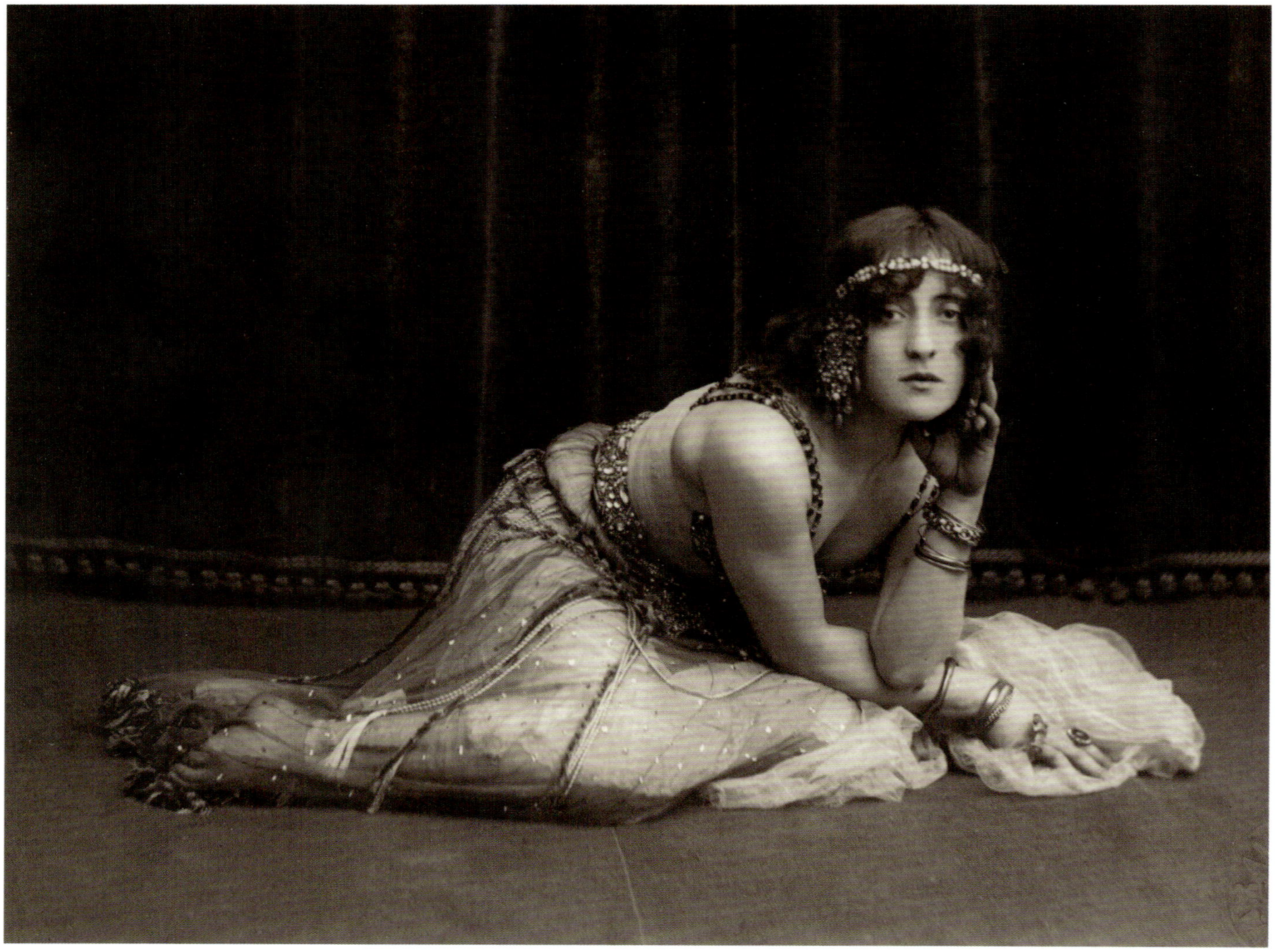

"At that time, between 1930 and 1950, there were two very wealthy captains of industry and collectors," recalls Anna Bulgari Calissoni, Costantino Bulgari's eldest daughter. *"Both had a palace in Venice and both were clients of Bulgari. They were Count Cini and Count Volpi. I knew Count Cini. He was a man of perfect courtesy and he really looked the part of a 'Grand Seigneur'. I remember going to Venice to estimate the value of his jade. The collection was fabulous. During lunch – I was seated at his right – he spoke to me at length about my father Costantino and my uncle Giorgio."* [3]

The destinies of these two millionaires could just as well have been those of two adventurers, two explorers or two conquerors of the New World. Both are marked by an extraordinary spirit of enterprise. The elder, Giuseppe Volpi, was born in Venice in 1877. By this time, Venice – *La Serenissima* – was no more than a shadow of its former self. A sleepy city that had lost its commercial influence and was not yet a destination for tourists. The young Giuseppe was studying at the University of Padua when the death of his father forced him to look for work. Faithful to the Venetian tradition, he travelled and settled in the Ottoman Empire, where he built his fortune in the export of tobacco. In 1905, at the age of 27, he returned to Venice to embark on a new adventure: the Adriatic Society of Electricity (SADE). Not content with being a bold entrepreneur, Volpi was also a visionary. He understood that the electrification of Italy was one of the industrial gambles of the early twentieth century. A year later, he married a lovely young aristocratic woman Nérina Pisani. She would

309.	"	27.10	Ing. Giacomo Recupito.	" V. Gregoriana, 54.	Servizio thè argento.	8.000.=
310.	"	"	Ing. Luigi Macallini	" V. Verona, 7	Filo 85 perle	66.590.=
311.	"	7.11	On. Sen. Vitt. Cini	Venezia, S. Vio 732.	39 oggetti antichi in oro e argento.	325.000.=

give him two daughters. Nérina and her husband are mentioned often in the Bulgari accounts. After Nérina's death, Giuseppe Volpi went on to marry his second wife, Nathalie Kanoui, who would give him a son, Giovanni.

Vittorio Cini was eight years younger than Volpi. A native of Ferrara, Venice soon became his adopted city. If Volpi was an entrepreneur, Cini was a financial genius. He inherited some land from his father and very quickly doubled his income by draining and developing the marshlands. In the aftermath of the First World War, the capital at his disposal enabled him to embark on an industrial adventure. He was the head of the group of businessmen who undertook the construction of Marghera, the new industrial port of Venice. In 1918, he also married. And this union made all the front pages. His wife was the first star of Italian cinema: Lyda Borelli.

Unlike many women celebrities of the Belle Epoque, whose reputation of beauty can be difficult to understand in modern times, Lyda Borelli was a woman who would still be considered extremely attractive by modern standards. Her ethereal physique was very far from the curves that were fashionable at the beginning of the 20th century. Although she is largely forgotten – her career ended in 1918 on her marriage to Cini – Lyda Borelli is a legend in her own right. She was the exact contemporary of Theda Bara, one of the most famous partners of Rudolph Valentino. Theda, who often embodied disturbing and evil characters, was often described as a "Vamp".

Facing page: *Lyda Borelli, the future Countess Cini. Before World War I, she was the greatest star of Italian silent films.* **Above:** *A purchase by Senator Vittorio Cini (later Count Cini) recorded in the Bulgari archives, dated 1935.* **Overleaf:** *Diamond and emerald sautoir signed by Bulgari, 1928. Bulgari Heritage Collection.*

For her part, Lyda Borelli was the first Italian actress to be called by the title previously reserved for female singers: "Diva".

Her career of 13 films was brief, but remarkable. Her performance in *Malombra*, directed by Carmine Gallone, would lead the public to create two expressions derived from her name: "Borellismo" and "Borellegiare". Both refer to her particular style of acting, a mixture of hallucinatory expressions and theatrical attitudes, very similar to those of Sarah Bernhardt, the famous legend of the theatre. In *Malombra,* Lyda portrays a young orphan aristocrat, 'Marina' who is summoned by her uncle to the castle of Malombra. The castle is haunted by a murdered ancestor. The ghost takes possession of Marina persecuted by her abusive uncle. The film, of which only clips remain, is a monument to the Gothic style so often used in silent cinema. Lyda was 34 years old, when she married Vittorio Cini, who decided to put a stop to his wife's career. According to Anna Bulgari Calissoni, *"Count Cini decided to buy all the rights of her films. He did not want anyone to see them. It is for this reason they have become so rare."* [4] While maintaining a residence in Rome, the two settled mainly in Venice in the palace Count Cini has just bought. Their son, Giorgio, was born in 1918. Three girls, including twins, Mynna, Ylda and Yana, followed in 1920 and 1924.

It was in 1924 that the two great lords of Venice became acquainted. When Vittorio Cini joined the SADE Board of Directors, he was already very close to Giuseppe Volpi. Their palaces in Venice were situated almost opposite each other on the two banks of the Grand Canal, not far from the bridge of the Academia. Both were involved not only in the industrial development projects of the Veneto, but also in its cultural programme. In 1932, Count Volpi launched the film festival in Venezia.

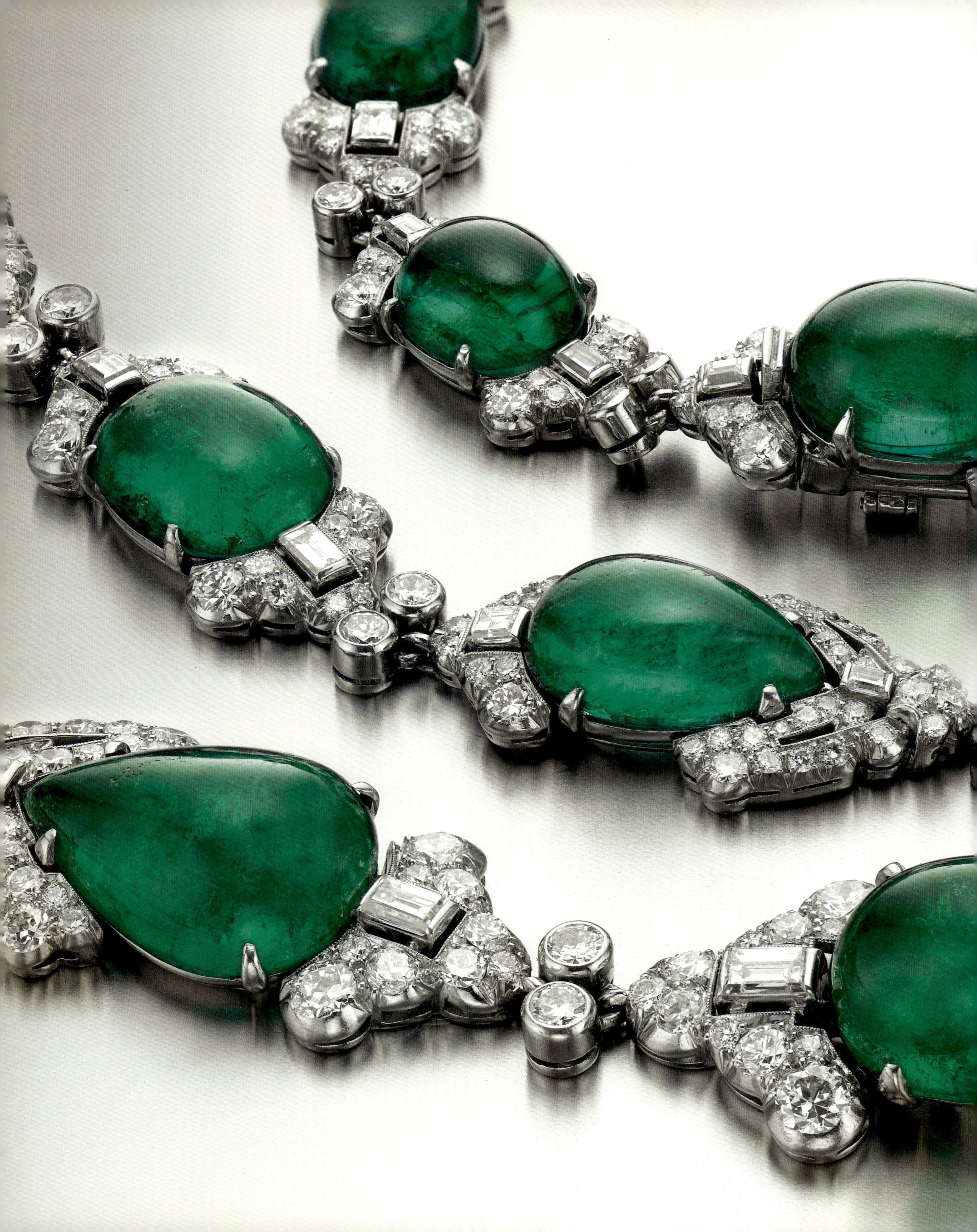

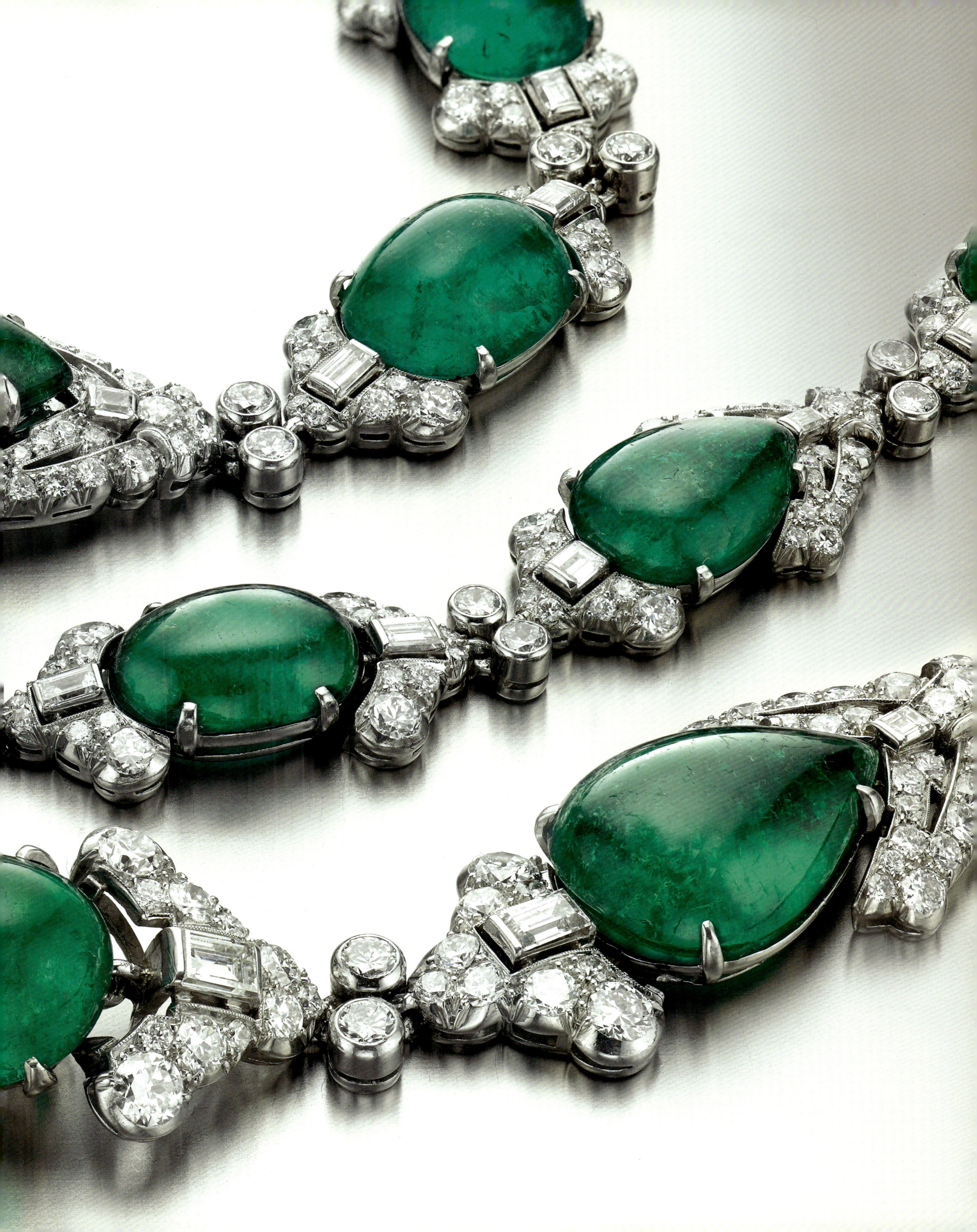

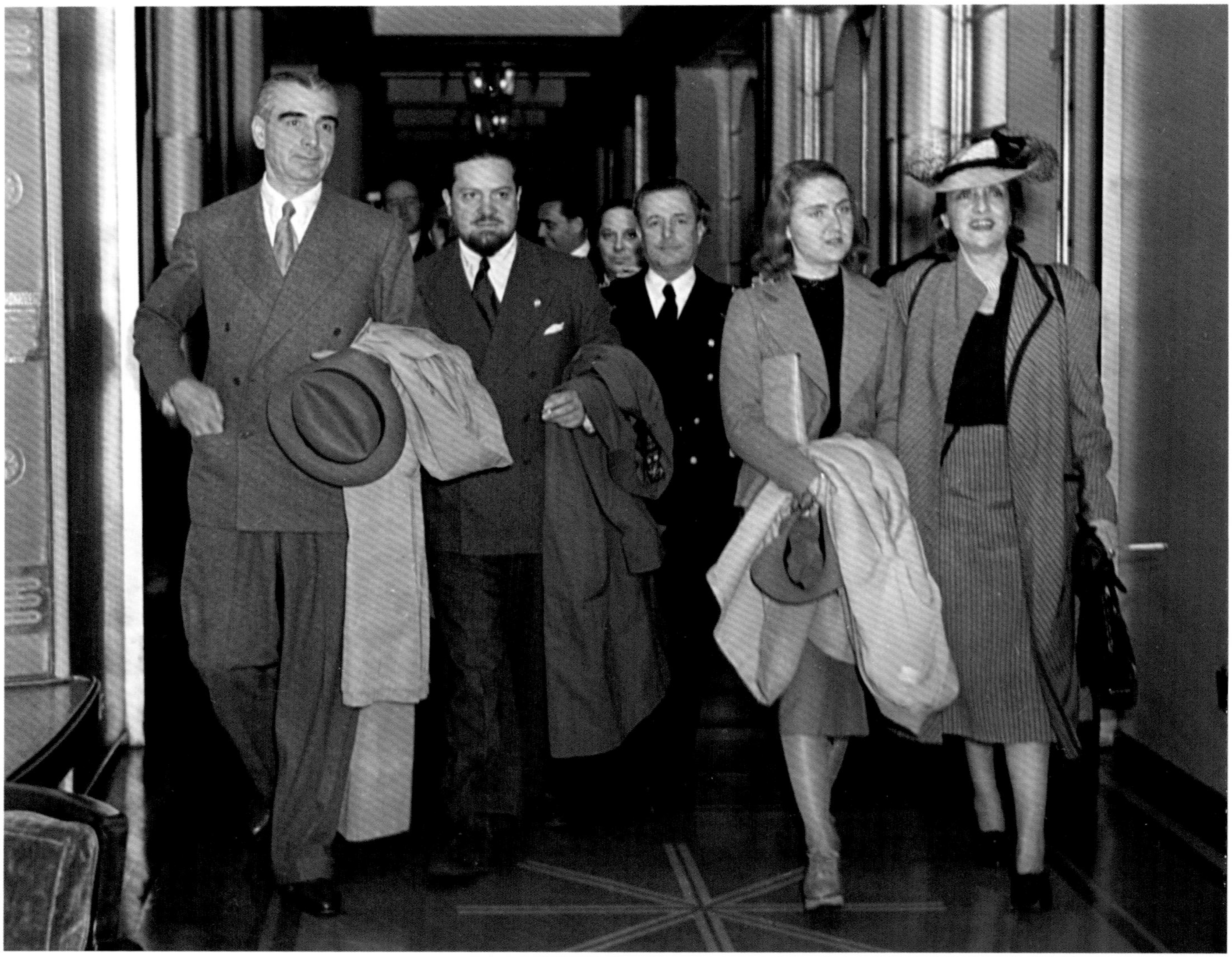

Both Giuseppe Volpi and Vittorio Cini would be ennobled by King Victor Emmanuel III. Volpi was granted the title Count of Misurata in 1925. And, on 16 May, 1940, Cini became Count of Monselice, after the medieval castle he owned in the south of Padua. Both were also arrested by the Germans in October 1943, after their official break with Mussolini. Volpi was detained for a few days, but his dire state of health secured his release. He was placed under house arrest in his home in Rome. He died in 1947. Count Cini was less fortunate. He was transferred to Germany, to the prison camp of Dachau. His wife was forced to take refuge in the Vatican.

Giorgio Cini's attempts to save his father by means of enormous bribes paid to the Nazis may seem implausible, but are corroborated by several testimonies, notably by Princess Marie Vassiltchikov, a White Russian who lived in Berlin during the Second World War. She published the story in her *Berlin Diaries:*

June 29, 1944: "I had to leave a message at the Hotel Adlon and in the hall, I ran into Giorgio Cini. He has come all the way to Berlin to try and bribe the S.S. in setting his father, the old Count Cini, free. When Italy changed sides last year, the latter (a one time minister of Mussolini) was arrested in Venice and has been in Dachau concentration camp, in an underground cell, for the past

Above: *Count Cini, on the left, with his wife, Lyda, on the right, and one of their daughters, 1930s.* **Facing page:** *Ring set with a sapphire of 4.50 carats encircled with diamonds. Made by Bulgari in 1925, it clearly heralds the style of the Trombino rings that the jewellery house would launch in the 1930s. Collection FD Gallery, New York.*

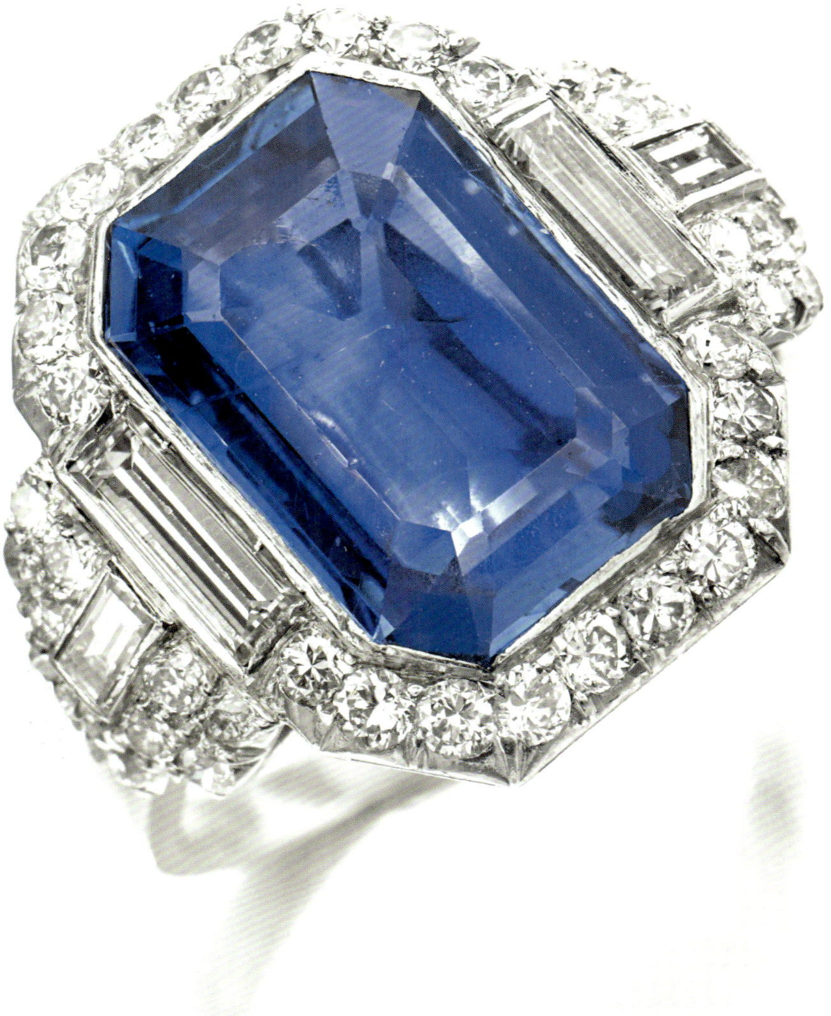

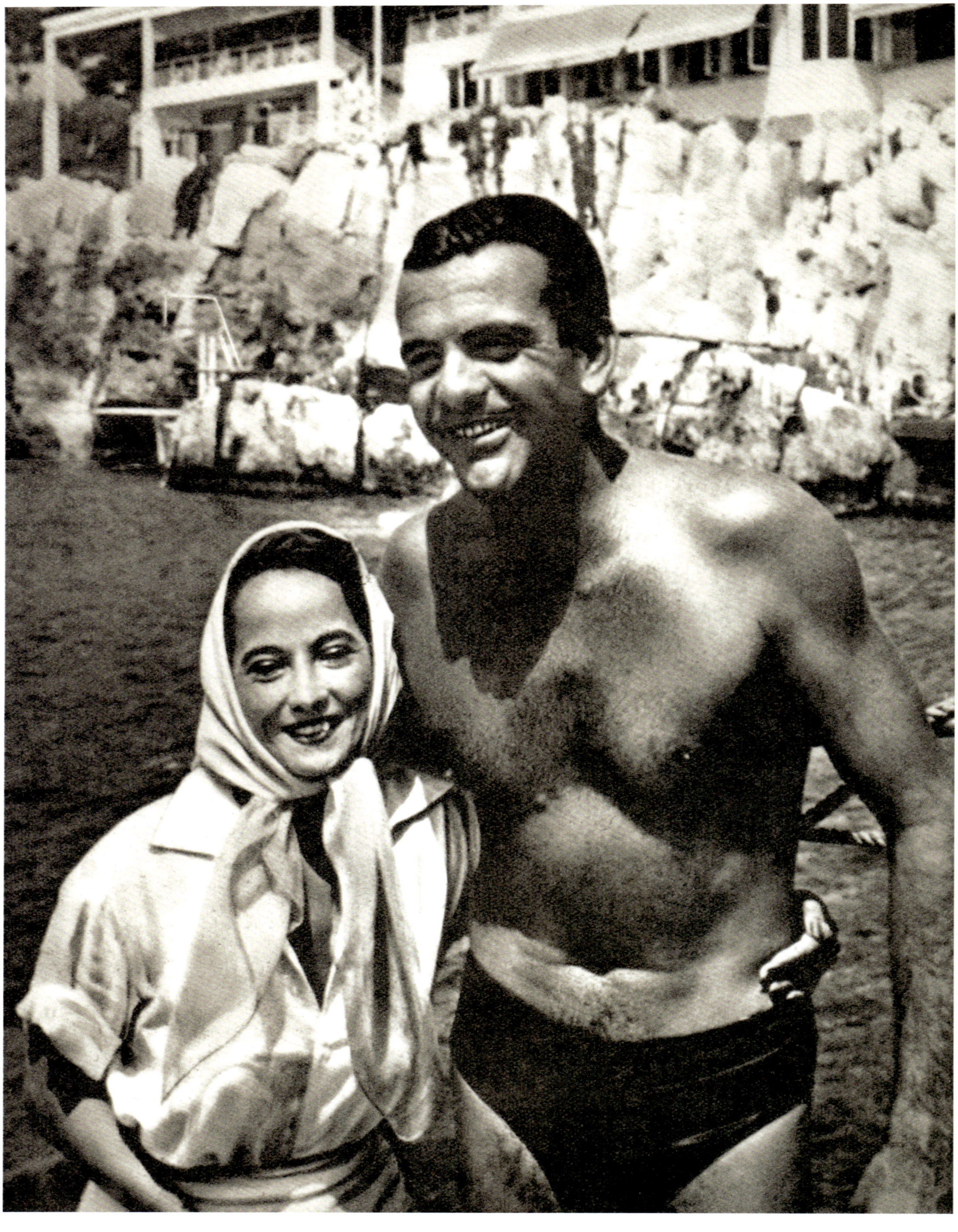

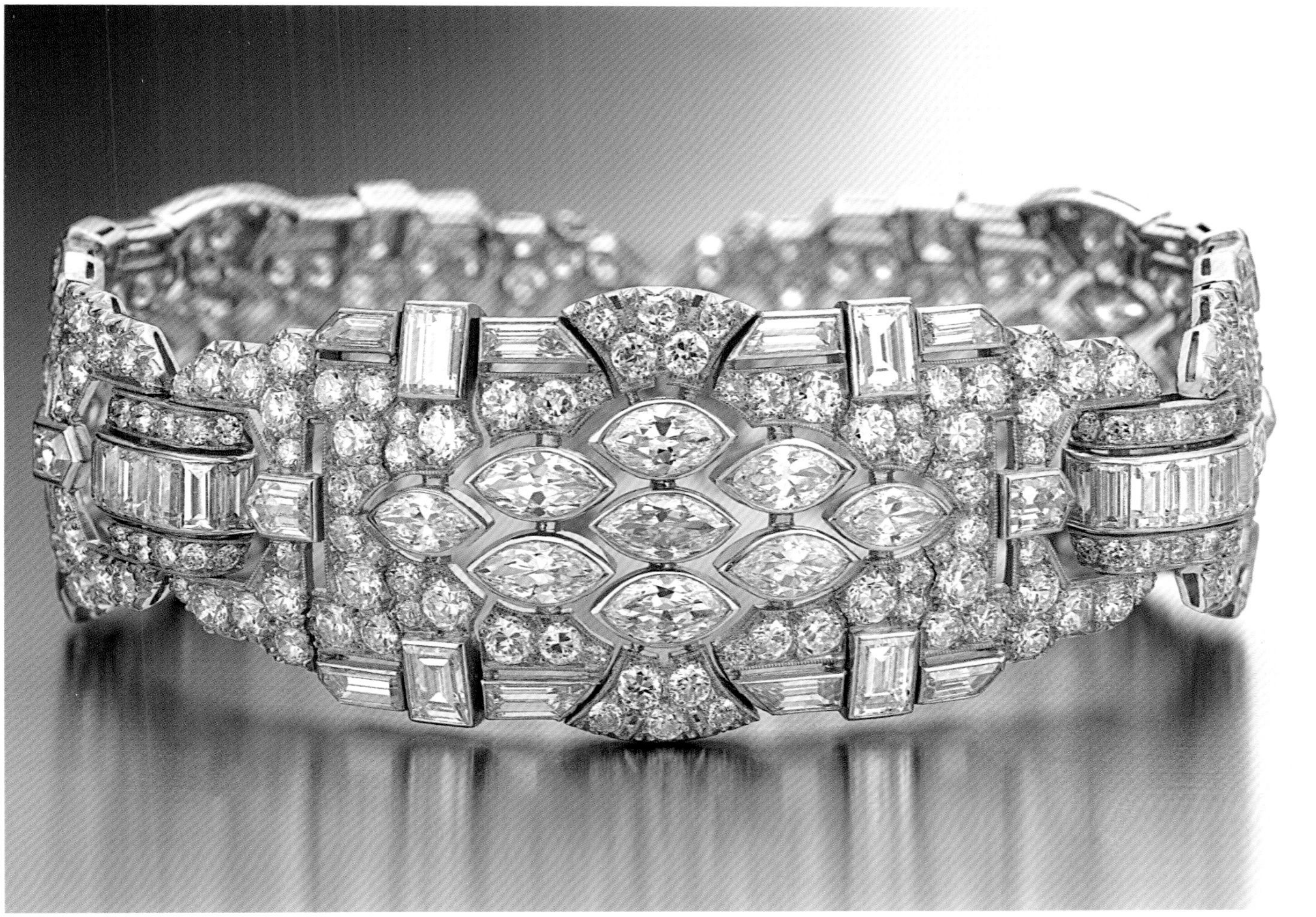

eight months. The Cinis have millions and Giorgio is willing to pay anything to get him out." [5]

As daring as it may seem, the journey to Berlin was a success. Count Cini was discreetly released by the Nazis. He travelled to Switzerland with his son and would not return to Italy until 1947. Unfortunately, his trials were not yet over. Very much weakened by his detention, Vittorio Cini asked his son to take over his financial affairs. Giorgio was not yet 30 years old. He was the heir to an important fortune. He was extremely good-looking and he was still single. During the summer of 1948, he spent several weeks in Rome. The Countess di Frasso, back in Italy after a few years of exile in the United States and Mexico during the war, gave a party in the magnificent stables at Villa Madama, where she now resided. It was here that Giorgio met the lovely British actress, Merle Oberon.

Facing page: *Giorgio Cini and Merle Oberon in Cannes, August 1949. Giorgio died a few days later in a senseless plane crash.*
Above: *Art Deco diamond bracelet. Bulgari Heritage Collection.*

The young woman was a star with more than thirty films under her belt since her debut in 1933. Her interpretation of the role of Cathy in *Wuthering Heights* with Laurence Olivier and David Niven brought her worldwide fame. Her love life was chaotic. There had been several flings with co-stars, including Leslie Howard. And she was in the process of divorcing her second husband, Lucien Ballard. Behind her very seductive smile and her brilliant career, there was an anxious and romantic character. Her complicated past would not be revealed until after her death in 1979. Far from being born in Tasmania, as she had always claimed, Estelle Merle O'Brien Thomson had actually been born in Bombay in 1911. Her father was a railway official. And her mother, Constance, had been only twelve years old at the time of her birth. All her life, Merle would present her as her elder sister.

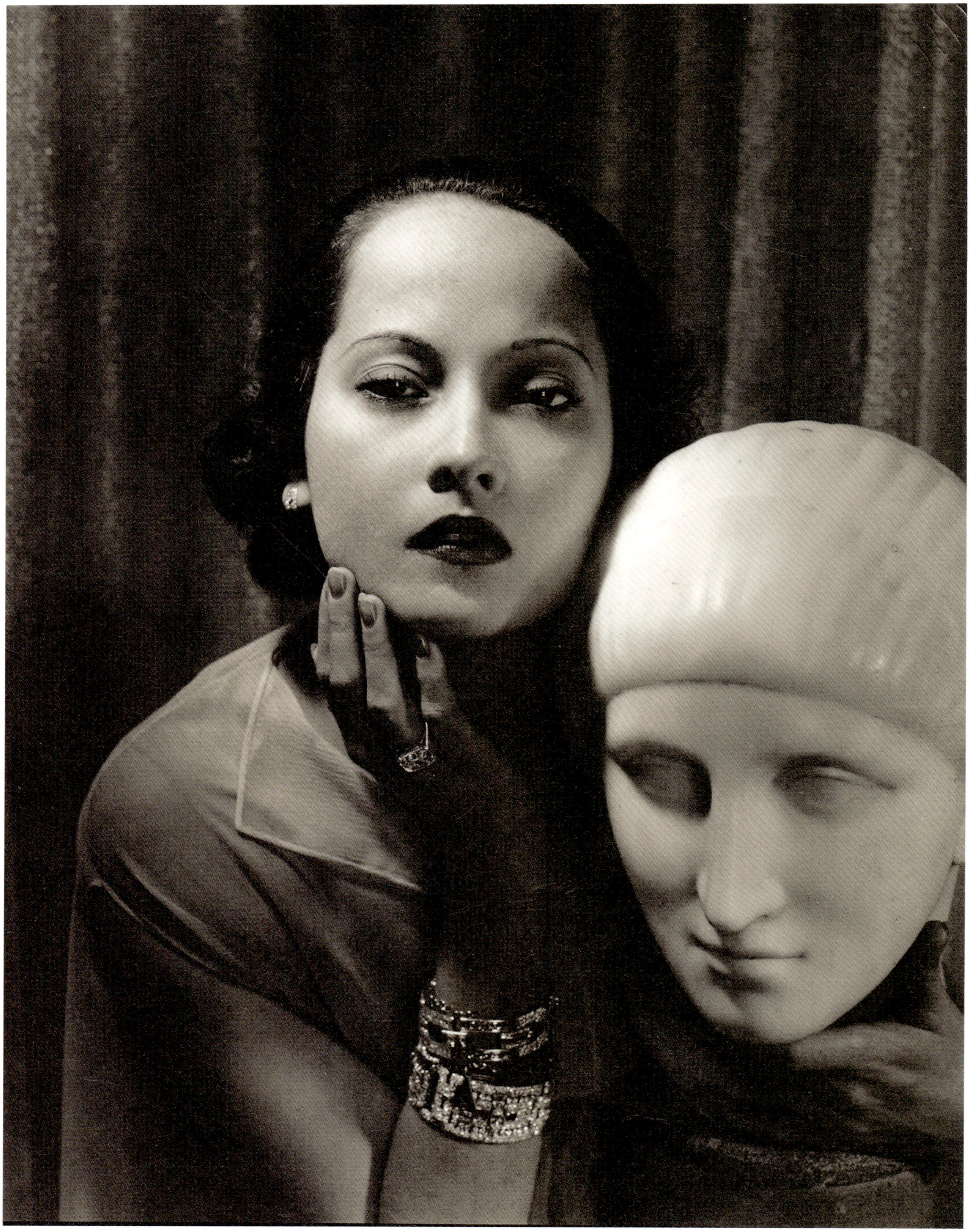

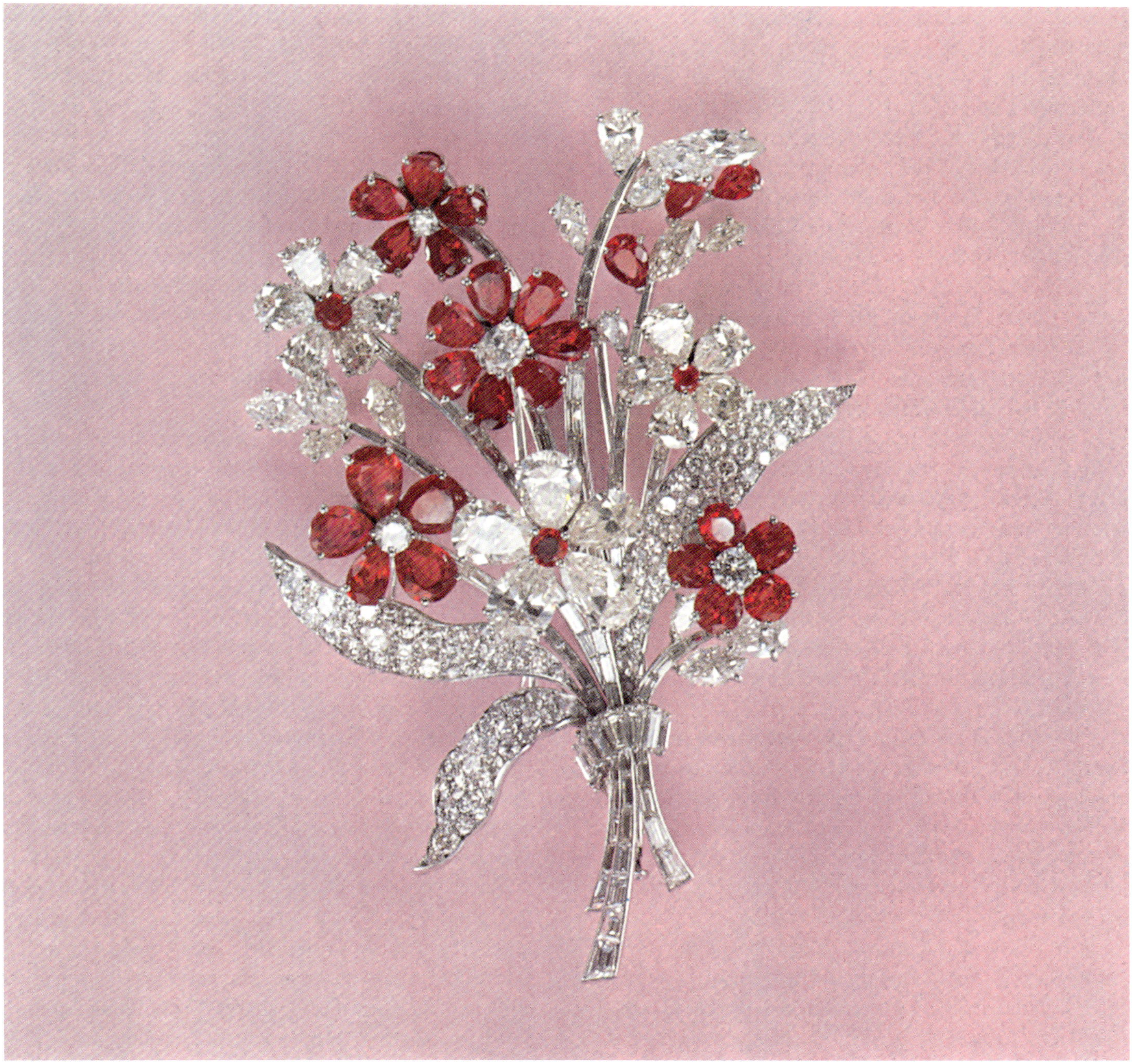

Above: *Diamond and ruby flower brooch, which was bought by Merle Oberon from Bulgari in the 1960s. It was later sold at Christie's in New York in 1980.*
Facing page: *One of the first portraits of Merle Oberon at the beginning of her acting career.*

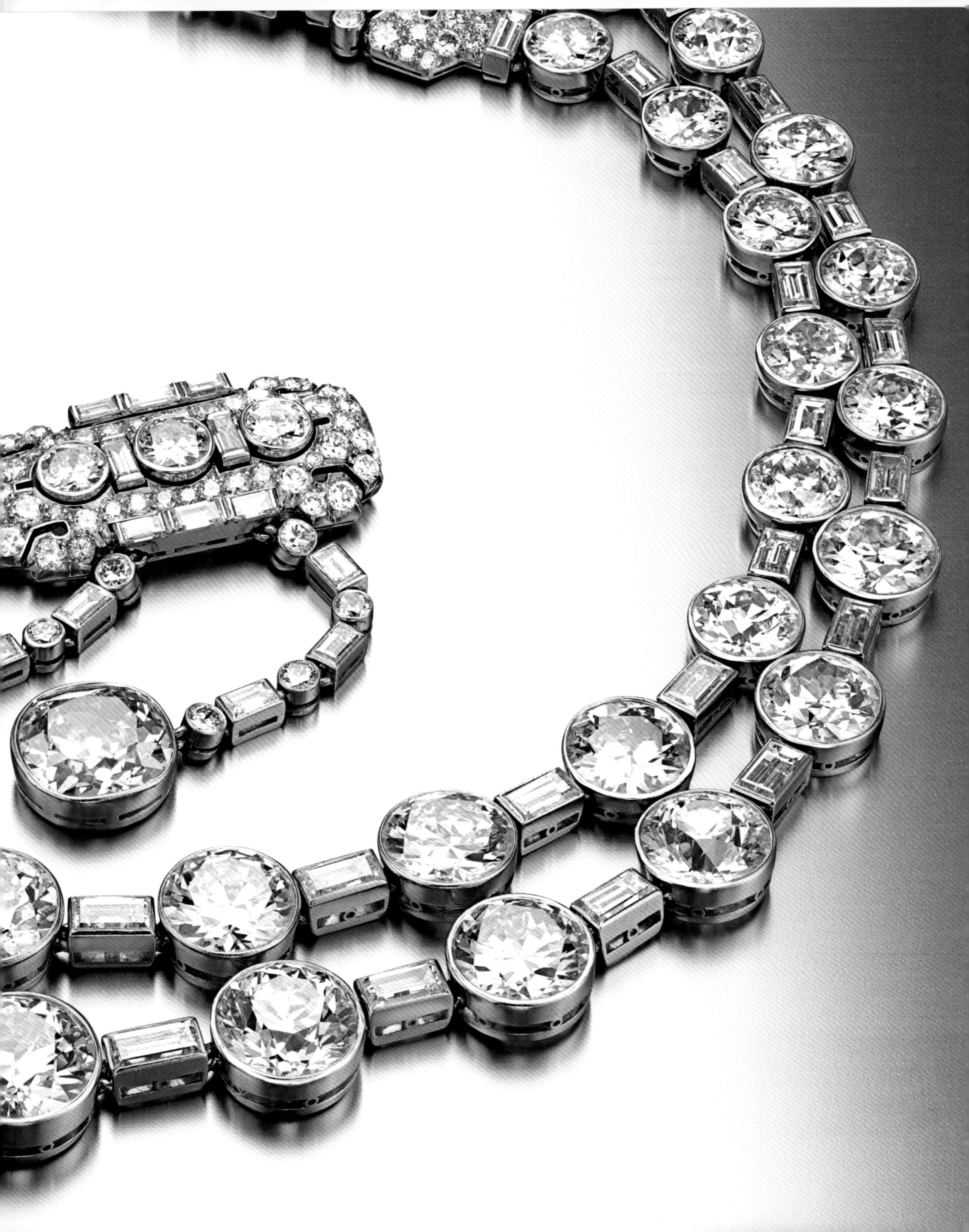

Chapter 4

A SPLASH OF DIAMONDS

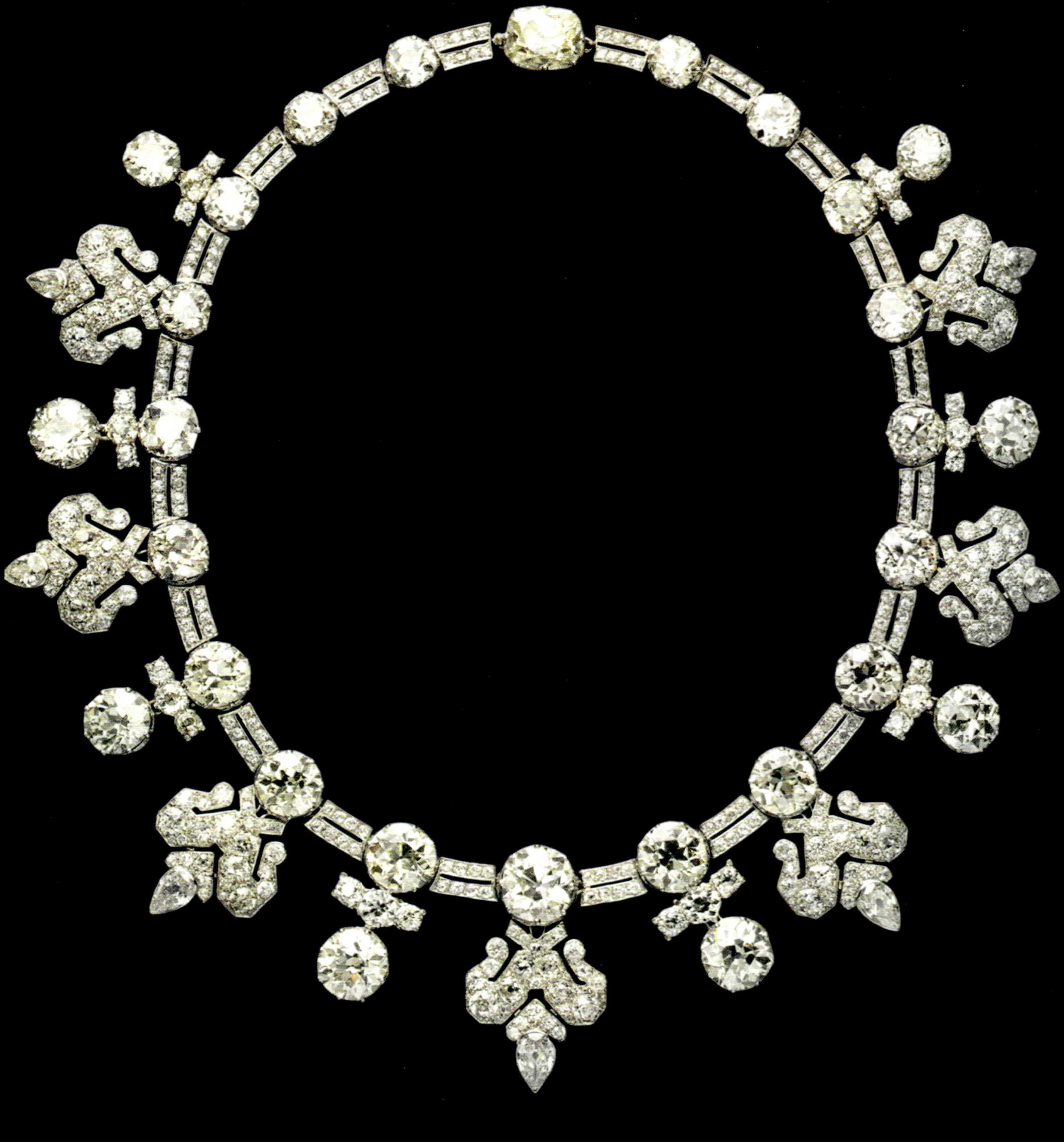

The creation of the Infanta Beatriz of Spain's diamond necklace in 1935 is a good example of the change in fashion that Europe experienced in the 1930s (see chapter 2). The long diamond sautoir of Queen Victoria Eugenie of Spain was outdated. Her Majesty transformed it into a shorter double necklace and offered the unused diamonds to her children. Her eldest daughter, Beatriz, entrusted hers to Bulgari. The diamonds were reassembled into a necklace that characterises the evolution of the style of the Maison at that time. The "*chaînes d'huissier*" – (long necklaces ending with a pendant that is often detachable to wear as a brooch – were by this point considered completely outmoded. A more classical necklace, closer to the neck was back.

One of the reasons for this stylistic revolution was, of course, the change in fashion. In the aftermath of the First World War, women who had often taken their husbands' places at work during the years of conflict had demonstrated that they were capable of independence. Their clothing evolved to reflect this. The corsets, in which the elegant women of the Belle Époque had been imprisoned, disappeared, especially spurred on by the young Parisian seamstress, Gabrielle Chanel. The lines of evening dresses had become fluid and almost tubular. The high neckline was often straight. There was no longer any question of an elegant woman showcasing her cleavage with silk and lace as fashion had required before 1914. And on these new dresses, often shaped in very supple fabrics, long jewelled pieces had bloomed. And Bulgari had followed this trend. The *haute joaillerie*, which Giorgio Bulgari had dreamed of during his famous stay in Paris before 1914, first expressed itself in this way. Several diamond and coloured "*chaînes d'huissiers*" signed by Bulgari, dating back to the mid-1920s, have survived.

In the mid-1930s, Paris still set the tone, but fashion has changed yet again. In 1933, a young Swiss designer opened his couture house in the French capital. His name was Robert Piguet and from his very first collection he returned to a very feminine, more sophisticated silhouette. The cut was again markedly new, but not in a stifling way as it once had been. The muslin chemisettes that hid the cleavage were gone and skin was revealed once again. Sleeves and shoulders were reduced to their simplest forms. Necklaces that encircled the neck found their natural place on this type of dress.

Impressive diamond necklaces were becoming a signature Bulgari piece, probably facilitated by the death of Sotirio in 1932. After this, his two sons had a free hand and they did not hesitate to take risks. The Bulgari archives track the very important purchases of gemstones that were made abroad, especially in Paris, but also in Germany and London, around that time. An invoice dating from 1936 details the arrival from Paris of 9,068 brilliants, with a total weight of 554.20 carats, which cost 556,000 francs at the time. Another invoice, also from 1936, describes "a brilliant emerald-cut, of the best colour, weighing 14.12 carats, ten baguette diamonds of 5.07 carats and 138 small

Facing page: *This diamond necklace was created by Bulgari in 1935 for the Infanta Beatriz of Spain, Princess of Civitella-Cesi. The most important diamonds were given to the Infanta by her mother, Queen Victoria Eugenie of Spain. The necklace was sold at auction by Christie's, Geneva in 1980.* **Previous page:** *Two-strand diamond necklace, 1930s. Bulgari Heritage Collection.*

brilliants". The total value was estimated at 69,351 francs.

Very often, as was the case with the Infanta Beatriz of Spain, the client would bring diamonds from an old piece of jewellery that she wished to be reset in a more modern jewel. Bulgari would add its own stylistic touch. For the Infanta, the large diamonds from Queen Victoria Eugenie's sautoir were reset as pendants on diamond flowers; it was very Art Deco in its purified design. The motifs evoke the fleurs-de-lis of the royal dynasty of the Bourbons, to which the royal house of Spain belongs. The rectangular links between the flowers were also made with diamonds removed from antique jewels belonging to the royal family of Spain.

The necklace that was sold to Countess di Frasso in 1939 was of similar structure, but with different flower motifs. This time, the design of the pendants was a modern adaptation of the papyrus flower. As before, the larger diamonds were suspended from the end of each flower. The house of Bulgari seems to have made several of these papyrus necklaces before and after the Second World War. One detail was always noticeable: the very special attention paid to the design of the clasp. It was often composed of a double scroll of diamonds, sometimes even highlighted with two pendants. The backs of the fashionable evening dresses plunged as deeply as at the front, and the idea was to provide an ornament as seductive at the back as it was on the décolleté.

One of the most touching anecdotes related to these diamond necklaces is told by Enza Tomassi, one of the saleswomen of the house, in her memoires, *Tre volte il cielo: "I think that it was in 1955 that Henry Ford and his wife, Ann, came to the shop. He wanted to buy an evening bag for his wife. I presented them with various models before he decided on the most modest, with no diamonds on the clasp. I asked him if he did not prefer another model, more graceful, because ten tiny diamonds were set on the clasp. He looked at me and answered a little dryly: 'Mrs. Tomassi, I cannot afford it.' At the time, Ford factories were in trouble. A few years later, he came back alone, and asked me to choose a very beautiful jewel that he wished to give to his wife. 'You know her, you know her tastes. You have carte blanche,' he said. 'Even for a diamond necklace?' I asked. 'Absolutely, choose one.' He bought it. Clearly, Ford no longer had problems at that time."* [1]

Facing page: *This long diamond chain is called a* "chaîne d'huissier" *(literally, "bailiff's chain"), it is typical of Art Deco jewellery. On such chains, the pendant is usually detachable and can be worn as a brooch and the necklace can be divided into bracelets. Bulgari Heritage Collection.*

1. *Tre volte il cielo* [lit. Three times the sky] by Enza Tomassi von Heuduck Kiskis, Ed. Fermenti, 2000.

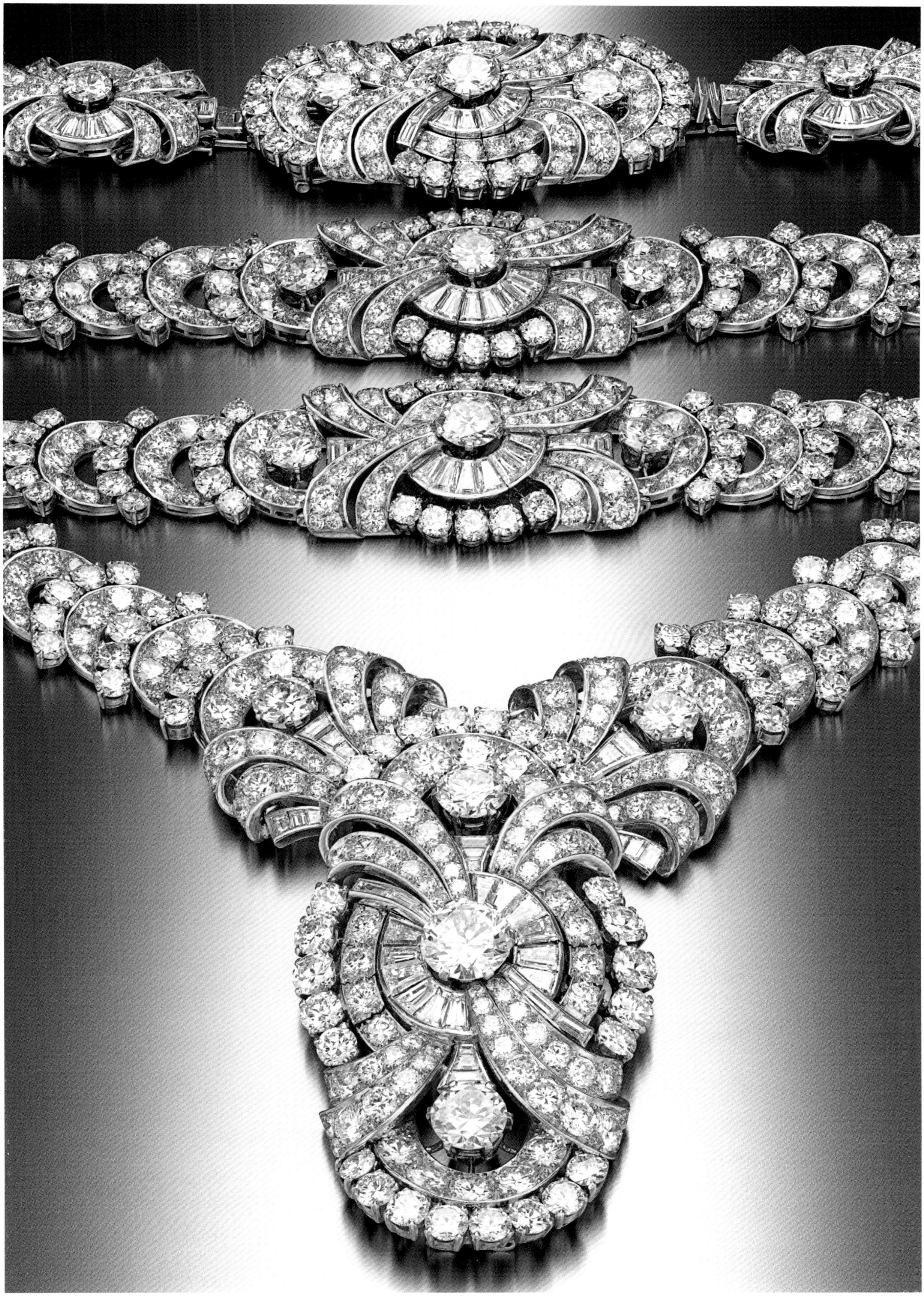

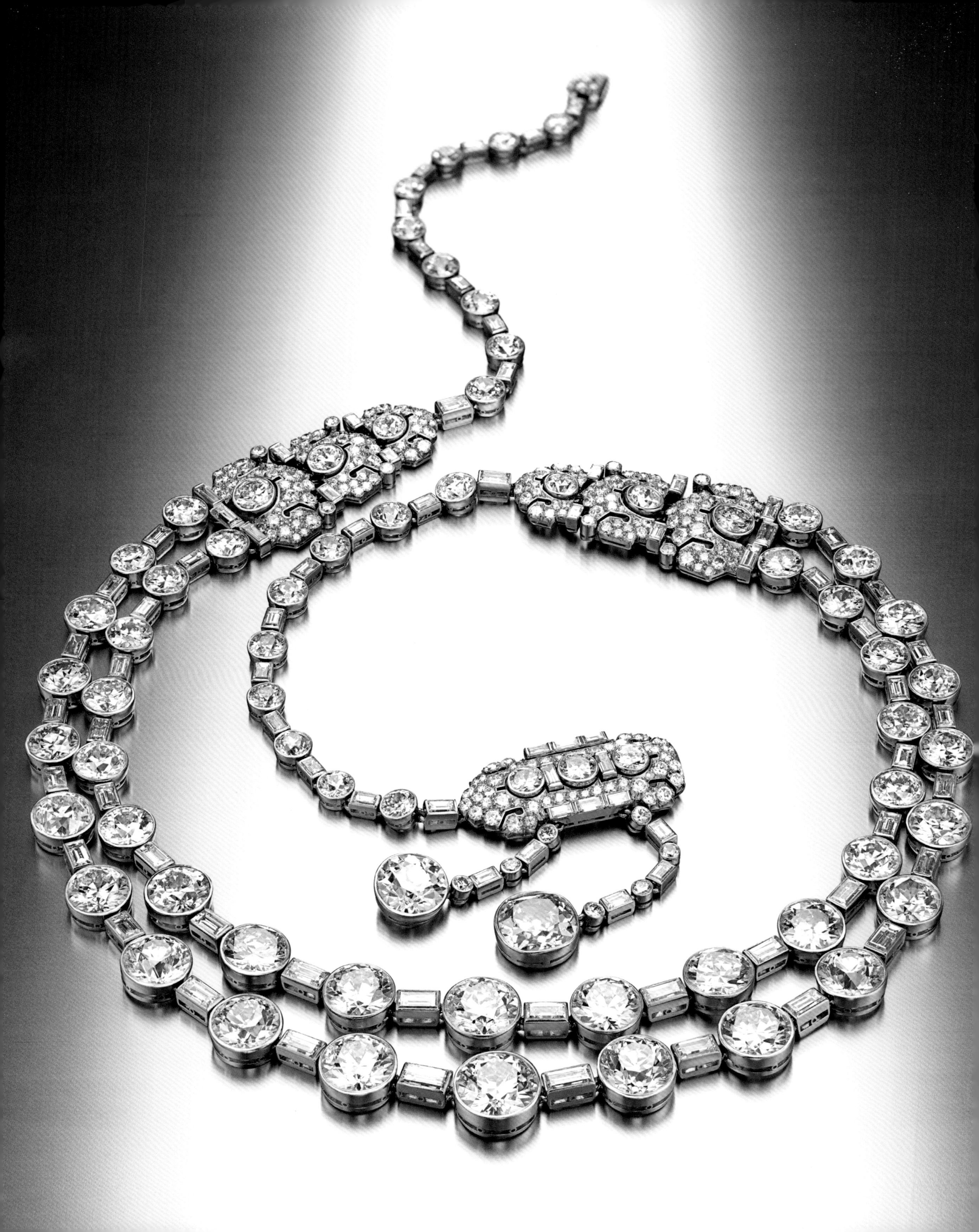

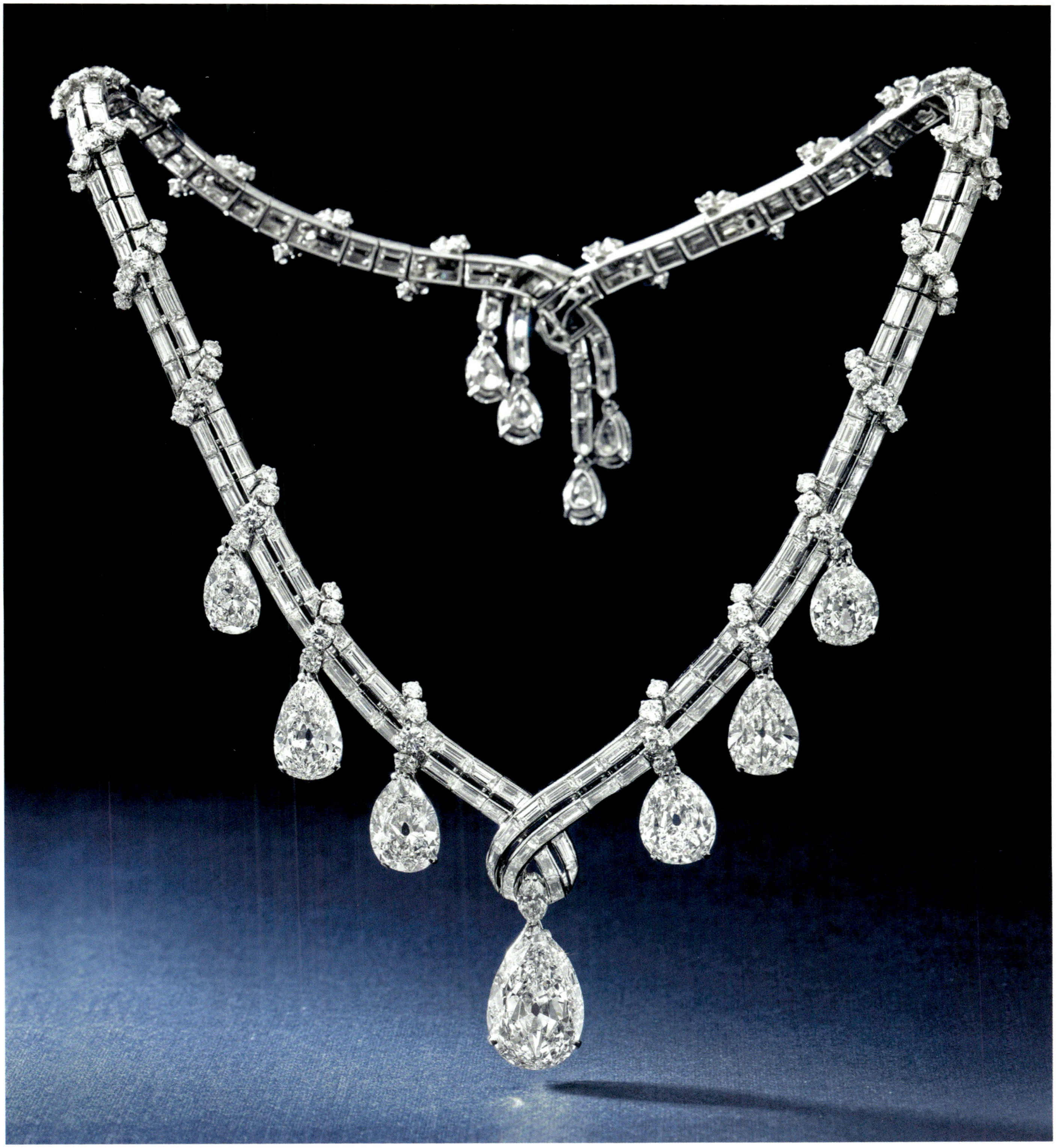

Above: *This diamond necklace is very typical of the Bulgari style during the 1950s. It was sold by Sotheby's, Hong Kong in April 2015.* **Facing page:** *A two-strand diamond necklace created by Bulgari in the 1930s. Bulgari Heritage Collection.*

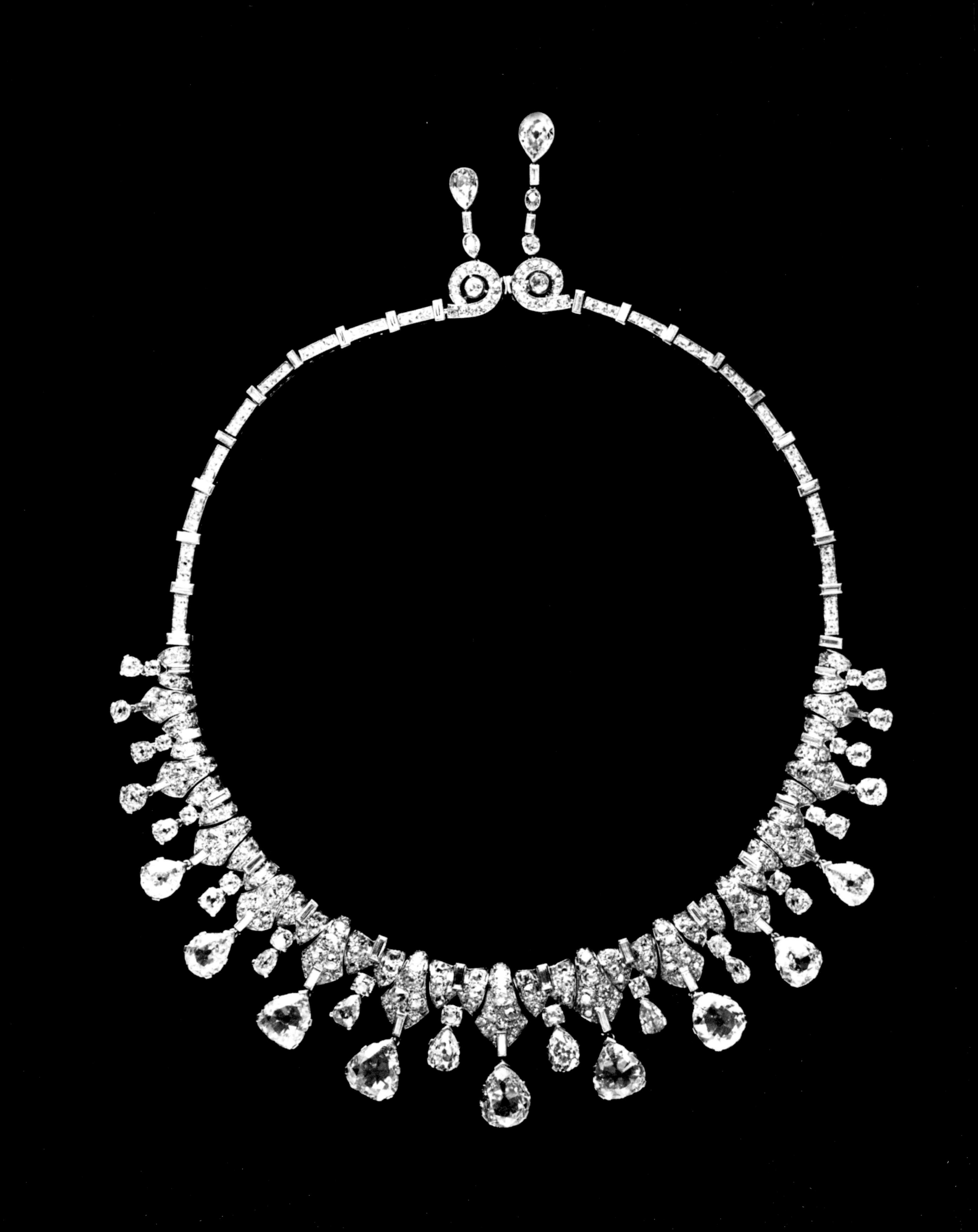

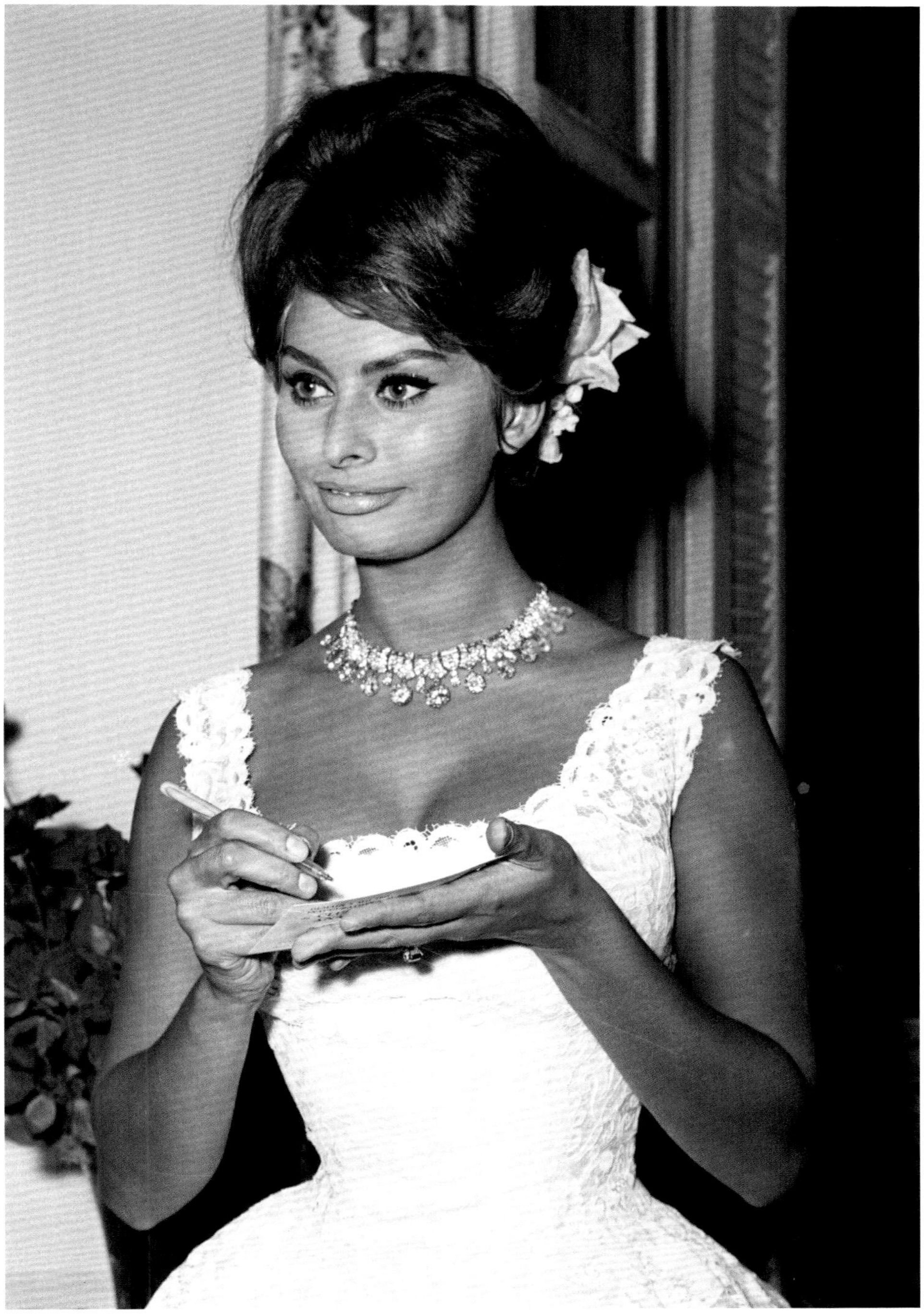

Above: *Sophia Loren in the 1960s. She is wearing a diamond necklace created by Bulgari, which is very similar in style to the necklace bought by Dorothy di Frasso in 1939.*
Facing page: *A Bulgari diamond necklace of the same style, sold by Christie's, Geneva in 1981.*
Overleaf: *Diamond necklace with five sunburst motifs, which can be detached and worn as brooches. The necklace was created by Bulgari in 1953 and bought by Queen Soraya of Iran. It was sold at auction in Paris, in 2002, by Etude Beaussant Lefèvre.*

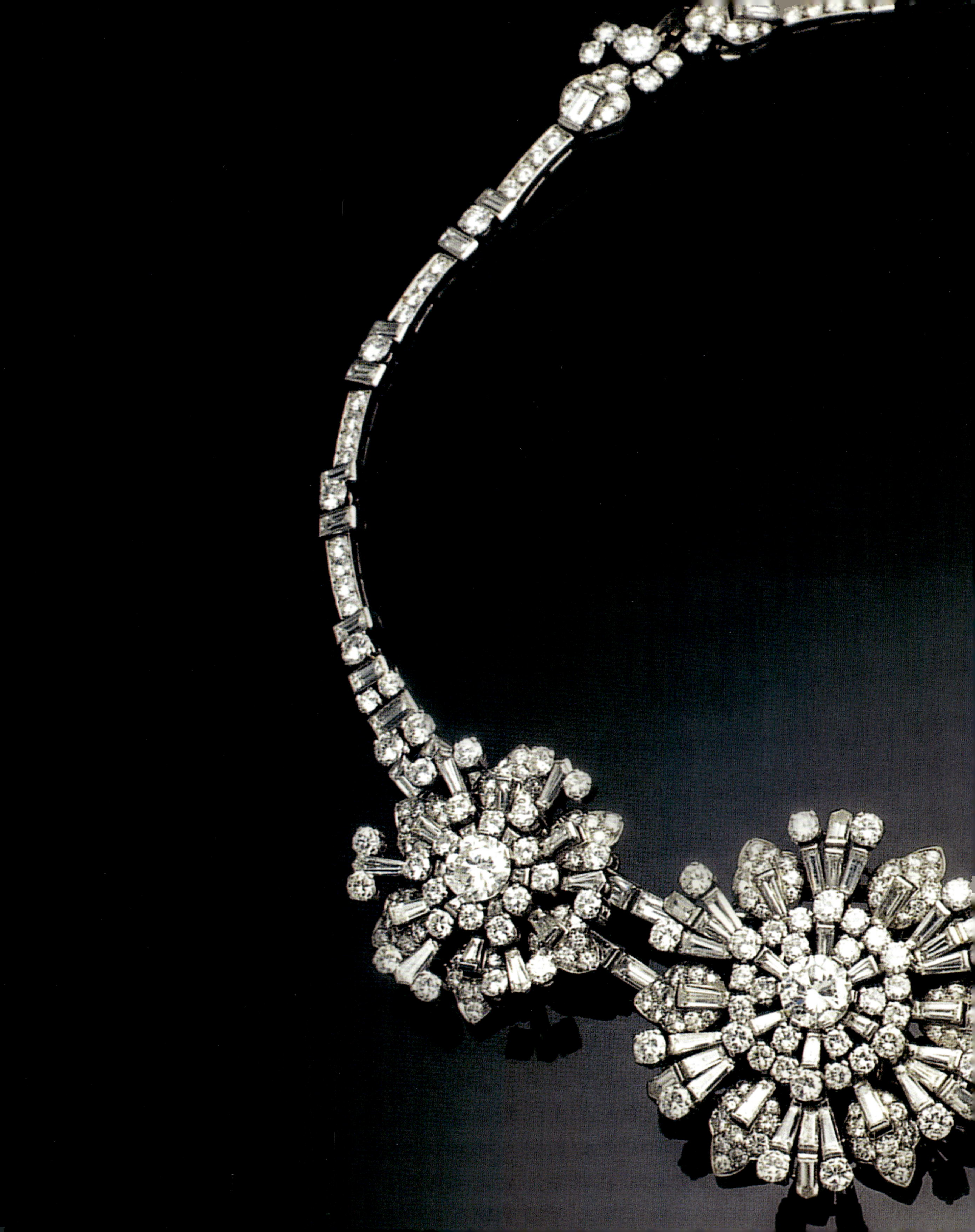

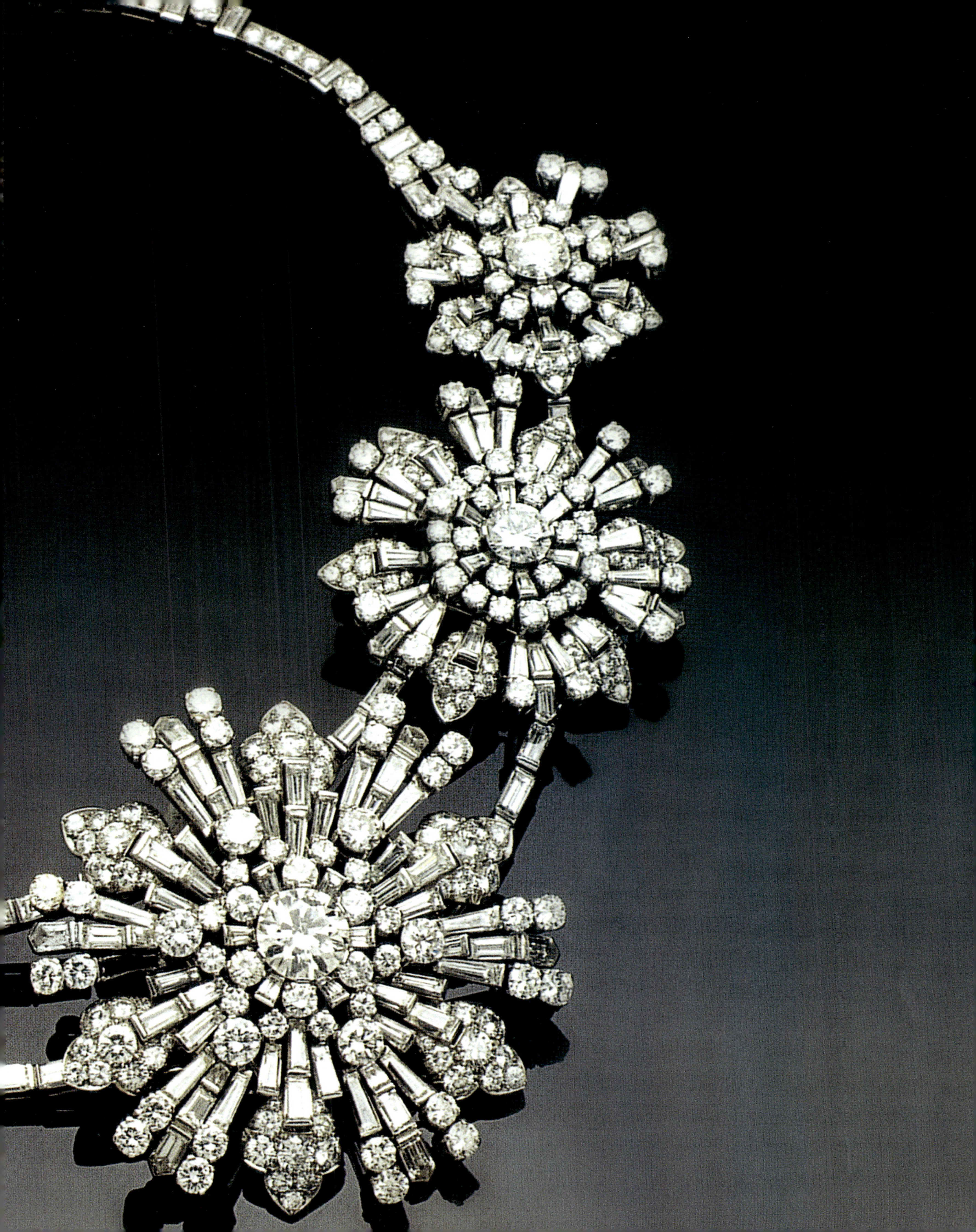

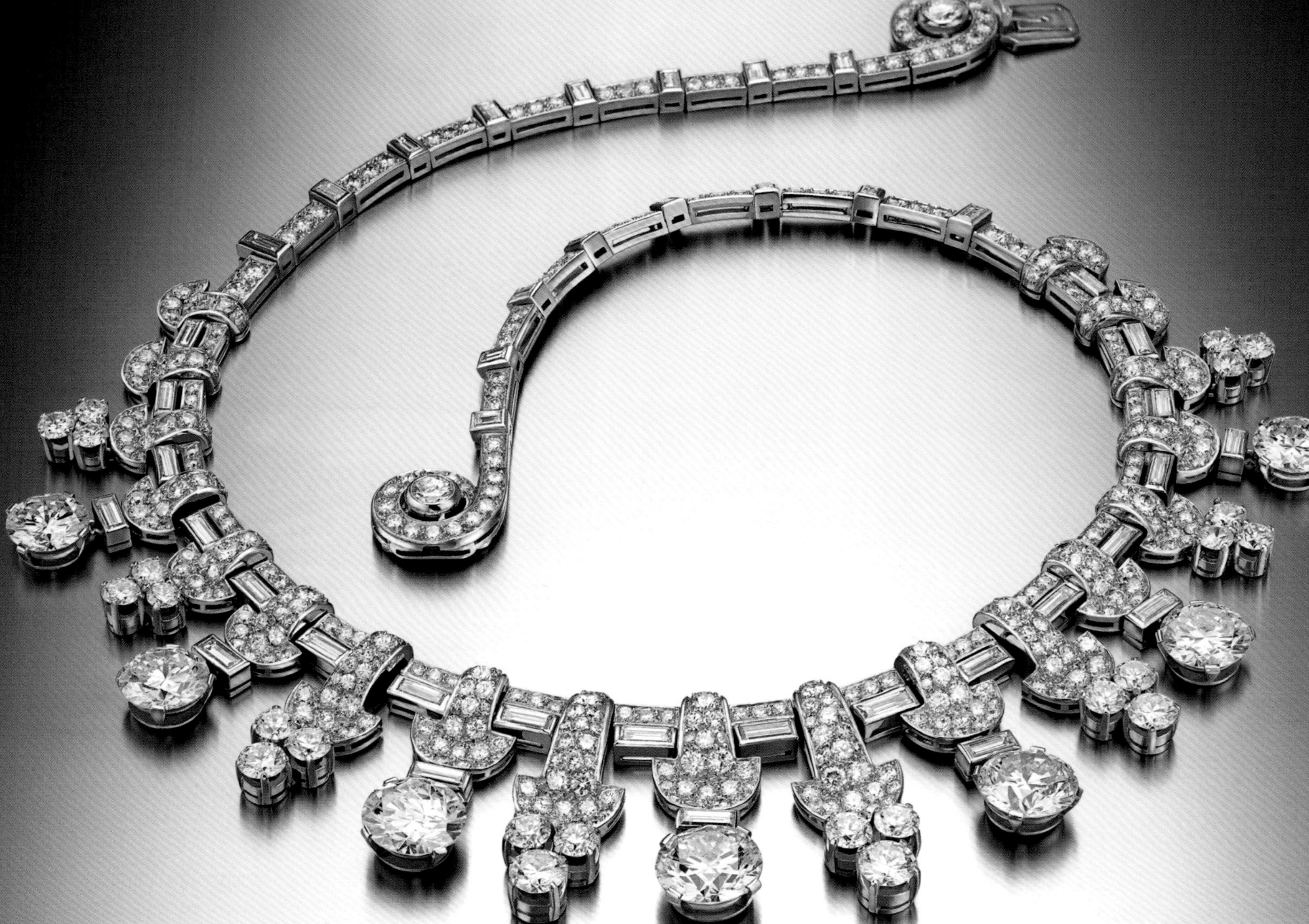

Above: *Diamond necklace with the typical Bulgari lotus flower motif. Bulgari Heritage Collection.* **Facing page:** *Art Deco diamond necklace set in platinum created by Bulgari in 1935. FD Gallery collection, New York.*

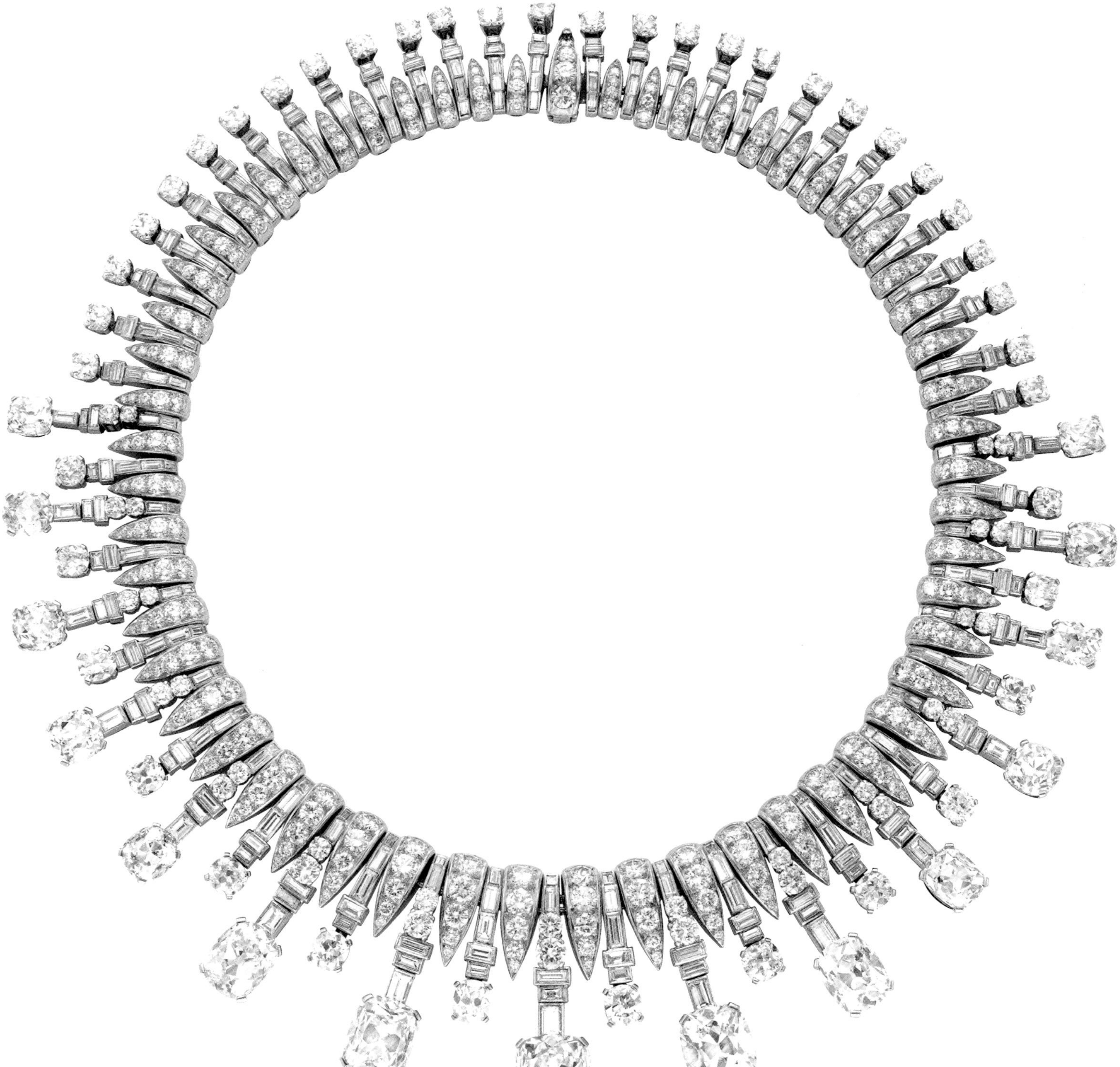

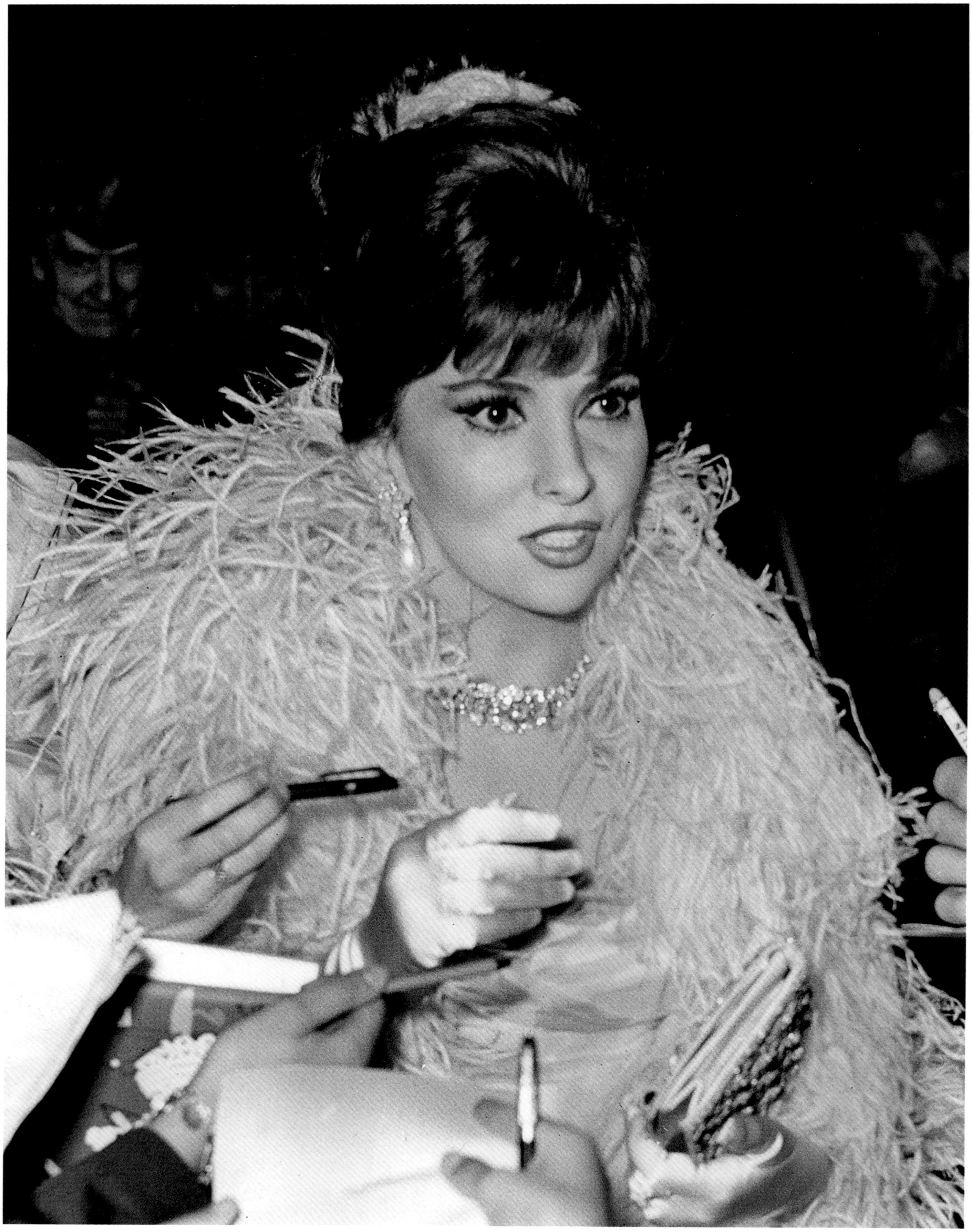

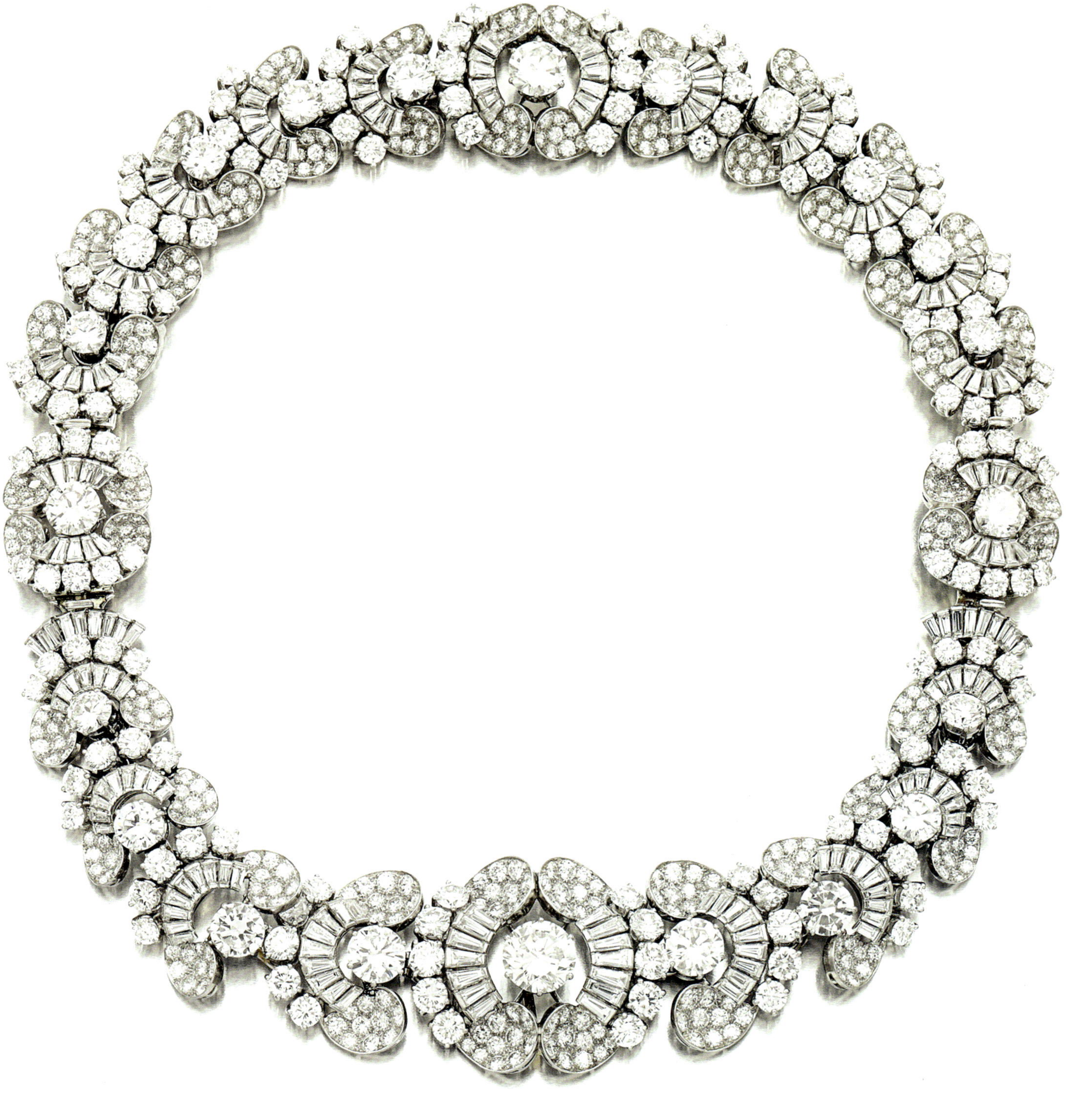

Above: *Diamond necklace sold to Gina Lollobrigida in the 1960s. It can be transformed into two bracelets. It was sold at Sotheby's, Geneva in 2013.* **Facing page:** *Gina Lollobrigida signing autographs during the Berlin Film Festival in July 1965.*

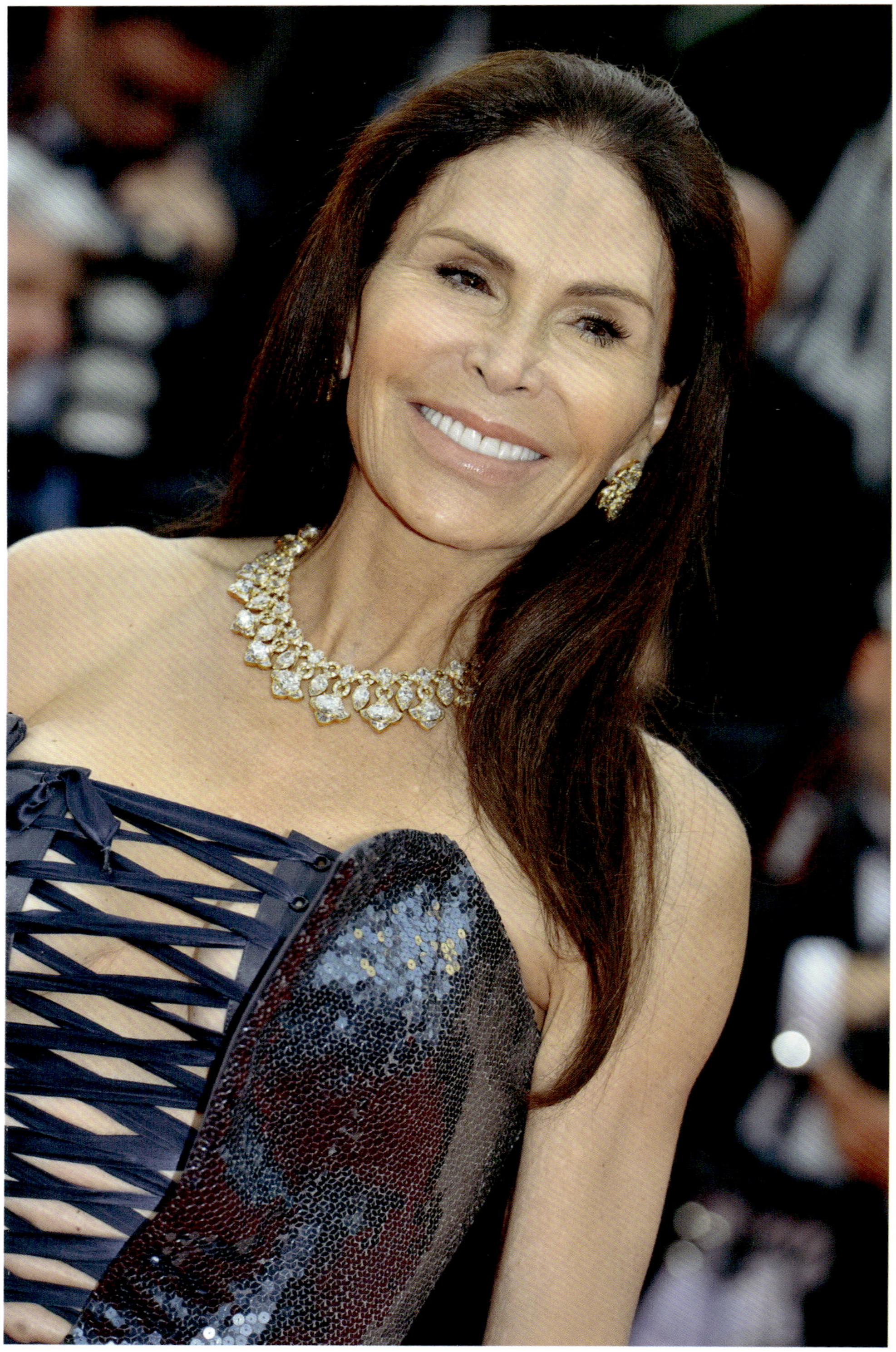

Above: *Mouna Ayoub wearing one of her stunning Bulgari diamond necklaces.* **Facing page:** *Mouna Ayoub's Bulgari diamond necklace and matching earrings. Private collection.* **Overleaf:** *Bulgari diamond necklace, which can be transformed into two bracelets. Bulgari Heritage Collection.*

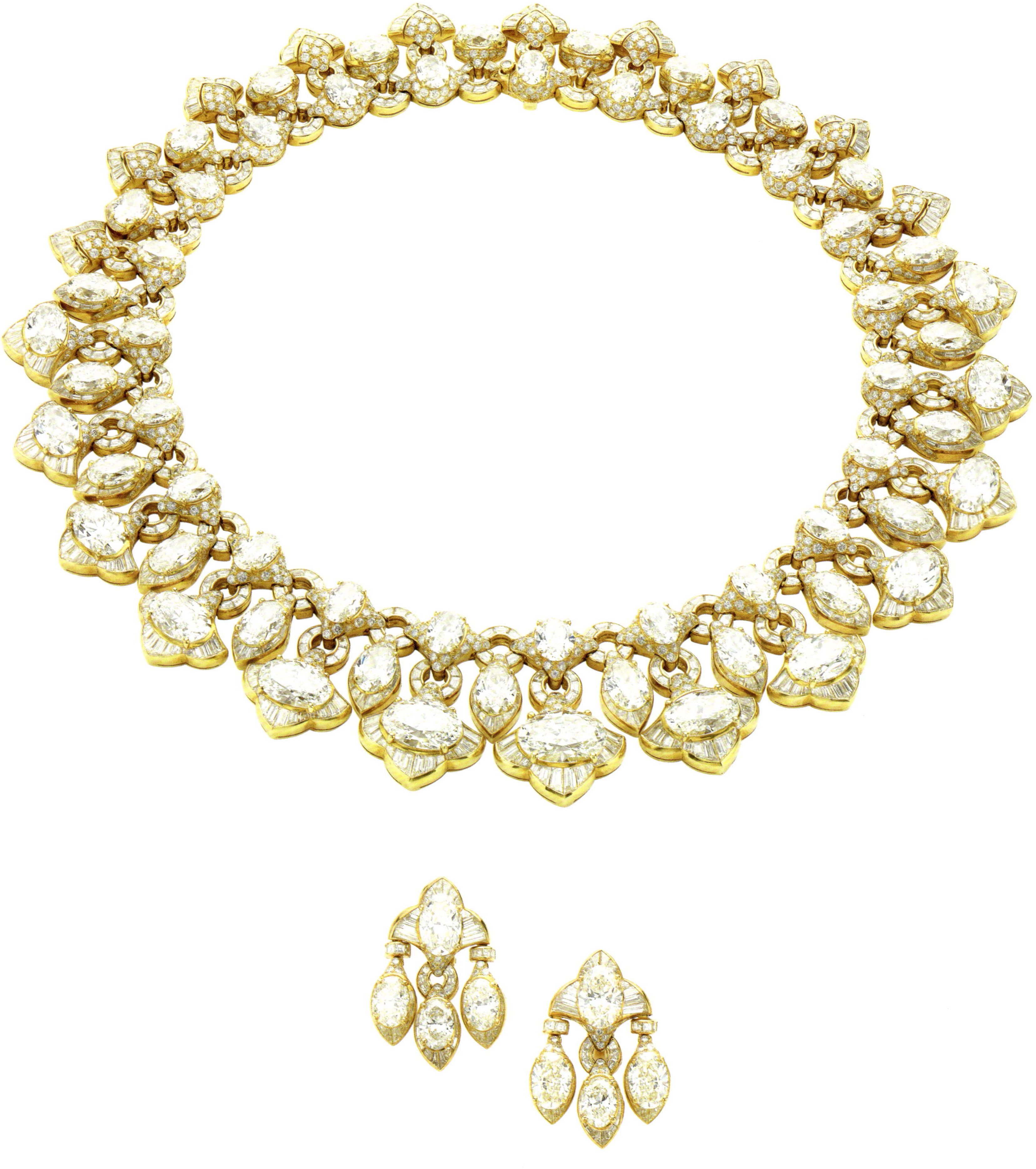

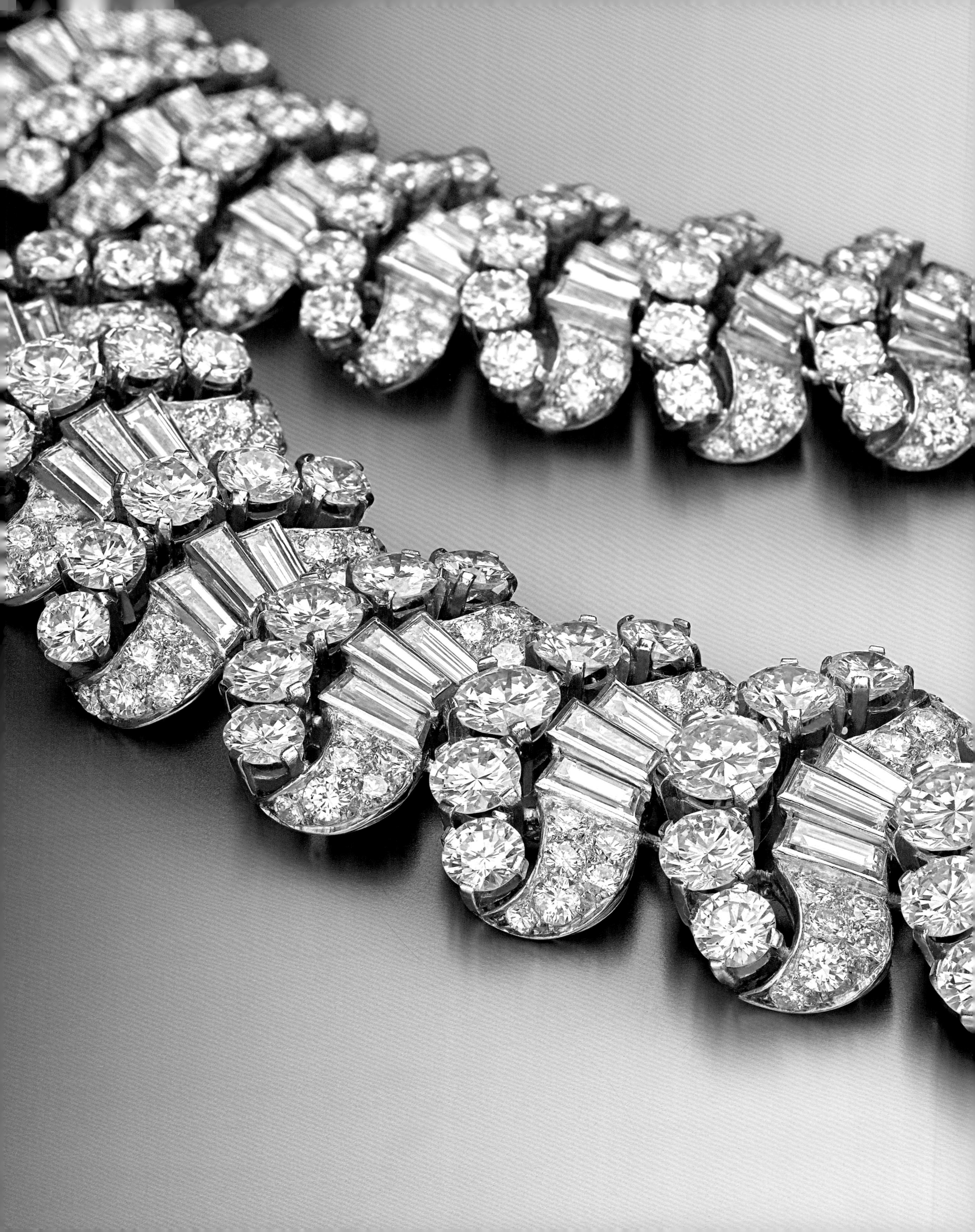

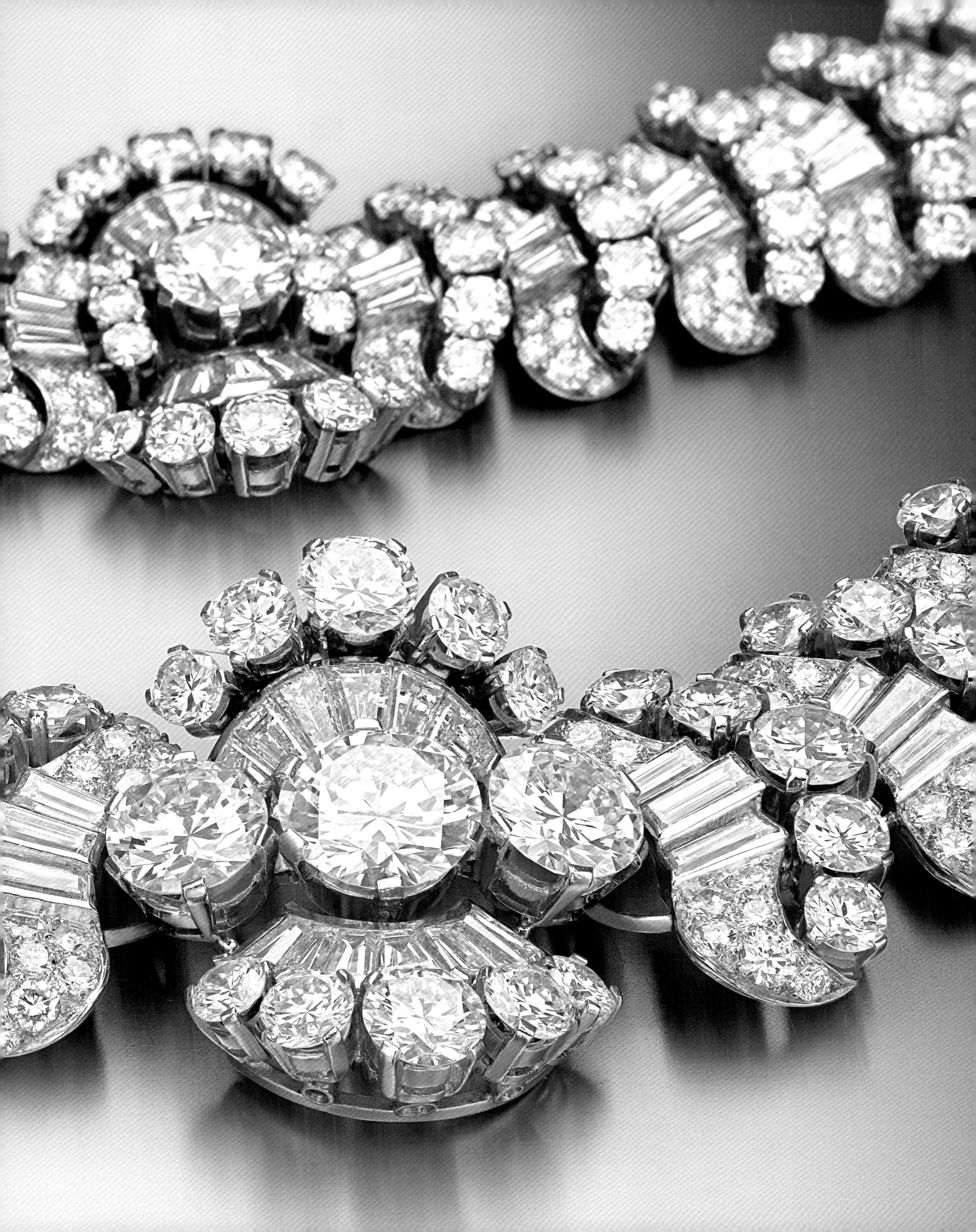

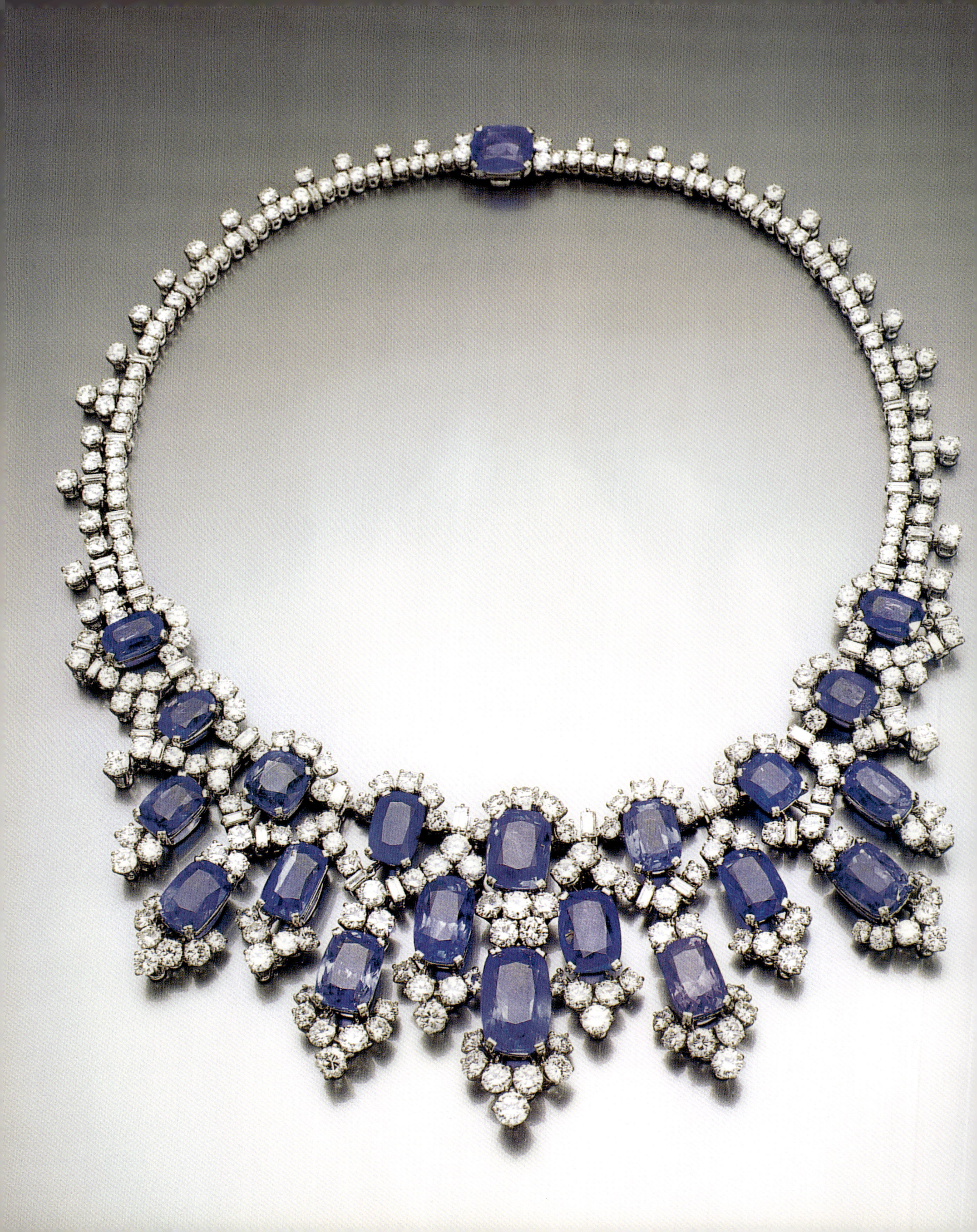

Chapter 5

THE LOVERS OF VIA DEI CONDOTTI

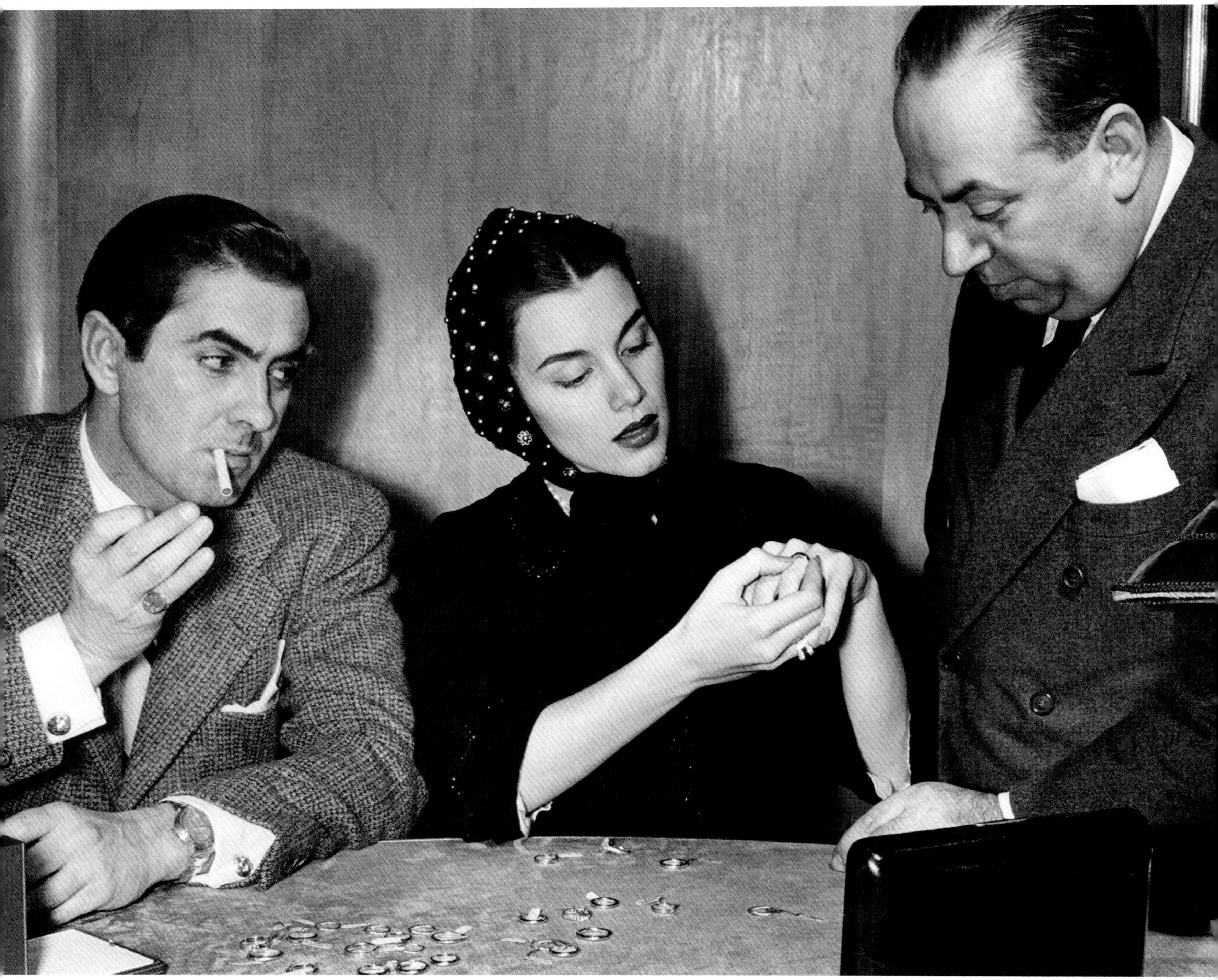

Above: *Tyrone Power and his fiancée, Linda Christian, in the Bulgari boutique in Rome. They are choosing their wedding rings with the help of Ubaldo Crescenzi, whose family still works for Bulgari.*
Previous page: *Sapphire and diamond necklace created by Bulgari for Princess Soraya in 1958.*

Tyrone Power and Linda Christian

Bulgari Boutique, Via dei Condotti, January 1949

In the picture, Tyrone Power looks rather nervous. He is lighting a cigarette as he watches his fiancée, Linda Christian, trying on a ring from the dozens of wedding rings in front of her. To the right of the image, Ubaldo Crescenzi, Bulgari's workshop chief at that time, contemplates the future bride and groom. They are seated in the small private room in the right of the shop on Via dei Condotti. It is a few days before their wedding, and they have come to choose their rings. A classic yellow gold model for him, something a little more sophisticated for her. Her wedding band is made up of two rings joined together: one in gold, the other in platinum. The two bands are engraved with this sentiment: *"Tyrone loves Linda"*. The young woman wants to be able to use one or the other of these two wedding rings. The first when she wears gold jewellery. The second with her engagement ring, a diamond solitaire mounted on platinum. She has just uttered a few words that may explain Tyrone Power's slightly worried look: *"I love emeralds, even if I do not have any yet."* [1]

Giorgio Bulgari, who was also present on that day, was waiting for an opportunity to show her some of the fabulous parures kept in the Bulgari safe. Not only was Tyrone and Linda's wedding in Rome the world's most publicised marriage since that of Princess Elizabeth in England two years before, but it was also quickly becoming one of the most expensive. Outside the shop, the paparazzi and the fans waited for a glimpse of the celebrity lovers. The two stars probably left by the side exit that opens into the inner courtyard where their car would have been waiting.

Rome, Italy… the whole world was talking about this wedding that would take place on 27 January. All the preparations had been made in the Italian capital. The jewels were from Bulgari. Domenico Caraceni, the tailor who had created Gary Cooper's wardrobe in the early 1930s, designed the groom's suit. The bridal gown was made by three young dressmakers from Parma who opened a boutique in Rome in 1943: Zoe, Micol and Giovanna Fontana. In appreciation of the considerable publicity that this commission would earn them, the Fontana sisters offered the dress to the star for free. However, it was also true that Linda bought her spectacular trousseau from Sorelle Fontana, at a cost of $5,000. It consisted of about twenty dresses and tailored suits, five fur coats, including a leopard and two minks, and even – as the couple would be honeymooning in the Italian Alps – an haute couture ski suit. The only foreign note in this all-Italian ensemble was Linda's French perfume. She always wore the same fragrance: Shalimar by Guerlain.

All of this was a far cry from the *"discreet little wedding"* Linda had announced in an interview with American journalist Robert Peer a few months earlier. The ceremony would take place in Florence, she explained: *"We want a very simple marriage. No extravagant trousseau. No champagne. No crowds. Our only guests will be my parents, my sister Ariadne and her husband, Jim Denton."* [2]

Three years previously, Linda Christian, a dazzling Mexican starlet, had become a celebrity overnight, thanks to the carefully orchestrated machinery of

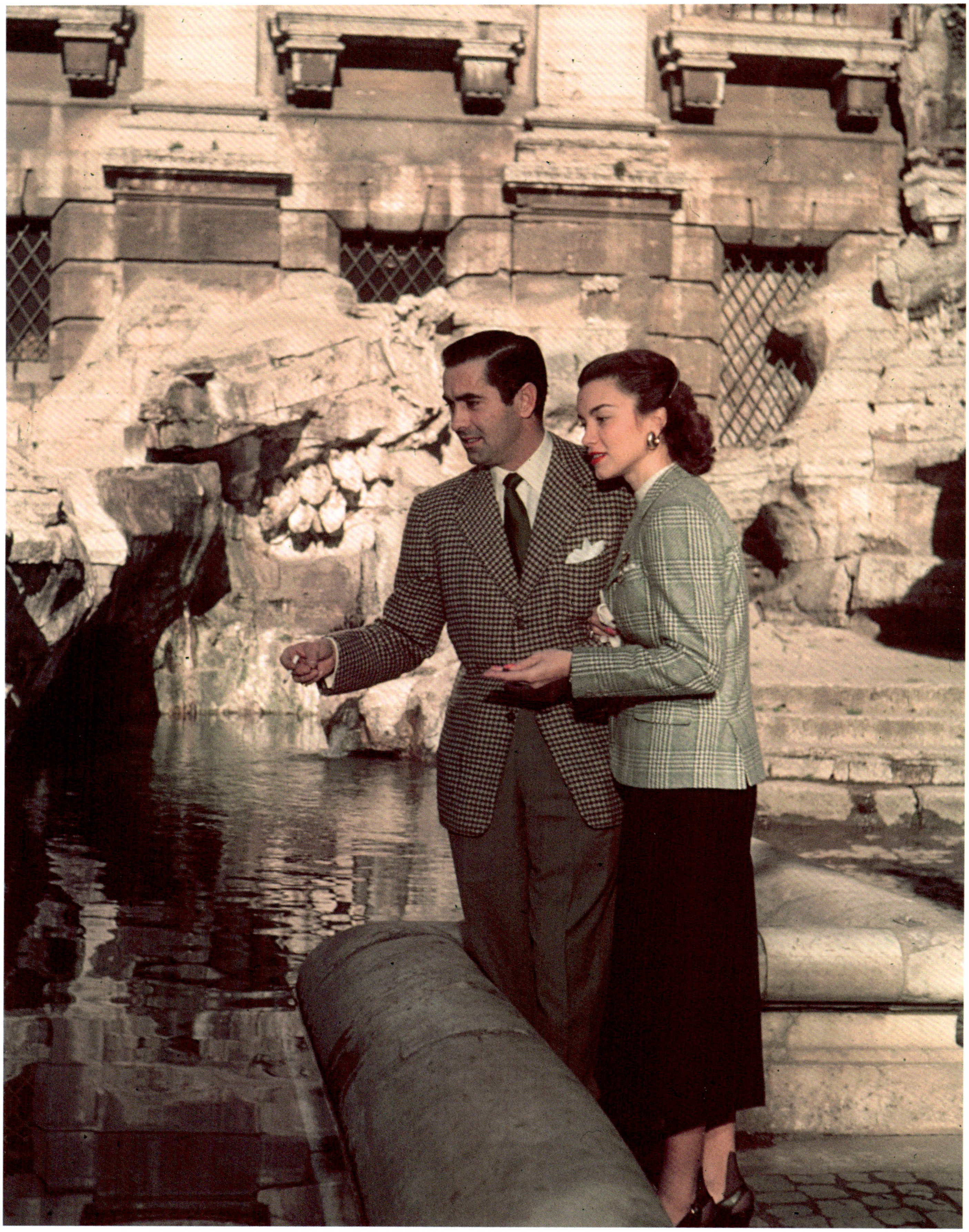

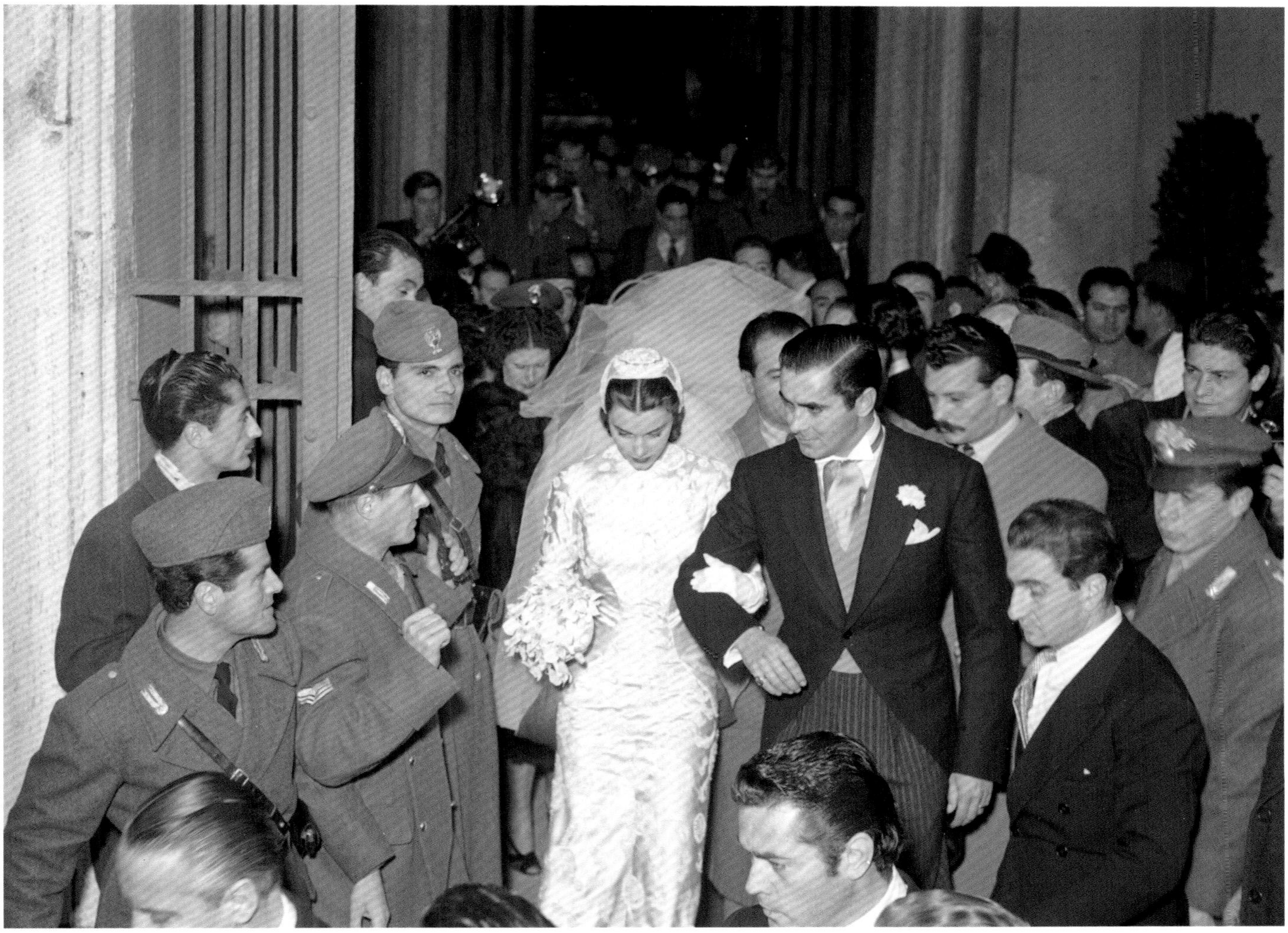

Above: *The wedding of Tyrone Power and Linda Christian in Rome on 27 January 1949. The ceremony took place in the church of Santa Francesca Romana, one of the oldest churches in Rome.* **Facing page:** *Tyrone Power and Linda Christian in front of the Trevi Fountain in Rome, a few days before their wedding.*

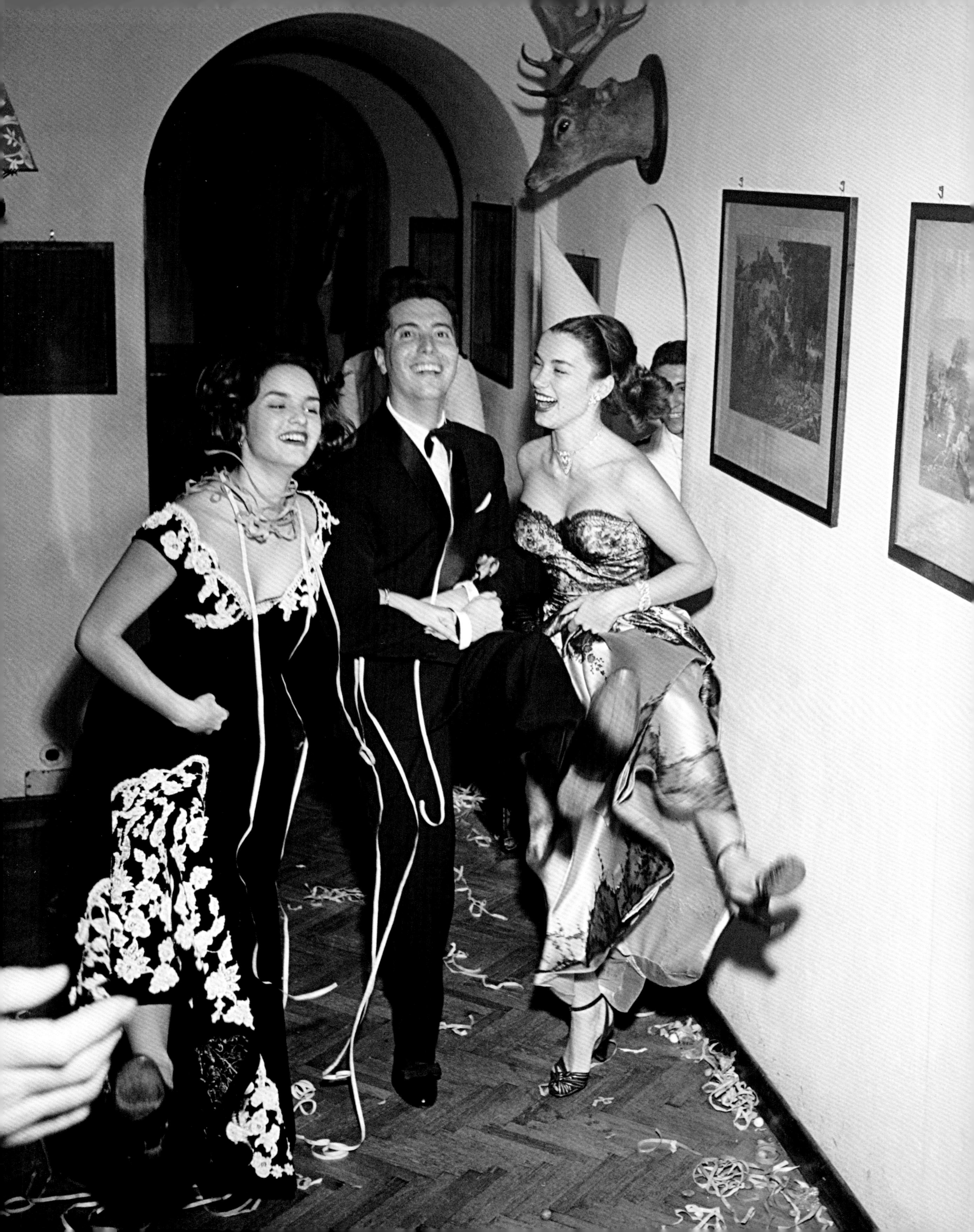

Hollywood. An advertising campaign, not really in the best taste, had launched her career. In its 3 September, 1945 edition, *Life* magazine stated: *"Even before the ink announcing the release of the atomic bomb on Japan is dry, Hollywood has turned the information into a good advertisement. Thanks to the Metro-Goldwyn-Mayer, Linda Christian, an obscure starlet, was solemnly proclaimed the Anatomic Bomb. Half Mexican and half Dutch, Miss Christian was born in Tampico, Mexico, twenty-two years ago. Her real name is Blanca Rosa Welter. Her father, director of an oil company, traveled extensively in the world with his family. She speaks six languages: Spanish, French, English, Dutch, German and Italian."* [3]

Another star, Errol Flynn, one of Hollywood's greatest seducers, had discovered the "anatomic bomb" during one of his visits to Mexico in the early 1940s. In his memoirs, Flynn explains, not very gallantly, that he advised the young woman to consult a good dentist in order to remodel some of her teeth, the only flaw in her smile. He even offered to pay the bill. It seems this was good advice. A few weeks after her arrival in Hollywood, Linda signed a seven year contract with Metro-Goldwyn-Mayer. Her stage name of Linda Christian was also one of Errol Flynn's ideas. Christian was the name he used in one of his first Australian films. And then he played the role of 'Fletcher Christian', the mutinous officer who led the rebellious sailors of the *Bounty*.

It cannot be denied that the young actress's first films were not all masterpieces. Her best role came from director Robert Florey, in 1948, in *Tarzan and the Mermaids*. In it Johnny Weissmuller makes his last appearance as the character that earned him worldwide fame. Naturally, the gossip columns all speculated on a possible romance between the two actors. Would Tarzan marry his mermaid? But the rumour was completely unfounded. By that time, the mermaid was already very fond of another star: Tyrone Power.

In our era of quick and ephemeral celebrity it might be difficult to comprehend the degree of fascination that Hollywood stars aroused in the mid-20th century. Their slightest movement unleashed floods of people. A star's arrival at a port or airport would trigger such crowds that the entire police force of the city had to be mobilised. For more than ten years, Tyrone Power had been one of these media phenomenon, someone who inspired thousands of fans simply with a smile. His audience was mainly female, as he was the undisputed prince of romance, especially historical romance. In 1949, the year of his marriage to Linda, he was 34 years old. During his 15-year career in Hollywood, he had successively portrayed 'Count Axel de Fersen' opposite Norma Shearer in *Marie-Antoinette,* 'Ferdinand de Lesseps' in *Suez,* a conquistador in *Captain from Castile,* a loveable brigand in the title role of *Jesse James,* and the handsome doctor 'Major Safti' in the first film adaptation of *The Rains Came,* the famous novel by Louis Bromfield.

His personal love stories were equally as famous and numerous. His first wife was the French film actress Annabella. The marriage lasted ten years, on paper at least, though in reality they only lived together for three years. By coincidence they had honeymooned in Rome in 1939. The war distanced them. Tyrone had volunteered for duty and when he returned to Hollywood in 1944, the husband and wife found themselves face to face once again, but without much to say to each other. With his star status, his involvement in the marine corps during the Second World War, his success, Tyrone was considered one of the most seductive men in the world. And if legend is to be believed, he didn't know how to say no, to anyone. Annabella grew tired of the situation. However, the couple parted on fairly good terms.

Tyrone's second official love story began in 1946. Once again he met an actress, but this one was American, and she was considered the sexiest of all the Hollywood ladies: Lana Turner, the platinum sweater girl of the 1940s. He was the actor that all women dreamed of. She was the actress who fed the fantasies of all men. For almost a year, they were inseparable. In 1947 Linda Christian met the couple on the set of *Green Dolphin Country.* Ironically, Lana had one of the lead roles and Linda played her maid. At this point, the American press was still fascinated by the Power-Turner couple, but in fact the love affair was turning sour. Lana dreamt only of marrying Tyrone, but she had made a mistake. A few months previously

Facing page: *Count Rodolfo Crespi, Linda Christian (on the right) and her sister, Ariadne, at Dorothy di Frasso's party at the Whip Club in Rome.*

the throng outside was such that several guests sitting inside the church later said that they did not hear any of the ceremony as the noise drowned out the words of the bride and groom. Officiating at the ceremony was Monsignor Hemmick, a World War II hero, who was the first American priest to be named a Canon of St Peter's Basilica.

Immediately after the ceremony, Pope Pius XII received the bride and groom for a private audience. The Vatican had hesitated to agree to this. It was only after receiving confirmation that the marriage of Tyrone and Annabella had only been a civil union that the Pope finally accepted the principle of an audience. In the eyes of the Catholic Church, the actor had never been married. Is it a coincidence? Eight hours *after* Tyrone and Linda had exchanged their vows in Rome, an American court declared the divorce decree of Tyrone and Annabella. During those eight hours, according to American law, Tyrone had been bigamous.

Despite the Papal blessings, this sumptuous ceremony, and the birth of two daughters, Romina and Taryn, the marriage of Tyrone and Linda would last barely seven years. Their divorce was announced in 1956. Tyrone died suddenly just two years later, in November 1958, at the age of 44, during the filming of *Solomon and Sheba.* His co-star was an Italian actress named Gina Lollobrigida. He would be replaced in the role by Yul Brynner. Just a few months before, in May, Tyrone had married again, to Deborah Montgomery Minardos. Deborah would bear him a son, Tyrone William Power IV, who was born in January 1959, two months after his father's tragically early death.

For her part, Linda would also remarry in 1962, to British actor Edmund Purdom. This second marriage would last less than a year, ending in divorce in 1963. She died in Palm Springs, California, in 2011. She has remained famous for being the first James Bond girl in history. Not in the cinema, but on television as 'Valerie Mathis' in the television adaptation of *Casino Royale* in 1954; this was eight years before the famous appearance of Ursula Andress in the first James Bond film *Doctor No.*

Tyrone and Linda's marriage was also one of the last appearances of Dorothy di Frasso in Rome. At 62, the Countess of Hollywood no longer enjoyed the rude health she once had. Her death on 4 January, 1954, was as surprising as her life had been. She has spent the end of the year in Las Vegas. On 31 December, her friend Marlene Dietrich had started the first of her legendary singing tours. Literally sewn into the flesh-coloured dress embroidered with rhinestones, which Jean Louis, the most famous costumier of Hollywood, had designed for her, Marlene conquered the room in a single refrain. Dorothy attended the show, sitting in the front row. She was one of the few to be admitted into the star's dressing room after the show. Unusually, she complains of being a little tired. Marlene massaged her neck and advised her to go to bed, unaware that Dorothy had heart problems and that she abused the nitroglycerin pills that her doctor had prescribed. The next day, the actor Clifton Webb entered her suite at the El Rancho hotel, to find her still bedridden. *"It's too bad that I am going to die so soon. I have been having such a good time."* [5] she said.

She returned to Los Angeles and, on the evening of 4 January, she boarded a sleeping car on the Union Pacific. It was Clifton Webb who discovered her body on the morning of 5 January. Flamboyant Dorothy had succumbed to a heart attack shortly after the train's departure. Her brother, Bertrand, was informed, but he was in Europe and it would take at least 48 hours to arrange a flight and return to the United States. The police took the necessary interim measures. The jewellery, precious objects and furs that were found in the sleeping car were kept secure, but not before being photographed. The body was taken to a funeral chapel and then on to Woodlawn Cemetery in New York. Dorothy was eventually buried in her family's vault, but while waiting for her brother's return to The States, her friend Barbara Hutton agreed that the coffin rest in her own family vault. It was Cary Grant, ever the gentleman, who kept vigil beside the coffin the first night. When her will was filed, it revealed assets in excess of $1 million. Important legacies were left to her faithful maid, Philomena, and to her butler in Rome. Her niece, Mary Taylor, received most of the inheritance. Sadly, her jewels would soon be sold off at auction in Los Angeles, never to be seen again.

Facing page: *Dorothy di Frasso wearing her sumptuous Bulgari diamond necklace at a party in New York during the 1950s. With her is Claude Terrail, the famous owner of La Tour d'Argent in Paris. Terrail family archives.*

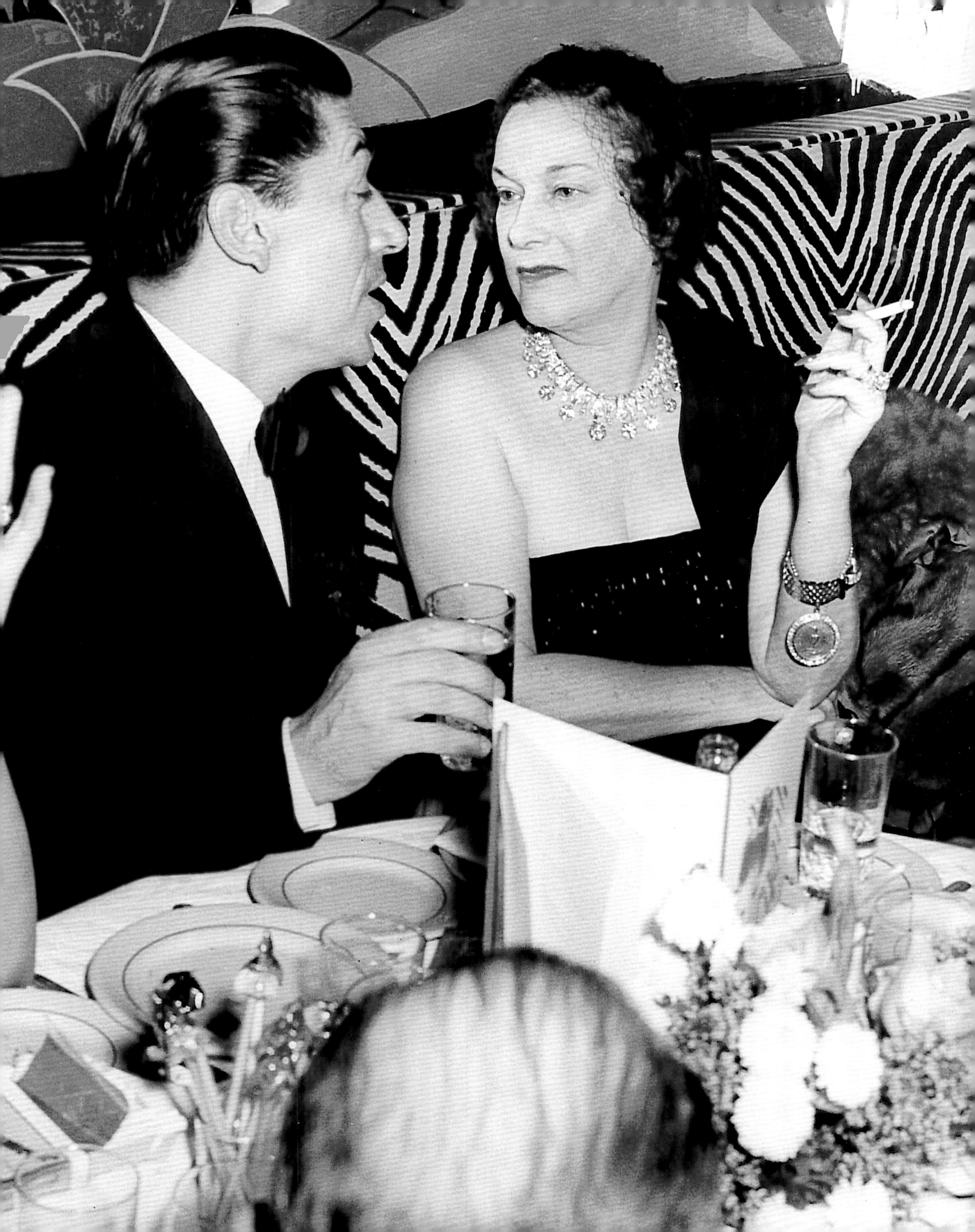

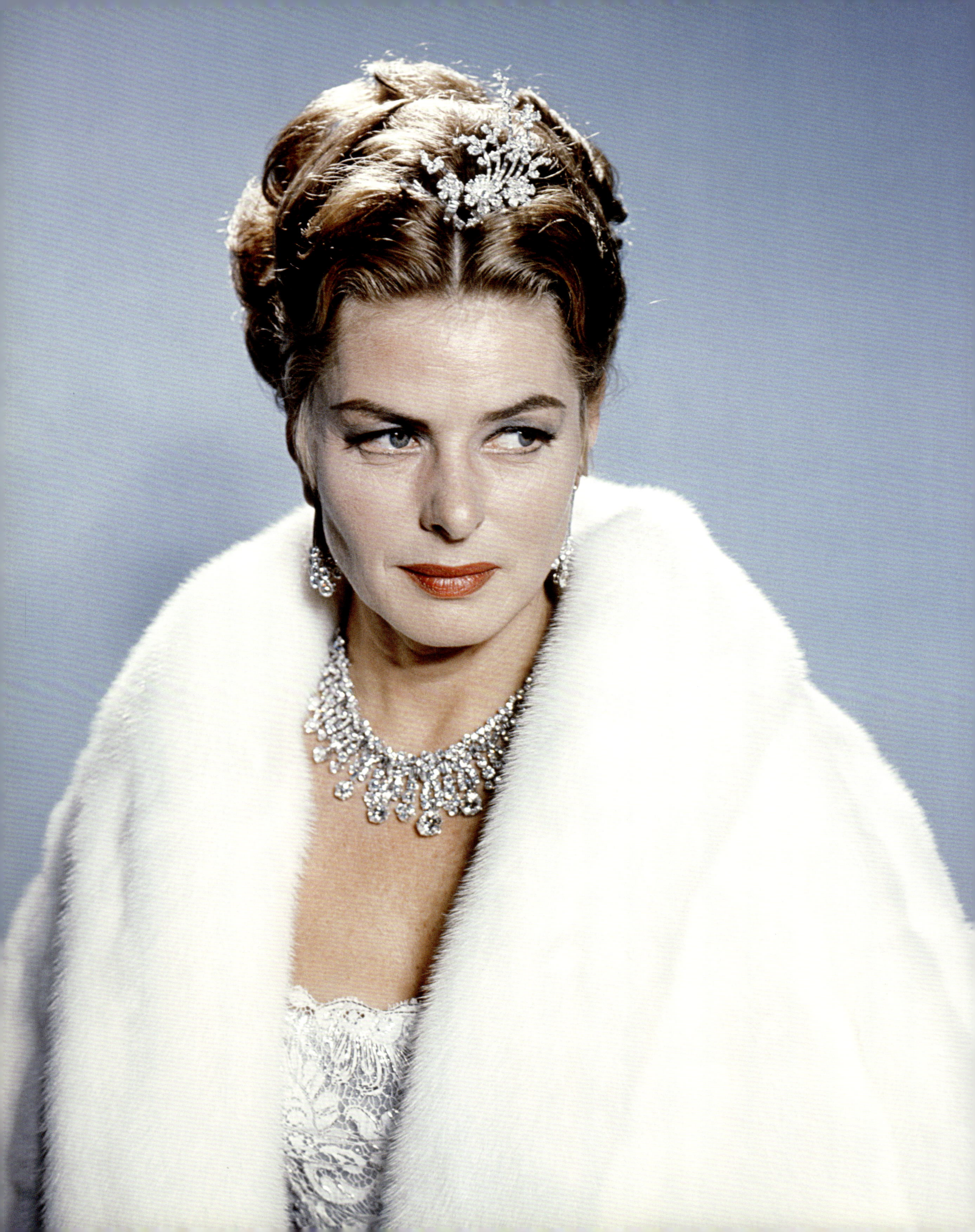

Ingrid Bergman, Roberto Rossellini and Anna Magnani's spaghetti

The article was dated 31 December 1951. It was signed by Inez Robb. It was published in the *Press & Sun-Bulletin*, a regional newspaper in Binghamton, New York. For New Year's Eve, Inez Robb drew up a list of everything from 1951 that she wanted to forget to begin the year 1952 well. She included a litany of personalities who had had problems with the tax authorities, had made bad movies, or who had simply turned out to be unpleasant. Two names were granted a special place: Ingrid Bergman and Roberto Rossellini.

For over a year, both had been vilified by the American press on a weekly basis. This was the woman who had been the star of *For Whom The Bell Tolls*, *Joan of Arc*, *The Bells of St Mary's* and *Spellbound*, the actress who had received three Academy Award nominations in the category of Best Actress and who had won the coveted "Oscar" in 1944 for *Gaslight;* the most popular Swedish actress after Garbo had become one of the most hated women in the world. The morality leagues, the Catholic and Protestant Churches, women and men all over the world castigated her conduct. She had openly committed adultery. She had left her husband and her child to live with the Italian director. She had divorced and remarried without conscience. In addition to this, she had agreed to play the role of an unrepentant sinner in *Stromboli,* a scandalous film signed by her lover, Roberto Rossellini.

Facing page: *Ingrid Bergman in 1963, during the shooting of* The Visit. *All the jewellery she wore for the film was created by Bulgari.*

The disapproval was such that some religious leaders, like the Catholic bishop of Galveston in Texas, called for a boycott of the film. According to him: *"The case of Ingrid Bergman-Roberto Rossellini highlights the most shocking and despicable conduct that has been seen for centuries. It is impossible to dissociate the film (Stromboli) from its performers and its director. If you love your wife, your mother or your children, you can not go and see this movie."* [6] In a surrealist development, an American senator even proposed a law controlling the morality of actresses. He accused Ingrid Bergman of having launched an attack against the institution of marriage. According to him, she was one of the most powerful women on the planet and had put her power at the service of evil. Fortunately, others, especially in Italy, were less fierce. *Il Popolo*, the official newspaper of the Christian Democracy party that supported the government of Prime Minister Alcide De Gasperi, condemned the attacks of the American newspapers. They were, for him, *"the act of American critics against a great actress and her work. Everyone, and we first, must deplore the scandal, but everyone must also judge a work calmly. And certainly, there is nothing scandalous about this film."*

Today, nearly seventy years later, it is clear that *Stromboli*, the film that caused so much ink to flow, has not aged very well. It tells the adventures of Karen, a young Lithuanian who was the mistress of a German officer during the war. She is imprisoned in a refugee camp in Italy. Antonio, a young Italian, offers to marry her and she follows him to his home on the volcanic island of Stromboli. Of course, the volcano erupts the very moment they set foot on the shore ...

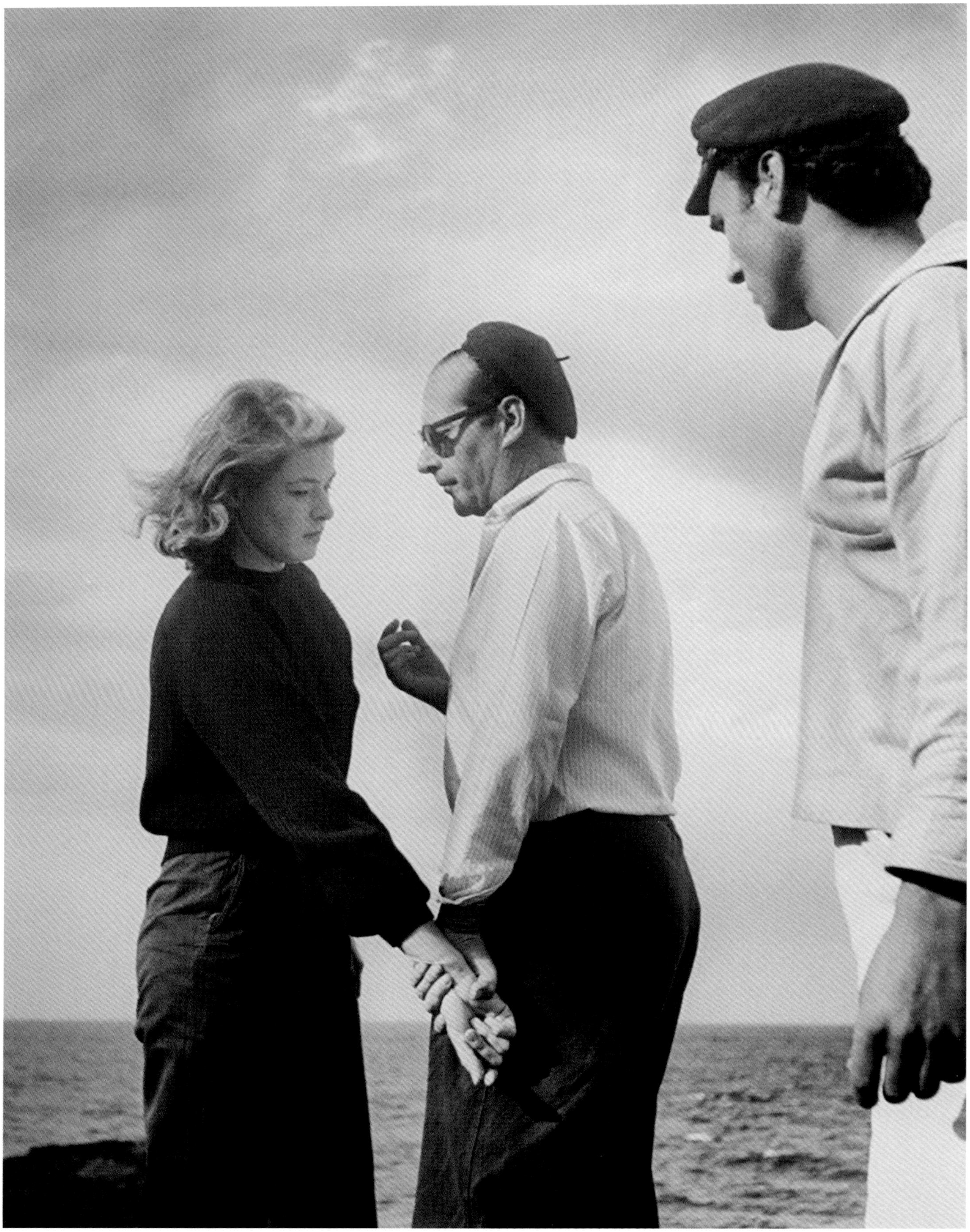

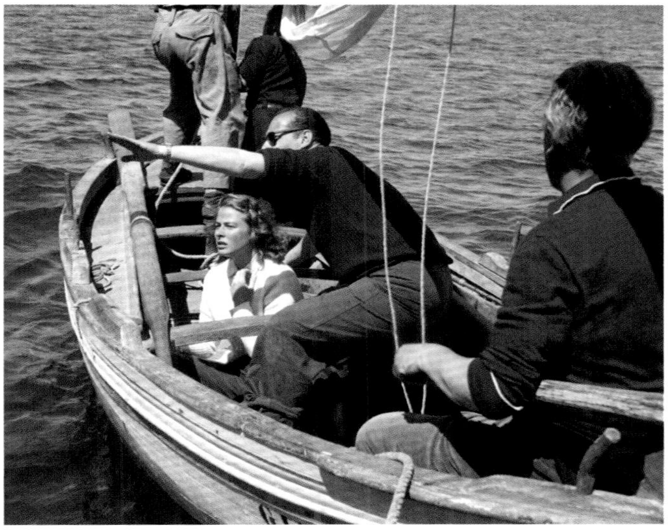

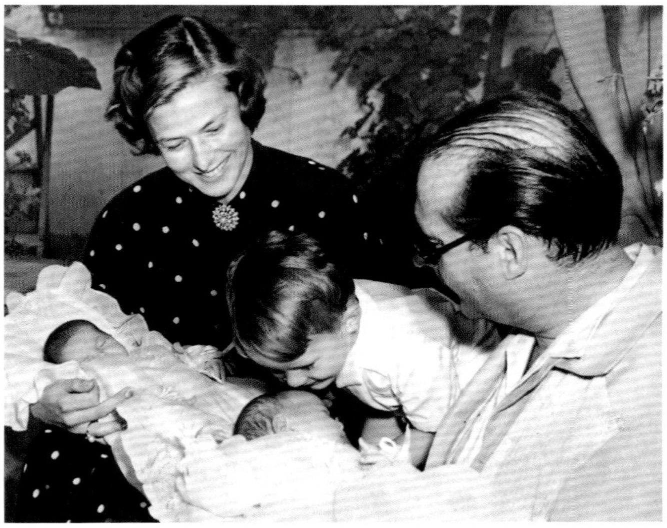

Everything in the film is rather kitsch and sometimes even a little boring. Perhaps it is this dullness that was the source of the scandal.

It all began one evening in the spring of 1948, in a small cinema on La Cienega Boulevard in Los Angeles. Ingrid Bergman was already a star. As a young Swedish actress, she had landed in Hollywood in 1939. Her producer, David O. Selznick, was a little worried because she did not speak a word of English and her name sounded rather German. Even worse, her eyebrows were very thick and black. However, he asked her to reprise the role that had brought her glory in Sweden in 1936 in the film *Intermezzo,* in an English version. Leslie Howard had been offered the lead male role. Against all odds, *Intermezzo: A Love Story* was a success. From then on, Ingrid has bound to the world of films. Her husband Petter Lindström, a Swedish dentist, joined her in 1941, with their daughter Pia, aged three. Before their arrival, Ingrid, alone in California for two years, had lived her own discreet love story with the famous photographer Robert Capa, which she revealed years later in her memoirs *My Story.*

Did Petter Linström pretend to ignore his wife's infidelity? Or was he also cheating on her? In any case, by 1948, they were still married to each other. Ingrid continued her career, and Petter was able to validate his dentist degree in California. Together, one evening in the spring of 1948, they discovered *Rome, Open City* in a Los Angeles cinema. The film, which tells of the misery in Nazi-occupied Italy, marks the beginning of Italian neo-realism. A few months later, in New York, the actress discovers another Rossellini film: *Paisan.* She was dazzled and immediately took it upon herself to write to this man, a complete stranger:

Dear Mr. Rossellini,
I saw your films, Rome, Open City *and* Paisan, *and enjoyed them very much. If you need a Swedish actress who speaks English very well, who has not forgotten her German, who is not very understandable in French, and who, in Italian, knows only "ti amo", I am ready to come and make a film with you.*
Ingrid Bergman.

"This letter had the most peculiar journey of any letter in history." Bergman recalls in her memoirs.[7] Ignoring Rossellini's address, the star sent it to the production company, Minerva Films, in Rome. She did not know that the director was involved in a lawsuit with his producers. Moreover, the day of the arrival of the famous letter in Rome, the offices of Minerva were devastated by fire. Inspecting the rubble the following day, an employee discovered the letter, which had miraculously escaped the flames. Intrigued by Ingrid Bergman's signature on a letter addressed to Rossellini, the company directors decided to call Rossellini, recalls Bergman. *"When he picks up, they announce: 'Minerva Films here, Mr. Rossellini.' Roberto:*

Facing page and above left: *Ingrid Bergman and Roberto Rossellini during the filming of* Stromboli. **Above right:** *Ingrid Bergman with her husband Roberto Rossellini, and their children, Robertino and the twins, Isabella and Isotta Ingrid in 1952.*

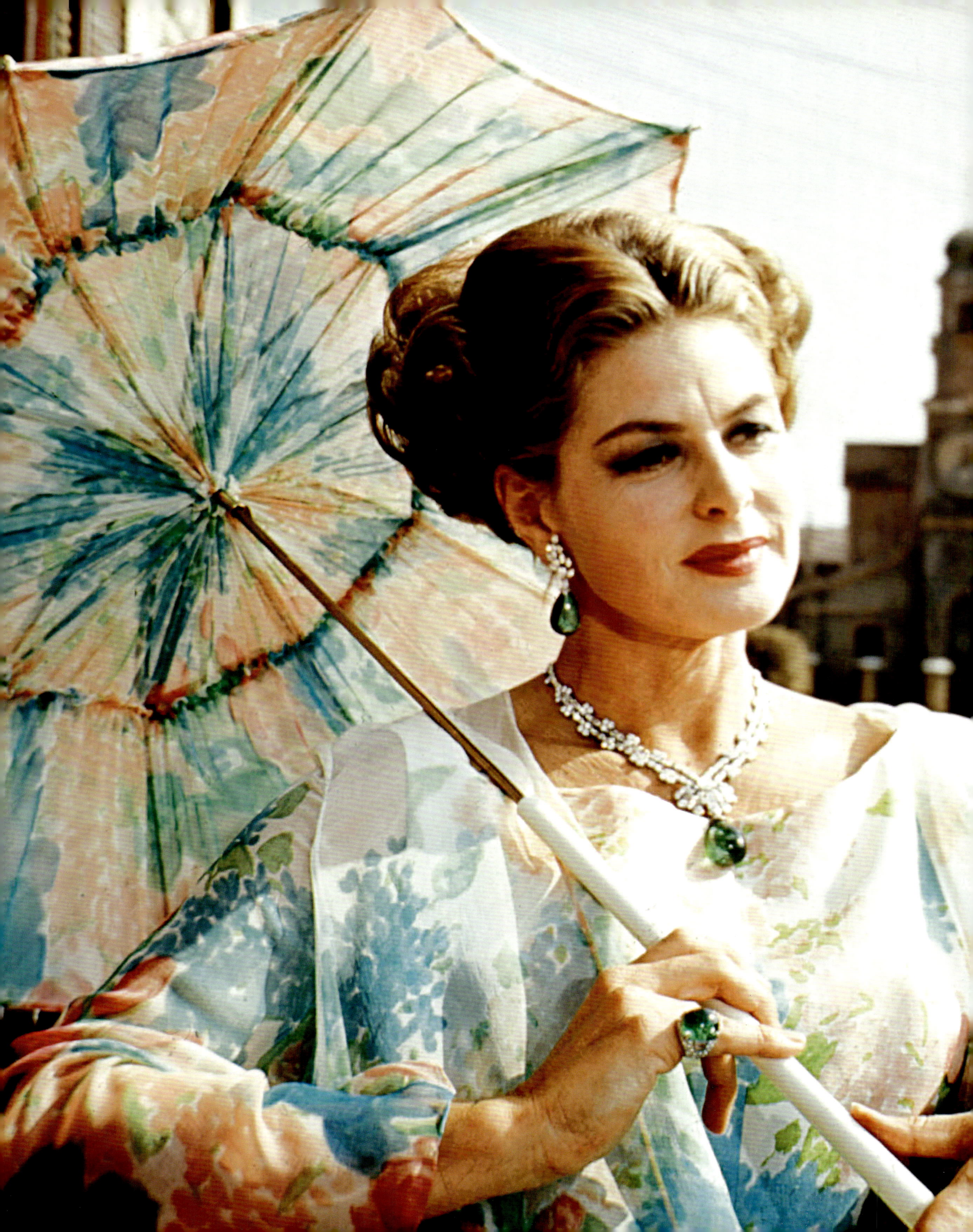

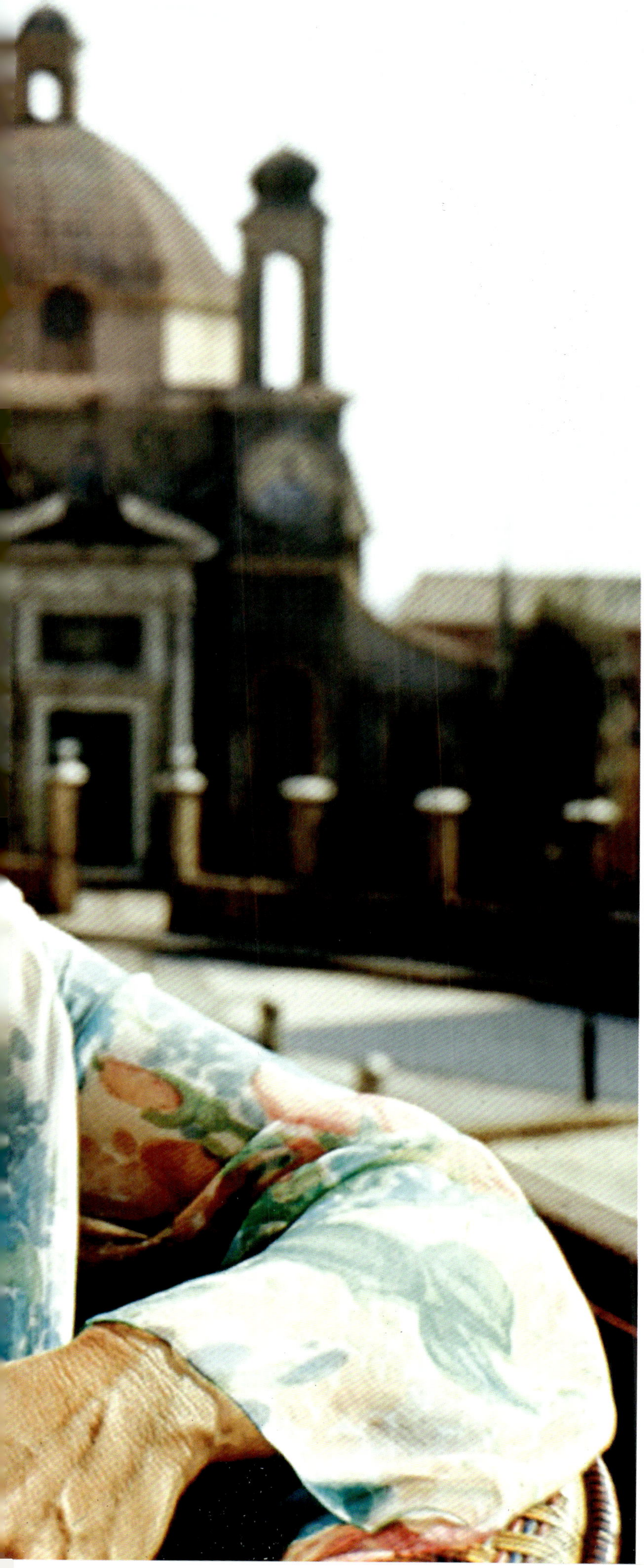

'I am not talking to you,' before hanging up."[8] At the end of the fourth telephone call, the Minerva directors decided to send the letter by courier. Rossellini did not speak a word of English. Intrigued by the American stamp, he asked one of his friends to translate the contents. When he was told the signature, he asked: *"Ingrid who?"* It was only after long explanations that he remembers seeing, just before the war, a Swedish film entitled *Intermezzo,* with a young actress named Ingrid Bergman.

On 8 May, 1948, a telegram signed by Roberto Rossellini arrived in Beverly Hills at the home of Dr Petter Lindström and Ingrid Bergman: *"I just received with great emotion your letter, which happens to arrive on the anniversary of my birthday as a most precious gift."* [9] A long letter describing the scenario of the next film Rossellini intended to shoot – not yet named *Stromboli* – followed a few days later. An agreement in principle was exchanged. During the summer of 1948, Bergman was staying in England, where she was shooting *Under Capricorn* with Hitchcock. Planning to spend a few days in Paris, she sent a telegram to Rossellini at the beginning of July proposing to meet him at the Hotel Georges V. At the time, Rossellini was still married to his second wife, Marcella, from whom he was separated. Also, he was openly living with the Italian actress Anna Magnani.

"I had no idea that I was going to create a domestic explosion. I did not know he had an affair with Magnani. And she did not know much about me or my career. But as she was a woman, she soon felt that there was something in the air," [10] Bergman recalls in her memoirs. La Magnani, who would a few years later become a very famous client of Bulgari, was at the beginning of her glorious career. Her temperament was as volcanic in real life as it was on the screen. Like everyone in Italian cinema, she had heard of the famous letter written to Rossellini by this Hollywood actress. The two lovers were spending the summer on the Amalfi coast. And Rossellini, who knew his companion's bad temper well, asked the hotel staff to hand him any post bearing a foreign stamp as discreetly as possible. Bergman's telegram arrived late in the morning. Rossellini and Magnani were having lunch in the enormous dining room of the Hotel Luna Convento.

Ingrid Bergman bedecked in Bulgari emerald and diamond jewels during the filming of The Visit *in 1963.*

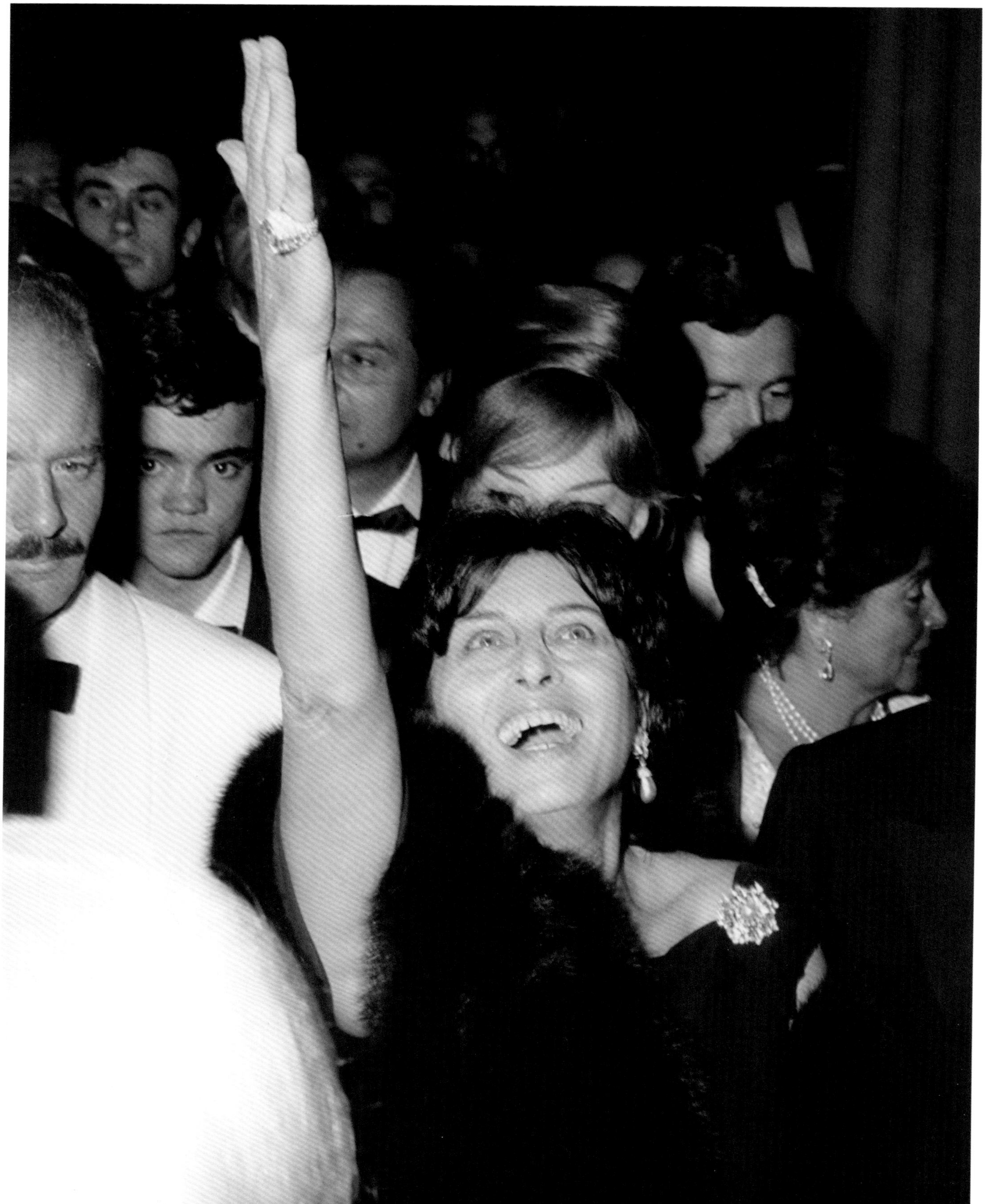

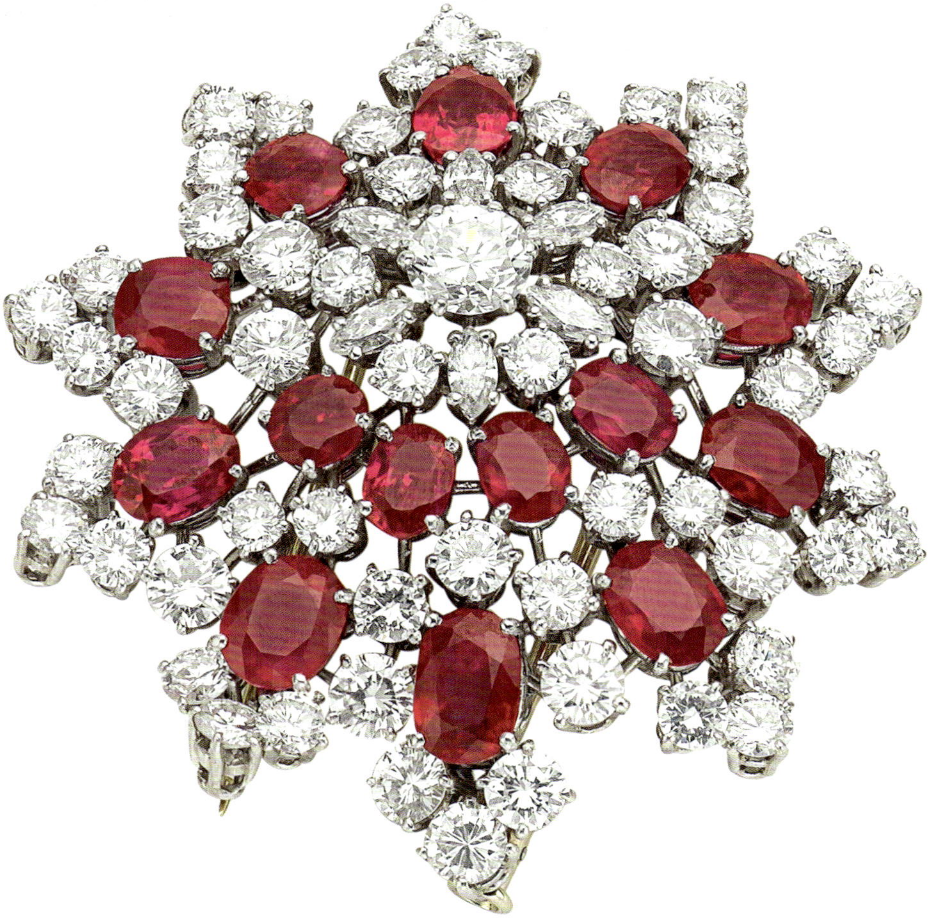

to a village bent on revenge – it was Bulgari that she called on to lend the sumptuous jewellery she wore on the screen. She died in 1982, after receiving a third Oscar for her supporting role as a simple-minded Swedish nurse in *Murder on the Orient Express.*

Five years earlier, Roberto Rossellini had gone to the cinema heaven, Anna Magnani already having preceded him in 1973. After being abandoned by the man she loved, the Italian diva had devoted herself to her career and, particularly, to her son Luca. Most of the important Bulgari pieces in her collection date from that time. The most beautiful is a Trombino ring, set with a 25-carat diamond. She also owned a beautiful pair of brooches set with rubies and diamonds. Paolo Bulgari, Giorgio's second son, remembers very clearly the volcanic character of "la Magnani". One day, she pushed open the doors of the shop on Via dei Condotti. Paolo rushed to offer her his help: "*She treated me like a dog*," he remembers. *"It's a very funny memory. I was 22 or 23, it was the early sixties. I was very young. One day she arrived, and like everyone else had something to do, I had to take care of her. You can not imagine! She was a demanding woman. And when she saw this young guy who did not have much experience, she just could not resist!"* [12] In 1973, while she was suffering from cancer, Anna approached Rossellini. It is he who would look after her during her last months. She died in Rome on 26 September 1973.

Facing page: *Anna Magnani, the diva of Italian cinema, in the 1950s. Roberto Rossellini was the great love of her life.* **Above:** *Bulgari ruby and diamond brooch from Anna Magnani's personal collection. Private collection Carlo Ferrero Zendrini.*

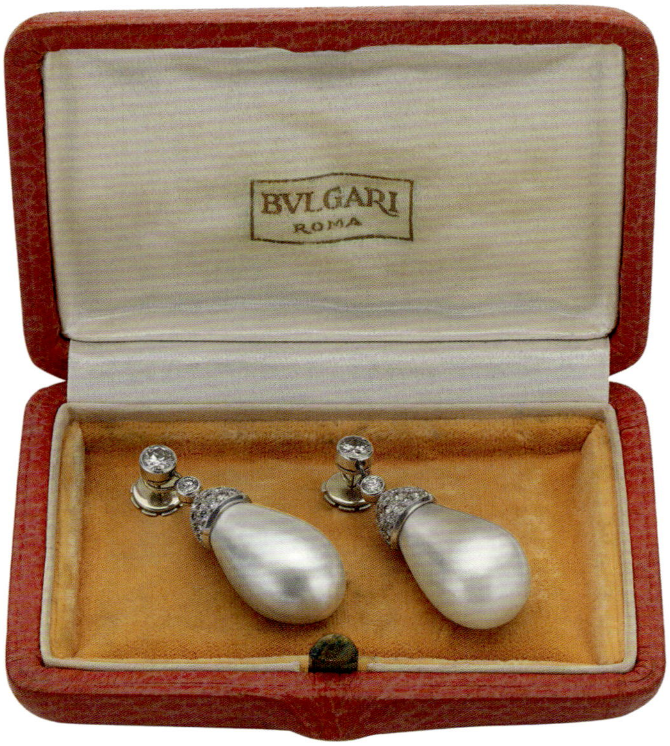

Bulgari jewels from Anna Magnani's personal collection. **Above:** *A pair of pearl and diamond earrings. Bulgari Heritage Collection.* **Below:** *A matching pair of pearl and diamond brooches. Bulgari Heritage Collection.*

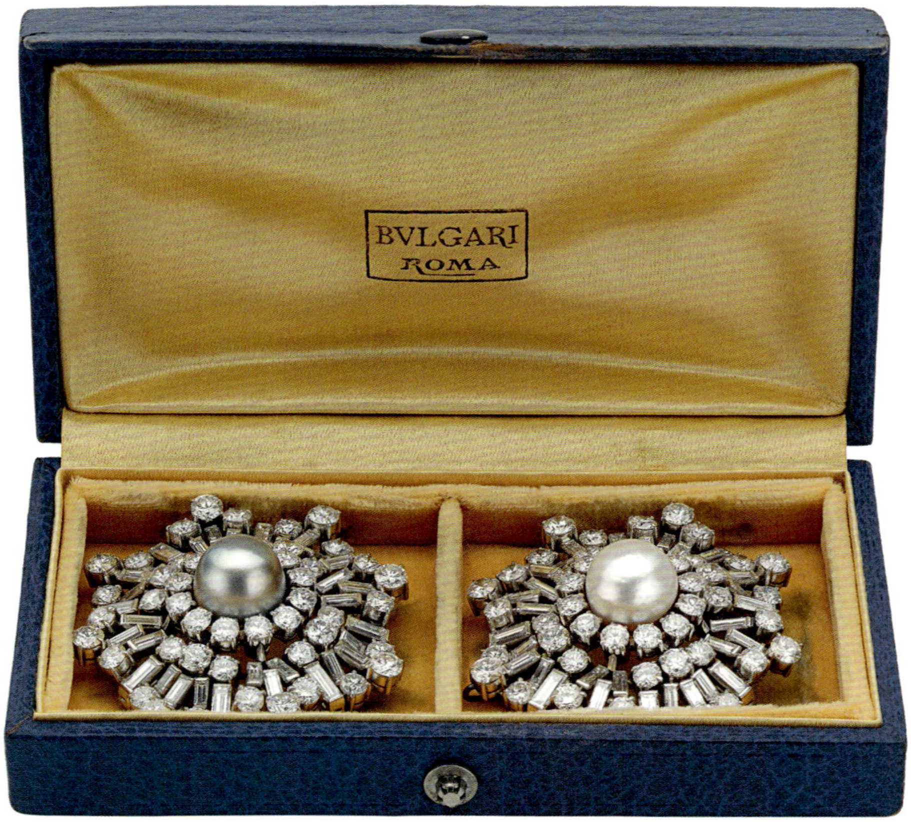

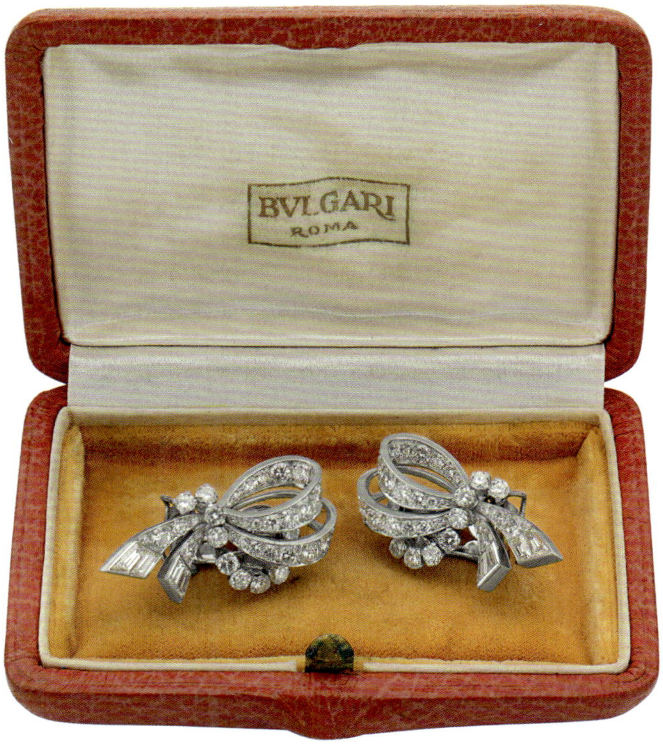

Above: *A pair of diamond earrings. Bulgari Heritage Collection.*
Below: *Five gold chain bracelets set with diamonds. Private collection.*

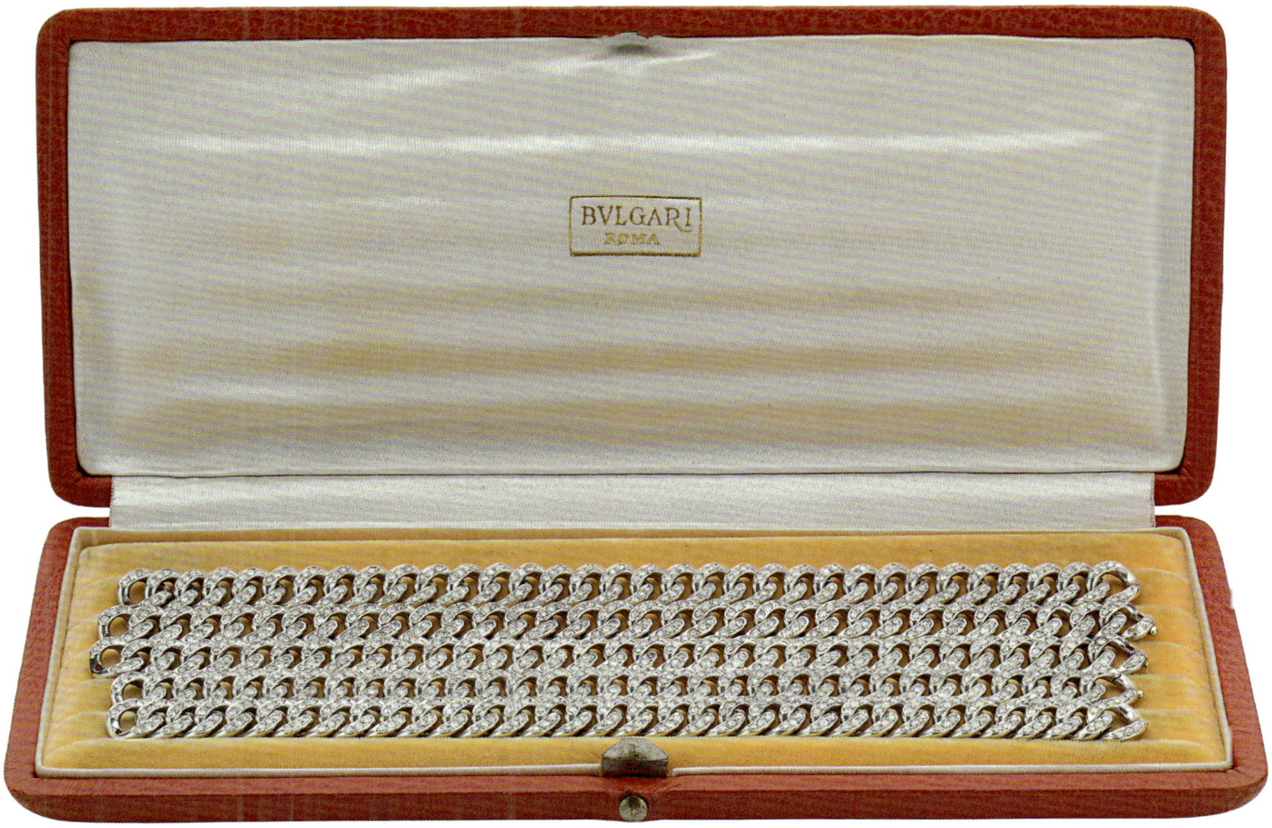

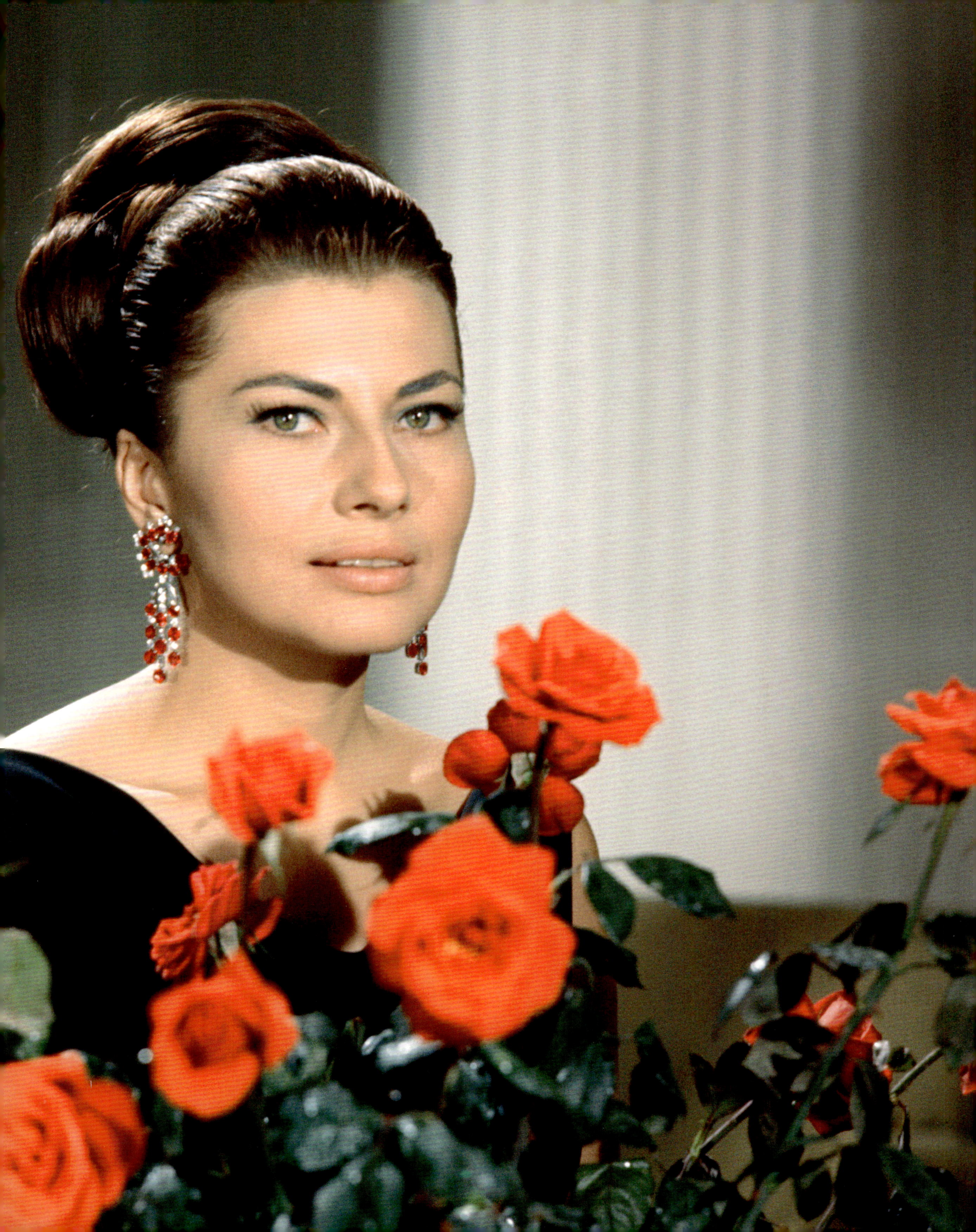

Shah of Iran and Soraya's Roman Holiday

Rome Airport, 17 August 1953

For the Shah of Iran and his lovely wife, Soraya, their arrival at Rome airport on the morning of 17 August, 1953, marked the true beginning of their exile. After a two-day visit to Baghdad where King Faisal had greeted them with all the honours reserved for reigning monarchs, the Iranian sovereigns had flown to Europe. So here they were on the day of their arrival: two slender and elegant silhouettes, a woman in a summer dress and a man in a light suit. Their sunglasses hid the disappointment in their eyes at the rather meagre reception that had been prepared for them. Not a single minister or official representative of the Italian government was present. The ambassador of Iran, who would normally have welcomed his king was absent. It was obvious that Iranian oil weighed heavily in international diplomatic relations. And the Shah no longer controlled that oil since his *coup d'état* failed.

Two days previously, the sovereign played his ace card in the tense game that saw him in opposition to his prime minister, Mohammad Mossadegh. And it seemed that he had lost. In the spring of 1951, however, both agreed on the principle of the nationalisation of the Anglo-Iranian oil company. England, who had the upper hand over the main wealth of the country, had been compelled to retire, but not without a struggle. It had even appealed to the International Court of Justice in The Hague, which had dismissed its complaint. The oil wells having returned completely to Iran, the Shah and his Prime Minister began wrestling over control of the army. A confirmed constitutional monarchist, Mossadegh insisted that it pass under the direct control of the government. The Shah, the son of a soldier and conscious of political instability in this period of the beginning of the Cold War, did not intend to let go of what he considered his ultimate recourse. On the morning of 15 August, the Sovereign sent an official messenger to his Prime Minister with the order to resign. Mossadegh had contented himself with replying by arresting the messenger. The Shah who was staying by the Caspian Sea decided that he had lost the struggle. Not stopping to return to Tehran, he had left the country.

The face he offered to photographers on his arrival in Rome was that of a weary man, unsure of his future. To a few close friends, he confided that his personal resources were limited: "Barely enough to buy a farm in the United States to settle in." Soraya's demeanour was a little more comfortable, as though she was not totally sorry to be back in Europe.

Their love story was one of the most famous of the 20th century. It began in the aftermath of the Second World War. At the time, the Iranian sovereign considering the needs of State wanted at all costs to ensure his succession with a son. At the time, there was only his younger brother, Prince Ali Reza, to succeed him. And for now Ali Reza had no son either. The four other princes of the Pahlavi family were born from the marriages of their father, Reza Shah, to Qadjar princesses belonging to the previous dynasty. The constitution forbad them to inherit the crown. Also, from his first marriage to Princess Fawzia of Egypt, the King of Kings had had only one child – a daughter, Princess Shahnaz. As a female, she could not succeed her father either. In 1945, Fawzia, who was very bored in Tehran, had left the country to return to Egypt. The divorce has been announced three years later.

The Shah remarried in 1950. His eldest sister,

Facing page: *The Empress Soraya of Iran wearing her Bulgari ruby and diamond earrings.*

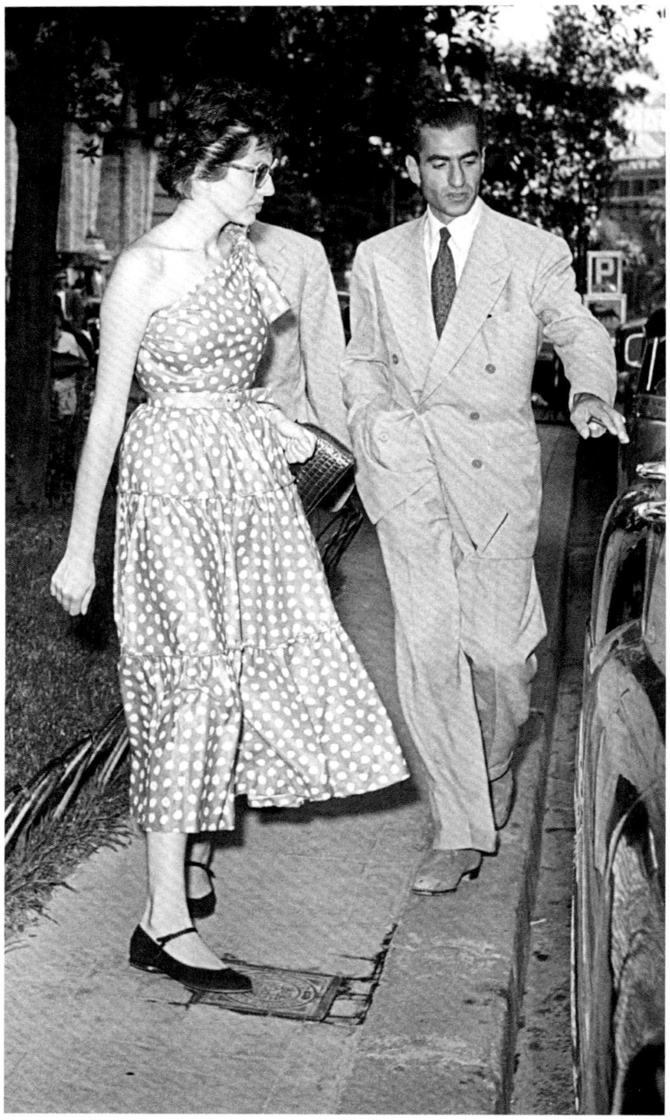

Princess Shams, found the ideal candidate in the person of Soraya Esfandiary-Baktiari, an 18-year-old girl. Her father, Khalil Esfandiary-Baktiari, belonged to the powerful tribe of the Baktiar, who for more than twenty years has been among the political opponents of the Pahlavi reign. Her mother, Eva Karl, was German. Soraya was a dazzling girl with green eyes. She had spent much of her youth in Europe. She had had a modern education, which should enable her to play the role of a truly active sovereign. Her reaction to the Shah's marriage proposal, was exactly as that of any young Iranian girl of her age would have been. Flattered, and seduced by the smile of the young king, she accepted. Unquestionably, the Shah was crazy about her. At an official dinner, a few months later, he confided: *"The queen is exactly the type of woman I like."* Soraya's feelings were harder to pin down. At the same dinner, she replied, *"I'm not sure I can say the same."*

The wedding ceremony that the Shah wanted to be sumptuous turned out to be a disaster. A few days before the appointed date, Soraya succumbed to typhoid. Everything had to be delayed for several weeks. The Shah visited her as often as possible and, according to tradition, every day he sent her a new jewel, which was placed on his fiancée's pillow. The marriage ceremony eventually took place on 12 February, 1951. Soraya was not yet fully recovered; she had lost over 20lbs and was very frail. Her shoulders were covered with a white fur cape designed by Christian Dior and under her beautiful dress she wore woollen socks to keep her warm. Shortly before the reception she was so exhausted that the Shah and one of his aides used their swords to cut off much of her heavy bejewelled train.

After two years, still no children had been born to the couple. Political and family pressure was becoming difficult to bear for the young queen. This exile in Rome at least had the merit of removing the couple from the atmosphere of intrigue that reigned in Tehran. Barely installed in a suite on the fourth floor of the Excelsior Hotel, the royal couple, who had arrived with just a few suitcases, crept outside the hotel through a side door. Their destination – Via dei Condotti for a shopping trip. The photographers who were ubiquitous in Rome at that time, spotted them quickly and their pictures flew around the world. The Shah, very chic, always wore his light suit. On the other hand, Soraya had changed her style. She was wearing a rather audacious silk summer dress, with white polka dots. The asymmetric dress was held up by a simple knot over her left shoulder. Of course, on that afternoon, the couple drove past Bulgari's shop, but they do not seem to have stopped on this occasion. This early exile was not the best time for jewellery purchases.

Two days later, their situation was reversed. Mossadegh had fallen and the Shah was recalled to

Above: *The Shah of Iran and his wife on the streets of Rome during their brief exile in 1953.* **Facing page:** *The ruby and diamond bracelet and earrings bought at Bulgari by Empress Soraya c.1953-54. After her death, the pieces were sold in Paris by Etude Beaussant Lefèvre.*

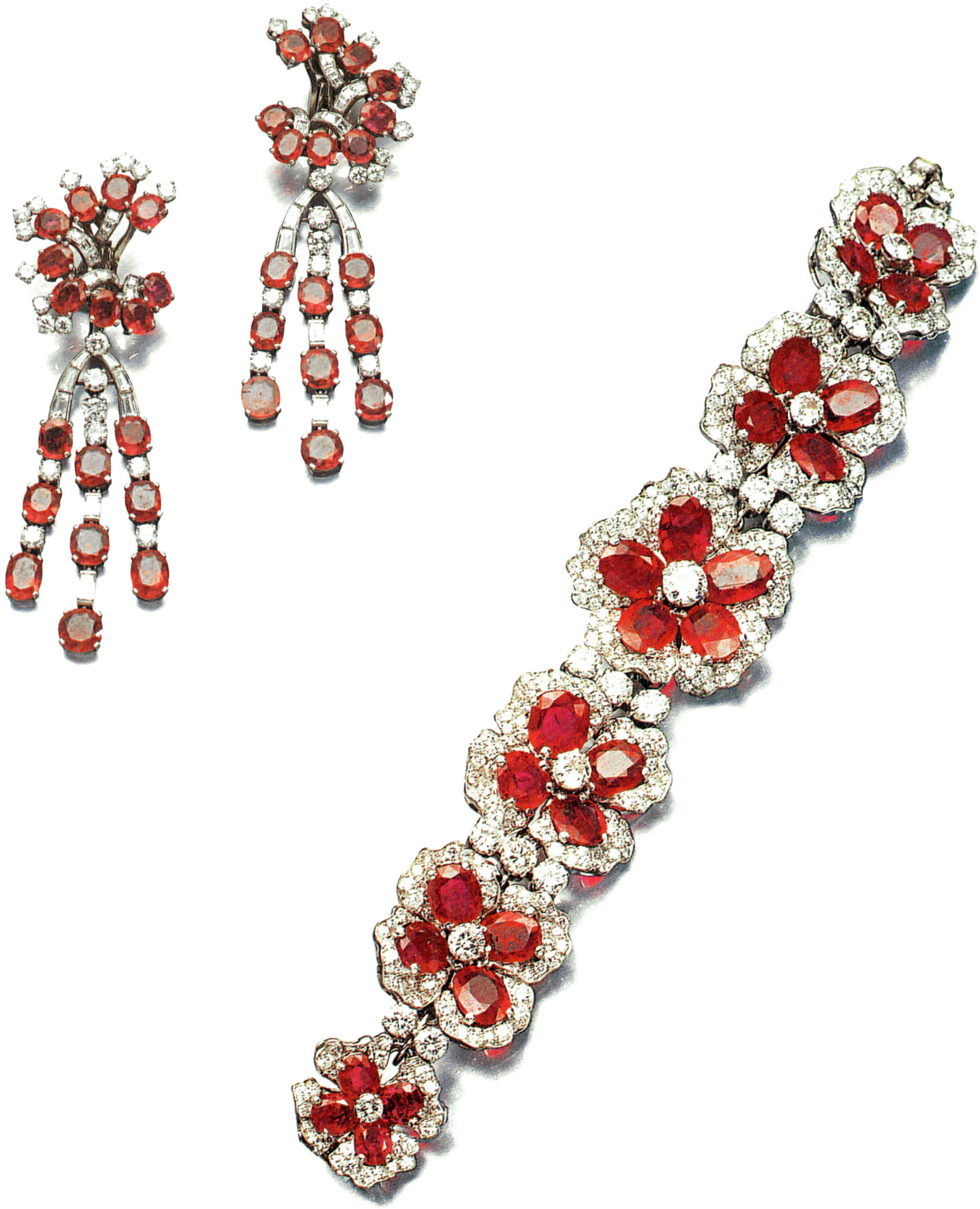

Iran. He asked his wife to remain in Rome for a few days, to be sure of the situation back home. Soraya did not hesitate to agree. She loved this city with its carefree air. A memorandum, dated 9 September, 1953, signed by Giorgio Bulgari, and recently acquired by the Bulgari archives, proves that she visited the shop on Via dei Condotti during the second part of her stay in Rome. The document, which comes from the personal archives of Soraya, concerns a ring set with a "white blue", emerald-cut diamond, weighing 24.50 carats. It is a simple descriptive note accompanied with the price of the jewel, but it is addressed to: *"H.M. the empress Soraya Pahlavi of Iran"*. Nothing, however, confirms that she bought this diamond. A second memorandum of the same period identifies four diamond rings, weighing 17.50, 18.33, 22.65 and 32.45 carats, and a pair of earclips decorated with two pear-shaped diamonds with an overall weight of 28.33 carats. But again, there is no indication that these jewels were actually purchased.

Soraya's first acquisitions from Bulgari arrived in Tehran in April 1954. Two jewel cases contained a ruby and diamond bracelet and a pair of matching earrings. The floral motifs of the bracelet are interesting. The six flowers prefigure the famous flower jewels that would become characteristic of Bulgari house style from the early 1960s. Two more cases contained a diamond necklace, the five star motifs of which could be dismantled and worn separately as brooches, and matching earrings.

Other memoranda, written this time in French and accompanied by photographs, concern a whole series of jewels in pearls and diamonds, including a very important necklace. Interestingly, the descriptions of these jewels all note in brackets the phrase *"en exécution"* (in production), which indicates that they were actually manufactured. Soraya sold several important jewels in the years following the Islamic Revolution of 1979. Therefore, it is not beyond imagination that some of the jewels delivered to her in the 1950s were those sold discreetly in the 1980s to provide funds after her exile. The hypothesis is all the more likely as two photographs included in the same archive file show a diamond and sapphire necklace and clips, the stones and general form of which closely resemble the diamond and sapphire necklace created by Bulgari in the 1970s for Princess Soraya. It seems that this last necklace was mounted with the stones of an older jewel, also from Bulgari. The archive file containing all these documents ends with a letter dated 19 October 1956, addressed to the *"Grand Master of the house of H.I.M. the Shah-of-Shahs at the Excelsior Hotel in Rome"*. It is accompanied by drawings and photographs of four rings set with large emeralds, two pairs of earrings and a diamond necklace that *"Her Majesty has deigned to take into consideration"*.

The sapphire necklace, the ruby and diamond bracelet and ruby earrings, and the diamond necklace bought in 1954 all appear in the catalogue of the auction of Princess Soraya's belongings, organised in Paris by Messrs Beaussant & Lefèvre, in May 2002.

Indeed, when she died in Paris on 26 October, 2001, Soraya had not been Queen for over forty years. A year after the return of the Imperial couple to Teheran, Prince Ali Reza, the Shah's only brother able to succeed him, had died in a plane crash. The pressure to produce a son increased. And after many disappointments, the Shah had to accept the fact that Soraya would never have children. As he was still in love with her, he offered to take a second wife simply to ensure the succession. She refused. She left Iran in 1958. Their divorce was announced that same year.

She would never see her country or her husband again. The Shah would die in exile in 1980 in Cairo. Living in Europe – Rome, Munich and finally Paris – Soraya became an elegant yet lonely and melancholic legend of the jet set. She even made a film in Italy, *The Three Faces of a Woman;* it was rather a disaster. All her subsequent love stories ended badly. Around the world, the press called her "the princess with the sad eyes".

Facing page: *The Bulgari diamond bracelet bought by Empress Soraya. It was sold after her death by Etude Beaussant Lefèvre.*

1. *Look* magazine, 12 April, 1949. **2.** *Modern Screen*, October 1948. **3.** *Life* magazine, 3 September, 1945. **4.** Interview with the author, October 2014. **5.** Film Museum Berlin, newsletter no 66. **6.** *The Shreveport Times*, 9 February 1950. **7., 8., 9., 10.** Ingrid Bergman and Allan Burgess, *My story*, Delacorte press, 1980. (Translated by Ingrid Bergman and Allan Burgess from the French edition, *Ma Vie*, Fayard, 1980). **11.** Enza Tomassi von Heuduck Kiskis, *Tre volte il cielo*. **12.** Interview with the author, October 2014.

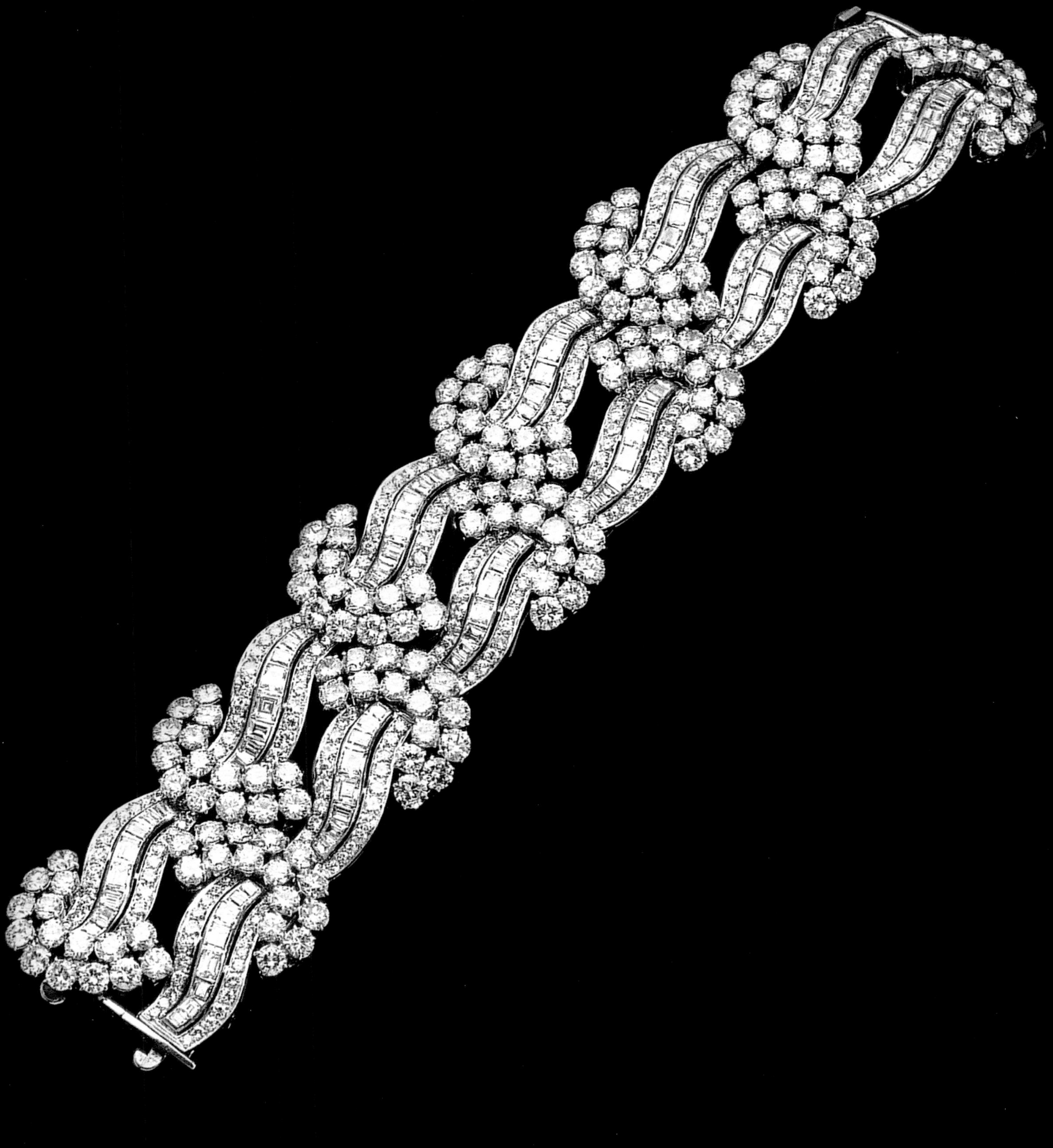

Jewellery designs sent to Empress Soraya and the Iranian court by Bulgari in the 1950s.

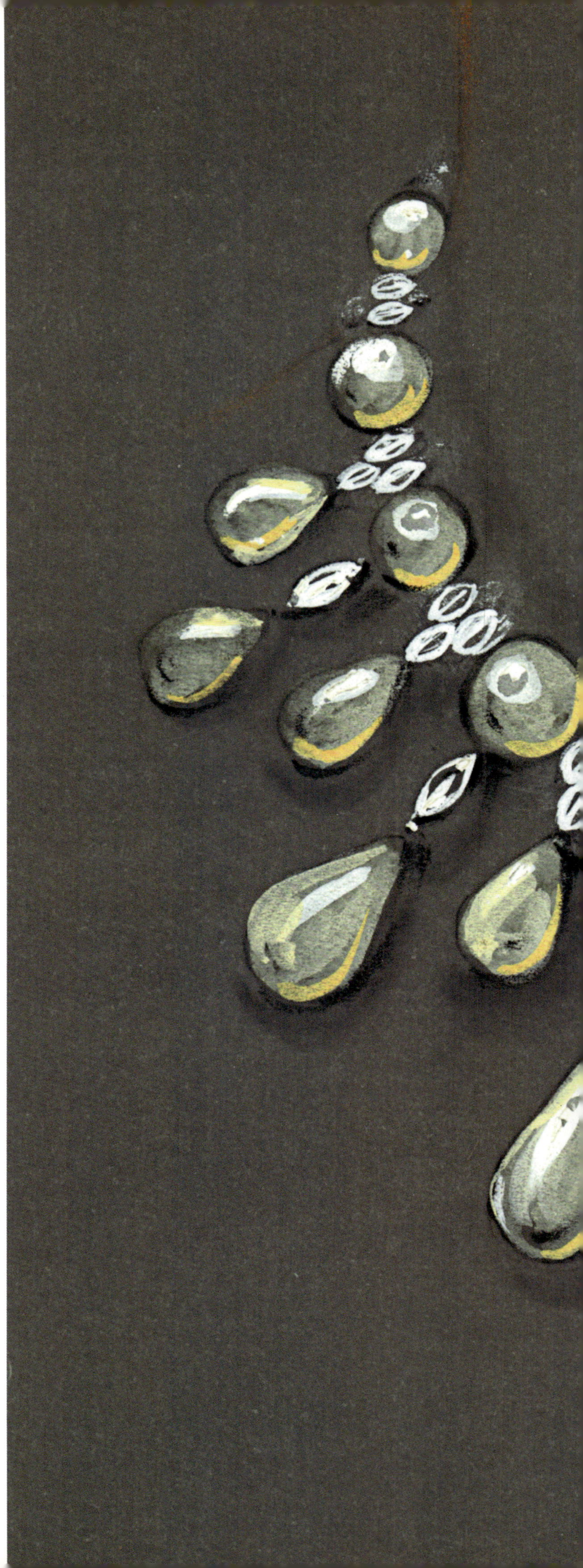

Design for a diamond and pearl necklace sent by Bulgari to the Empress for approval. It seems that the piece was never created. Bulgari Historical Archives.

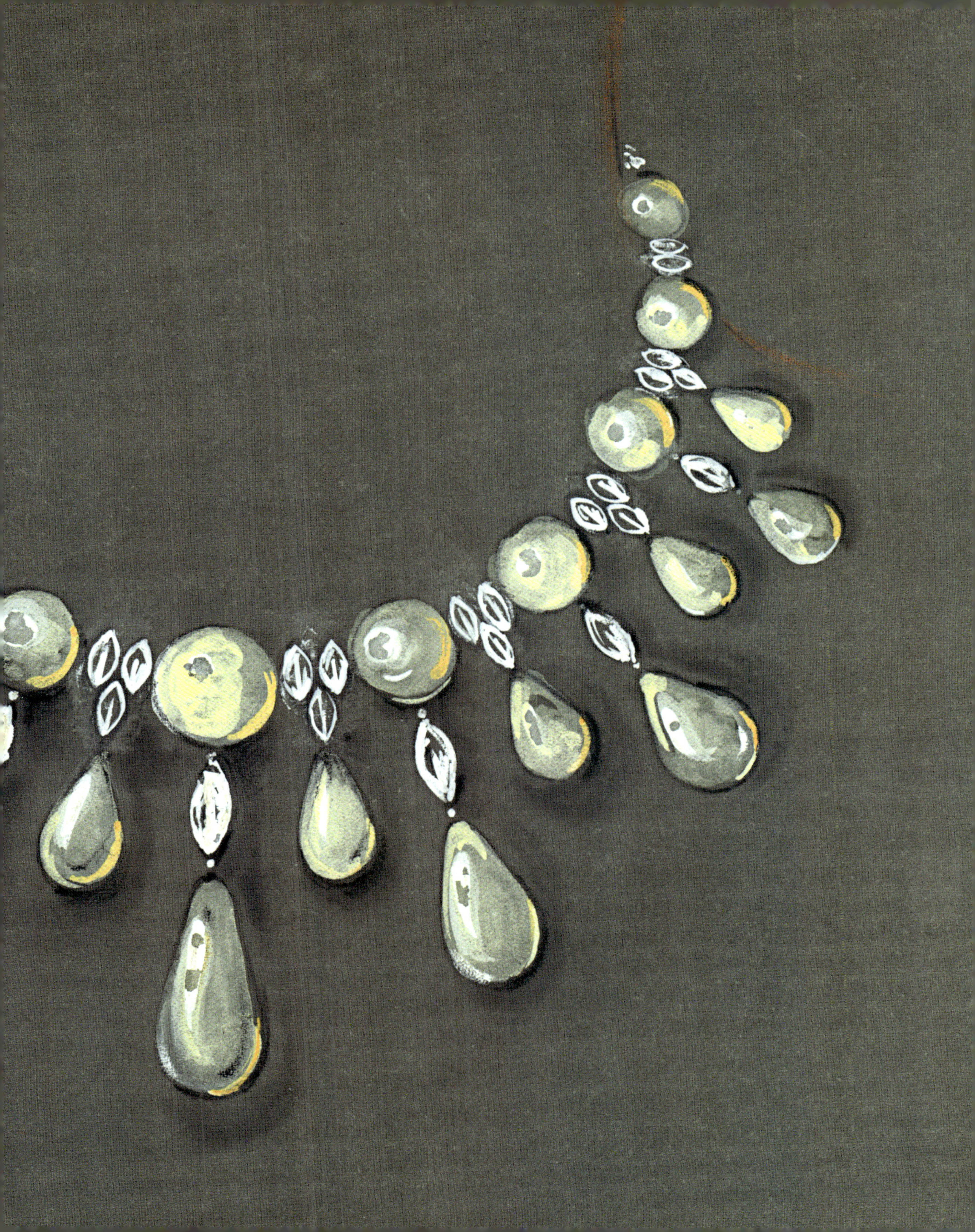

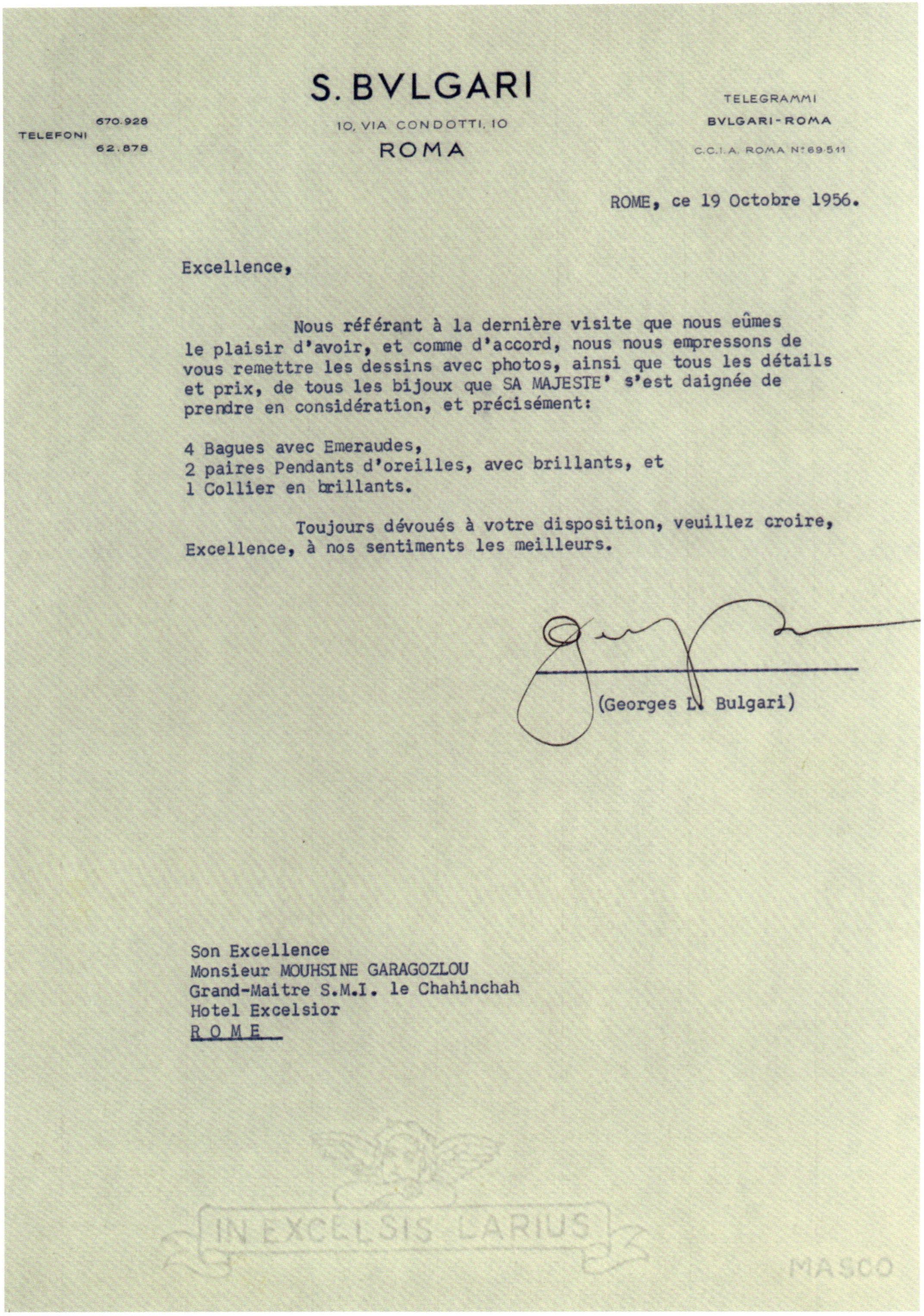

S. BVLGARI
10, VIA CONDOTTI, 10
ROMA

TELEFONI 670.928 62.878

TELEGRAMMI BVLGARI-ROMA
C.C.I.A. ROMA N. 69.511

ROME, ce 19 Octobre 1956.

Excellence,

Nous référant à la dernière visite que nous eûmes le plaisir d'avoir, et comme d'accord, nous nous empressons de vous remettre les dessins avec photos, ainsi que tous les détails et prix, de tous les bijoux que SA MAJESTE' s'est daignée de prendre en considération, et précisément:

4 Bagues avec Emeraudes,
2 paires Pendants d'oreilles, avec brillants, et
1 Collier en brillants.

Toujours dévoués à votre disposition, veuillez croire, Excellence, à nos sentiments les meilleurs.

(Georges L. Bulgari)

Son Excellence
Monsieur MOUHSINE GARAGOZLOU
Grand-Maitre S.M.I. le Chahinchah
Hotel Excelsior
ROME

IN EXCELSIS LARIUS
MASCO

Letter signed by Giorgio Bulgari and sent to the grand master of the court of the Shah of Iran with various designs for a pearl and diamond bracelet to match the necklace shown on the previous page. Bulgari Historical Archives.

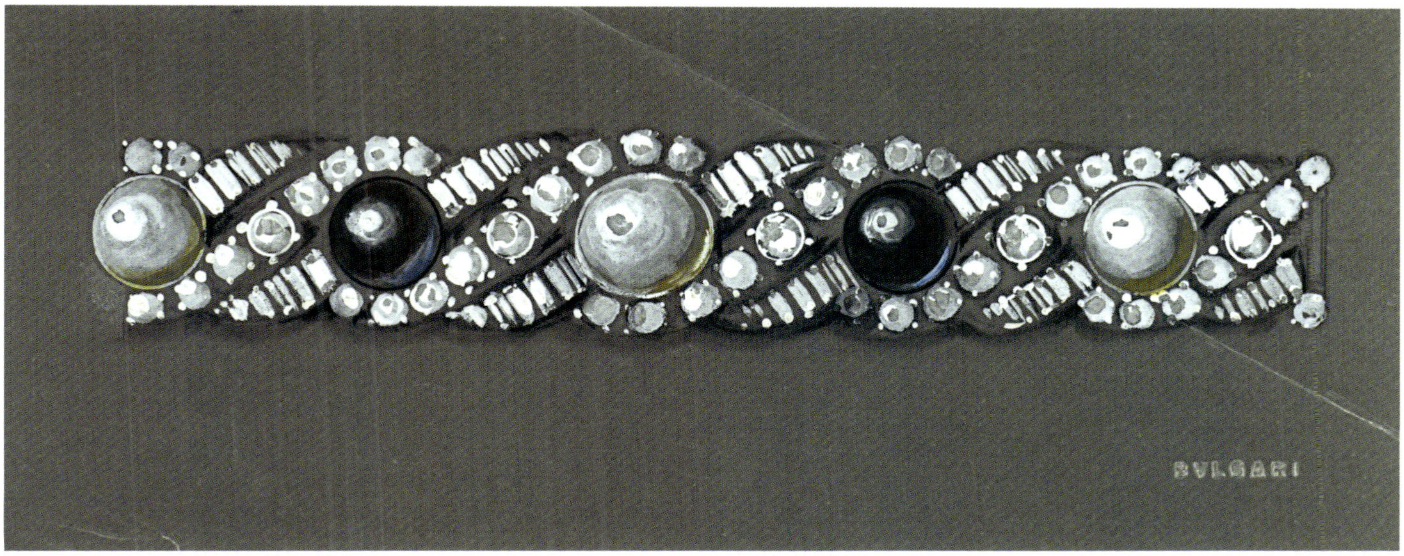
BVLGARI

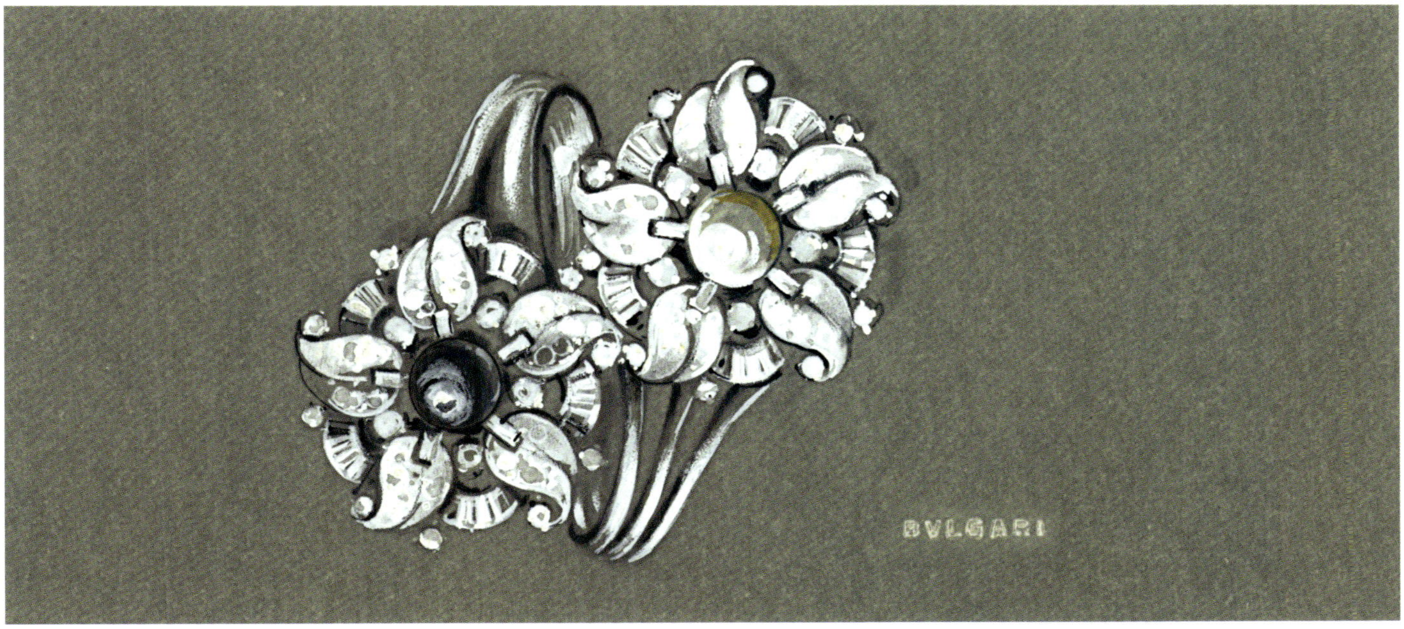
BVLGARI

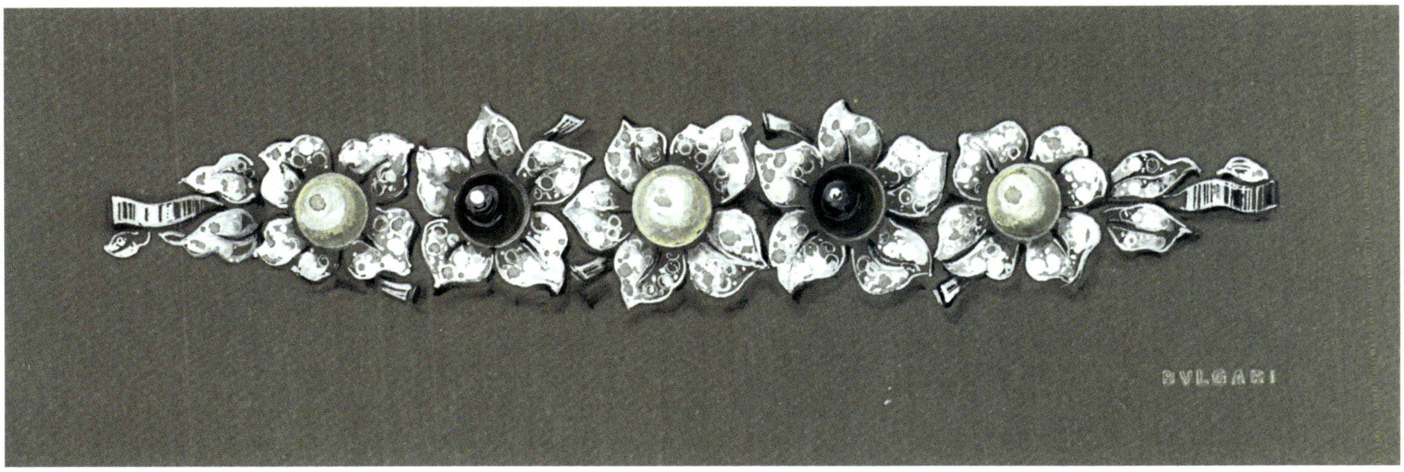
BVLGARI

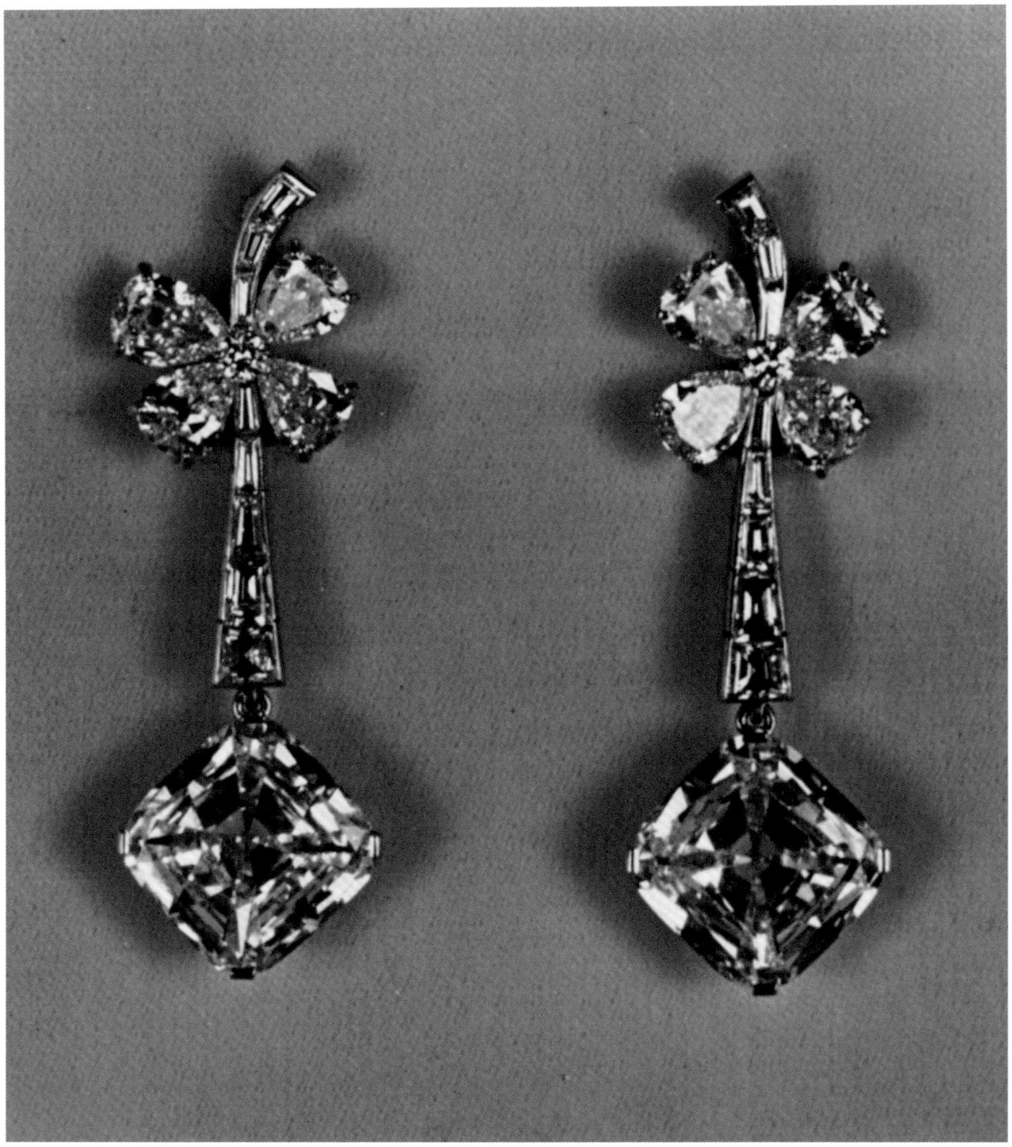

A pair of diamond pendant earrings and a list of jewels "in progress" submitted by Bulgari to the Iranian court for Empress Soraya. Bulgari Historical Archives.

BVLGARI

= MEMORANDUM.=

N°.455.D.
334.0/3 = One pair of EARCLIP = PENDANTS in platinum with :

2 blue-white,pure, EXTRA pearshaped DIAMONDS
weighing together carats 28.33
(but showing at least the weight of
35 carats) , mounted with :
30 round diamonds, baguettes and
navette diamonds weighing cts.8.08......

.... Lit.130.000.000 at I750.........£g. 74.285:=

Special price...£g. 67.000:=

N°1206.B/2 = One platinum RING with :

1 blue-white, extra fine, pure
emerald-cut DIAMOND of carats I8.33,
mounted with :
2 extra fine baguette diamonds.......

........Lit.63.000.000 at 1750..........£g. 36.000:=

Special price....£g. 32.500:=

N°942.B/3 = One platinum RING with :

1 blue-white ,extra fine, pure
round DIAMOND of carats 22.65,
mounted with :
2 shaped diamonds ,carats I.I8........

.......Lit.110.000.000 at 1750..........£g. 62.855:=

Special price....£g. 56.500:=

N°/VC. = One white, pure, emerald-cut DIAMOND
weighing carats 32.45..........

.........Lit. 70.000.000 at 1750..........£g. 40.000:=

Special price....£g. 36.000:=

(NB.: This stone is not available at the
present moment.)

Her Majesty
The Empress SORAYA PAHLAVI of Iran.

IN EXCELSIS LARIUS

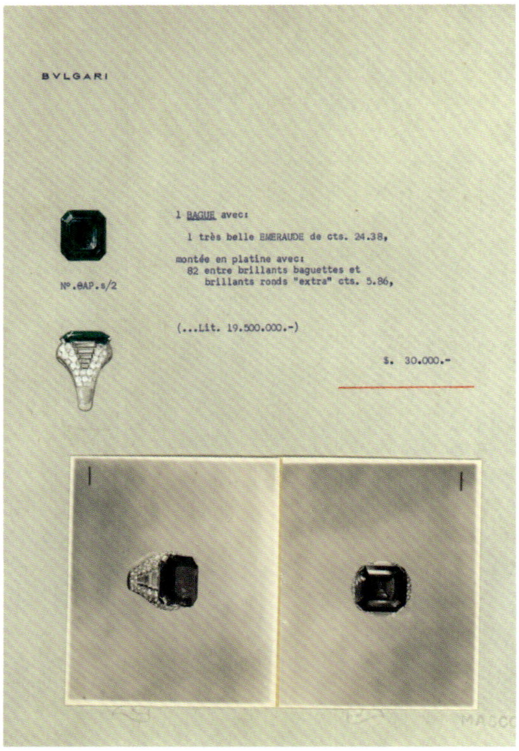

BVLGARI

1 BAGUE avec:

1 très belle EMERAUDE de cts. 24.38,

montée en platine avec:
82 entre brillants baguettes et
brillants ronds "extra" cts. 5.86,

N°.0AP.s/2

(...Lit. 19.500.000.-)

$. 30.000.-

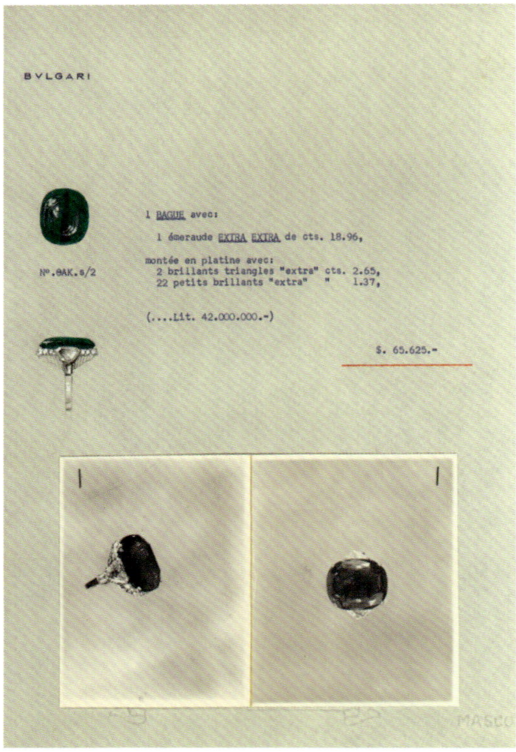

BVLGARI

1 BAGUE avec:

1 émeraude EXTRA EXTRA de cts. 18.96,

montée en platine avec:
2 brillants triangles "extra" cts. 2.65,
22 petits brillants "extra" " 1.37,

N°.0AK.s/2

(....Lit. 42.000.000.-)

$. 65.625.-

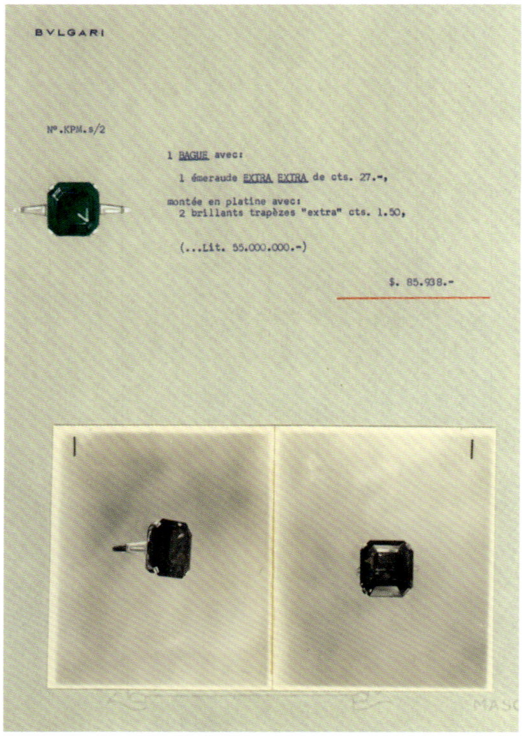

BVLGARI

N°.KPM.s/2

1 BAGUE avec:

1 émeraude EXTRA EXTRA de cts. 27.-,

montée en platine avec:
2 brillants trapèzes "extra" cts. 1.50,

(...Lit. 55.000.000.-)

$. 85.938.-

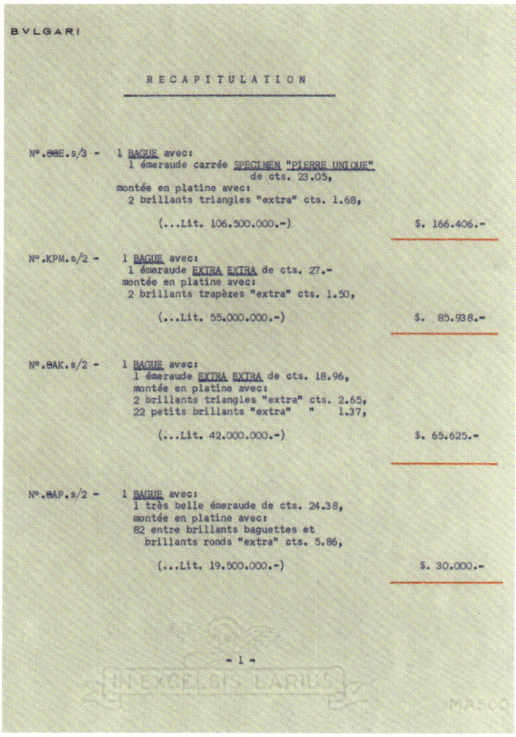

BVLGARI

RECAPITULATION

N°.00E.s/3 - 1 BAGUE avec:
1 émeraude carrée SPECIMEN "PIERRE UNIQUE"
de cts. 23.05,
montée en platine avec:
2 brillants triangles "extra" cts. 1.68,
(...Lit. 106.500.000.-) $. 166.406.-

N°.KPM.s/2 - 1 BAGUE avec:
1 émeraude EXTRA EXTRA de cts. 27.-
montée en platine avec:
2 brillants trapèzes "extra" cts. 1.50,
(...Lit. 55.000.000.-) $. 85.938.-

N°.0AK.s/2 - 1 BAGUE avec:
1 émeraude EXTRA EXTRA de cts. 18.96,
montée en platine avec:
2 brillants triangles "extra" cts. 2.65,
22 petits brillants "extra" " 1.37,
(...Lit. 42.000.000.-) $. 65.625.-

N°.0AP.s/2 - 1 BAGUE avec:
1 très belle émeraude de cts. 24.38,
montée en platine avec:
82 entre brillants baguettes et
brillants ronds "extra" cts. 5.86,
(...Lit. 19.500.000.-) $. 30.000.-

- 1 -

A diamond and emerald necklace and a list of rings "in progress" submitted by Bulgari to the court of Iran for Empress Soraya. Bulgari Historical Archives.

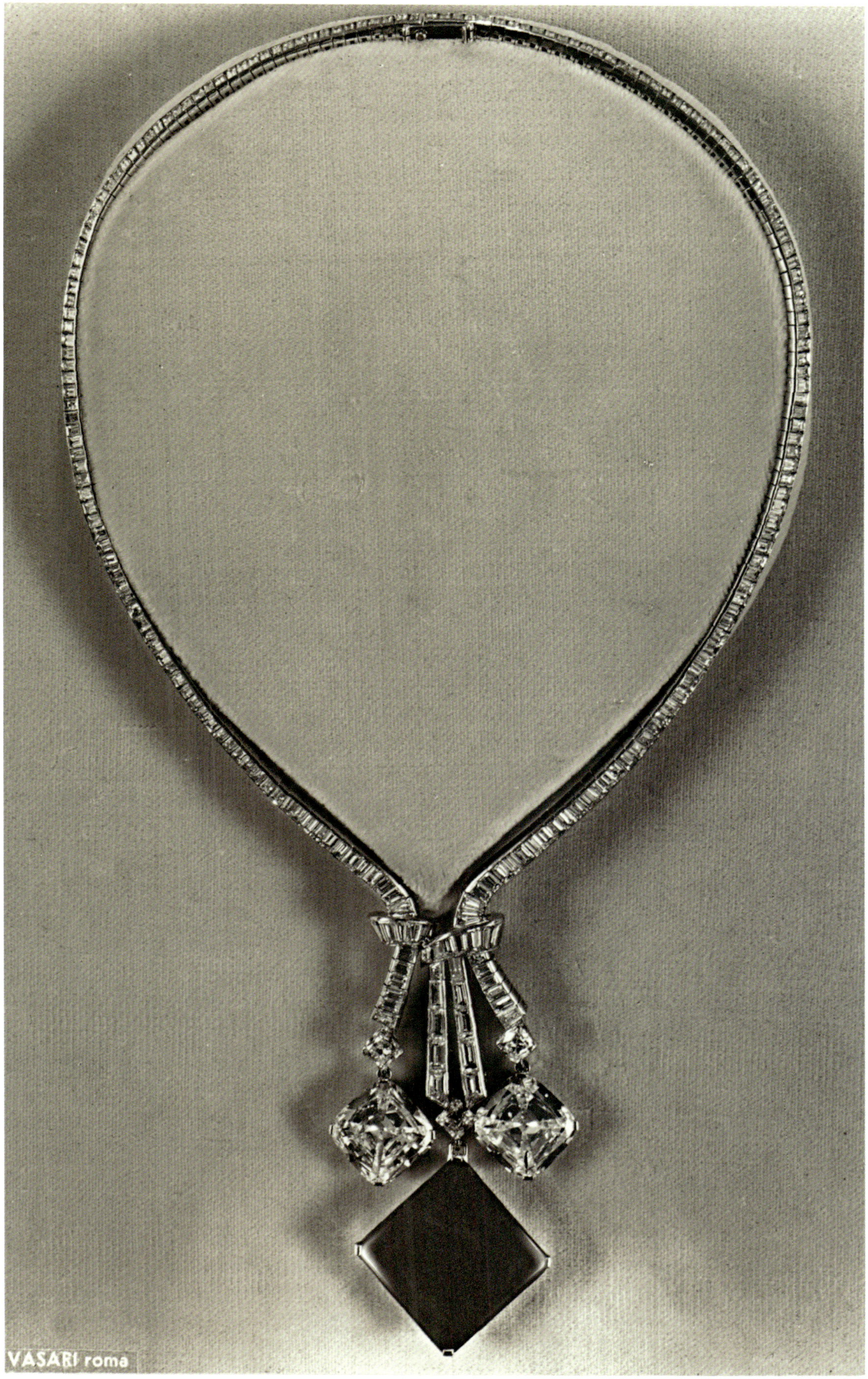
VASARI roma

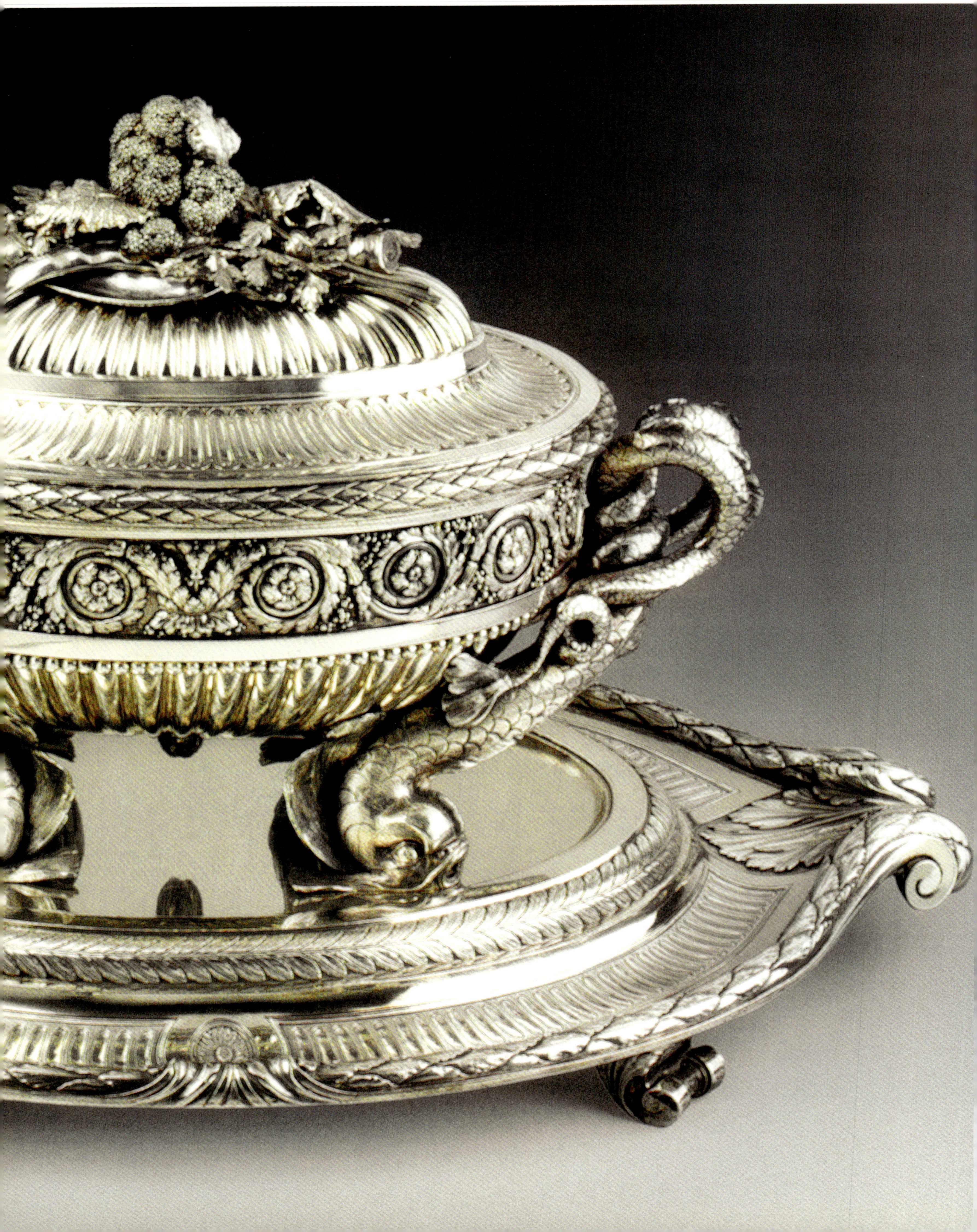

Chapter 6

THE CHAMBER OF TREASURES

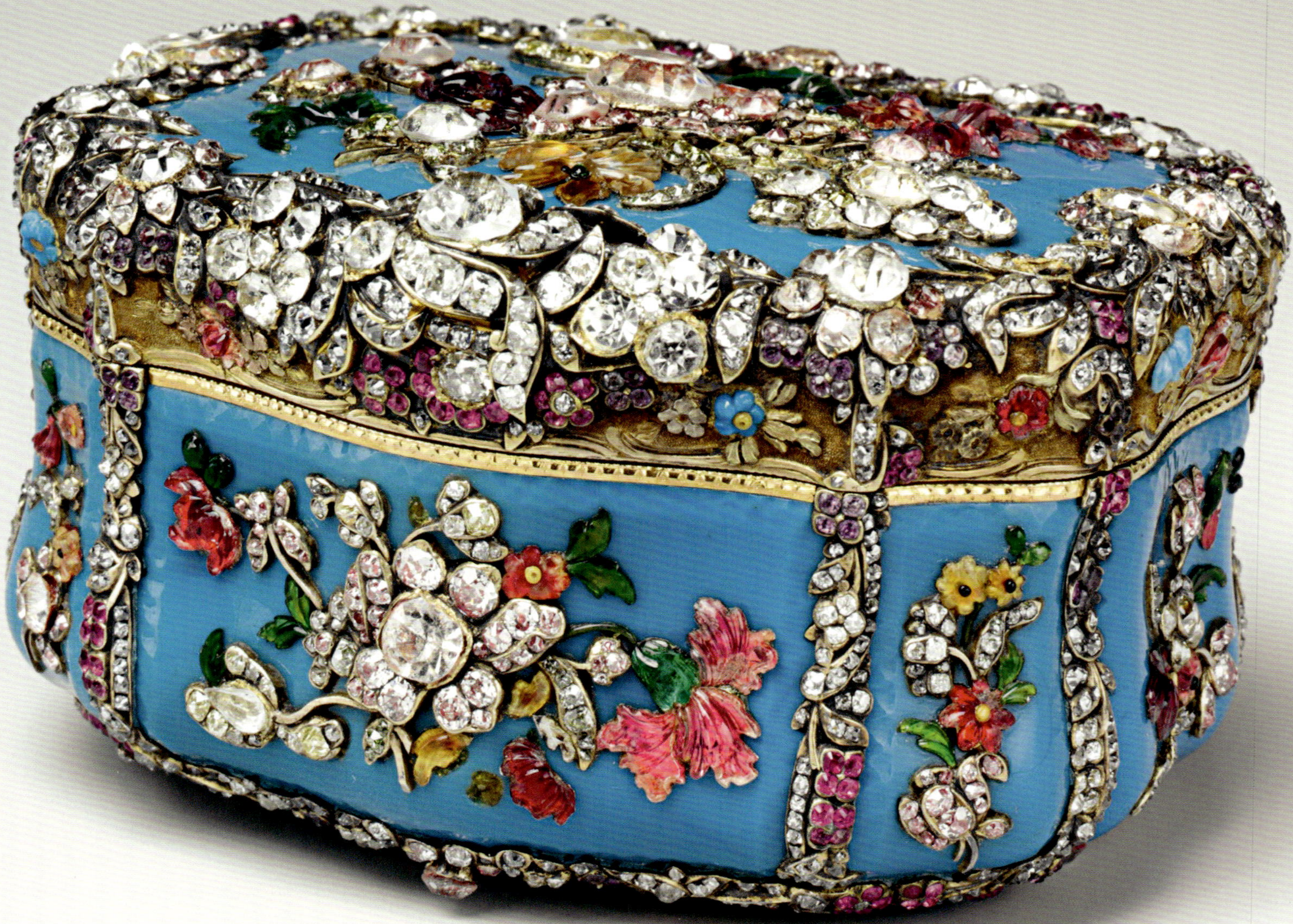

The sale was expected to last nearly a week. Sotheby's, the British auction house chosen by the Egyptian government, had published a catalogue in several volumes detailing the magnitude of the treasures offered to enthusiasts from all over the world: jewellery, silverware, gold coins, photographs, antiquities... The personal collection of former King Farouk of Egypt, confiscated the year before by the Egyptian government, was spectacular.

Overthrown in July 1952, Farouk had gone into exile three days after the coup that had cost him his crown. At the time he had been staying in his summer palace of Montazah in Alexandria. It was from here that he had left Egypt, on board his yacht *Mahroussa*. The officers who had seized control of the country had not even given him time to go to Cairo to collect his personal belongings or a few of the precious objects he had accumulated during his 20 years on the throne.

A year later, the monarchy was abolished and the royal palaces and their contents were confiscated. Soon, the Egyptian Revolutionary Government announced its decision to sell many of the items. After several months of procrastination, a team of experts was appointed to make an inventory of the best of the hundreds of *objets de vertu*.

News of the royal auction had piqued the interest of merchants and jewellers all over the world. King Farouk was in the unfortunate habit of not settling his bills immediately, so some invoices had still not been paid at the time the monarchy had been abolished. And most creditors had already announced their intention to claim part of the proceeds of the sale.

Facing page: *A snuffbox by Jean Guillaume George Krüger made for Frederick the Great, King of Prussia in gold, opaline turquoise and diamonds and precious stones. It was bought by Bulgari at the King Farouk auction in Cairo in March 1954. It was then purchased from Bulgari in 1956 by Robert Lehman, who gave it to the Metropolitan Museum of New York where it is exhibited today.*
Previous page: *Silver tureen by Ignaz Joseph Würth.*

Although the Egyptian royal collection was very varied, with a certain number of objects of only average quality, several lots aroused the envy of connoisseurs. One such lot was a sumptuous turquoise opaline snuffbox mounted on gold, the panels and lid of which were set with floral motifs of diamonds and precious stones. Costantino Bulgari had identified it immediately. This snuffbox belonged to an exclusive set of *objets de vertu*: 125 similar boxes all encrusted with gems and known as the "Potsdam snuffboxes".

They were created between 1753 and 1774 by Jean Guillaume George Krüger, an English goldsmith based in Berlin. These had all been commissioned by the same collector, Frederick the Great, King of Prussia (1712-1786). They were arranged on consoles, in his personal apartments at the Sanssouci Palace in Potsdam. The decoration of these rooms being a riot of rococo, the snuffboxes were in their perfect environment. When Frederick died in 1786, his kingdom and most of his personal property was inherited by his brother and successor, Frederick William II, who survived him by ten years. After that, the snuffboxes were scattered among his numerous descendants.

One box went to Russia at the beginning of the 19th century with a tsarina, born Princess of Prussia. It was sold by Christie's in London in 1927. It is now in the collections of Queen Elizabeth II. Another box is in the Louvre Museum in Paris. Four are in the Victoria and Albert Museum. Several have remained the property of the Hohenzollern family and are exhibited at Hohenzollern Castle in Germany.

And it was one of those legendary boxes that Costantino Bulgari managed to buy at the sale of King Farouk's collection in 1954. Immediately after the auction, the snuffbox was sent to Rome and displayed in a showcase in the area of the Via dei Condotti boutique that was reserved for *objets de vertu*. Anna Bulgari Calissoni, who began working at the firm with her father and her uncle, a year prior to the King Farouk sale, remembers how dazzling that treasure room was: *"All the left part of the shop was reserved for these objects,"*

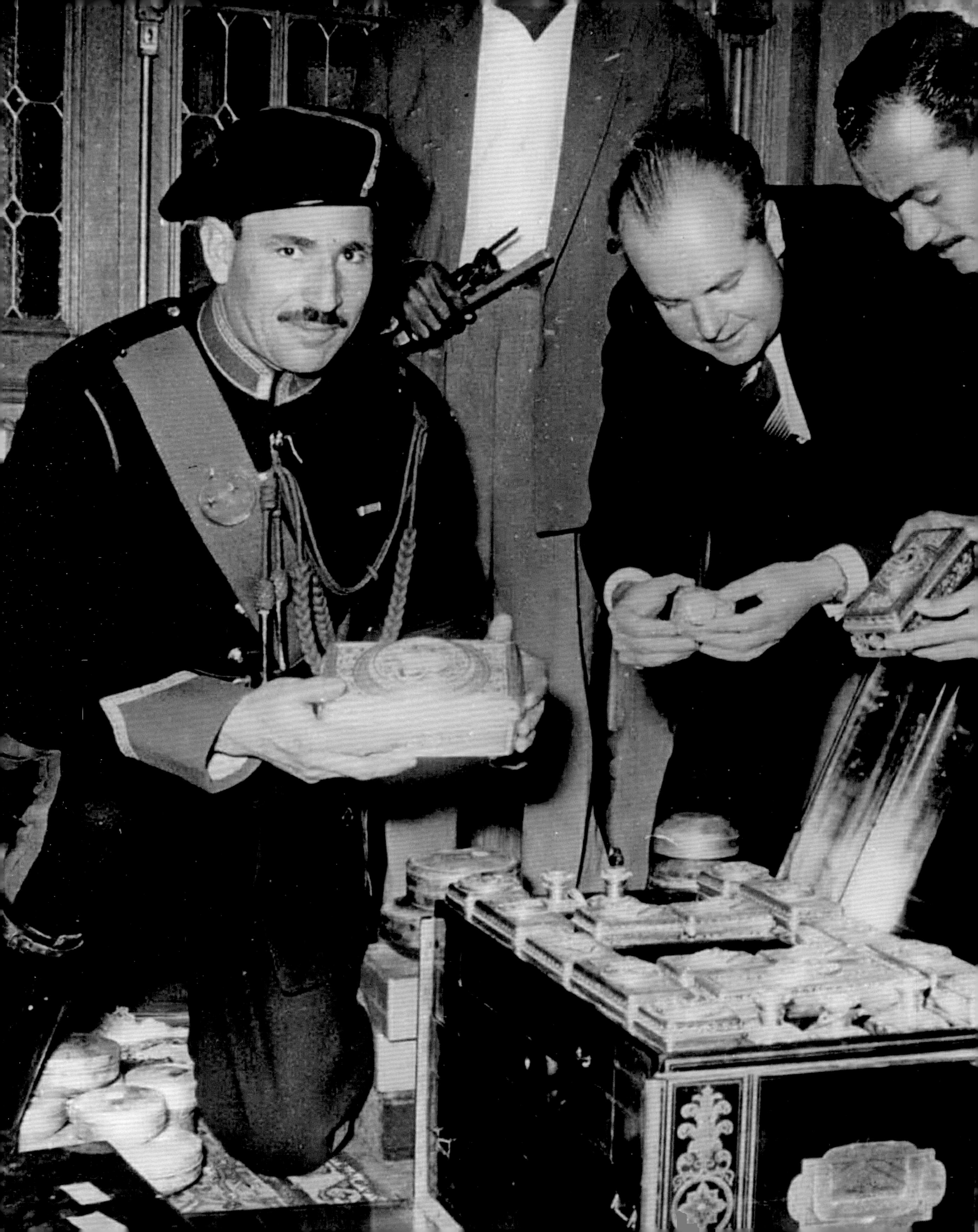

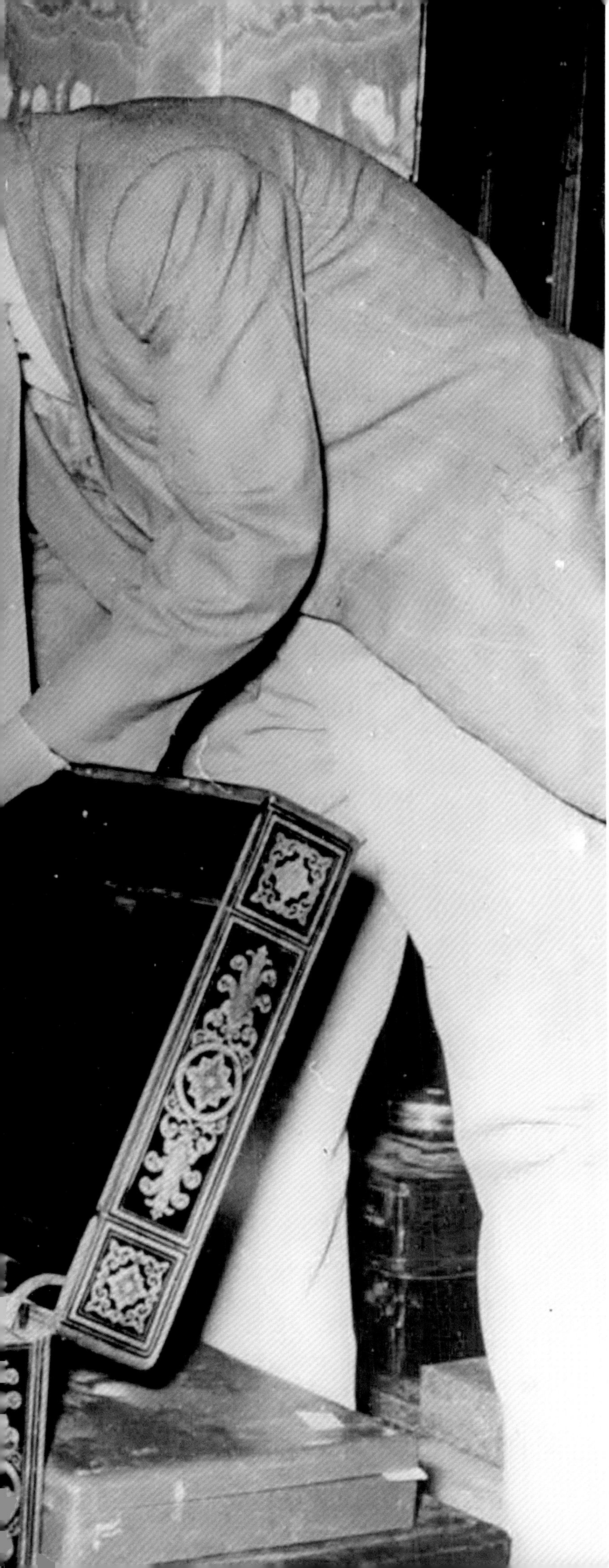

The auction of King Farouk's personal collection in Cairo in 1954.

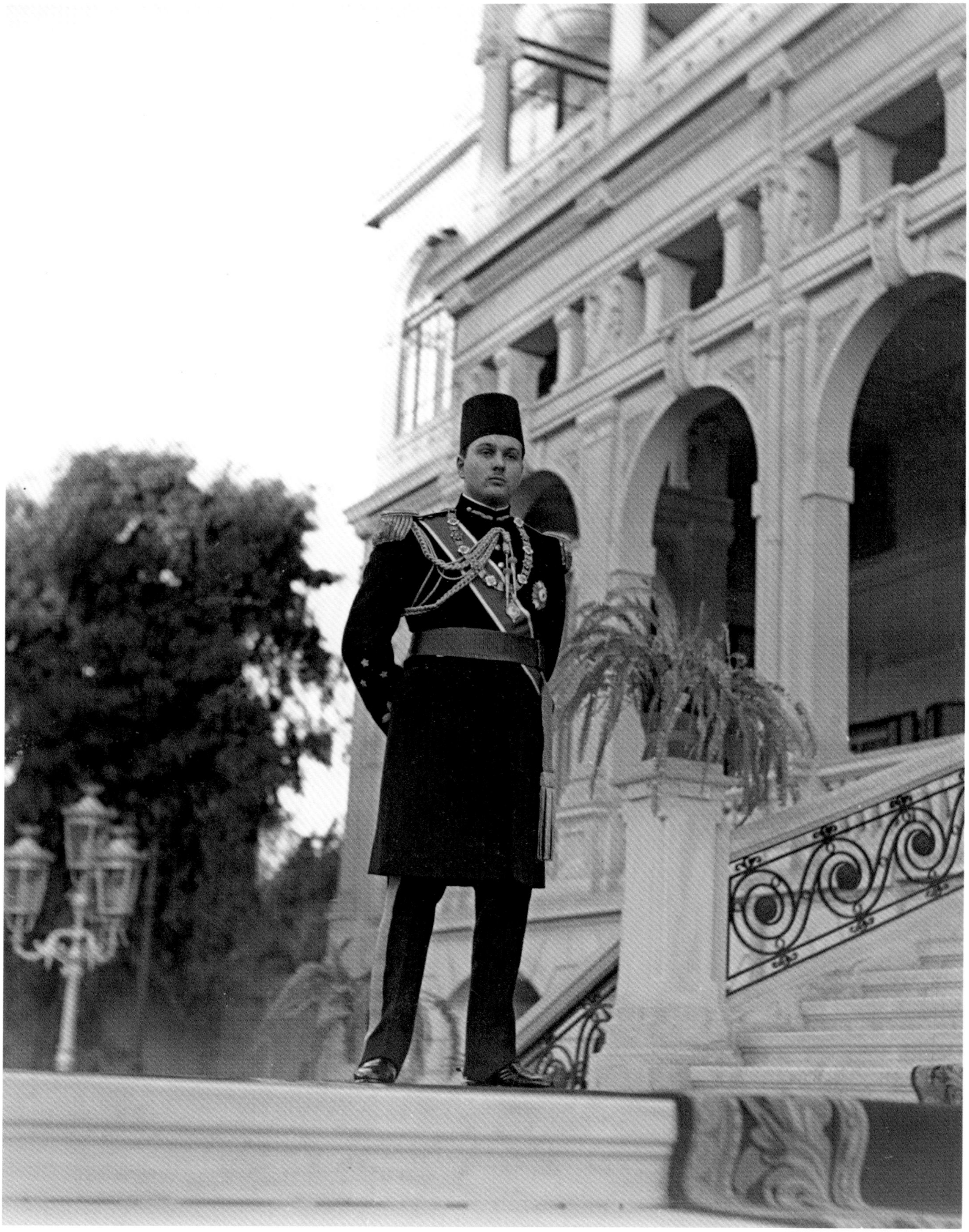

she recalls. *"It was truly an impressive sight that you would discover as soon as you walked through the door. My father Costantino and my uncle Giorgio worked in the same office. They got on very well, but they had different specialities. My uncle Giorgio may have had an easier character. He was in charge of fine jewellery. My father was the specialist in silverware. It was he who bought these precious objects. Later, I also began to buy."* [1]

This tradition of trade in precious metal, gold and silver, and hard stone is evidently a continuation of Sotirio Bulgari's work on the silver objects he made and sold throughout his life. The name of his first boutique on Via dei Condotti "Old Curiosity Shop" was more a reference to this type of work than to jewellery. In the same way that Giorgio gave an unparalleled boost to *haute joaillerie*, Costantino showed unfailing knowledge and expertise in the selection and trade of *objets de vertu*. He even published a monumental series of books devoted to Italian goldsmiths, which has become the reference work in this field. Anna, his eldest daughter, continued her work by writing and publishing the last volume of this set. *"I must say that my father gave us a very strict education, but it was thanks to him that I learned everything: goldsmithing, jades and precious objects in general. He also taught me to play chess, one of his passions."*[2]

The 20th century and its two world wars, which shattered empires, fortunes and social classes, was a propitious period for the sale of small precious objects. The sale of King Farouk's collection was not unique. Already in 1928, when the Soviets had organised the dispersion of collections seized in the Romanov palaces in St Petersburg, a representative of Bulgari (possibly Costantino himself) had gone to Berlin to the Rudolph Lepke auction room, and succeeded in buying some of the tsar's treasures. Another gold snuffbox enamelled with pastoral scenes, also of German manufacture and dating from the 18th century, was acquired during this sale.

As it happened, both boxes – the Egyptian one and the Russian one – were sold to the same customer: Robert Lehman, in 1956. The American collector and philanthropist, donated both of them, along with hundreds of works of art, to the Metropolitan Museum in New York, where they are exhibited.

Facing page: *King Farouk of Egypt in the garden of the Koubbeh Palace in Cairo in 1938.*

Actually, the Russian Revolution played a major role in the wealth of Russian *objets de vertu* in Rome during the interwar years. After the Bolsheviks seized power, two European capitals became refuges of the Russian aristocrats: Paris and Rome. Numerous and illustrious Russian refugees settled in the Eternal City. Queen Elena of Italy, wife of King Victor Emmanuel, and born a princess of Montenegro, had been raised at the Smolny Institute in St Petersburg under the protection of the Tsars. And two of her sisters had married Grand Dukes of Russia. So it was natural for her to grant special protection to Russians fleeing the new regime. The three most important Russian émigrés in Rome were the Grand Duchess George of Russia, born Princess of Greece (1876-1940), her cousin the Grand Duchess Peter of Russia, born Princess Milica of Montenegro (1866-1951)) – one of the sisters of Queen Elena of Italy – and Princess Zenaïde Yusupova (1861-1939).

The latter, mother of Prince Felix Yusupov, the assassin of Rasputin, settled in Rome in 1920. She remained there until her husband died in 1928. The sole heiress of Russia's richest family, the greater part of her legendary jewellery collection had been left behind in Russia. She had, however, succeeded in bringing with her into exile a considerable number of precious objects, including snuffboxes, hard stone statuettes and dozens of small *objets de vertu* signed *"Fabergé"*, the great goldsmith of the Russian court.

According to the oral tradition of the Bulgari family, some of these pieces were purchased by Costantino Bulgari. A blue and white enamel snuffbox sold recently in Paris confirms this theory. It bears a label indicating the two provenances: Yusupov and Bulgari, Rome.

According to Anna Bulgari Calissoni: *"One of the most beautiful objects I have ever seen in the shop of Via dei Condotti was an icon. The riza, the precious frame that reveals only the face of the saint or the Virgin, was in purple enamel. It was signed Fabergé".*[3] These transactions with personalities from among the Russian immigrants were certainly eased by the presence on the Bulgari team of Vittorio Lombardo, an Italian jeweller, who had lived in Russia until 1918. *"He was a grand seigneur with incredible looks,"* recalls Anna Bulgari Calissoni. *"His father had settled in Russia where he had a jewellery store. After the revolution, he managed to escape in the nick of time. He really had been on the verge of being shot by the Bolsheviks."* [4]

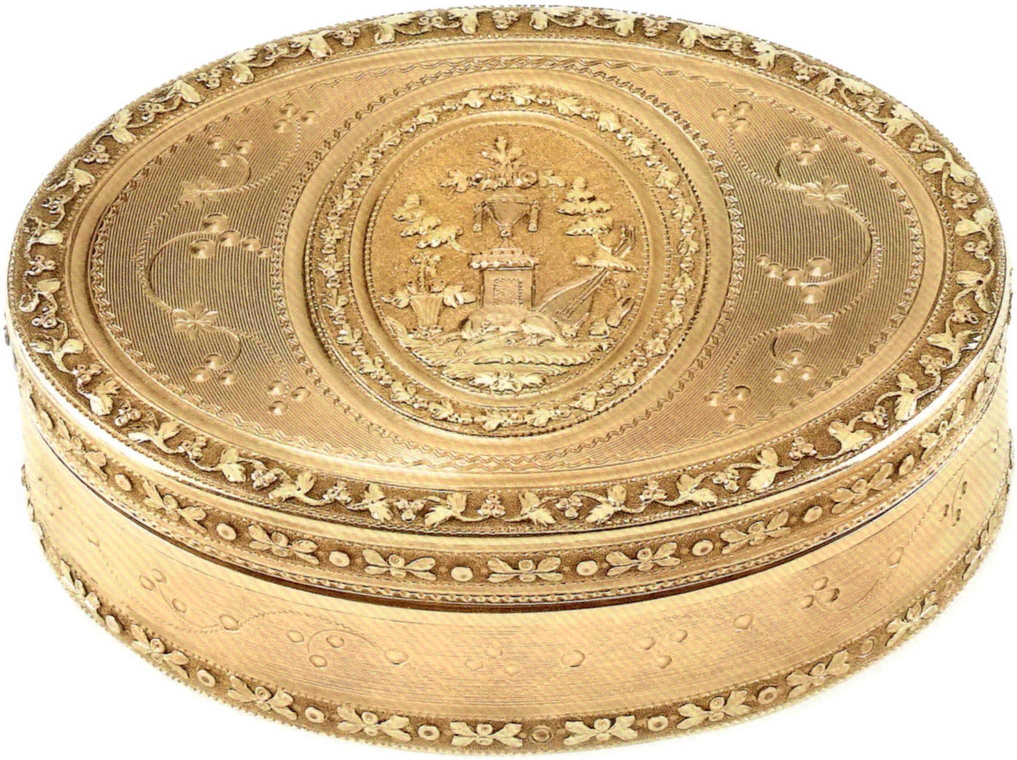

A Swiss coloured-gold snuffbox (1780–1790) sold in Rome by Bulgari. It was sold again at Christie's London, November 2012.

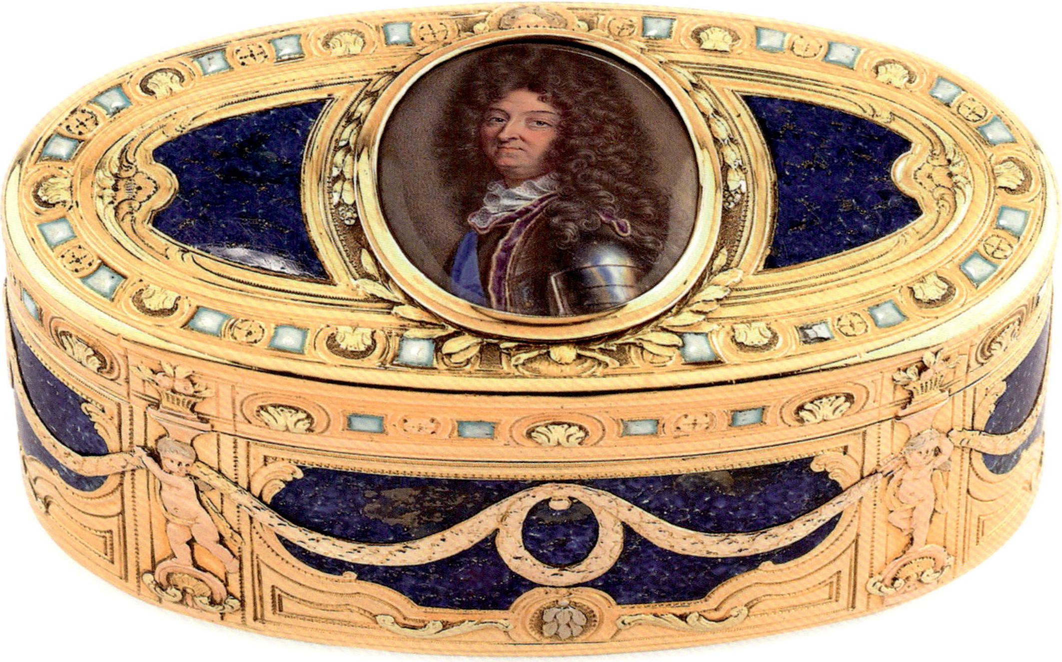

A Louis XV snuffbox in gold and enamel with a miniature of King Louis the XIV of France. Sold in Rome by Bulgari. It was sold again at Christie's London in May 2012.

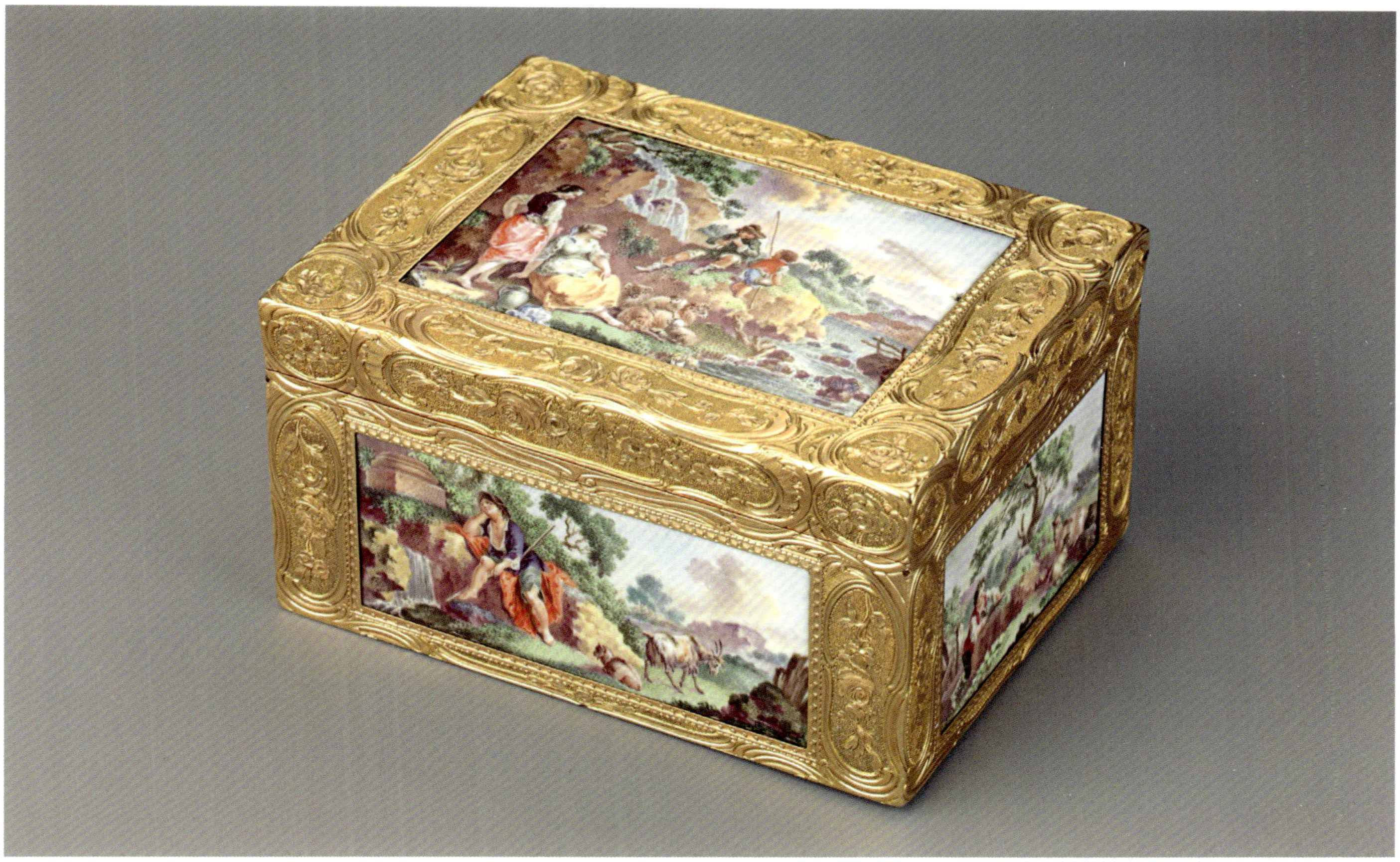

Of course, silverware occupied a very special place in this treasure chamber. One of the most spectacular pieces ever seen in the showcases at Via dei Condotti was a fabulous tureen, with its display stand, bearing the stamp of Ignaz Joseph Würth. It dates from 1779-1781 and was part of the "second service" of the Duke of Saxe-Teschen, who was the son-in-law of the great Empress of Austria, Maria Theresa. The tureen was sold by Bulgari to one of the greatest collectors of the second half of the 20th century: Commander Paul-Louis Weiller (1893-1993).

The man was a legend. Born to a wealthy Jewish family in the Alsace, he had been baptised in the Catholic religion. His father, Lazare Weiller, was an industrialist who would become a pioneer of television. His mother, Alice Javal, who died in a concentration camp in 1944, was one of the first women pilots of aeroplanes in Europe. Paul-Louis was also a pilot. During the First World War, his plane was shot down several times. Thanks to a series of miracles, he always escaped. And for his amazing bravery in action during the war, he was made an officer of the Legion of Honour. Returning to civilian life in 1918, he founded an aircraft engine manufacturing company that made him a fortune.

Stripped of his French citizenship by the Vichy government, he narrowly escaped arrest by the Gestapo in January 1942, fleeing abroad. In 1945, with the liberation of France, he returned home and decided to embark on patronage, so that Paris would regain its place as the capital of world culture. He supported museums, artists, created a ballet company and bought houses that he filled with works of art.

Paul-Louis Weiller was also at the centre of an extremely brilliant social life. Members of the European royal families and the most famous movie stars of the time were all received at his homes in Paris, Versailles or on the French Riviera. From his two marriages – to Princess Alexandra Ghika and Aliki

Above: *German snuffbox, c.1765, in gold and enamel. This box was part of the Russian imperial family treasure that was sold in Berlin in 1928 and apparently bought by Costantino Bulgari. It was sold by Bulgari in 1956 to Robert Lehman, who gave it to the Metropolitan Museum of New York, where it is exhibited today.*

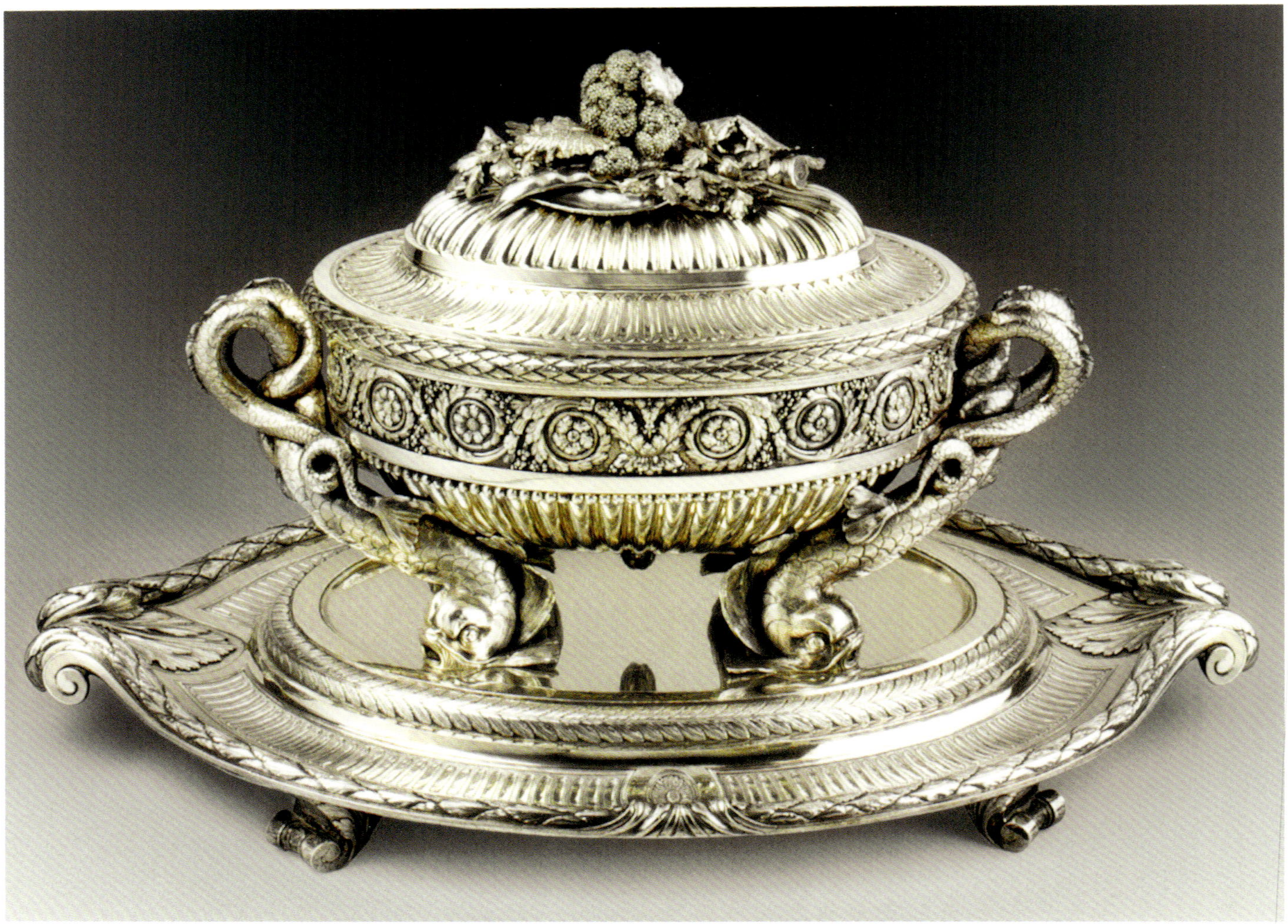

Diplarakou (Miss Europe in 1930) – two children were born: Marie-Élisabeth and Paul-Annik. It was doubtless Paul-Annik's marriage to Princess Olimpia Torlonia in 1965, that led Paul-Louis Weiller to discover the Bulgari shop in Rome.

In addition to the Duke of Saxe-Teschen's silver tureen, he acquired a good part of of Bulgari's stock of jade objects. His purchases, comparable to those of Count Cini before the war, are counted in dozens of pieces. Some remained with his descendants, others were sold in April 2011, in Paris, by Gros & Delettrez. The two most important pieces of the collection had been acquired from Bulgari in the 1960s. The first, in white nephrite jade, is a cup adorned with four butterflies and eight dragons. It dates from the Jiaqing era, early 19th century. It sold for 300,000 euros, three times its estimate. The second, even more spectacular, is a light green nephrite jade cup, dating back to the Qianlong period, which covers the last sixty years of the 18th century. A wedding gift, it is a virtuosity of dazzling sculpture and reprises the symbols of longevity and happiness. It sold for 810,000 euros.

Anna Bulgari Calissoni stopped working at Bulgari in 1984. In the early 1990s, the House stopped practically all activities related to *objets d'art* to devote itself exclusively to jewellery.

Above: *Silver tureen by Ignaz Joseph Würth, made in Vienna in 1779-1781 for the Duke of Saxe-Teschen. It was bought by Paul-Louis Weiller from Bulgari in Rome in the 1960s. Paul-Louis Weiller collection, Etude Gros & Delettrez, Paris, April 2011.*
Facing page: *Commander Paul-Louis Weiller with his second wife, Aliki Diplarakou in 1931.*

1. - 4. Interview with the author, 2015.

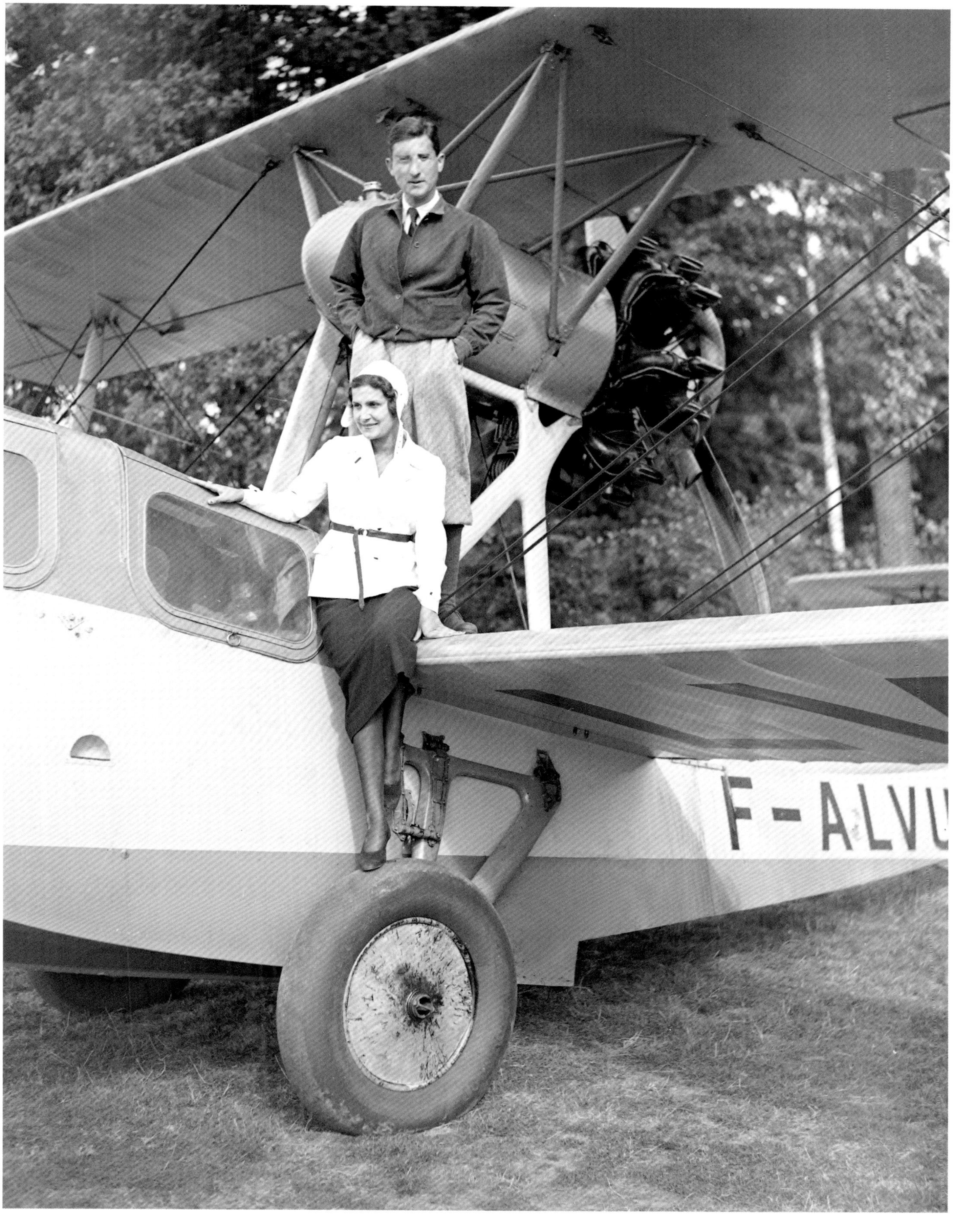
F-ALVU

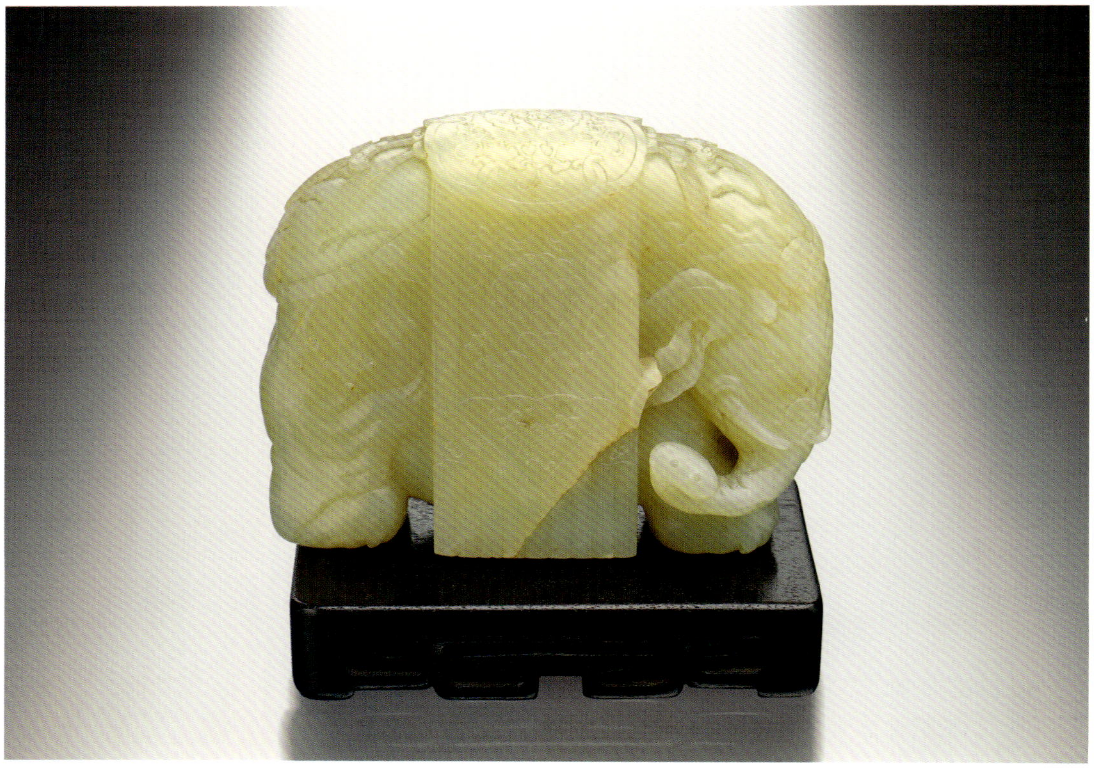

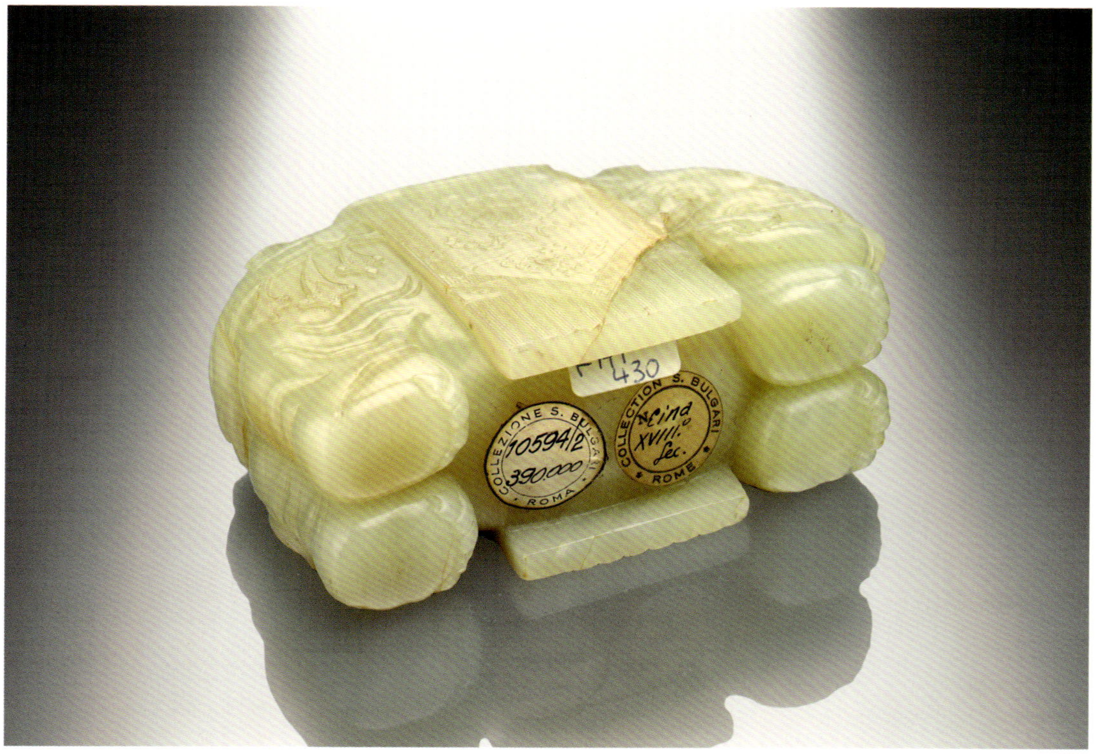

Chinese jade elephant, 18th century, from a private collection, bearing the label:
Collection S Bulgari Rome.

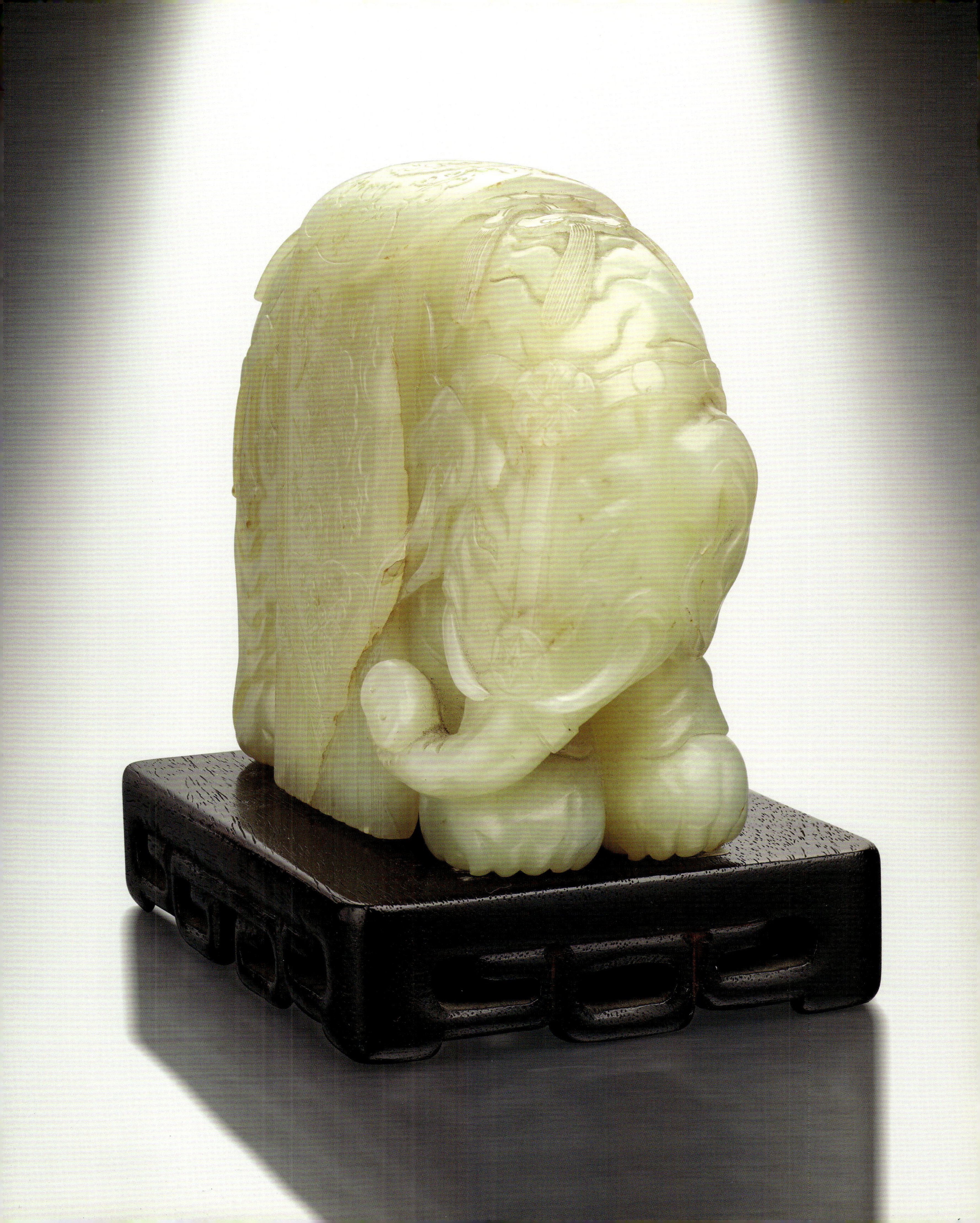

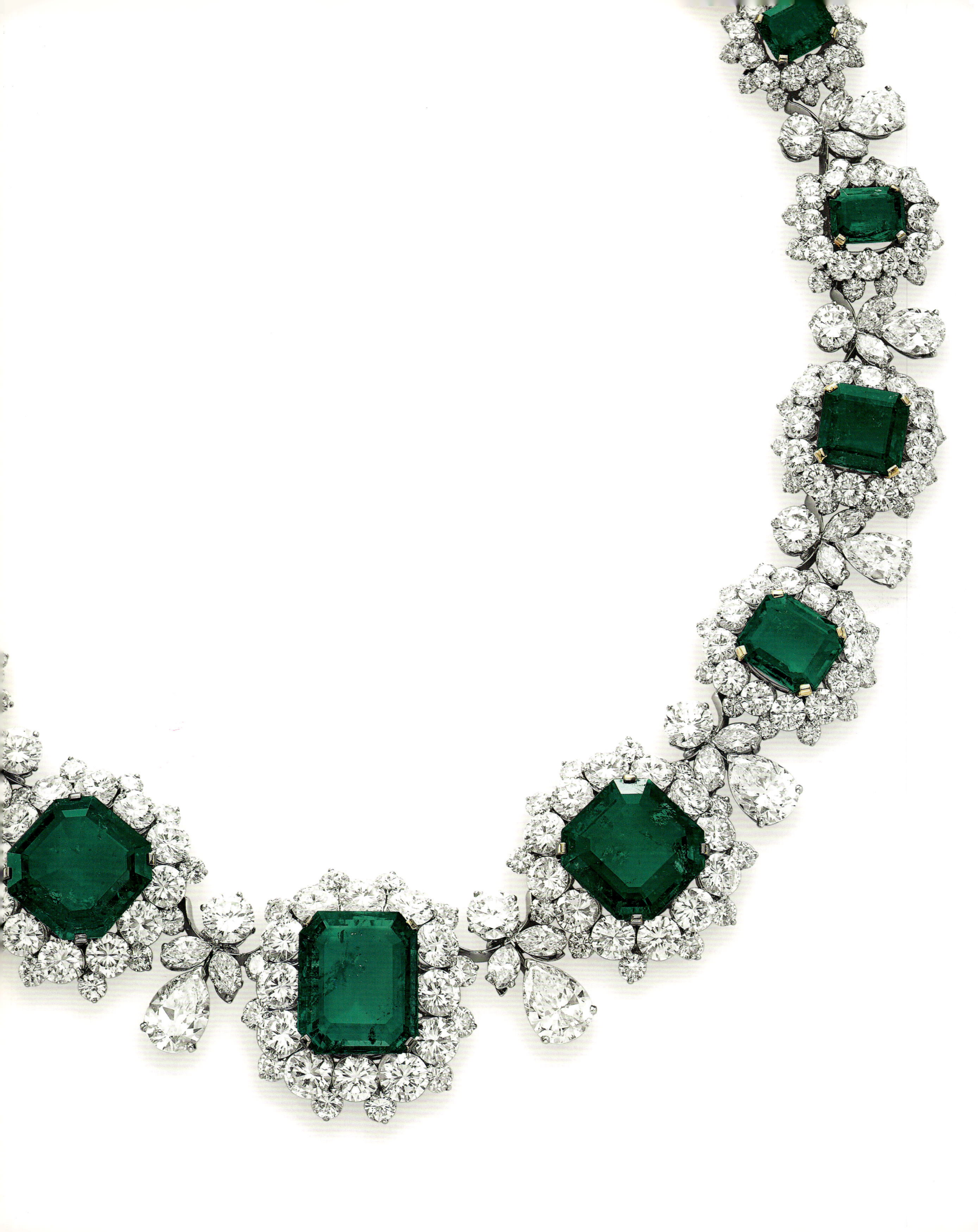

Chapter 7

HOLLYWOOD ON THE TIBER

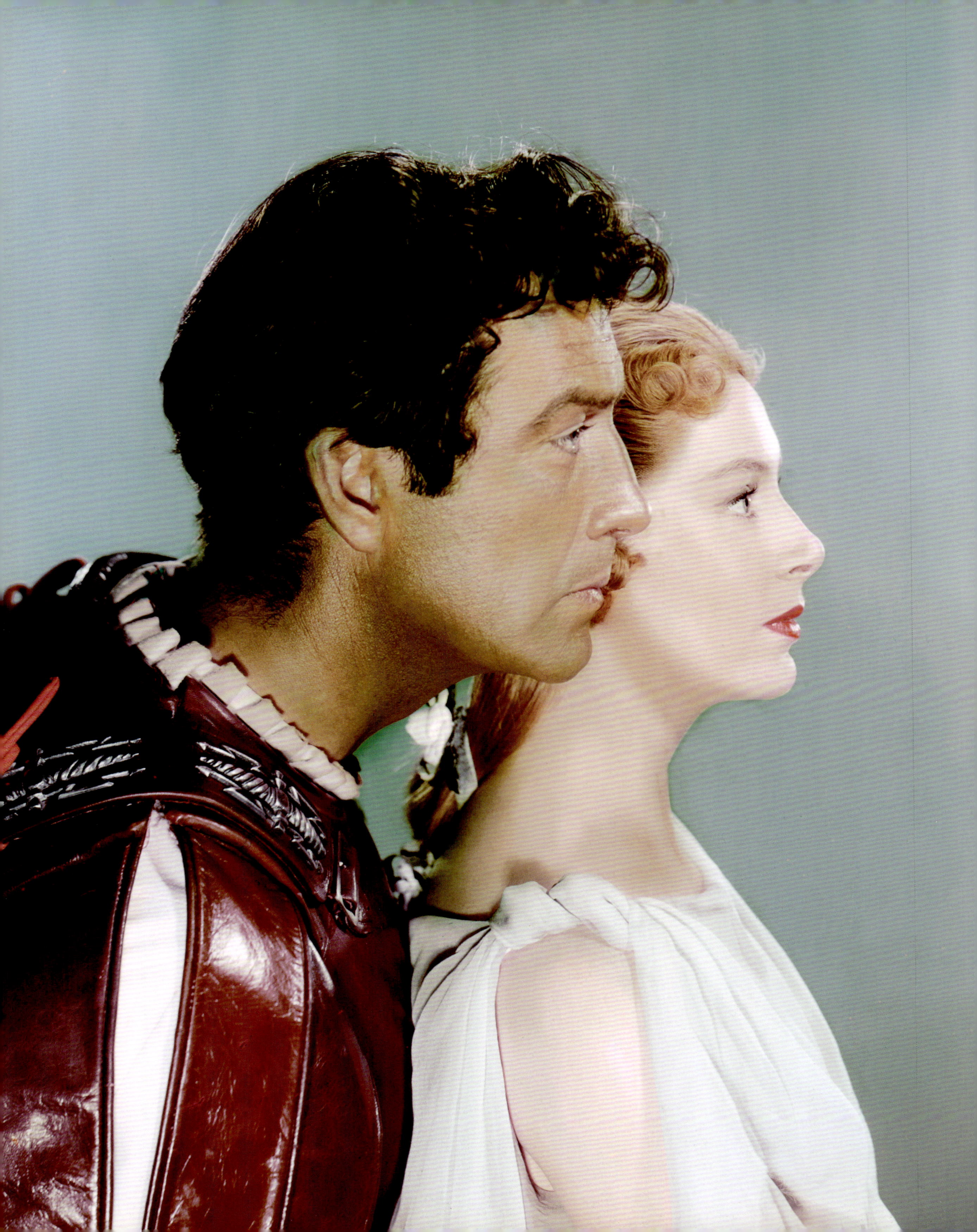

Clare Boothe Luce (1903-1987)

Rome, Via Veneto, September, 1955

In just a few minutes, the little group who surrounded the couple as they left the US embassy had turned into a crowd of a hundred or so people; photographers, journalists and simple onlookers were following without really knowing why. It is true, they made a fine couple. He was tall – 6ft 2in – and slim, with an engaging smile, and neatly combed hair. She was a little older, blonde, overwhelmingly stylish and impeccably elegant. The man was the most famous baseball player in the world and Marilyn Monroe's ex-husband. His name was Joe DiMaggio (1914-1999). His family, who settled in California half a century ago, was of Sicilian origin. The woman had been a fashion journalist and a war reporter, before being elected to the House of Representatives as a Republican. Now she was the American Ambassador in Italy, the first woman appointed to this post in the history of the United States. Her name was Clare Boothe Luce. Almost immediately after her arrival in Rome two years before, the press, the public and the political world nicknamed her *"La Luce"*, the Light. Her panache, courage and strong speeches earned her some fanatical enemies but also crowds of admirers. Now, thirty years after her death, few people realise that we owe some famous aphorisms, to *"La Luce"*, such as, *"No good deed goes unpunished!"* or *"A hospital is not a place to be sick"*.

With her innate sense of publicity, Madame Ambassador had improvised this scene on the streets of Rome. DiMaggio, who had just divorced Marilyn Monroe, came to Italy on a family pilgrimage. Arriving in Rome, he decided to stop at the Embassy for a courtesy visit. The Ambassador immediately saw an opportunity and said: *"Joe, let's go down to one of those little sidewalk cafés and have a cup of coffee."* [1] She knew that the press was always waiting in Via Veneto in front of the Embassy. And to cause a small riot around a man as famous as DiMaggio, would not be very difficult. The articles in Rome's newspapers the following day would certainly be positive.

Since her arrival in Rome, in April 1953, *"La Luce"*, had been one of the main topics of the Italian press. She had succeeded in finding her place in the very masculine universe of diplomacy in Rome. Even the Holy See recognised her ability. Her active support of the Italian government during the diplomatic crisis of Trieste forced the communist rule of Marshal Tito to yield. And Italy recovered the entire city and its territory. The whole country rejoiced at this victory. And in recognition, the US Ambassador was invited to an special dinner held in her honour by the Italian government at Villa Madama. Even the Italian Communist press, which did not like her very much, was sometimes amused by the stand that the Ambassador took. The ambassadorship in Rome was the culmination of an exceptional career.

It all started a quarter of a century earlier. Clare Boothe was one of the first female American journalists to write about something other than "social events" or "embroidery and cooking". While the gossip columnists, Elsa Maxwell, Hedda Hopper and Louella Parsons often displayed a rather vague idea of truth, Boothe was always scrupulously honest

Facing page: *Robert Taylor and Deborah Kerr in* Quo Vadis, *the first American epic shot at Cinecittà in Rome, in 1950. This film was the very beginning of Hollywood on the Tiber.* **Previous page:** *Elizabeth Taylor's emerald and diamond necklace. Bulgari Heritage Collection.*

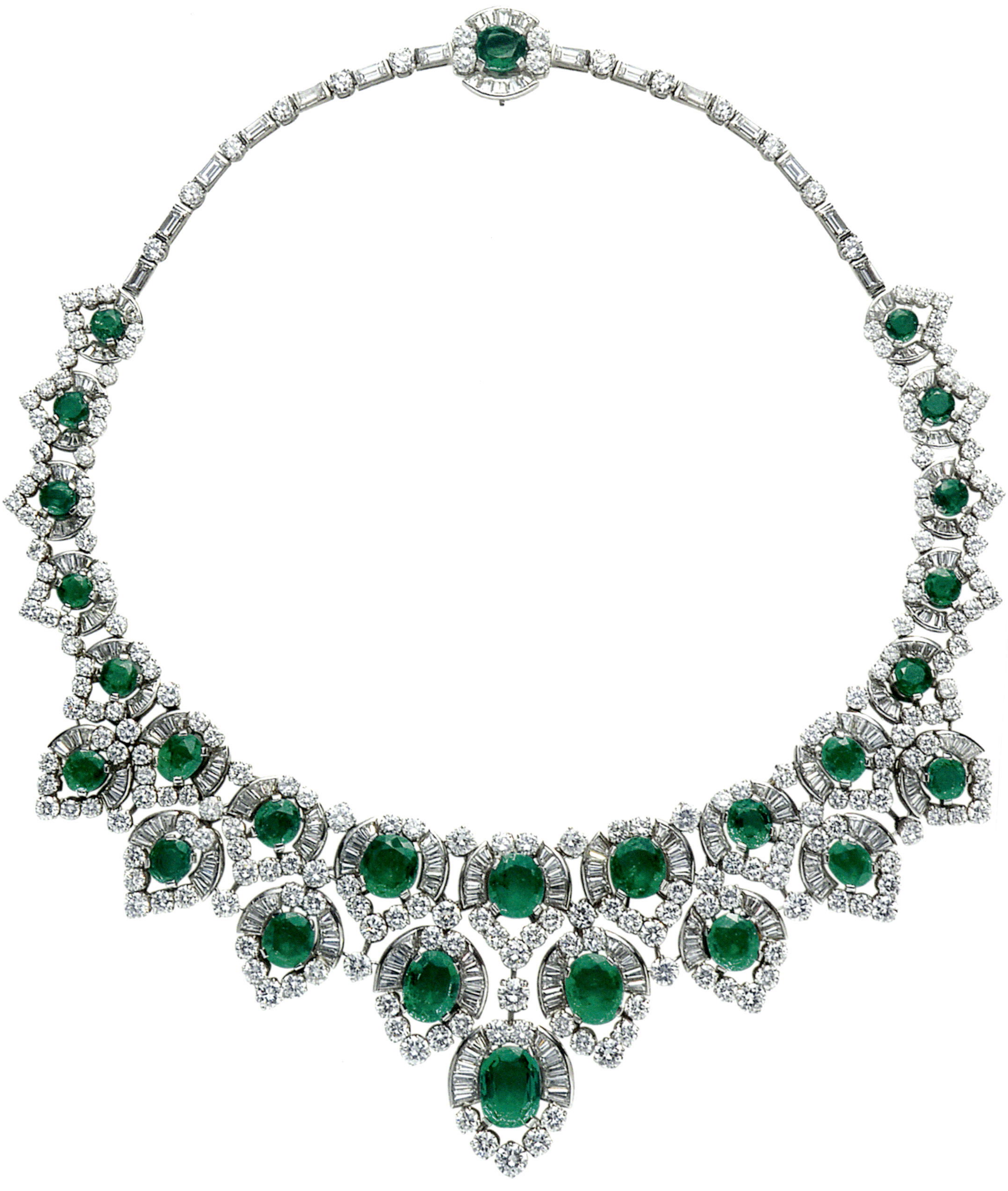

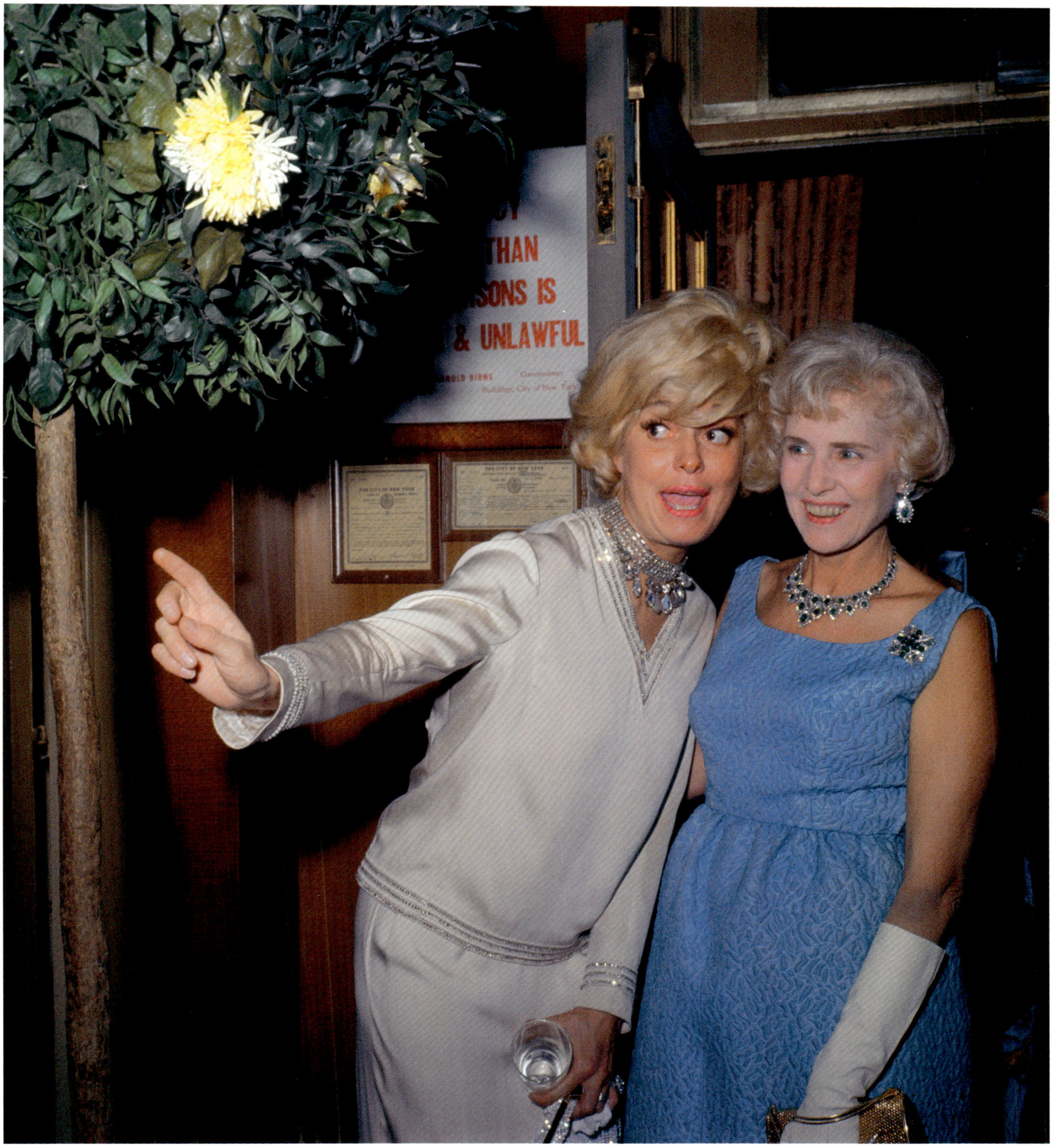

Above: Time *magazine's 40th anniversary dinner; Carol Channing with Clare Boothe Luce, who is wearing the emerald and diamond necklace created for her by Bulgari.* **Facing page:** *The emerald and diamond necklace bought from Bulgari by Ambassador Clare Boothe Luce during her posting in Rome, between 1953 and 1956. It was sold at Sotheby's, New York in 1988. Private collection.*

in her articles. She also wrote for the theatre and enjoyed her greatest success in 1936, with *The Women*. This play, with an all-female cast, features a group of elegant New York ladies who spend their time talking about... men. As it happens, one of the characters, "the Countess", was inspired by Dorothy di Frasso. The adaptation to cinema in 1939, with Joan Crawford, Norma Shearer and Rosalind Russell in the lead roles, remains a cult film. During the war years, Boothe's reports on the ground, especially in Asia, left their mark on American public opinion. In 1942, she entered the House of Representatives. Ten years later, the hundred or so speeches she had made during the presidential campaign to support Eisenhower's candidacy were rewarded by the Ambassadorship in Rome.

Her private life had been far less successful. Her first marriage to George Tuttle Brokaw, an alcoholic millionaire, ended in a divorce in 1929. She then married Henry Luce, an American press magnate. Sadly, in 1944, her only child, Ann Clare Brokaw died at the age of 19, in an unfortunate traffic accident. Clare Boothe Luce converted to Catholicism.

According to Nicola Bulgari, Giorgio Bulgari's youngest son, this dynamic woman's stay in Rome from 1953 to 1956 was a key element in the birth of what would later be termed the "*Dolce Vita*": "*Before being a film by Fellini, the* Dolce Vita *was above all a way of life,*" he explains. "*Clare Boothe Luce was a journalist, writer, politician and celebrity. She was the first woman in the history of the United States to be appointed ambassador in a foreign country. She arrived in Rome in April 1953. When she moved here, I think she found the city a little boring. My father knew her very well. And when she felt a little depressed, she would sometimes come to Bulgari to buy something or just chat with him. I remember her coming to dinner at my parents' home on via Parioli. She promoted Rome, and attracted all of these exciting personalities, and in particular the stars and Hollywood producers who started making films here. Production costs at Cinecittà were infinitely lower than in Hollywood. Clare Boothe Luce is certainly the reason why this city has become a meeting point for the rich and famous all over the world. Rome was ready at the time for this change. There are so many fabulous places in this city where you can give parties. The scenery was already there – she brought in the actors.*" [2]

In fact, Clare Boothe Luce gave momentum to a movement that had begun a few years before her arrival. In 1950, *Time* magazine – a publication that belonged to her husband, Henry Luce – was already calling the Italian capital "*Hollywood on the Tiber*" in reference to the river that runs though the city. The pioneer of the renaissance of Cinecittà was an American producer: Sam Zimbalist. Like Clare Boothe Luce, he belongs to the category of characters that are sometimes referred to as "larger than life". To him, no project ever seemed too big. Especially when he was dealing with movies. He liked big spaces and vast scenery. He had just produced *King Solomon's Mines,* with Deborah Kerr in the female lead, in Africa. As soon as that film had finished, he launched a new project of gigantic proportions: adapting Sienkiewicz's biblical novel, *Quo Vadis,* which recounts the persecution of Christians during the time of Emperor Nero. It had been a dream of all Hollywood producers for years. Of course, the difficulty lies in the sets and the extras. The action takes place in the Rome of Nero, between the palaces of the Palatine and the Circus Maximus. Tens of thousands of Romans were supposed to furnish the crowd scenes. Not to mention that one of the key scenes was the burning of the city. Originally written for Elizabeth Taylor and Gregory Peck, the screenplay had never been shot.

Zimbalist had the brilliant idea to shoot the film in Rome. The Italian studios had suffered from bombing during the war, but they were still standing and the labour force was far less expensive than in California. As Elizabeth Taylor and Gregory Peck were no longer available, they were replaced by Deborah Kerr and Robert Taylor. Two amazing actors, who would go on to find fame, made their debut in this film: Sophia Loren played a slave and Bud Spencer, the future hero of the Spaghetti Western, was cast as a Praetorian guard. On its release in 1951, *Quo Vadis* earnt record profits. The era of the movie epic had arrived. And in a few months, Rome became one of the world capitals of cinema. In a strange twist of fate, Zimbalist – who would later die from a heart attack during the shooting of *Ben-Hur* in Rome – married Mary Taylor in 1954; she was the niece and heiress of Dorothy di Frasso.

In 1953, the year of Clare Boothe Luce's arrival, there was another film promoting the Italian capital on cinema screens all over the world. Also shot in

Facing page: *Gold Bulgari handbag bought by the actor Rossano Brazzi for his wife.*

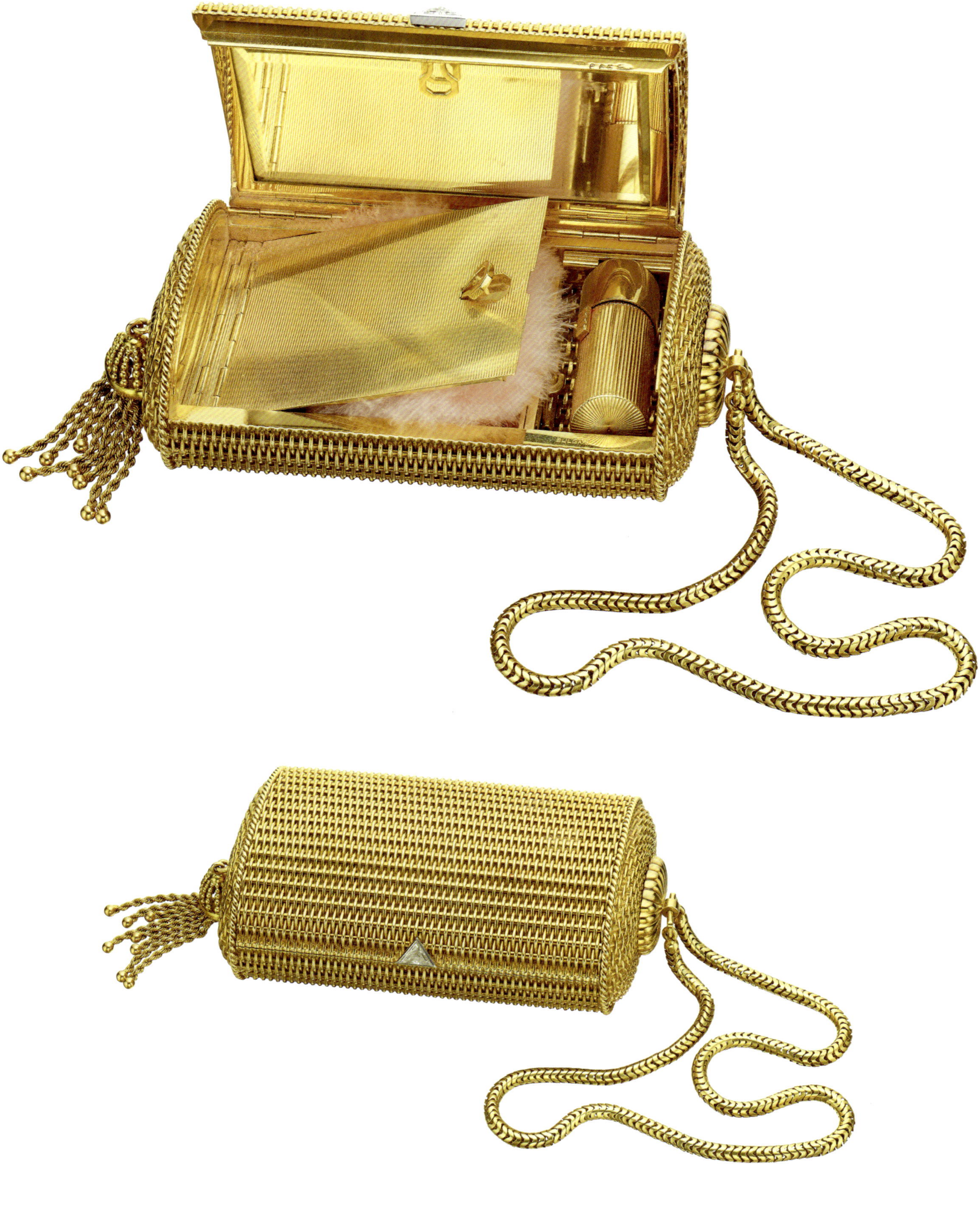

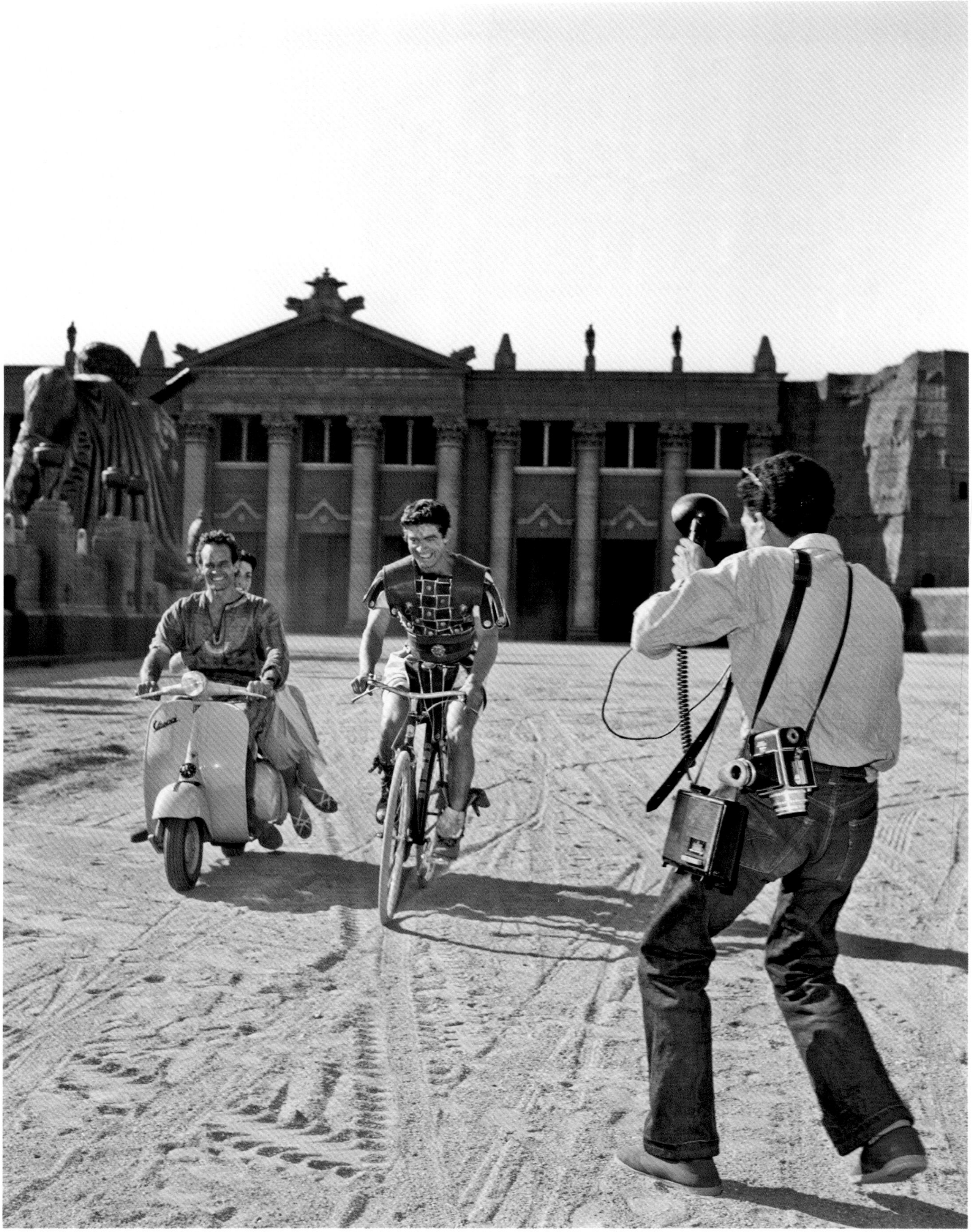

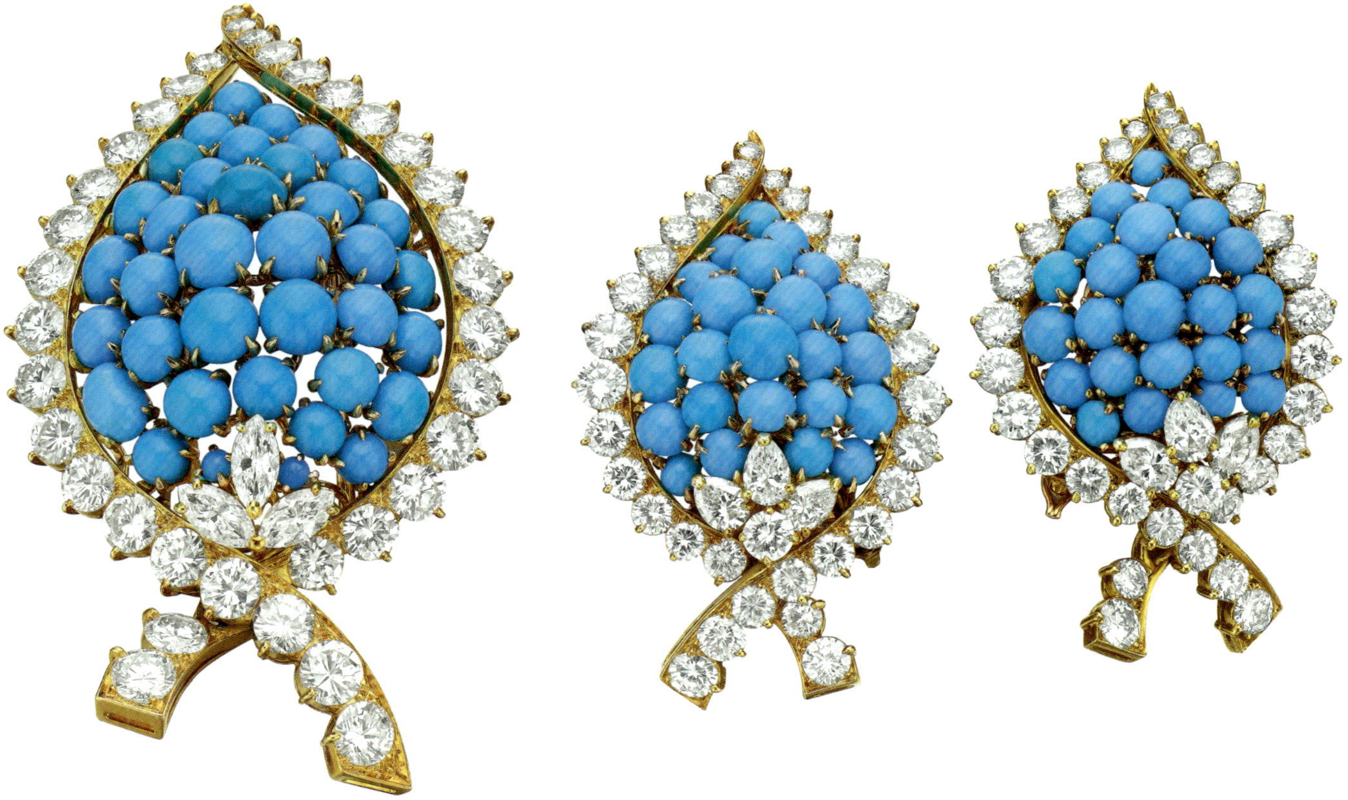

Rome, but in natural settings, this film was an early outing for the young actress Audrey Hepburn; it was, of course, *Roman Holiday.* It was a long and amazing advertisement for the wonders of the city. Audrey Hepburn and her co-star Gregory Peck, took walks along the Spanish Steps, St Peter's Square and some scenes were shot in the Colonna Palace and the most picturesque streets of the city.

Over the next ten years Audrey Hepburn would shoot several films at Cinecittà. The most surprising was *War and Peace* with the director King Vidor. Her two co-stars in that film were Henry Fonda and the young, good-looking and very romantic actor, Mel Ferrer. He would go on to become her husband. This time, the scenes were not shot in the ancient city of Rome but under the fake Russian sky of early 19th-century Moscow created by Cinecittà.

At the same time, Bulgari was undergoing some major changes. Sotirio's two sons, Giorgio and Costantino, were still in command, but this era also saw the arrival of the third generation of Bulgaris. Giorgio's sons, Gianni, Paolo and Nicola, and Costantino's daughters, Anna and Marina, gradually joined the team. The House of Bulgari had become an institution of life in Rome. The shop on Via dei Condotti had become a sort of club where one could buy jewellery and precious objects, but which was also part of the worldly ritual of the rich and famous, whether they were from Rome or were wealthy tourists. *"All the hotels were full,"* remembers Nicola Bulgari. *"The Excelsior on Via Veneto was the place to be. Rome had become a way of life with its rituals. The evenings usually started with a drink on the terrace of the Hotel Hassler. Afterwards, there were dinners, balls, evenings. And of course, the women were very elegant and wore jewellery. At this time, our shop of the Via Condotti was a social rendezvous."* [3]

Anna Bulgari, who joined the house in 1953, has a clear memory of this period of elegance: *"A man would never have entered the shop without being in a suit and tie. The women were all wearing make-up, often with hats and of course gloves. Among those who impressed me the most, I remember Princess Lilian of Belgium, the second wife of King Leopold III. She was perfectly dressed. I still have the vision of her clothes and yet it happened 60 years ago. She was in white and beige, bordering on fawn. All the accessories, the gloves, the handbag, the shoes, were perfect. It was truly a vision of refinement. I also remember Nina*

Facing page: *Stephen Boyd and Charlton Heston on the set of* Ben-Hur *at Cinecittà, Rome.* Ben-Hur *was an enormous box-office success.*
Above: *Pair of turquoise and diamond earrings and a matching brooch, which were bought from Bulgari by actor Rossano Brazzi for his wife.*

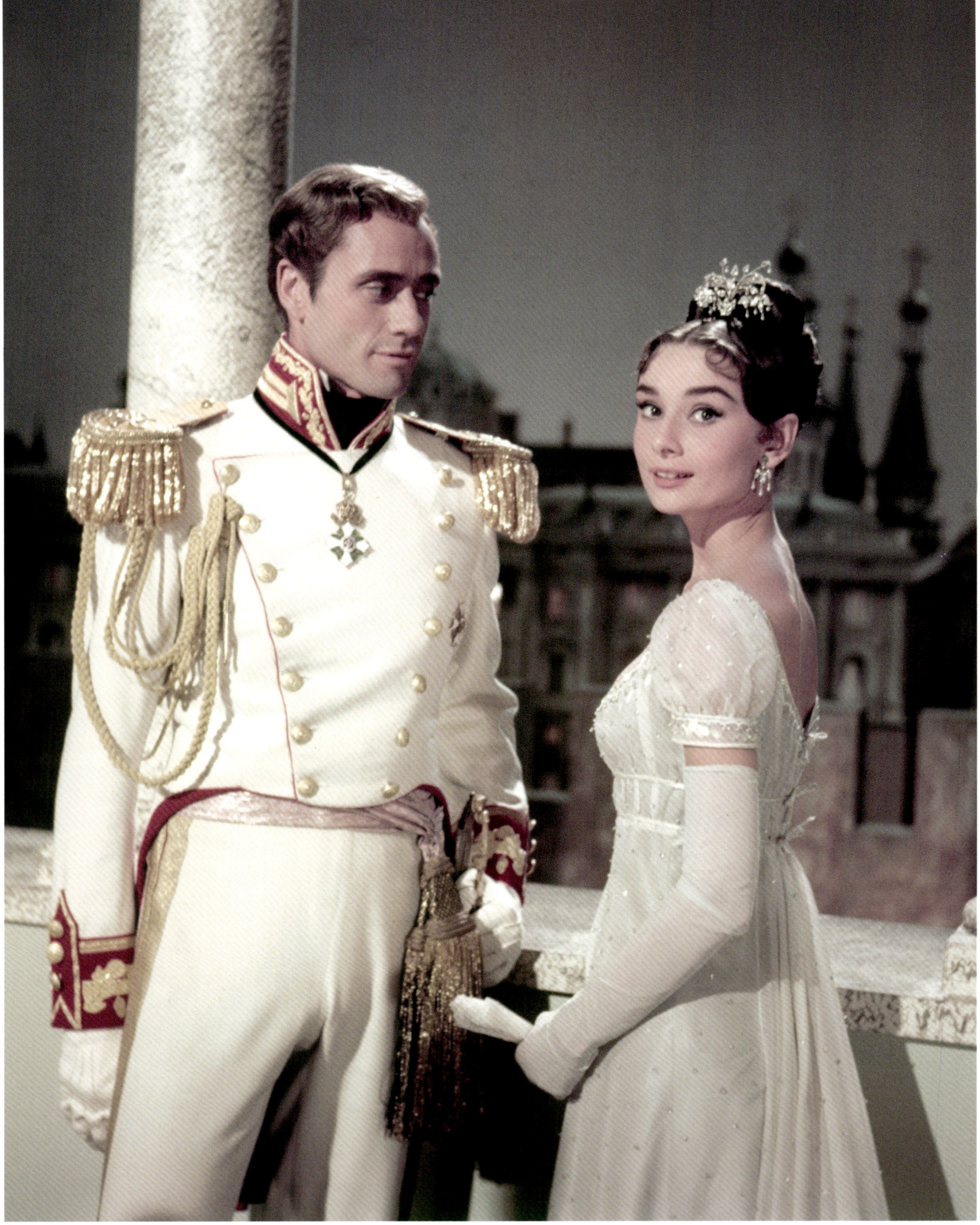

Dyer, a famous model who had married Baron Thyssen and Prince Sadruddin Aga Khan. And of course, later, there was Marella Agnelli." [4]

Vincenza Tomassi, who began working at Bulgari after the war, was another witness of this whirlwind: *"Among all those who were my clients at Bulgari, there were so many cinema and theatre actors that I can hardly remember all of them: Kirk Douglas, Orson Welles, Rock Hudson, Audrey Hepburn, Marlene Dietrich ... Kirk Douglas came with an actress Pier Angeli, who he wanted to marry. He gave her a diamond ring and she bought him a gold pendant, a small reproduction of Michelangelo's* Moses.*"* [5]

Unfortunately, the marriage never took place. Kirk Douglas would marry Anne Buydens in 1954. Pier Angeli would experience a tragic love story with James Dean before she died prematurely in 1971, at the age of 39, almost certainly from drug poisoning. Another love story that would lead to nothing, was that of Rock Hudson and Phyllis Gates. *"He was very beautiful and very attractive,"* remembers Vincenza Tomassi. *"He bought a gift for his secretary, whom he later married. And this made many of my colleagues laugh."* [6] The marriage of Phyllis Gates and Rock Hudson would be a disaster. It was orchestrated by Hudson's agent, in order to dispel the rumours of his homosexuality. Phyllis demanded a divorce in 1957. Rock Hudson died of AIDS in 1985. His highly publicised death greatly contributed to the global awareness of the need for medical research to fight this disease.

Clare Boothe Luce was a member of this extremely sophisticated universe. Not only did she know all the American celebrities whom she received at the Embassy, but she was also invited to the more conservative receptions given by the aristocracy of Rome. On 14 March, 1954, the Prince and the Princess of Civitella-Cesi held a party at Palazzo Torlonia to celebrate their eldest daughter, Sandra's 18th birthday. All the aristocracy of Rome was there, and the guest of honour was the birthday girl's grandmother, Queen Victoria Eugenie of Spain. Clare Boothe Luce, who was accompanied by her husband, was one of the few ladies not wearing a tiara that evening. Maybe it was in anticipation of this ball that she made one of her most sumptuous orders at Bulgari. Early in 1954, she acquired a necklace of 27 emeralds mounted on a diamond net. According to her biographer, Silvia Jukes Morris, one of the reasons she bought this jewel was to stand out amongst the Roman princesses who all had sumptuous jewels. It seems that a year later she acquired a second necklace. This one was composed of diamonds and drawn on a model very similar to the papyrus flower necklace created for Dorothy di Frasso in 1939. Clare Boothe Luce wore it during the farewell party she threw at the end of December in 1956. After attending the first act of *Iris* by Mascagni at the opera house, *"La Luce"* went to the fountain of Trevi. Bedecked in evening dress, fur stole and diamond necklace, she threw a coin into the fountain; according to tradition, this would ensure her to return to the Italian capital. Strangely, this diamond necklace does not appear in the catalogue of the Sotheby's sale of her jewellery after her death in 1987.

The incessant whirlwind of celebrities going in and

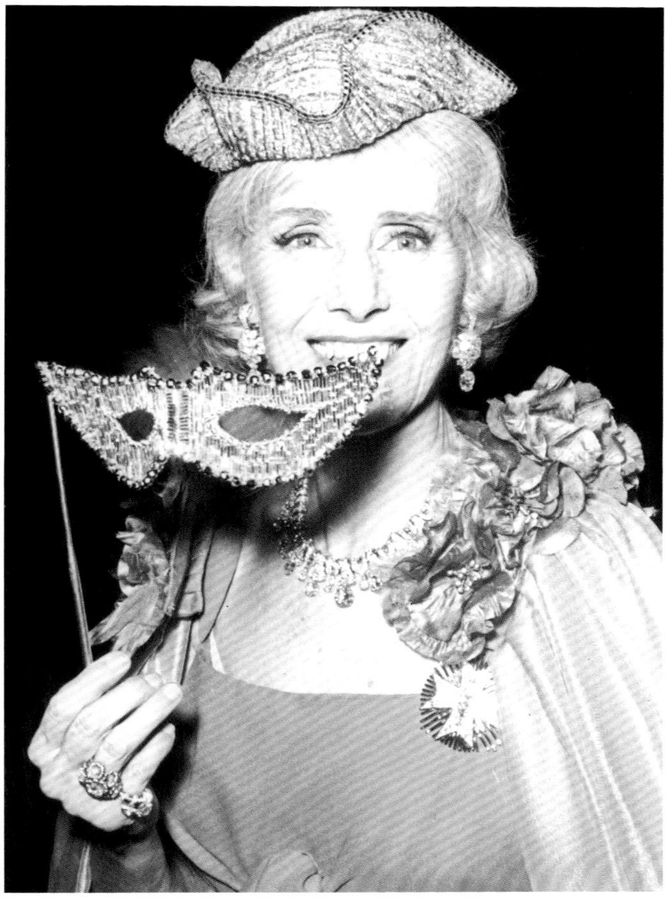

Facing page: *Mel Ferrer and his wife Audrey Hepburn on the set of* War and Peace, *which was shot at Cinecittà in 1955. Both were Bulgari customers.* **Above:** *Ambassador Clare Boothe Luce at a ball in 1967. She is wearing a Bulgari diamond necklace very similar to the one created for Dorothy di Frasso in 1939.*

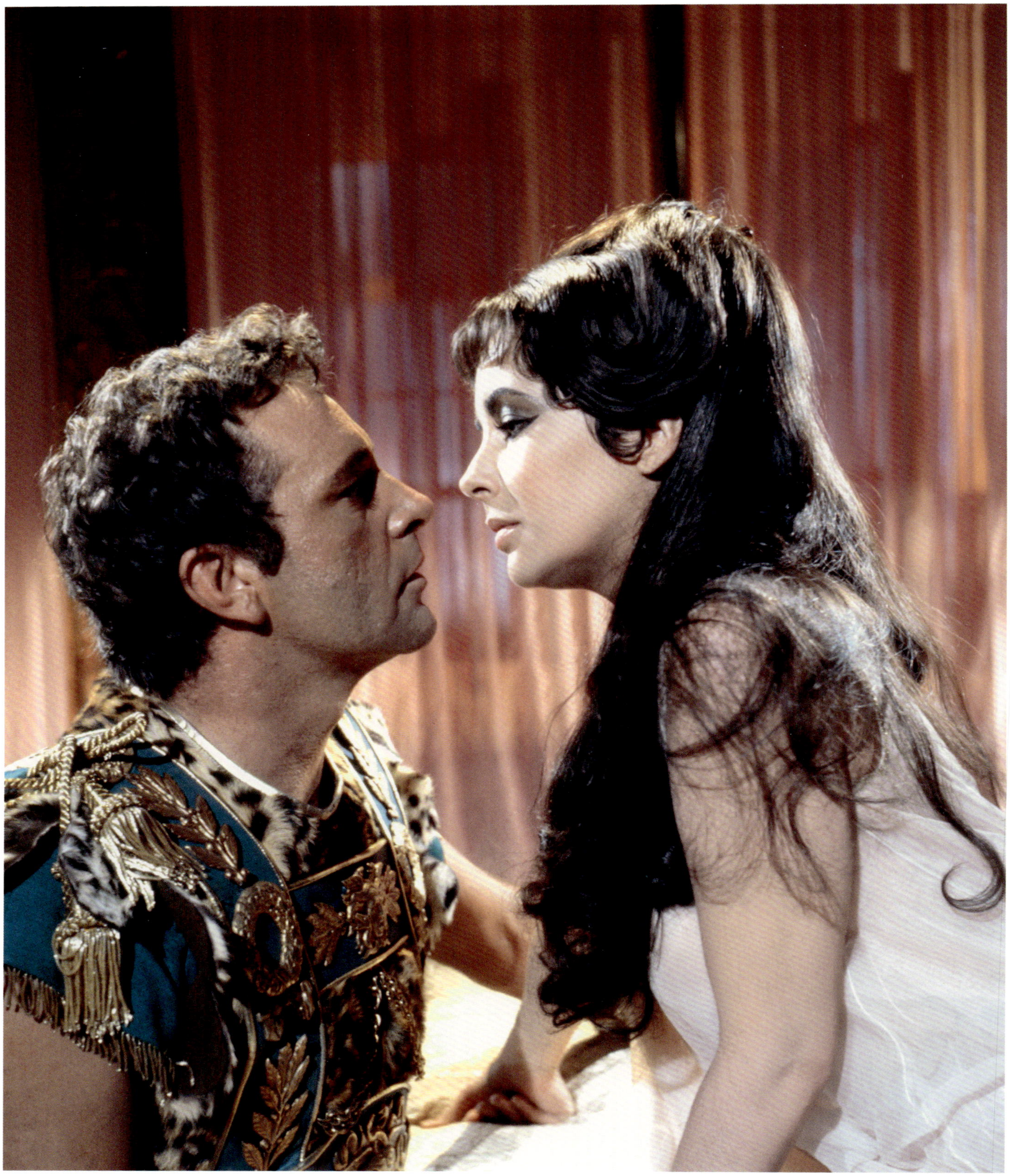

Above. *Elizabeth Taylor and Richard Burton in* Cleopatra, *which was shot in Rome in 1962.* **Facing Page:** *Gold and turquoise hand mirror made by Bulgari in 1962 during the filming of* Cleopatra. *The mirror was probably given as a gift to Elizabeth Taylor by the production company. Bulgari Heritage Collection.*

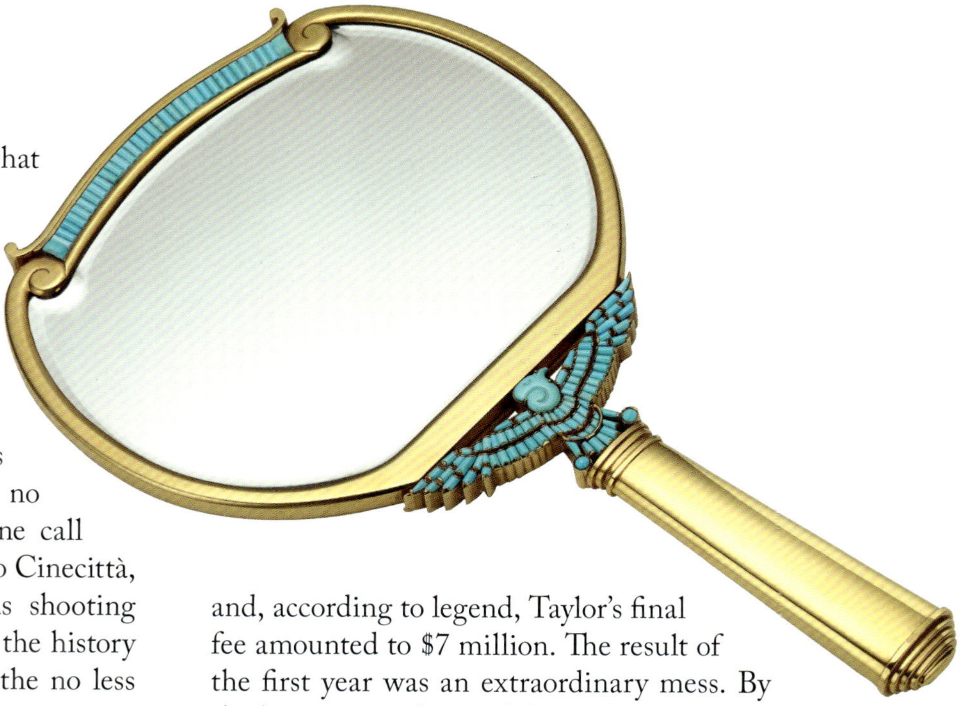

out of Bulgari during those years meant that staff had to show an exceptional sense of diplomacy. The side exit, opening into the inner courtyard, was not only useful for fleeing the paparazzi who were waiting in the street, but also sometimes to avoid crossing paths with a husband, wife, lover or mistress. In her book of memoirs, Vincenza Tomassi, remembers the famous year of 1962, during which, no doubt in January, she received a telephone call from Richard Burton asking her to come to Cinecittà, bringing jewellery. The Welsh actor was shooting the most famous and costly epic movie in the history of cinema, the legendary *Cleopatra,* with the no less legendary Elizabeth Taylor. The film and its two stars would leave glittering footsteps through the history of Rome and Bulgari. At the time, Burton was married to Welsh actress, Sybil Williams (1929-2013). Taylor was already twice-divorced (Conrad "Nicky" Hilton and Michael Wilding), widowed (Mike Todd), and now married to singer Eddie Fisher (1928-2010). There had been an enormous scandal in the United States. The weekly television show that Eddie hosted was even cancelled at the request of viewers. The singer had been married to Debbie Reynolds, the beloved child of the American public. Taylor and Fisher's affair and subsequent marriage made both of them extremely unpopular.

For several months, the Burtons and Fishers had been making regular trips to Rome, depending on the vagaries of the filming schedule for *Cleopatra.* The escalating costs of this epic production that started two years earlier, were ruining 20th Century Fox. Filming had begun in London in September 1960, under the direction of a Hollywood veteran, Rouben Mamoulian, and it had been a disaster. The weather, marked by rain floods, proved to be abysmal and made the recreation of Egypt under the British skies entirely unreliable. Filming had never been completed. The British hairdressers went on strike when they learned that Elizabeth Taylor would only use her personal hairdresser. Then, the star became ill and had to stay in hospital in London for several weeks. Fortunately for her, she had signed an iron contract, which stipulated a a fee of $1 million with a limited time span of filming, and an additional sum for each week of delay. In the end, filming ran to three years and, according to legend, Taylor's final fee amounted to $7 million. The result of the first year was an extraordinary mess. By the beginning of 1961, Mamoulian has resigned. He left behind him barely ten minutes of usable film and $7 million of deficit on the planned budget. As it was too late to turn back, the producers decided to entrust the film to a somewhat younger director, Joseph Mankiewicz. A serious relapse of Elizabeth Taylor's pneumonia stopped the filming once again. Mankiewicz seized the opportunity to rewrite the script. Taylor's ill health helped restore her image in the eyes of the American public. The actress who was regarded as a homewrecker had become the victim, a woman bravely fighting illness.

That summer, the producers took a radical decision, they moved the filming to Rome. The entire team was summoned to the Italian capital for the month of September. However, neither the set nor the script was completed. The actors, the extras, the technicians, wandered the Italian capital living on their expense accounts in luxurious conditions. Elizabeth Taylor and Eddie Fisher settled in a Roman villa; Richard and Sybil Burton were living in an hotel. The first scenes were finally shot in December. Against all odds, the two lead actors, who already knew each other and did not greatly appreciate each other, were finally getting on well. A little too well if one believed the rumours circulating Rome.

When Vincenza Tomassi arrived at Cinecittà to meet Burton: *"It was Elizabeth Taylor who opened the door (of the dressing room). (...) They chose a pair of earrings in emeralds and diamonds. I gave them a special price within the limit of the reduction I was allowed to offer, but Richard Burton wanted a better deal. So I had to talk to Giorgio Bulgari. I went to via Condotti leaving*

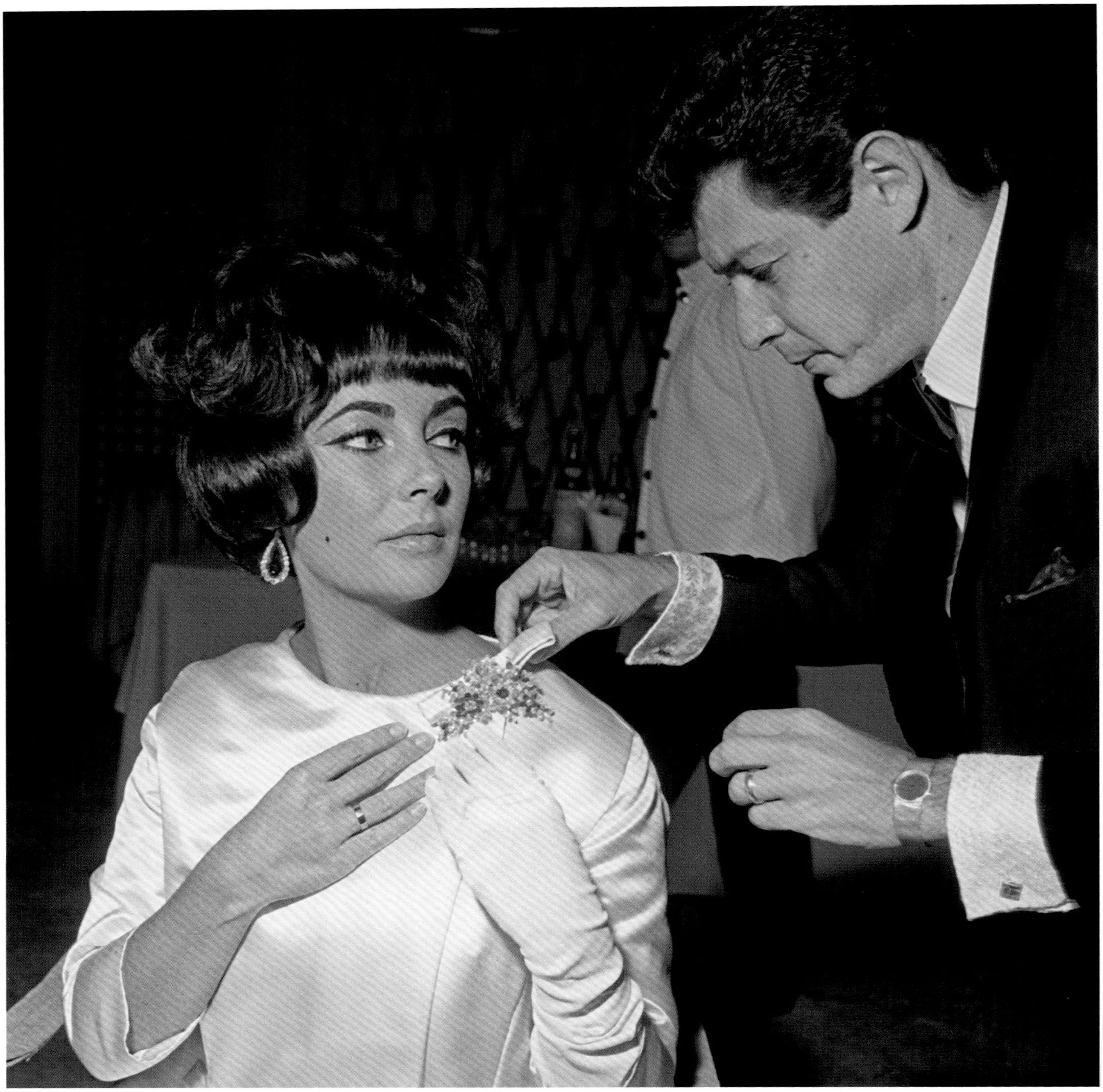

Above: *Elizabeth Taylor and her third husband, Eddie Fisher in Rome in 1961. She is wearing her Bulgari emerald and diamond flower brooch and earrings.*
Facing page: *The yellow and white diamond flower brooch bought from Bulgari by Eddie Fisher in 1961. It was sold at Christie's, New York in December 2011. Private collection.*

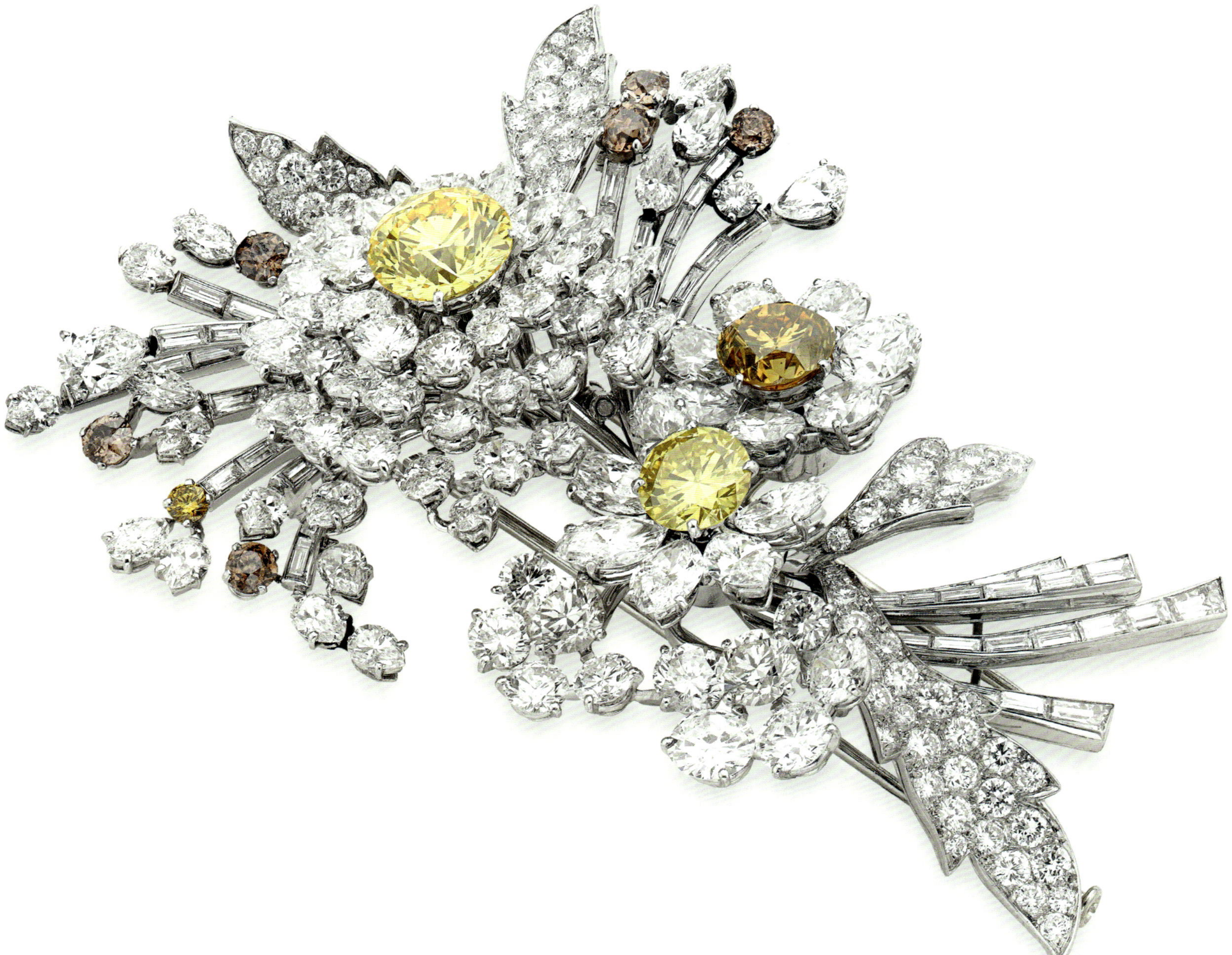

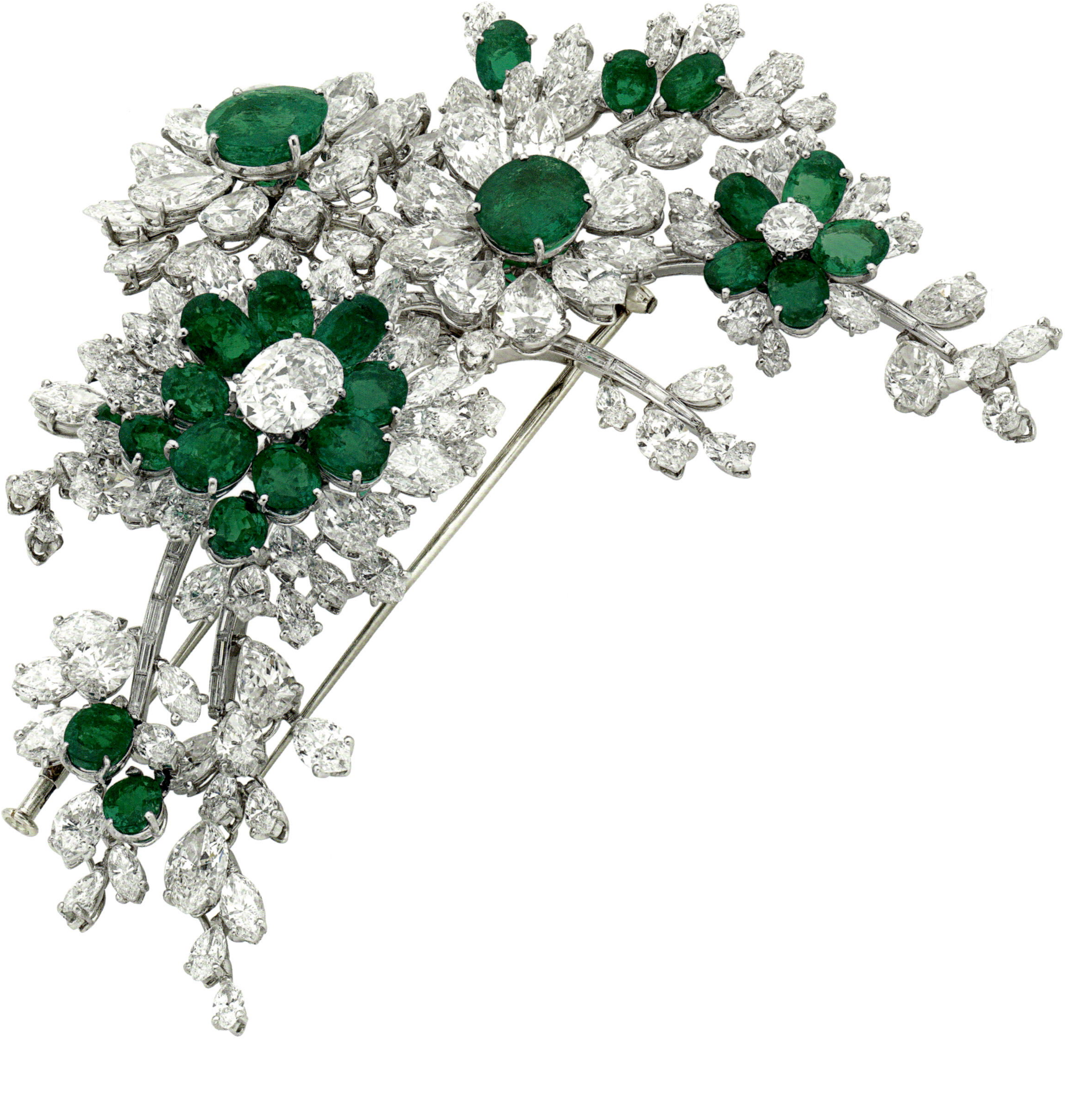

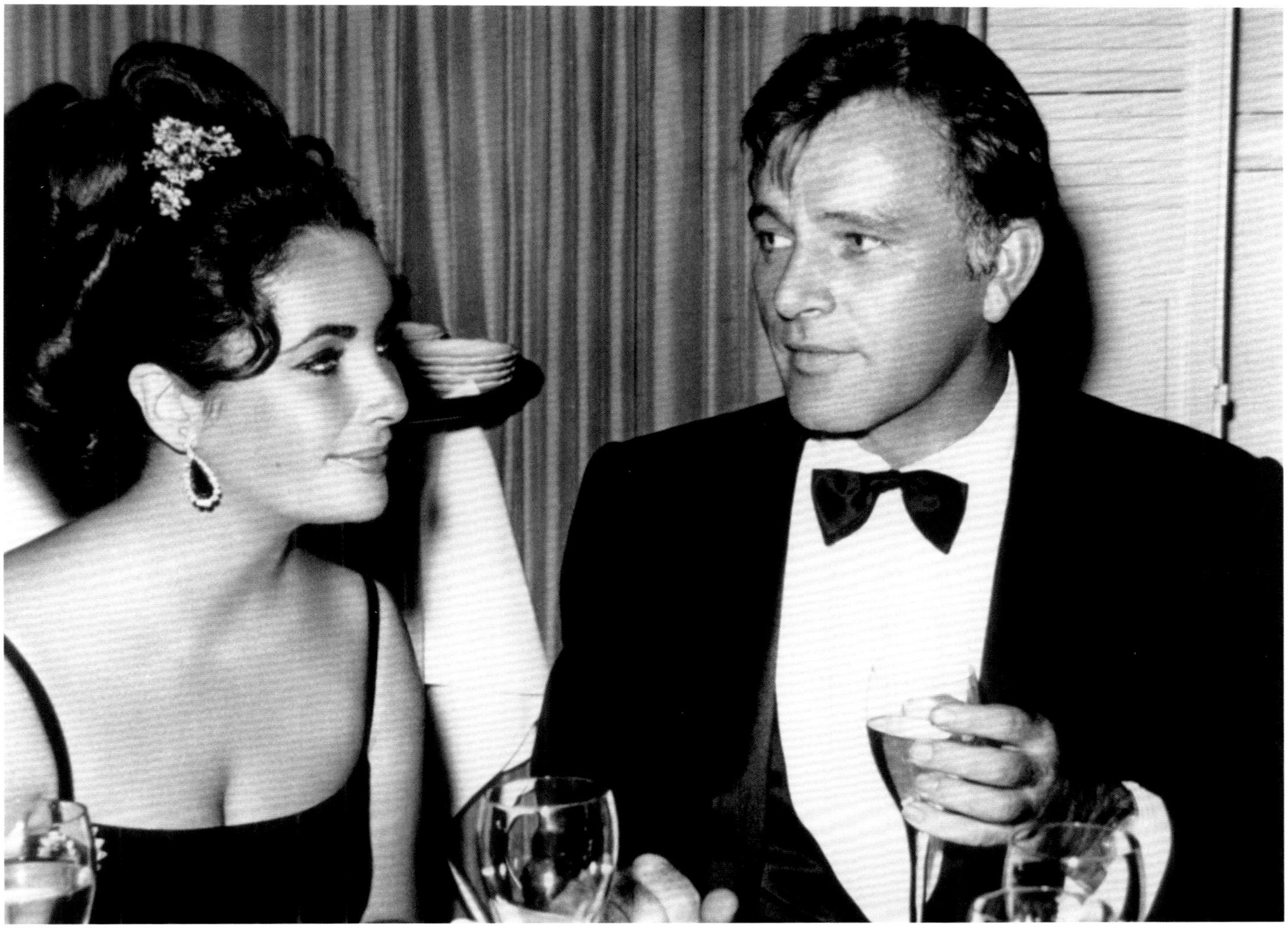

all the jewels I had brought with me on the table. 'Mrs. Tomassi' said Richard Burton *'You trust me that much?' 'Of course' I told him. 'If I cannot trust you, whom can I trust?' I returned an hour later and sold them a beautiful emerald and diamond ring. But two days later, I received a call from the shop in my office. A lady asked to speak to me. She was beautiful and elegant. 'I'm Sybil Burton,' she said, pointing to the ring I had sold. It was too big."* [7]

Photographs of the time show that by January 1962, Elizabeth Taylor already owned several Bulgari pieces. She attended the David di Donatello awards ceremony – the Italian equivalent of the Oscars – with Eddie Fisher. She was wearing her Bulgari emerald and diamond earrings, as well as a flower brooch and a bracelet set with the same stones. It is also certain that Eddie Fisher was aware of Bulgari, as three weeks later, he gave Elizabeth a yellow and white diamond parure, comprising a second flower brooch, a ring and a pair of earrings, set with two lemon-yellow pear-shaped diamonds of 15.60 and 15.38 carats for her 30th birthday All these jewels were signed Bulgari. By this point, Elizabeth and Burton had already started their legendary love affair, but they had agreed to remain discreet until filming had ended. *"Not because of the press,"* says Elizabeth in her book *My Love Affair with Jewelry*, *"but because of Sybil who is still married to Burton."* [8] However, according to Elizabeth Taylor, it seems that Eddie Fisher, who left his wife a few months later, decided not to settle the bill for his sumptuous gift. *"I received an invoice for the jewelry,"* she tells. *"Have I settled it? Mmm ... probably."* [9]

Facing page: *The emerald and diamond flower brooch bought for, or possibly by, Elizabeth Taylor from Bulgari in 1962. It was sold at Christie's New York in December 2011. Bulgari Heritage Collection.* **Above:** *Elizabeth Taylor and her fourth husband Richard Burton. She is wearing her Bulgari emerald and diamond earrings and the flower brooch pinned in her hair.*

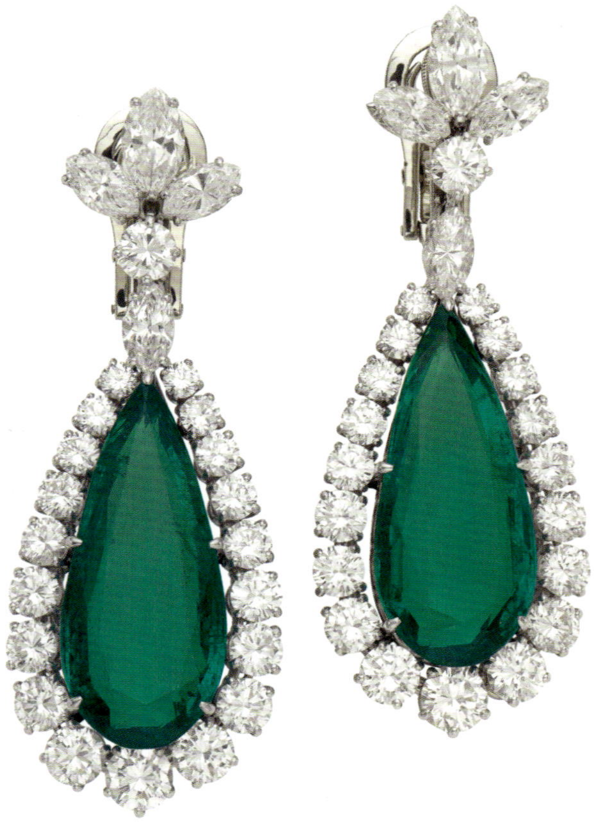

The emerald and diamond earrings bought from Bulgari for, or by, Elizabeth Taylor (wearing them in the picture opposite) circa 1961. They were sold at Christie's, New York in December 2011. Private collection.

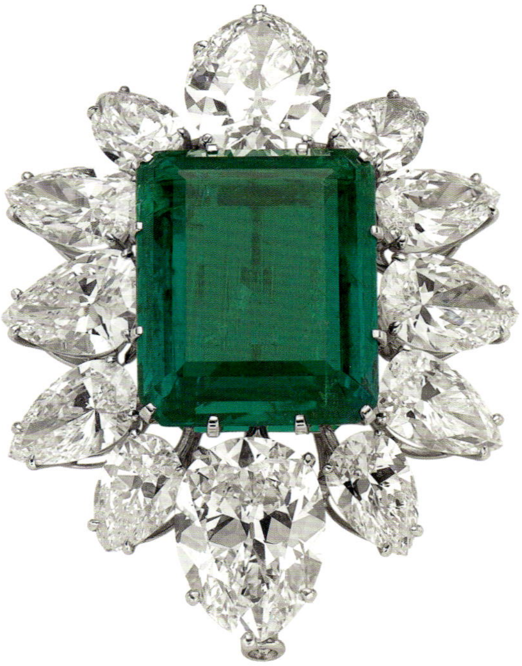

Above: *The emerald and diamond pendant/brooch purchased by Richard Burton from Bulgari. This piece must have been bought before 1962 as Miss Taylor wore it during the filming of* The VIPs *that same year. It was sold at Christie's, New York in December 2011.*
Facing page: *Elizabeth Taylor sparkling in her Bulgari diamond and emerald earrings and brooch/pendant.*

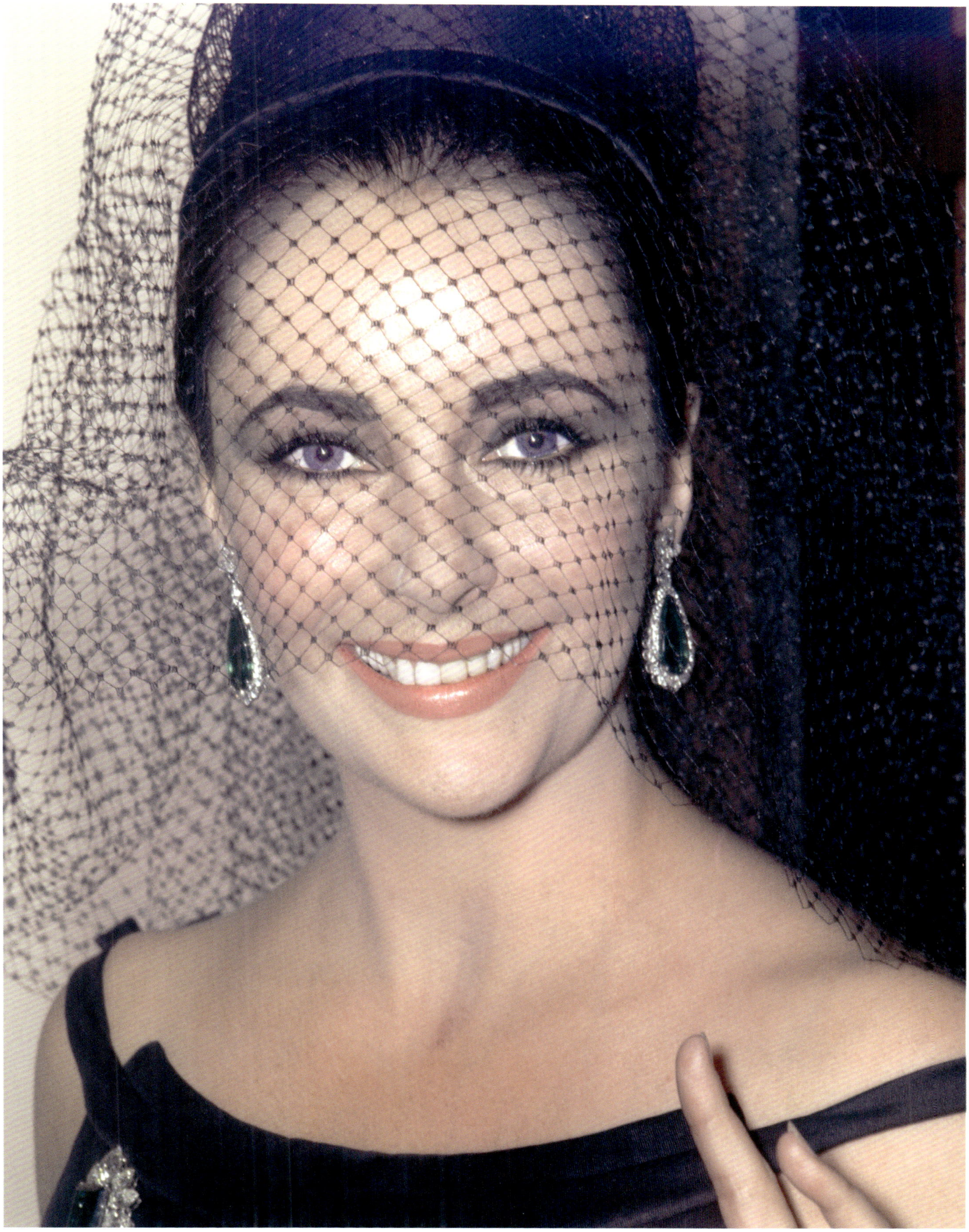

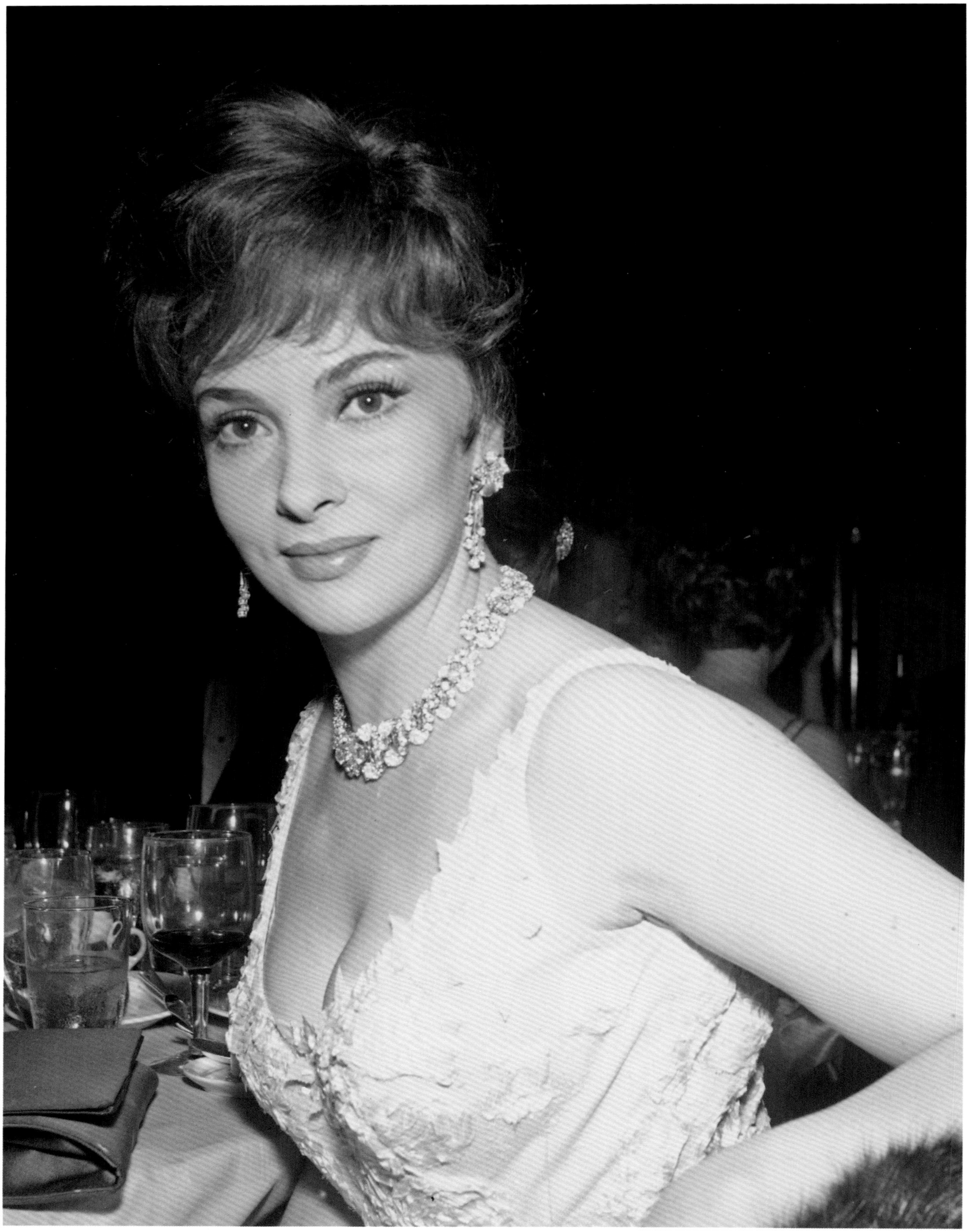

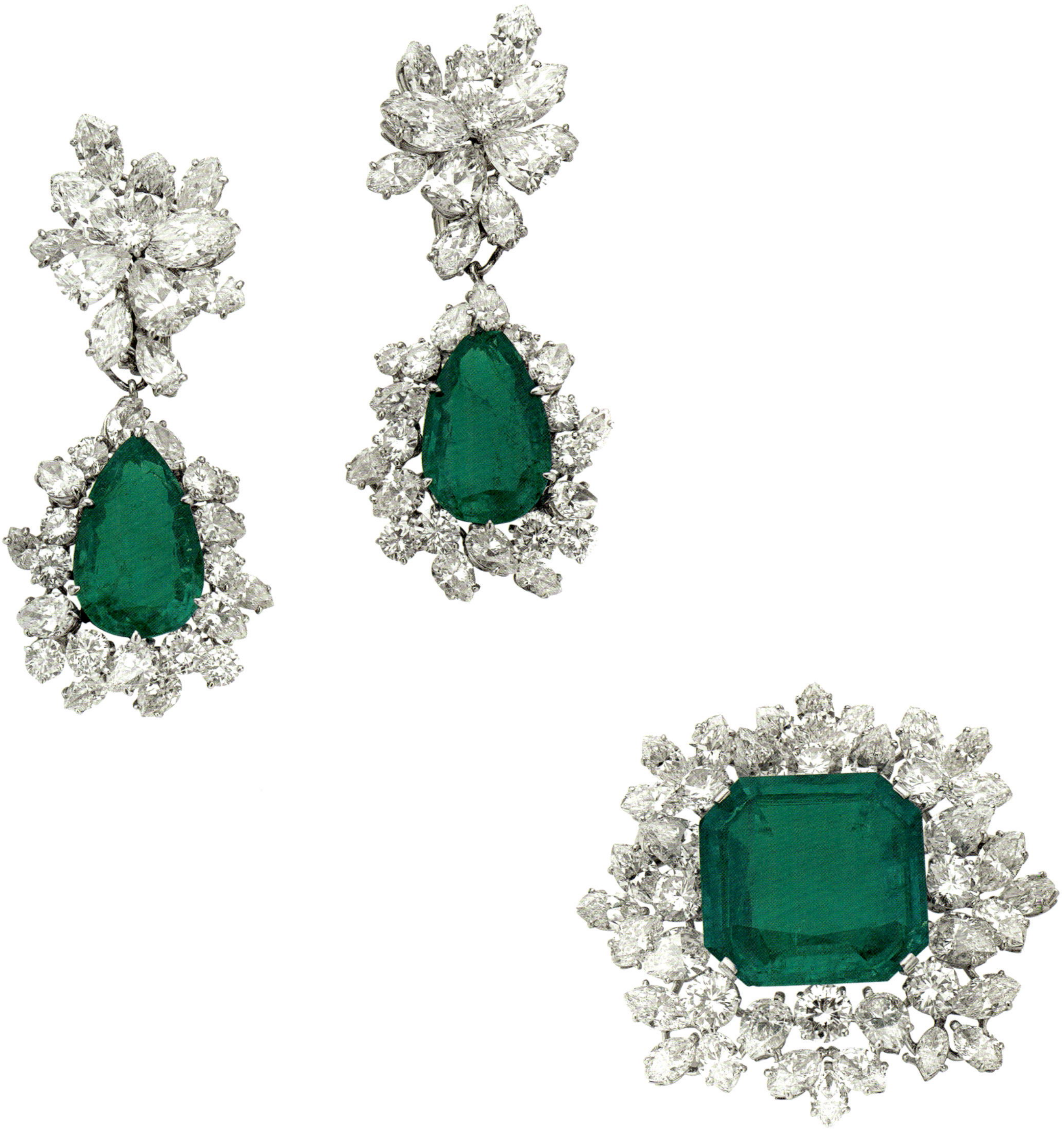

Above: *The emerald and diamond earrings (Bulgari Heritage Collection) and brooch (Private collection) bought from Bulgari by Gina Lollobrigida. They were sold at Sotheby's, Geneva in 2013.*
Facing page: *Gina Lollobrigida wearing her Bulgari diamond necklace.*

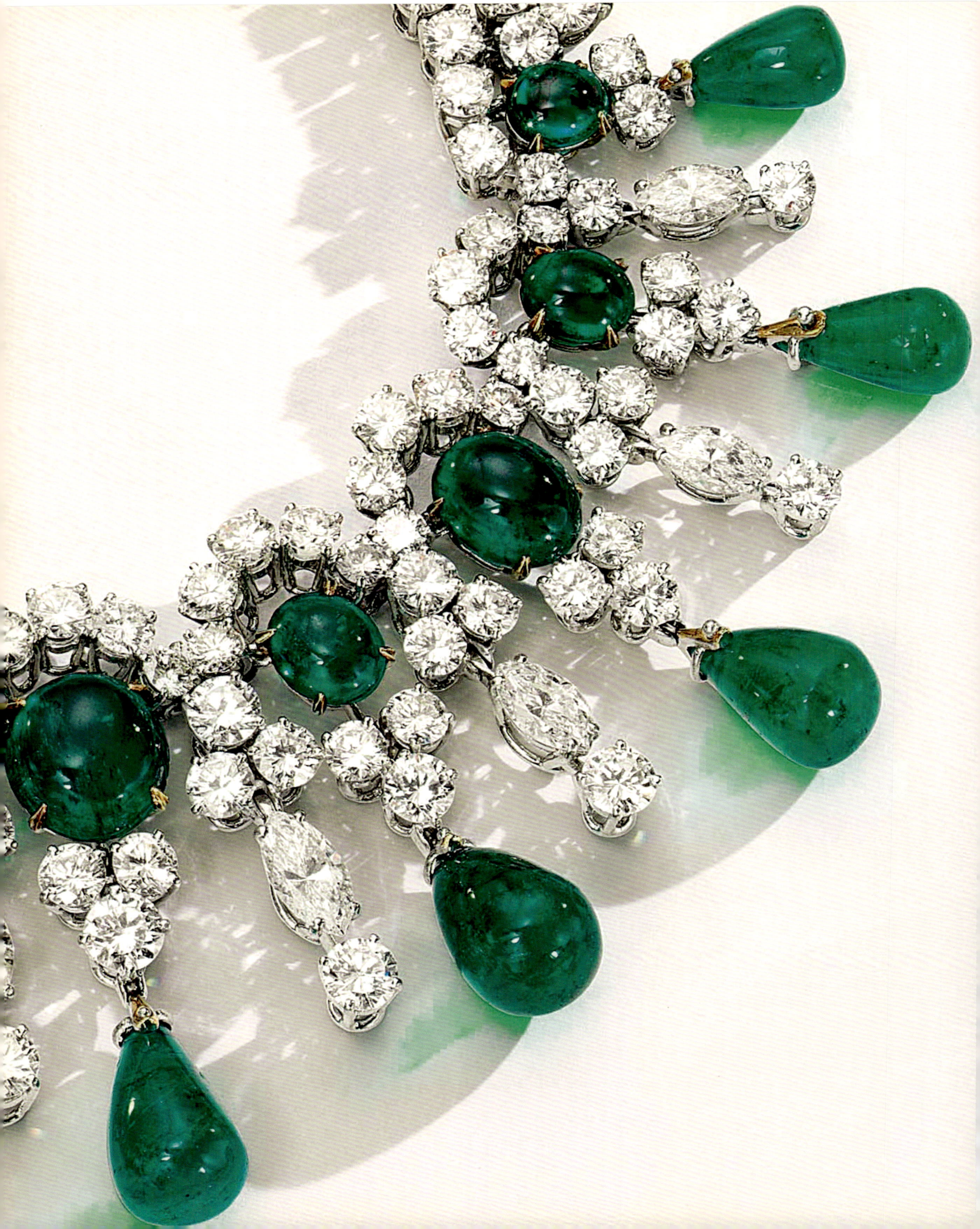

Chapter 8

THE QUEEN OF NEW YORK'S EMERALDS

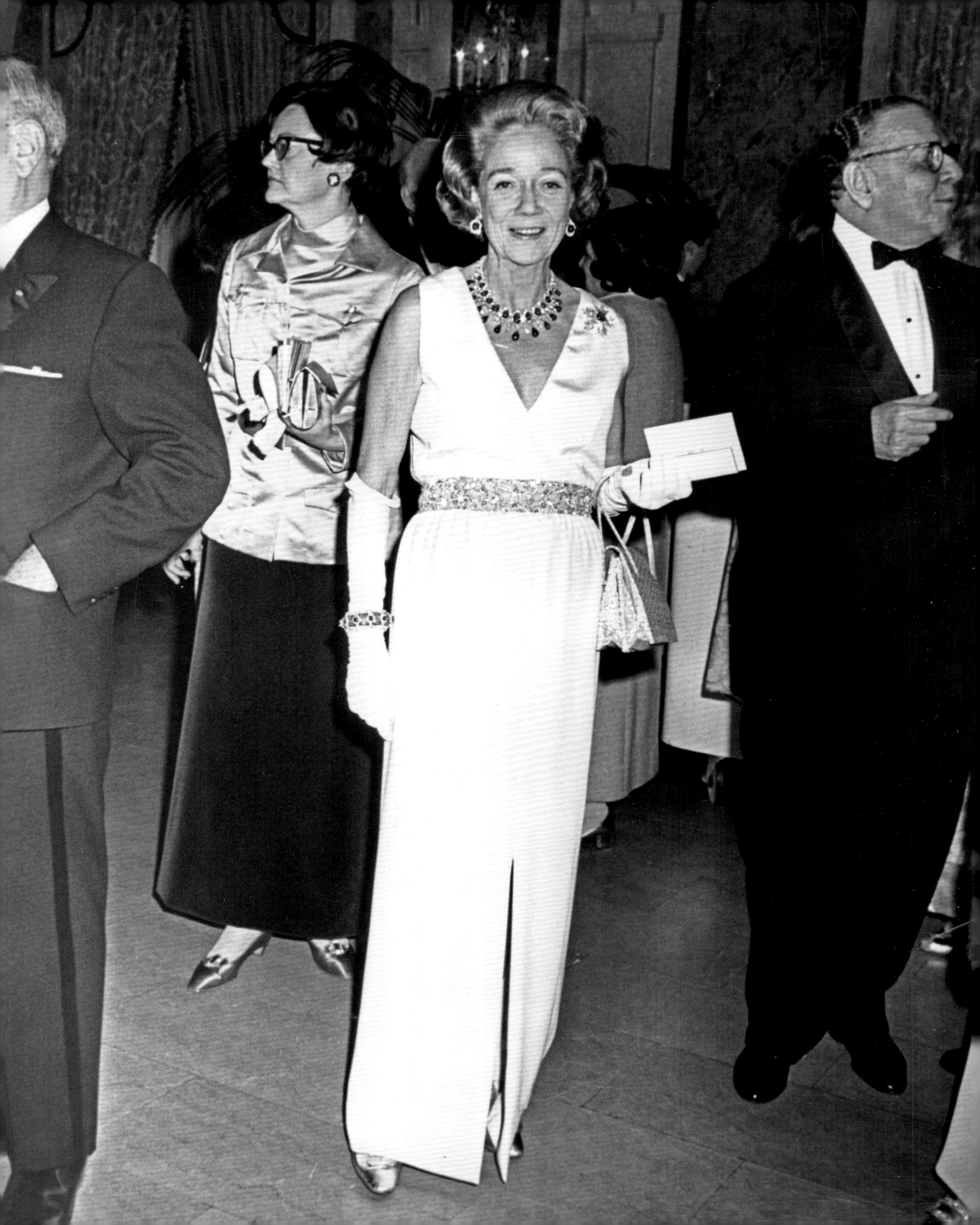

London, Autumn 1958.

Giorgio Bulgari had travelled from Rome for this exceptional client. Vincent Astor (1891-1959) was staying in London for a few weeks. This was not one of those wealthy Americans to whom Bulgari could send a salesman, even an exceptional one. This was one of the richest billionaires in the United States, almost a legend. He belonged to the most ancient and illustrious American dynasty: the Astors. His grandmother, Caroline, "*The* Mrs Astor" as she was referred to, had been the first lady of New York high society at the end of the 19th century. An imperious matriarch who issued decrees on worldly life in Manhattan. Haughty, elegant and always covered with jewels, she had laid down the first rules of American society. Her "reign" had begun at the end of the Civil War, when her husband, William Backhouse Astor Jr., had built an imposing mansion at 350 Fifth Avenue. He had chosen this site partly because his elder brother, John Jacob Astor, had settled right next door in a no less sumptuous home.

The centre of power in William Astor's house was the ballroom. In fact, Mrs Astor had placed a special condition on the architect: "her" ballroom should hold a maximum of 400 people. This was the limit of the elegant society that she had imagined. With the help of her friend, Samuel Ward McAllister, self-proclaimed supreme arbiter of elegance, she had undertaken to draw up an exhaustive list of these 400 people. Rumours of her plan spread quickly through the city and gaining entry to Mrs Astor's 400 Club became the ambition of all American multimillionaires. And especially of their wives. It took over twenty years for the ambitious Alva Vanderbilt to enter this closed circle.

Mrs Astor's snobbery had become such, that when her brother-in-law and neighbour, John Jacob Astor died in 1890, his son and heir, William Waldorf Astor, decided against living in his parents' house because he did not want to live so close to his aunt. Moreover, he left the United States to settle in England where he eventually became a viscount. To annoy his aunt, he had torn down his parents' home and in its place built the 13-storey Waldorf Hotel. His scheme was a grand success. After four years of living next door to the hotel's guests, Mrs Astor chose to move out and abandon her legendary ballroom. To annoy her nephew in return, she had her home pulled down and had her own hotel built on the plot: the Astoria. The two establishments would eventually merge to become the Waldorf-Astoria Hotel, which would be destroyed in 1929, to make way for the Empire State Building.

The turbulent saga of the American Astors did not stop with the death of Caroline in 1908. Her son John Jacob IV (Vincent's father) had an equally troubled fate. At the death of his father in 1892, he had inherited millions of dollars in property. A bit of a dabbler, he had invented several gadgets, including

Facing page: *Brooke Astor (1902-2007) the legendary society queen of New York. She is wearing the emerald and diamond necklace ordered by her husband at Bulgari a few months before his death.* **Previous page:** *Brooke Astor's Bulgari emerald and diamond necklace.*

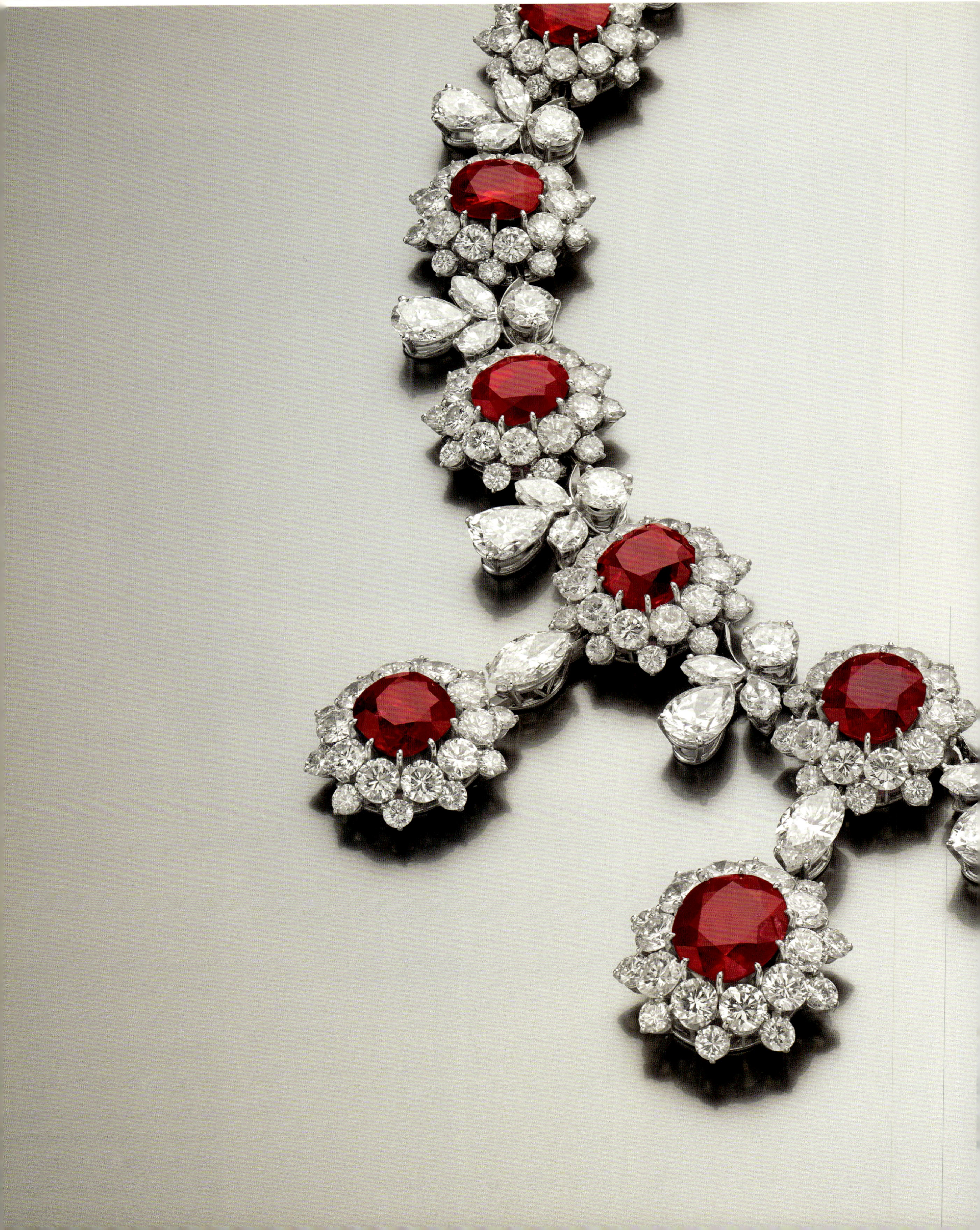

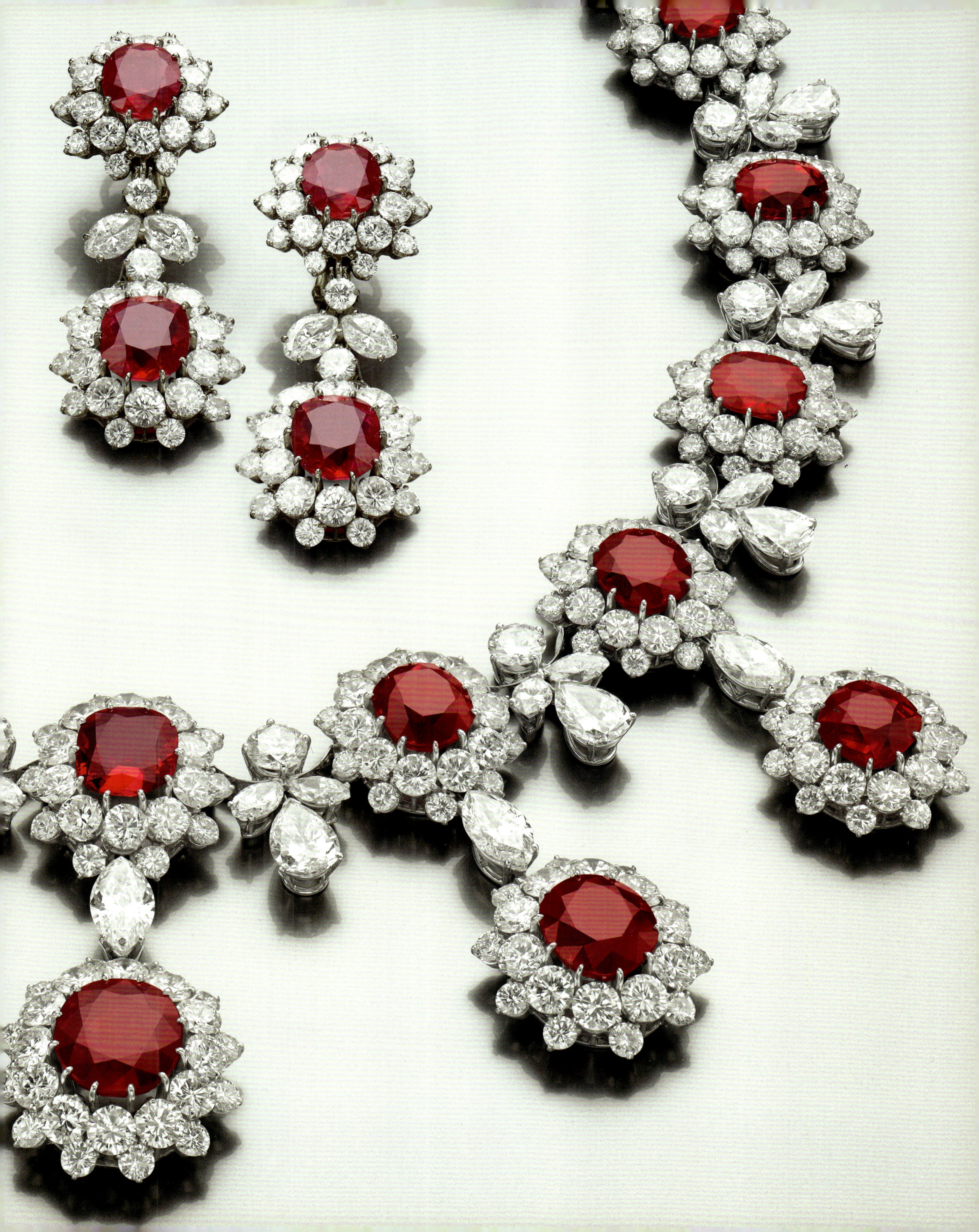

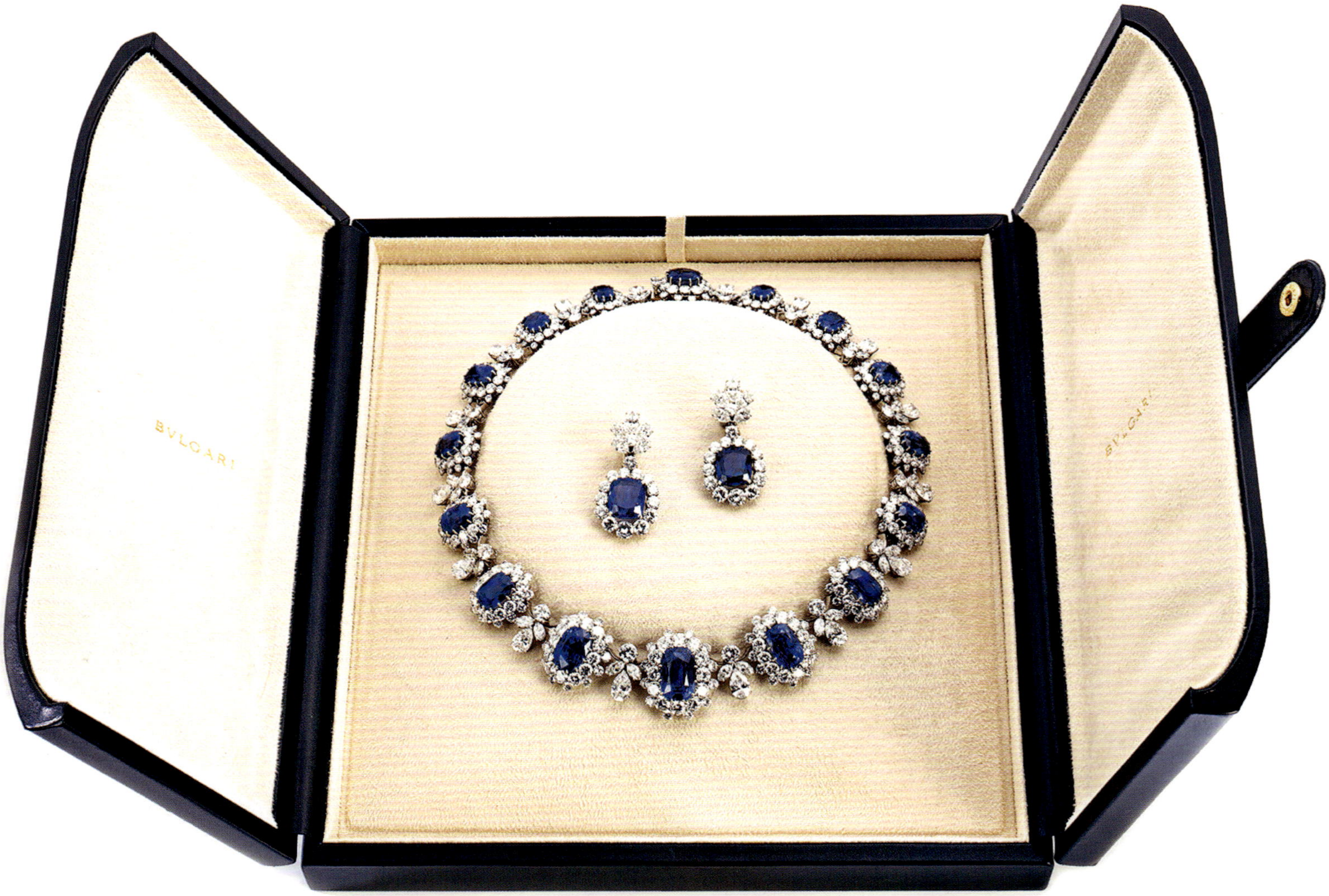

Previous page: *Ruby and diamond necklace created in 1962 for Princess Elvina Pallavicini. The set also includes a pair of earrings. Private collection.*
Above and facing page: *Sapphire and diamond parure in the same design. It was sold at Hampel Fine Art Auctions in Munich, June 2014.*

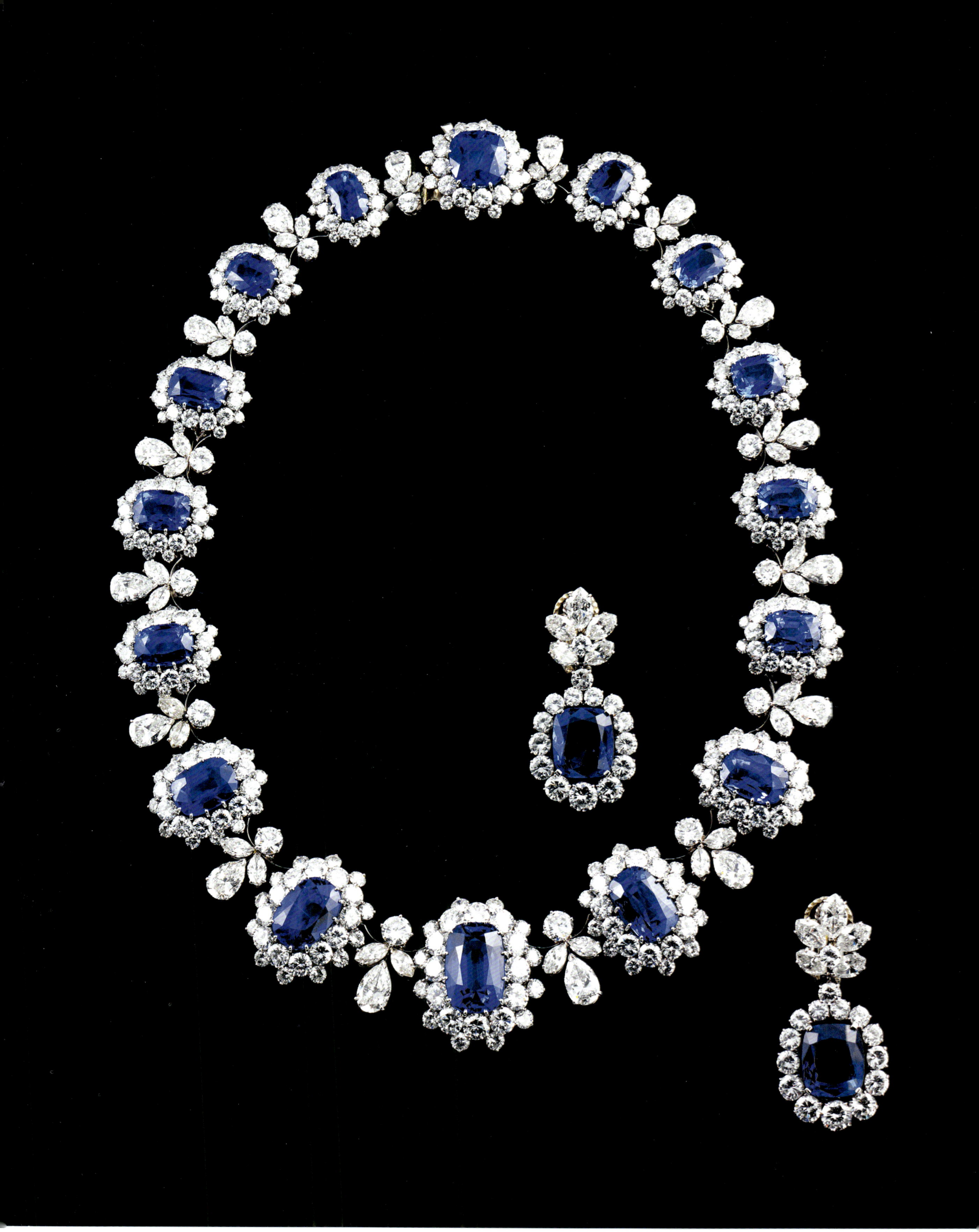

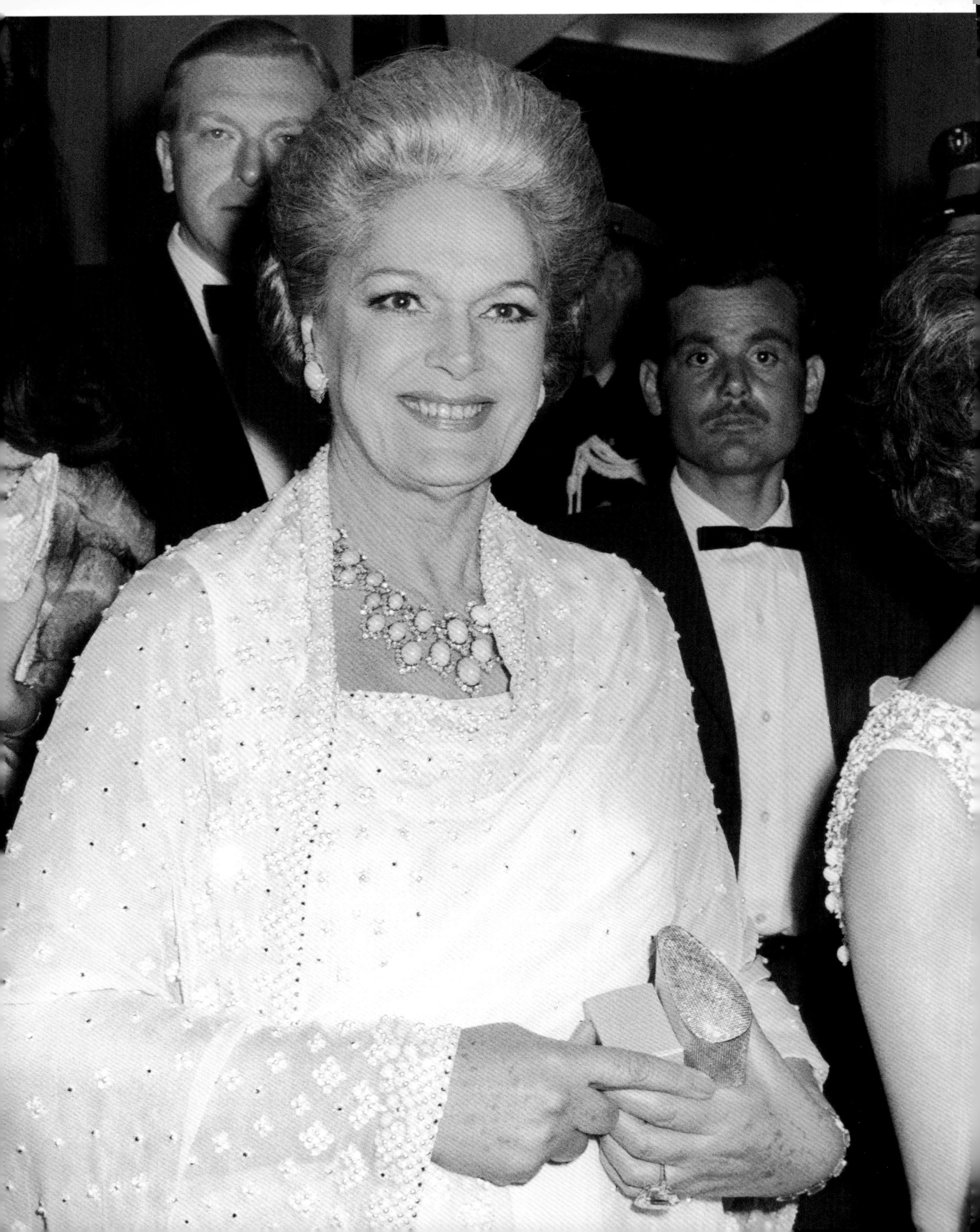

There were new codes, customs, fashions. *"My father was influenced by India,"* recalls Paolo Bulgari. *"His way of designing jewellery changed a little at that time. He was a master in the art of combining colours and it was this art that I learned from him. He caused a sort of revolution after the war by using heaps of different colours in the jewellery he created. Before the war, his creations were more classical, but after the war everything changed: the way of life, the way people dressed. And of course, American culture, music and art began to arrive in Italy. The Fifties brought a great opening to the world, it was a fantastic time."* [4]

Around this time, the sumptuous but rather classical jewels that alternate the red of rubies, the blue of sapphires and the green of emeralds with the white of diamonds, were gradually replaced with pieces in which all the colours blended with an extremely subtle harmony. The hues of the precious stones would be intensified or toned down by the use of the more pastel shades of turquoise, spinels, garnets, peridots, amethysts and other semi-precious stones. The Bulgari style was evolving and its clientele was growing. At the beginning of the 1950s, movie stars and billionaires were not the only people to stroll along Via dei Condotti and the Spanish square nearby. Kings and queens were also in Rome. In 1959, a young Roman aristocrat, Paola Ruffo di Calabria, became famous overnight after the announcement of her engagement to Prince Albert of Belgium. They would go on to become King and Queen of the Belgians. She was caught daydreaming in front of the Bulgari window. The royal family of Greece was also immortalized while walking in Via dei Condotti. King Farouk of Egypt, living in exile since 1952, had settled in the Italian capital. He would die there in 1965, at the age of 45, on a restaurant terrace while eating lobster. Certain members of his family would maintain that he had been poisoned by Egyptian spies.

Around 1955, an illustrious couple arrived at Bulgari. He reigned over millions of Ismaili Muslims. She was a former French beauty queen. They had married in 1944 in Geneva. One of the richest men in the world, everyone knew him by his title: His Highness the Aga Khan III. She was Yvette Labrousse, now known as the Begum Om Habibeh. A few years before, on 3 August 1949, she had been the victim of one of the most daring jewellery thefts ever committed. Just after their Cadillac had left their property at Le Cannet, Villa Yakimour, the Aga Khan and the Begum had been attacked on the roadside by four men who grabbed the Begum's red leather jewellery case. The booty was estimated to be worth FF220 million (the equivalent of nearly €10 million in today's money). The most important piece taken was a ring set with a 22-carat marquise-cut diamond. In fact, the theft had been a mistake. The gangsters had planned to kidnap American actress Rita Hayworth, who was staying at Yakimour with her fiancé, Prince Aly Khan, the eldest son of the Aga Khan III. The Begum retrieved some of her jewellery, but not all of it. Perhaps it was to replace the stolen pieces that her husband bought a diamond and turquoise parure signed "Bulgari". This would be one of the last jewels he would give to his wife. He died a year later. His grandson, Karim, who succeeded him, became His Highness the Aga Khan IV; he would also become a Bulgari customer, buying several parures for his first wife, Princess Salimah.

Facing page: *The Begum Aga Khan III at a gala party given in 1966 at the Paris Opera. She is wearing her Bulgari turquoise and diamond necklace and bracelet.* **Overleaf:** *The Bulgari turquoise and diamond necklace and bracelet, property of H.H. the Begum Aga Khan III, sold at Sotheby's in 2000. Private collection.*

1. *Footprints* by Brooke Astor, Doubleday, 1980. **2.** Anna Bulgari Calissoni, interview with the author. **3.** Paolo Bulgari, interview with the author. **4.** *Ibid.*

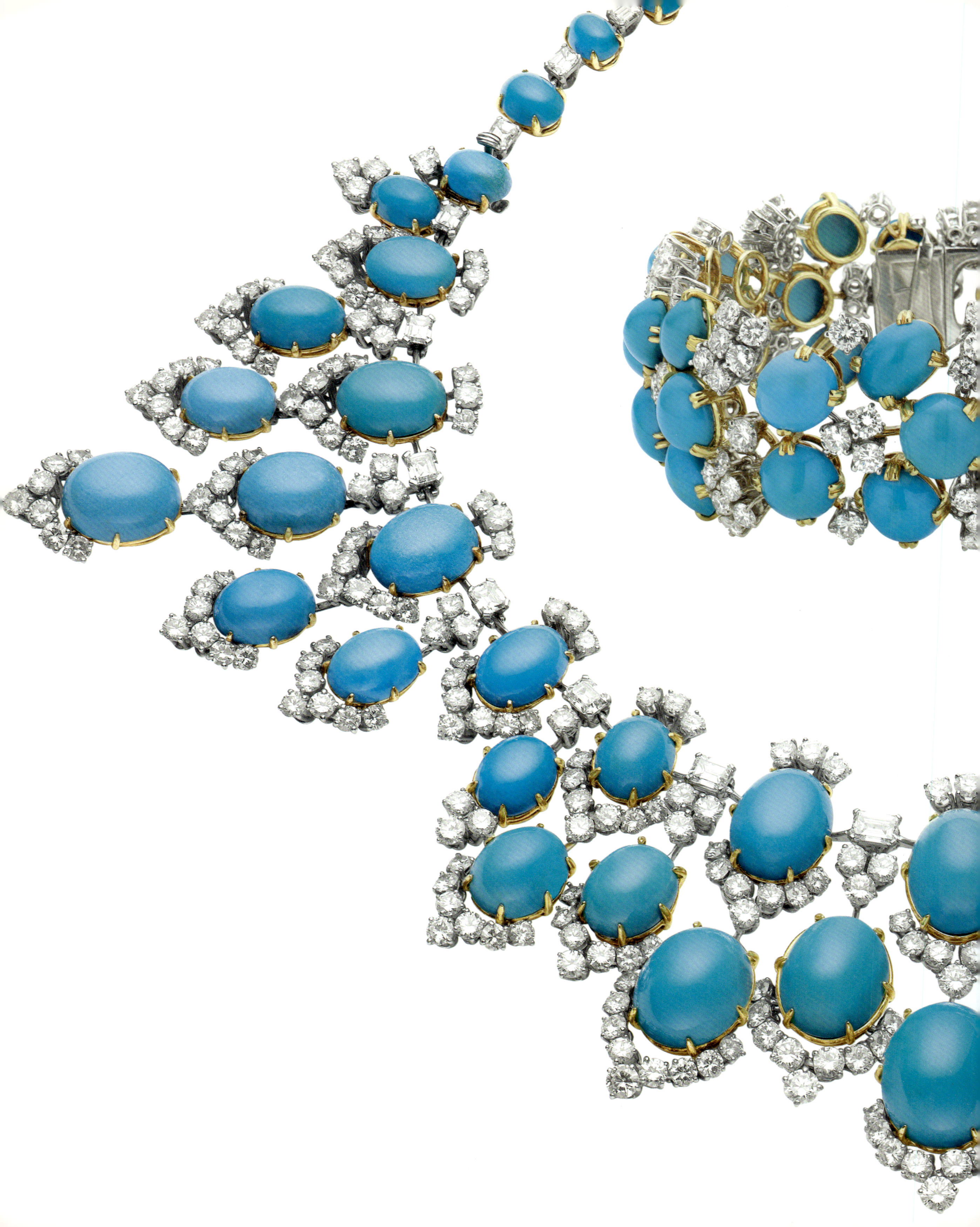

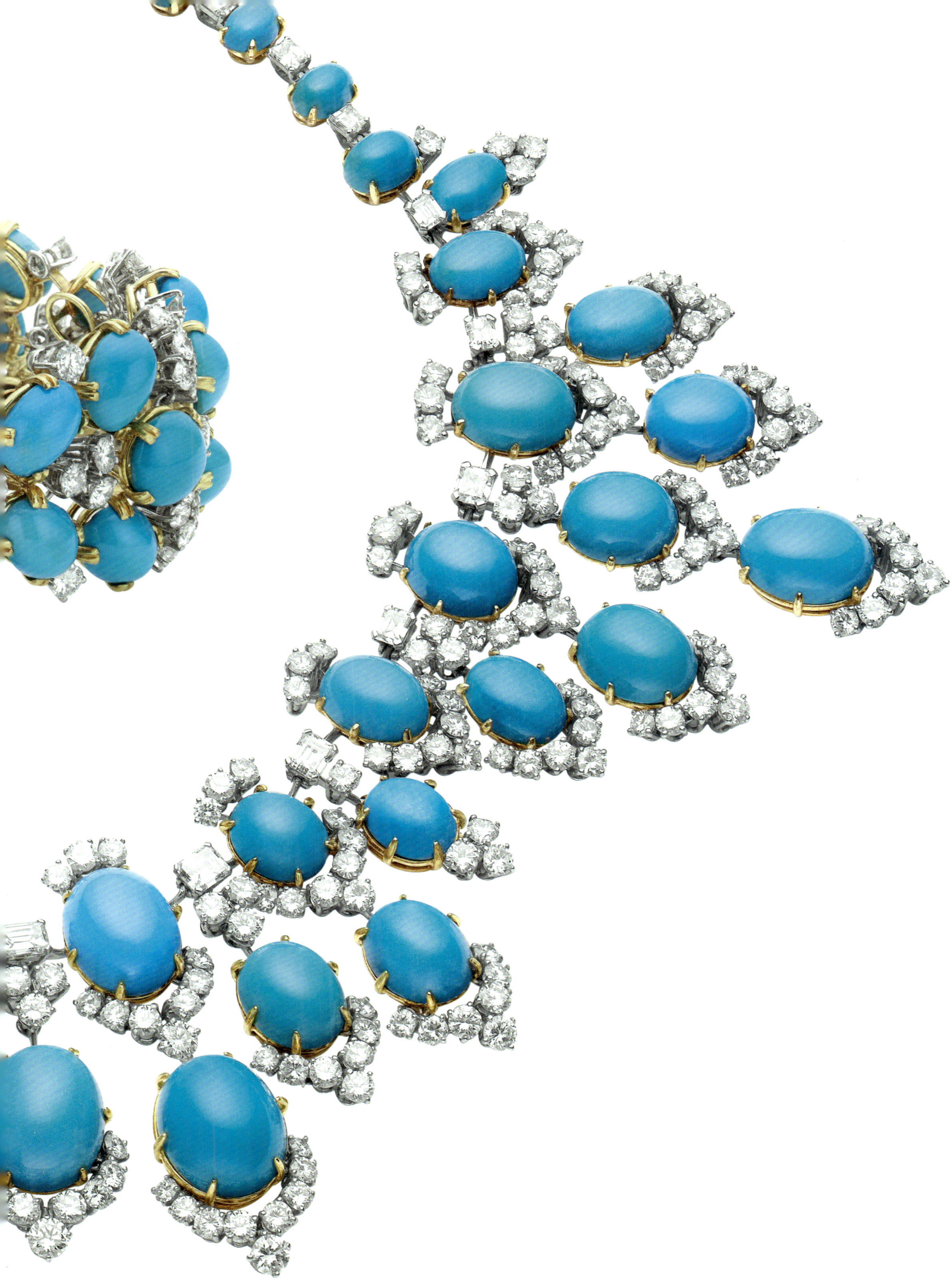

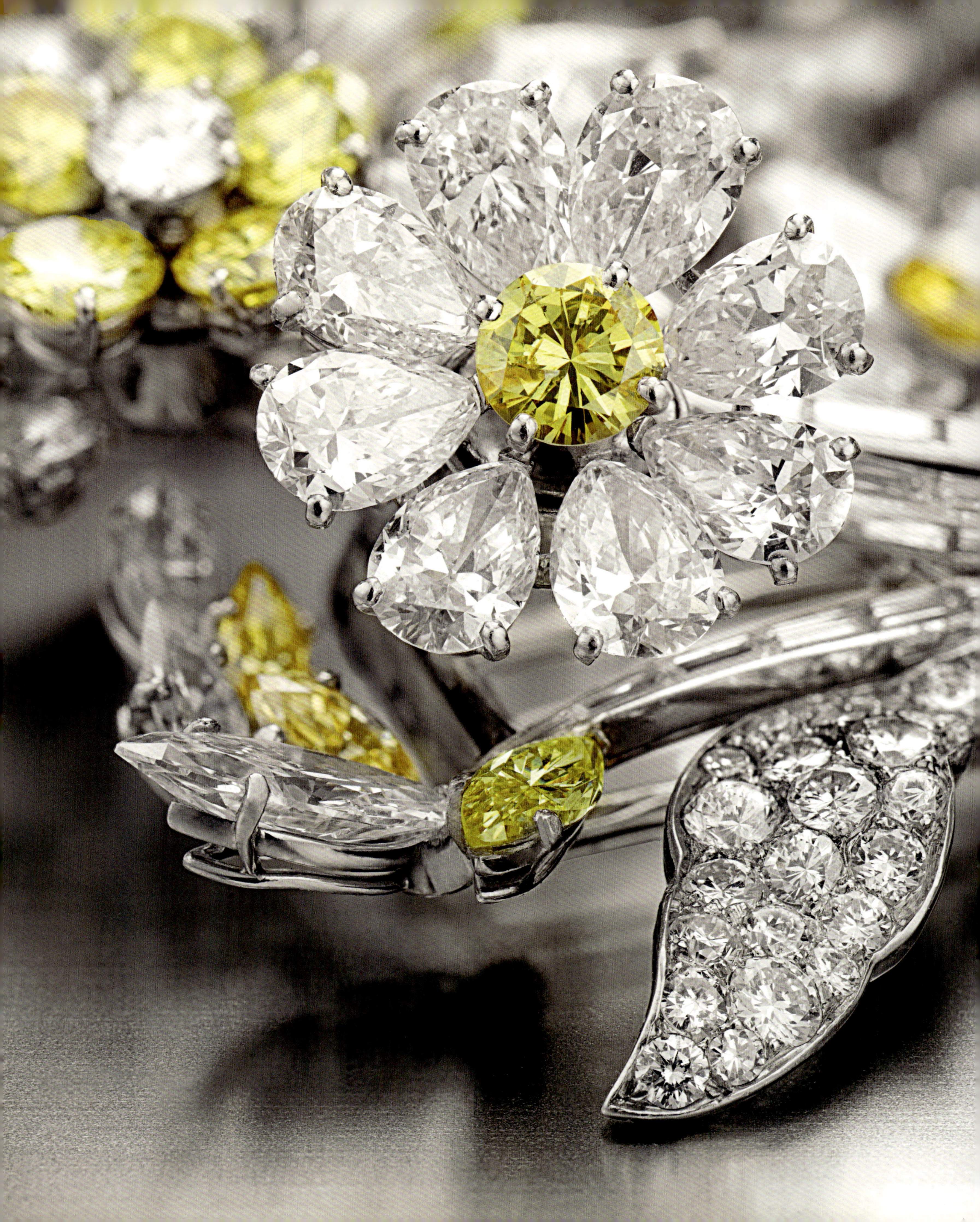

Chapter 9

ANOTHER ROMAN WEDDING

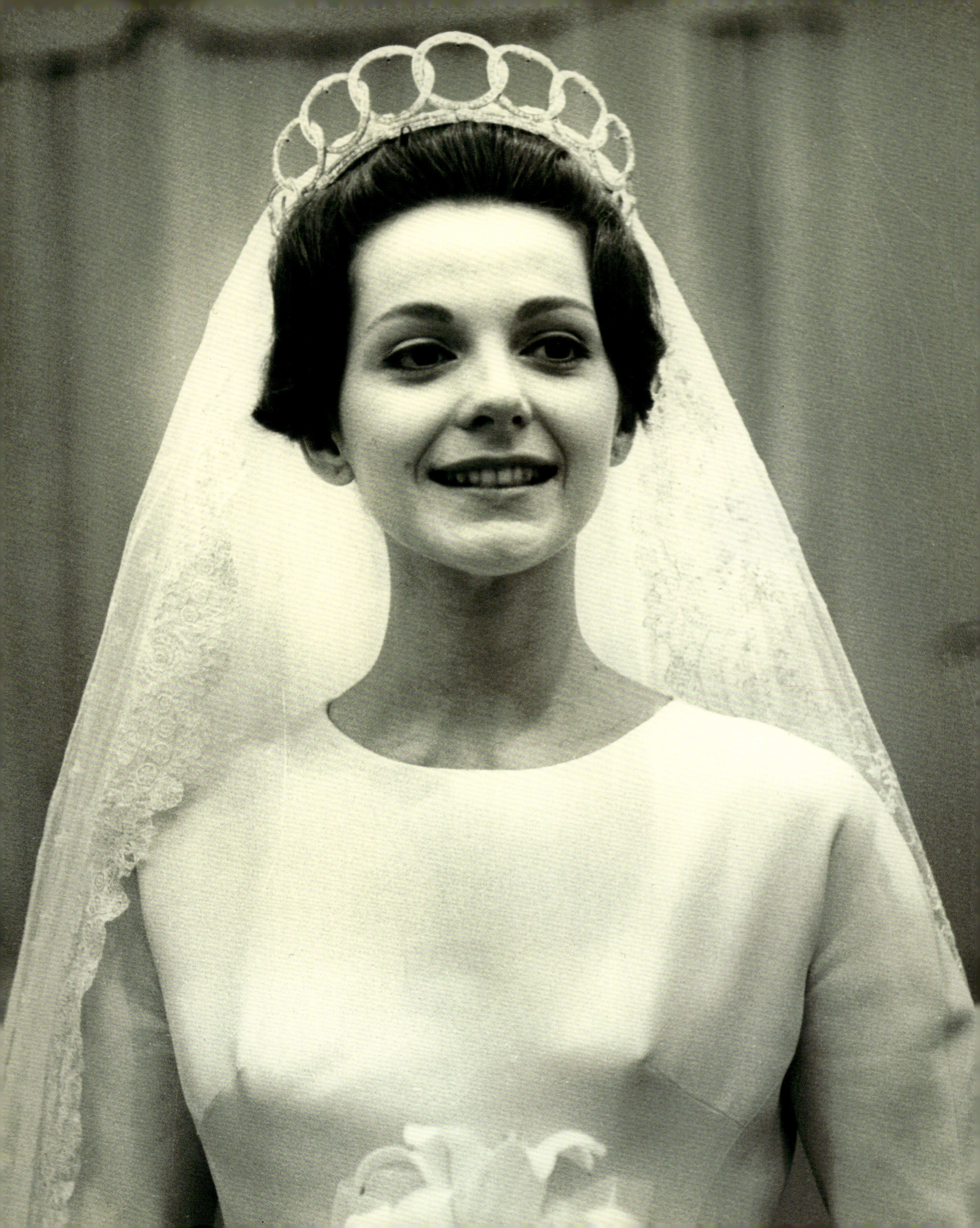

Olimpia Torlonia and Paul-Annik Weiller

The Basilica of Santa Maria in Trastevere, 26 June 1965

"On my wedding day, I wore the aquamarine and diamond tiara created by Bulgari for my mother in 1935 and that she had lent me, but without the aquamarines of course," recalls Princess Olimpia Torlonia, Mrs Paul-Annik Weiller. *"At that time, the rules were still very strict. Apart from a tiara – when the family owned one – a young woman did not wear jewellery on her wedding day, not even her engagement ring. And especially no coloured stones. It was not done. A woman could wear only her wedding ring on that day."* [1]

The wedding of Princess Olimpia Torlonia with Mr Paul-Annik Weiller, on 26 June, 1965 was a reprise of her own parents' wedding (Infanta Beatriz of Spain and Don Alessandro Torlonia) thirty years earlier (see chapter II). Though this occasion was even more sumptuous. For once, the extravagances of the *Dolce Vita* set made way in Roman newspapers for the description of the splendours of a far more traditional union. And the hundreds of journalists and photographers, who literally camped for days in front of the entrance of the Torlonia Palace, via Bocca di Leone, were not disappointed. *"It was truly an extraordinary ceremony that lasted three days,"* remembers the bride. *"First there was an evening at the Spanish Embassy, then a family dinner at the Grand Hotel and finally the wedding on 26 June 1965 in Santa Maria in Trastevere."* [2]

The Torlonia family, former bankers to the Pope, are one of the most illustrious of Rome. They are divided into several branches, possess the most beautiful palaces and the largest estates. Above all, since 1958 they have held one of the greatest honours of the pontifical court: they are one of only two princely families to hold the title of Assistant to the Pontifical Throne; the other is the Colonna family. This grants them the right to stand at the right of the Holy Father's throne during official ceremonies in the Vatican. (Traditionally, the Princes Colonna and Orsini shared this distinction, but after Prince Orsini's liaison with British actress Belinda Lee, Pope Pius XII withdrew this title and transferred it to the head of the Torlonia family.)

To add to the pomp, the mother of the bride was an Infanta of Spain, daughter of the late King Alfonso XIII. The King's widow, Queen Victoria Eugenie, who had not attended her daughter's wedding in 1935 (see Chapter 2) was now present for her granddaughter's. Her arrival at the church of Santa Maria in Trastevere was spectacular. As well as her three-strand necklace of enormous pearls she was wearing a brooch of two huge cabochon emeralds surrounded by diamonds; it had been a wedding gift from the last Tsar of Russia, Nicholas II. She was surrounded by her eldest son, Infante Juan, Count of Barcelona and the Grand Master of the Order of Malta, the Duchess of Aosta, the Begum Aga Khan III, and the daughters of the

Facing page: *Princess Olimpia Torlonia, wearing her mother's Bulgari diamond tiara on her wedding day in 1965. Private Archives.* **Previous page:** *Close-up detail of a Bulgari yellow and white diamond flower brooch. Bulgari Heritage Collection.*

last King of Italy, Princess Maria Pia of Bourbon-Parma and Princess Maria Gabriella of Savoy; and, of course, all of Rome's aristocracy.

The groom's family was quite colourful. Paul-Annik Weiller's father, Commandant Paul-Louis Weiller, a wealthy French businessman who was also an extraordinary collector and patron (see Chapter 6). The groom's mother, Aliki Diplarakou, was a former Greek beauty queen who had been elected Miss Europe in 1930. After divorcing Paul-Louis Weiller at the end of World War II, she had married Sir John Russell, a British diplomat who was currently the British Ambassador to Ethiopia. Far from seeing himself as a wealthy heir who simply had to wait to inherit his father's fortune, Paul-Annik was determined to assume his independence and to live outside of his father's circle. In 1954, having reached the age of majority, he took advantage of the financial independence that a small inheritance from his aunt had secured for him, to go to study in the United States. He then served his military service in the Air Force during the Algerian War. Returning to civilian life, he successfully embarked on business ventures. After his death, in 1998, it was said that he had succeeded in building a greater fortune than his father.

The ceremony was presided over by Monsignor Nasalli Rocca di Corneliano, Prefect of the Pontifical House. (A second Orthodox ceremony, in the groom's faith, would be celebrated at the Torlonia Palace later.) The photographs – the Infanta Beatriz was never without her camera – reveal details from another time. The church pews were covered with blue velvet, and in the aisles, at the end of each pew, hung a basket of white lilies. This decoration represents the heraldic coat of arms – fleurs-de-lys (lilies) on a blue field – of the Bourbon family, the dynasty to which the Infanta Beatriz belonged. On the left, in the choir of the church, the Queen of Spain, the Great Master of the Sovereign Order of Malta, and the Duchess of Aosta, were seated on gilded armchairs. In front of each of them was an antique golden prayer kneeler, also upholstered in blue velvet. Behind them were their lords- and ladies-in-waiting; and a little farther behind, stood several valets in liveries. On the right were the witnesses: Prince Alexander of Yugoslavia, the husband of Princess Maria Pia of Bourbon, and the Marquis of Crussol d'Uzès, for the bridegroom; for Olimpia, they were her uncle the Count of Barcelona and Prince Marco Torlonia, her brother.

Of the 800 or so women in the church that day, fewer than fifty were not wearing a hat. In 1965, the fashion was for rather small hats: turbans, floral straw hats or feather fascinators. Only a few Parisians chose to wear wide-brimmed hats. Either way, the heat was so stifling that most ladies had brought a fan with them. And, of course, all or almost all of them were wearing a pearl necklace, which was *de rigueur* at that time. *"It was almost a piece of uniform,"* Olimpia Torlonia remembers. *"The girls had one row, and when they married they received three. My three-strand pearl necklace was given to me by my husband and the clasp is an emerald. It was created at Bulgari. Like much of my jewellery. At the time, there were still strict rules. For make-up, for example, the only constraint was to never shine, so we would get a lot of powder. And we never went out without lipstick. On the other hand, one never wore foundation. The maximum of extravagance was a stroke of eye liner."* [3]

After the ceremony, the nearly 2,000 guests were invited to the reception at the Torlonia Palace. After congratulating the bride and groom in the courtyard in front of the fountain, they were invited to go to the salons on the first floor of the palace, where the reception was held and where the wedding presents were displayed. Dishes, silverware, crystal, dozens of *objets de vertu* and, of course, jewellery. To display the jewels, a showcase has been borrowed from Bulgari, whose store is located less than 100 metres from the Torlonia Palace on Via dei Condotti. Actually, the jeweller's signature is on most of these pieces. Everything was created by special order, with fittings, just as for an haute couture dress.

"At that time," recalls Olimpia Torlonia, *"women did not buy jewellery. It was the husbands, the betrothed, or the fathers who went to the jewellers to buy the jewels. Moreover, one did not necessarily buy jewellery already made, often one took along one's own stones and the jeweller created something according to what you had brought. My father, my husband, my father-in-law, all went to Bulgari. We, I mean wives or daughters, went there only*

Facing page: *Diamond necklace and earrings created by Bulgari in 1965 for the wedding of Princess Olimpia Torlonia. Private collection.*

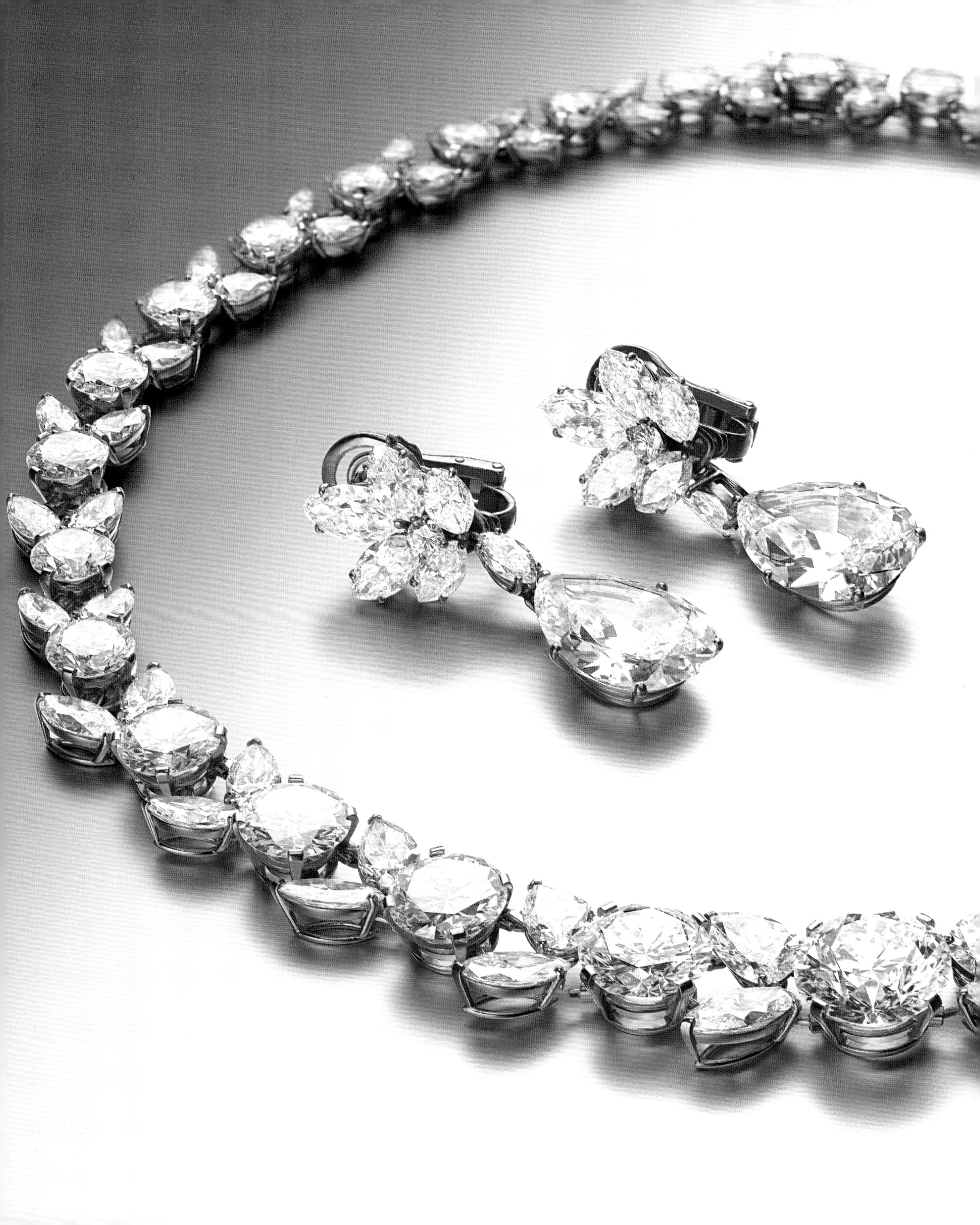

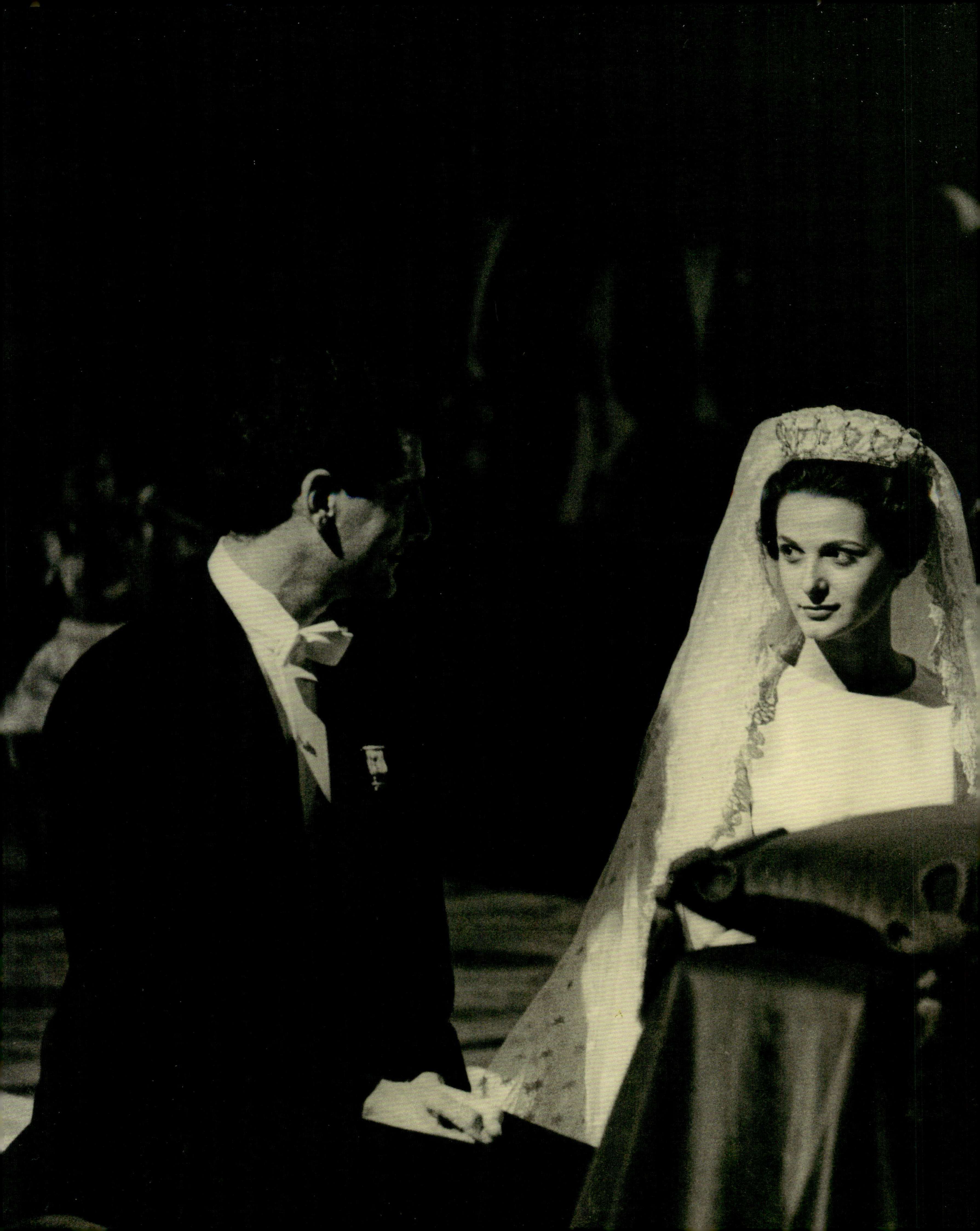

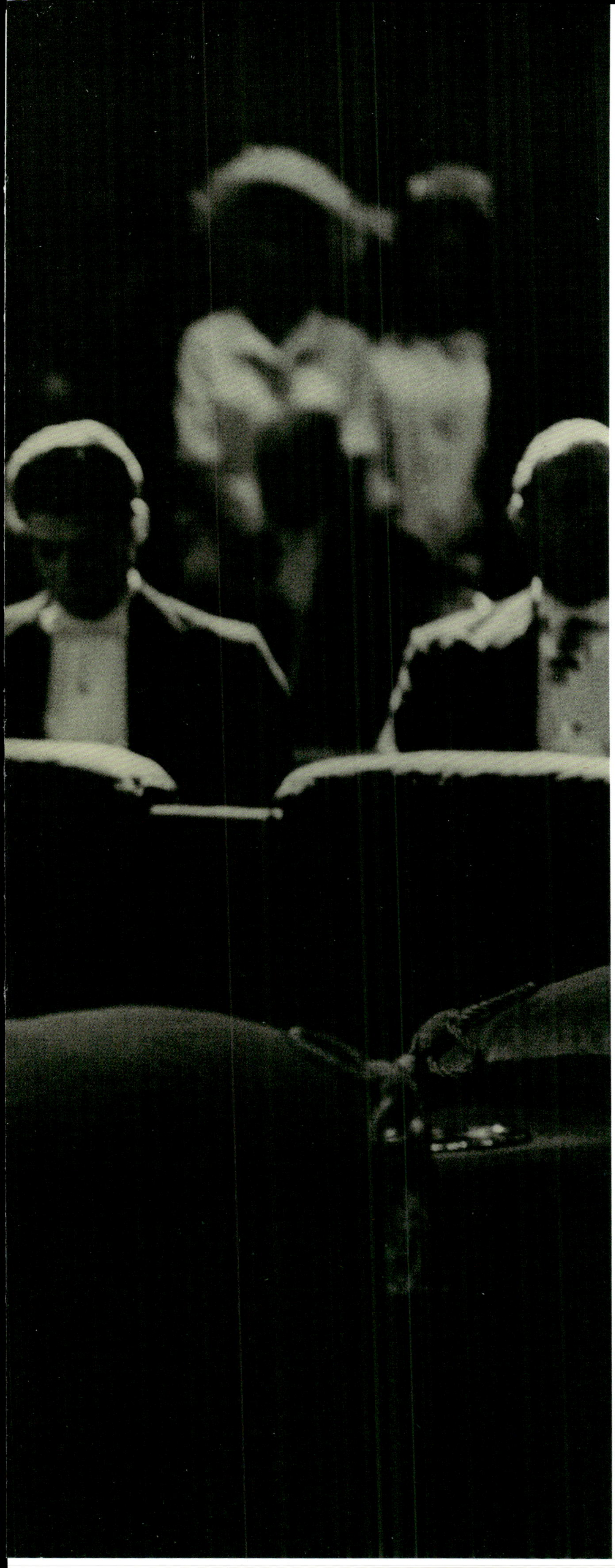

Princess Olimpia Torlonia and Paul-Annik Weiller on their wedding day in the Basilica of Santa Maria in Trastevere. Private Archives.

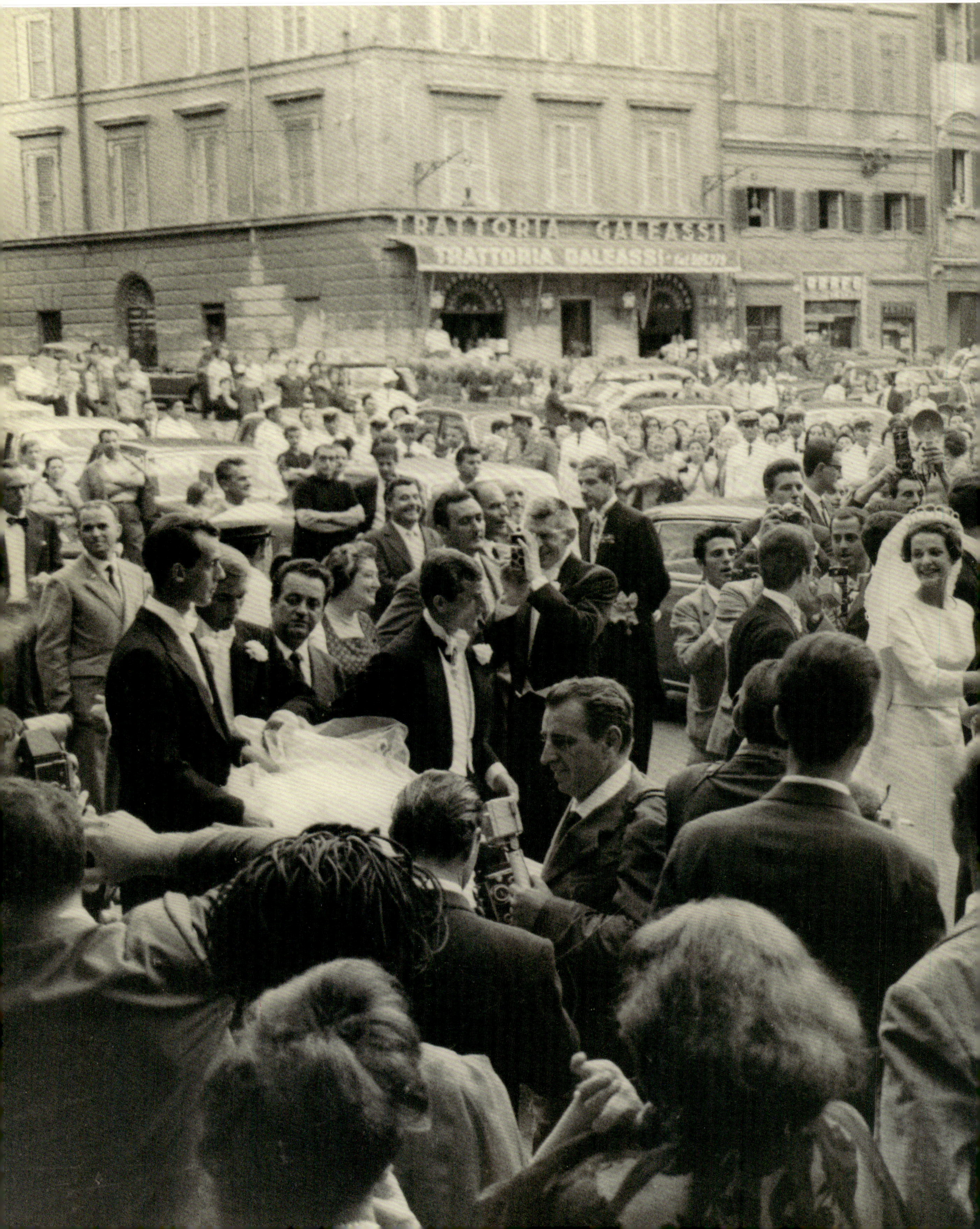
TRATTORIA GALEASSI
TRATTORIA GALEASSI

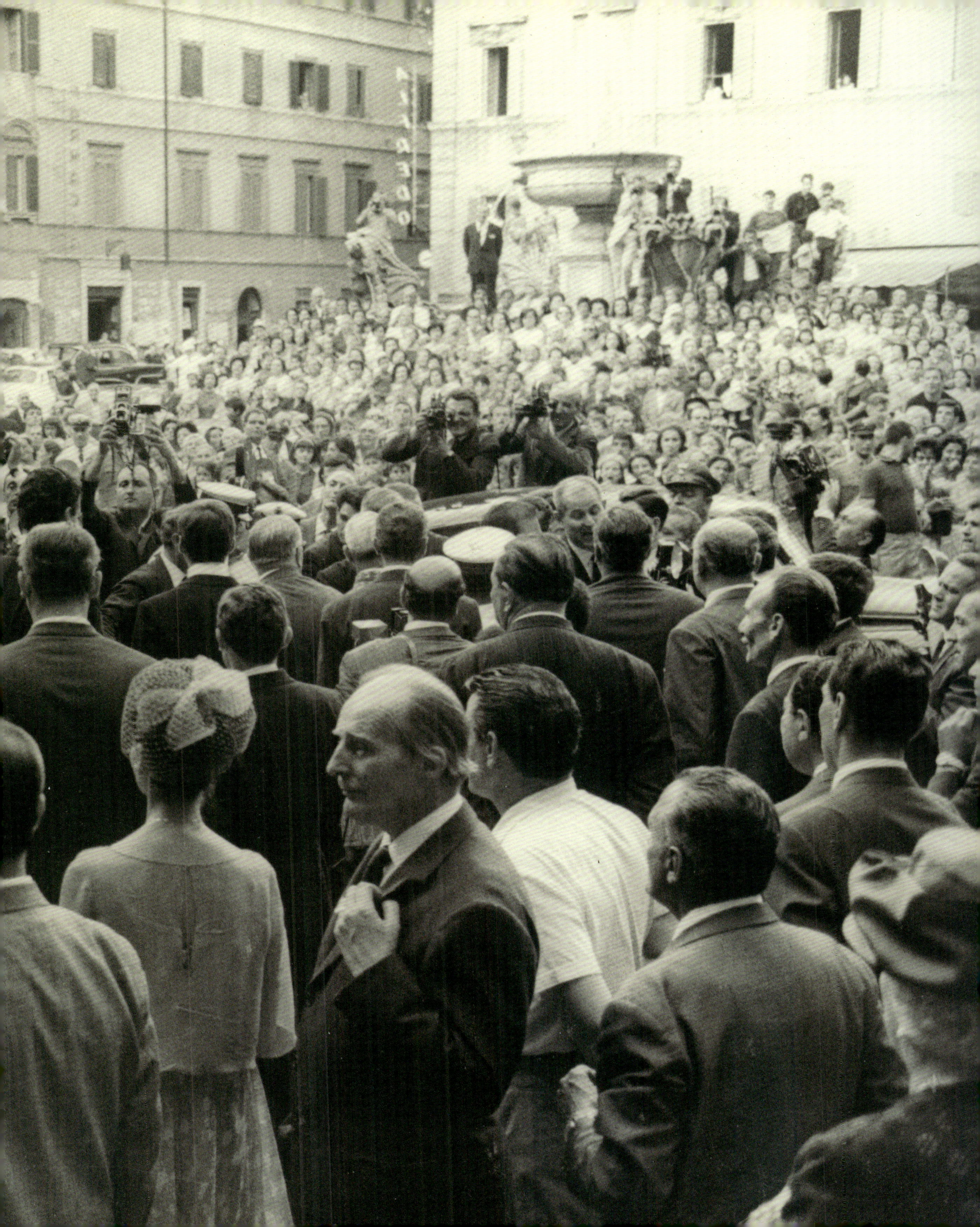

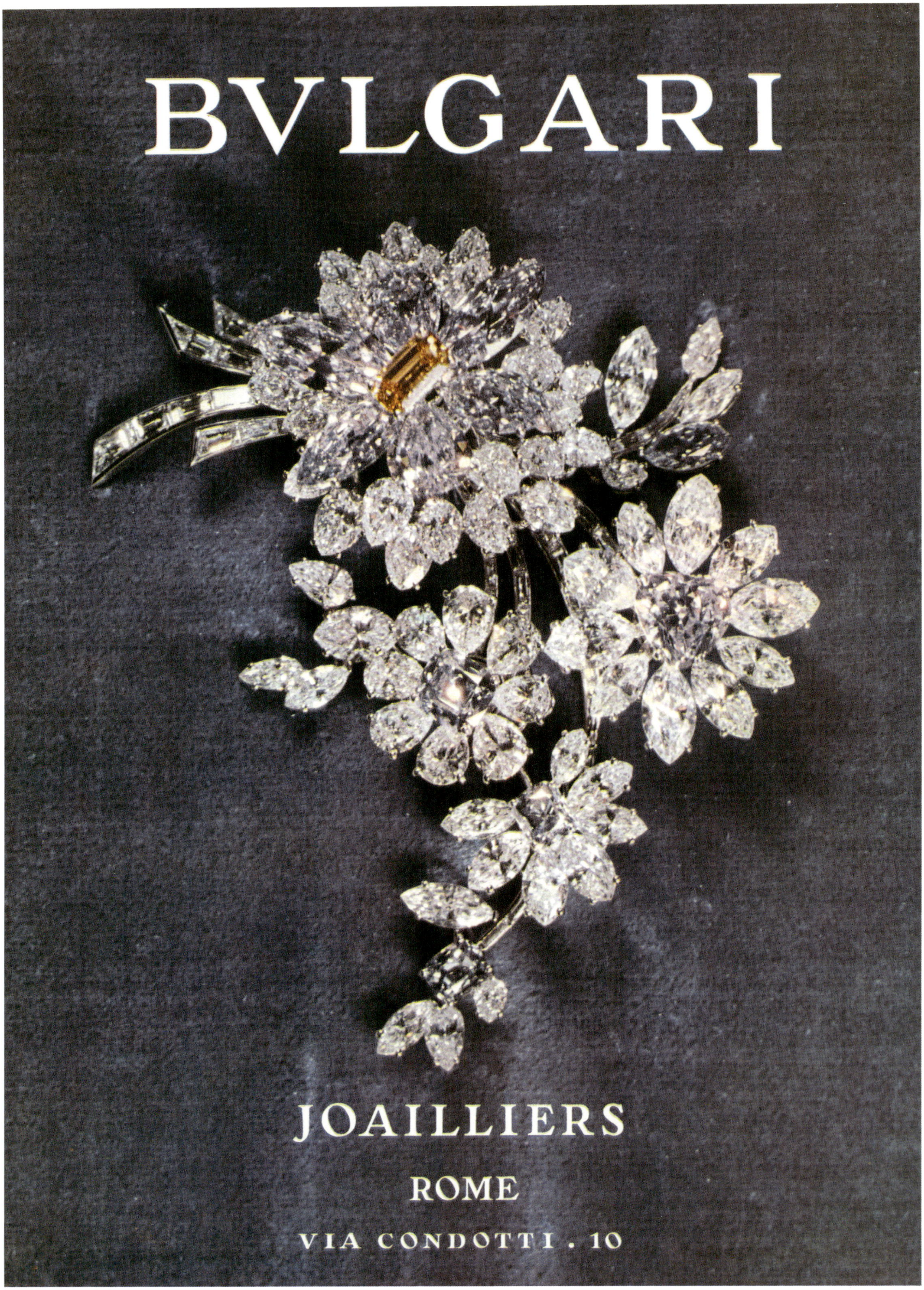
BVLGARI
JOAILLIERS
ROME
VIA CONDOTTI . 10

Flower jewellery from Bulgari

It all began in the early 1960s with the purchase of some unique coloured diamonds. *"It was the collection of one of the greatest diamond merchants of the time,"* recalls Paolo Bulgari. *"His name was Myran Eknayan (1892-1985), he lived in Paris and he was a friend of my father. He was also the husband of a famous French actress, Jacqueline Delubac. He had collected coloured diamonds for years and he had an extraordinary collection that included all the shades of yellow, blue, pink. Every year, my father would ask him to sell his collection. And one day, Eknayan said yes. We bought the whole lot. Hundreds of coloured diamonds. It is for this reason that we decided to create the flower brooches of coloured diamonds that have become so famous. It was necessary to do something with these diamonds."* [7]

Hundreds of coloured diamonds suddenly arrived in the Bulgari workshops. They were set according to a very special French technique dating from the end of the 19th century: the *trembleuse.* The idea was to give these stones movement, in addition to colour. Each of them was set on a light spring. Every movement made the jewel vibrate. In certain light the effect is striking. Emeralds, rubies and sapphires were soon added to the coloured diamonds, set in brooches and also in necklaces. The coloured diamond flower brooch given by Eddie Fisher to Elizabeth Taylor was one of these very special pieces, which are symbolic of Bulgari.

The refinement was not only limited to jewellery. Bulgari had became a real lesson in style at that time. The saleswomen and men were always extremely elegant and of course they could speak several languages. Some of them had rather aristocratic attitudes, which would be unacceptable today. The dazzling Marisela Federici, born into a family of Venezuelan diplomats, began working at the Via Condotti shop in the late 1970s. *"It was a world apart, really fascinating,"* she recalls. *"I arrived a little by chance. At the time, a young girl from a good family could come to work for a firm like Bulgari. We had an address book that could be helpful. But, we did not have a very commercial attitude. I remember one of my first big sales. A couple had bought several million dollars' worth of jewellery from me and I let them go with the jewels, without asking them to pay. I was sure they would do it, but they gave absolutely no guarantee. I remember that Gianni and Paolo Bulgari almost collapsed. 'You are crazy,' they said to me. In fact, these customers paid without any hassle the next day and they sent me a bouquet of 500 roses."* [8]

"This kind of detail was a particular feature of this universe at that time. One of the Bulgari services that fascinated me most was packaging. It took several people to make a package. The boxes came from a special supplier. The wrapping paper was gray. And on each package it was necessary to apply a wax seal. It took quite a long time, but the result was always perfect." [9]

1. Dona Olimpia Torlonia, Mrs Paul-Annik Weiller, interview with the author, 2015. **2.** *Ibid.* **3.** *Ibid.* **4.** *Ibid.* **5.** *Ibid.* **6.** *Ibid.* **7.** Paolo Bulgari, interview with the author, 2014. **8.** Marisela Federici, interview with the author, 2015. **9.** *Ibid.*

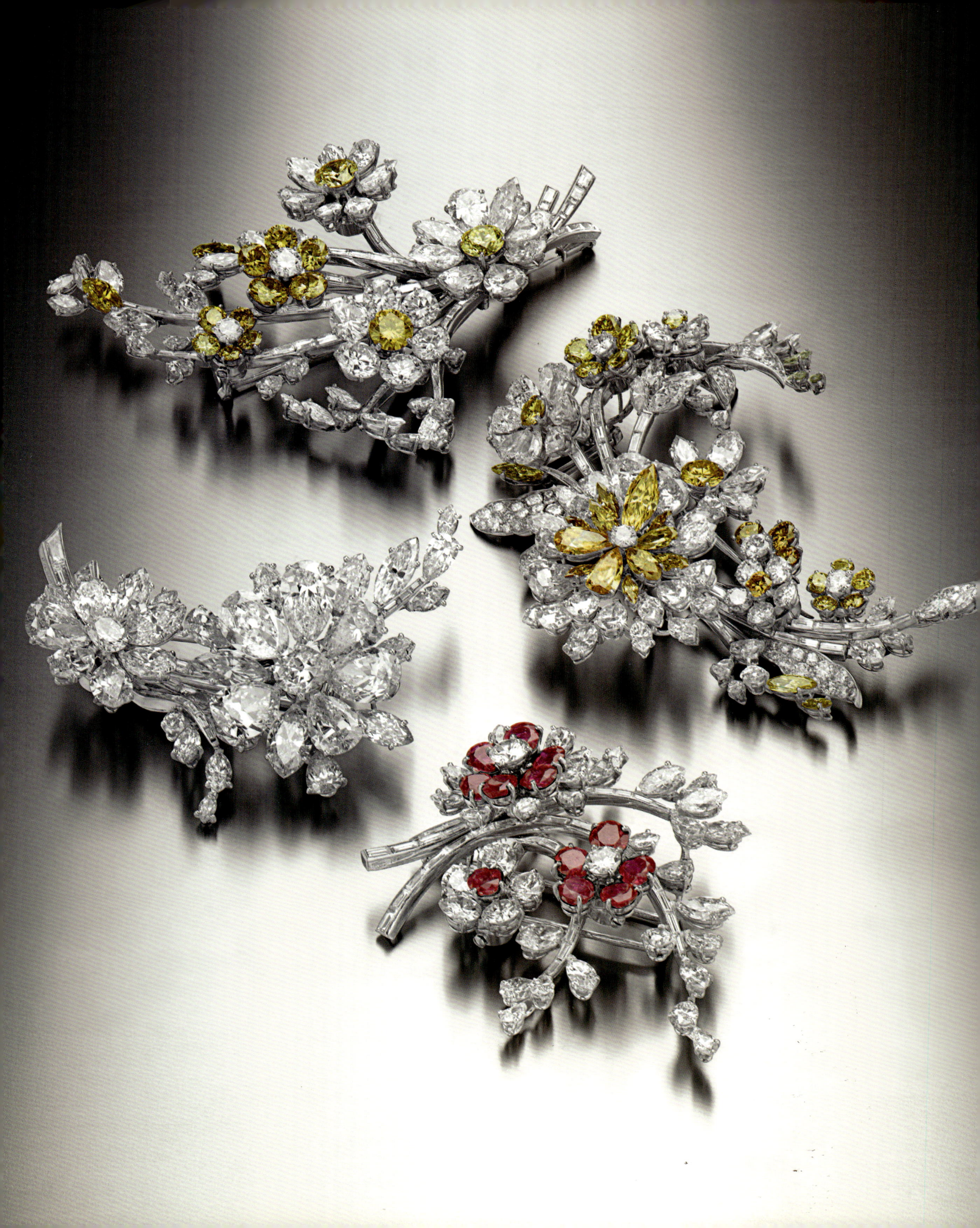

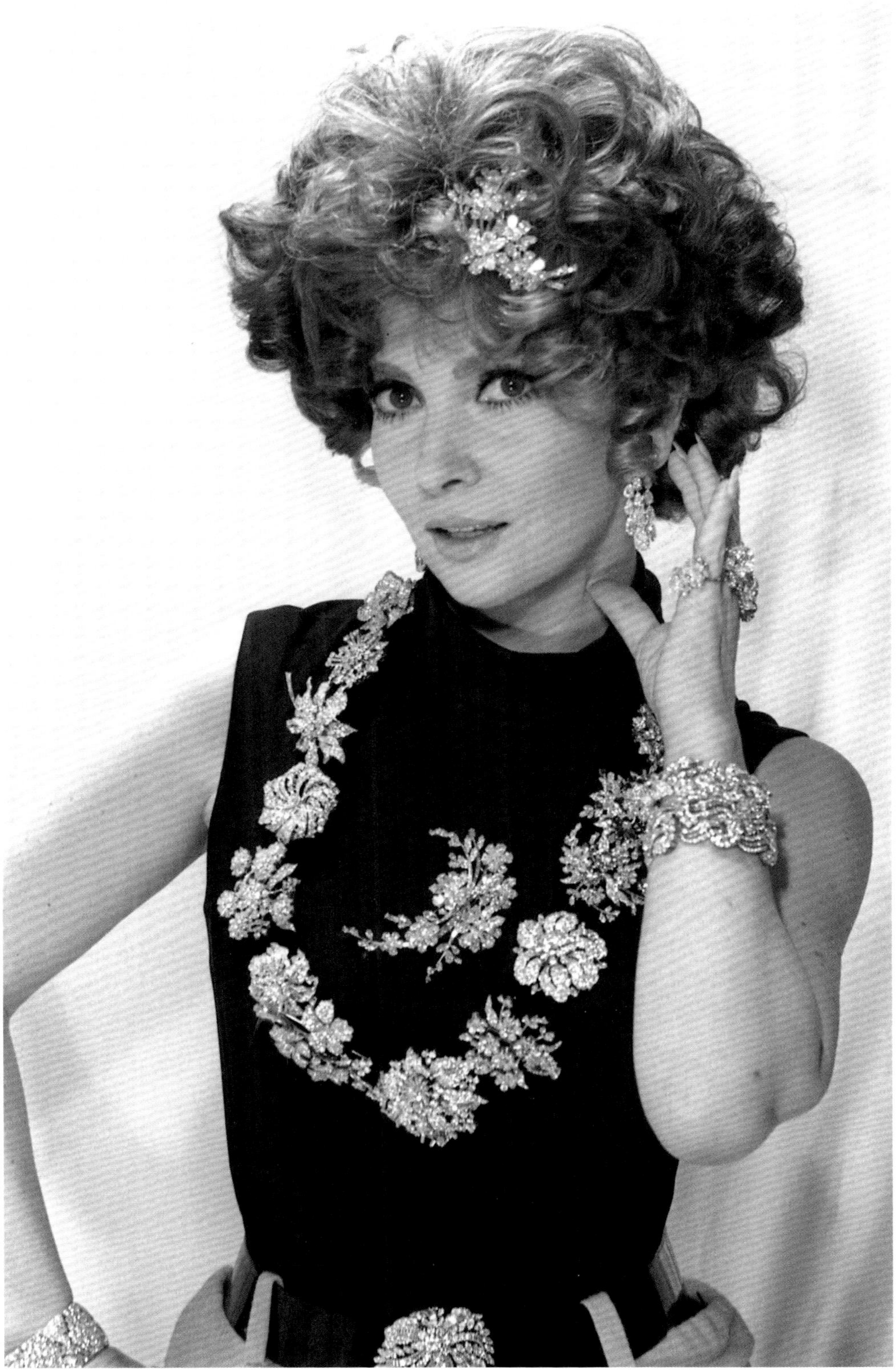

Facing page: *Bulgari flower brooches set with diamonds, yellow diamonds and rubies. Bulgari Heritage Collection.* **Above:** *Gina Lollobrigida wearing dozens of Bulgari flower brooches, 1960s.* **Previous page:** *Bulgari advertisement featuring a flower brooch, 1960s.*

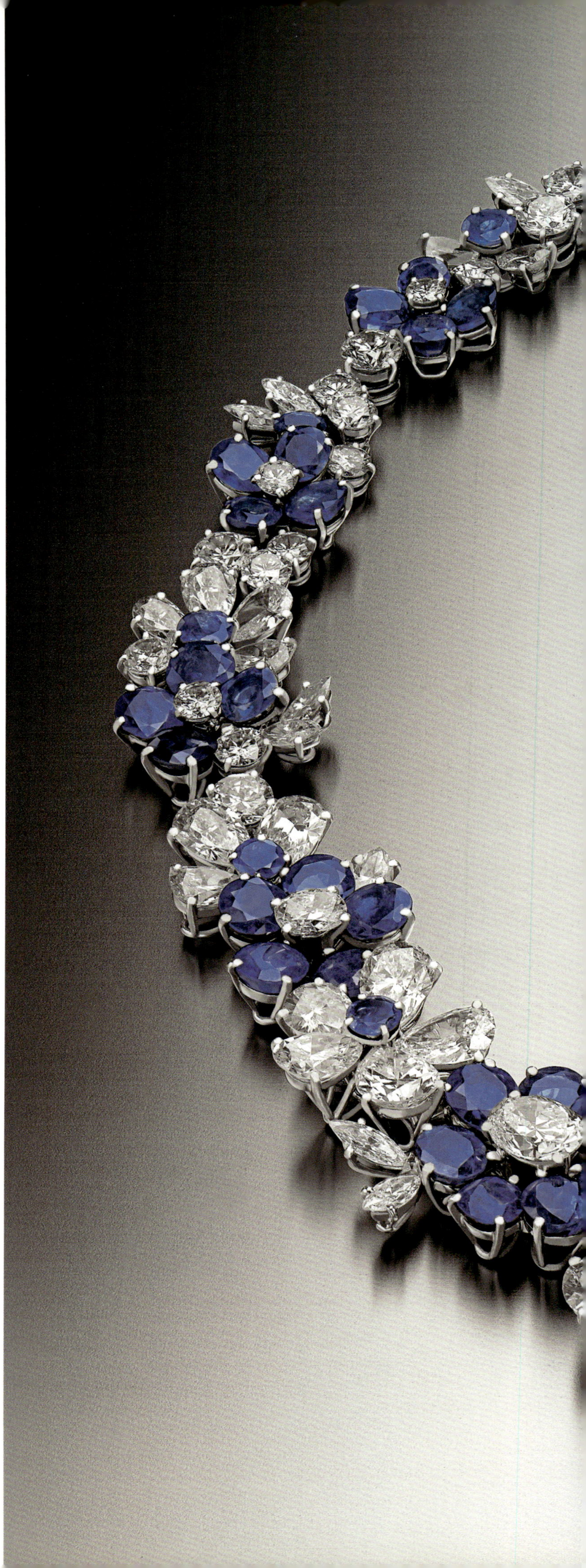

Sapphire and diamond flower necklace, 1960s. Bulgari Heritage Collection.

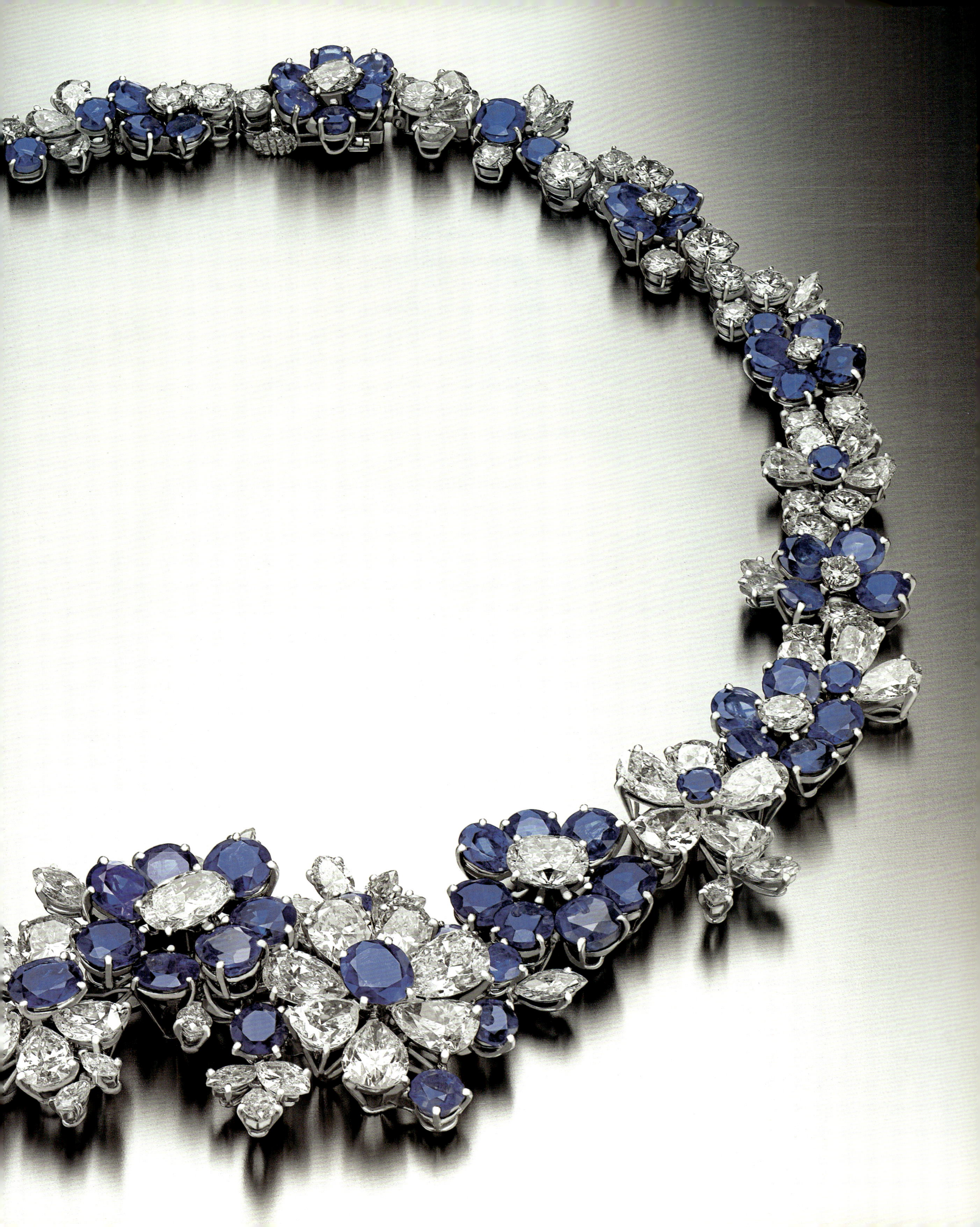

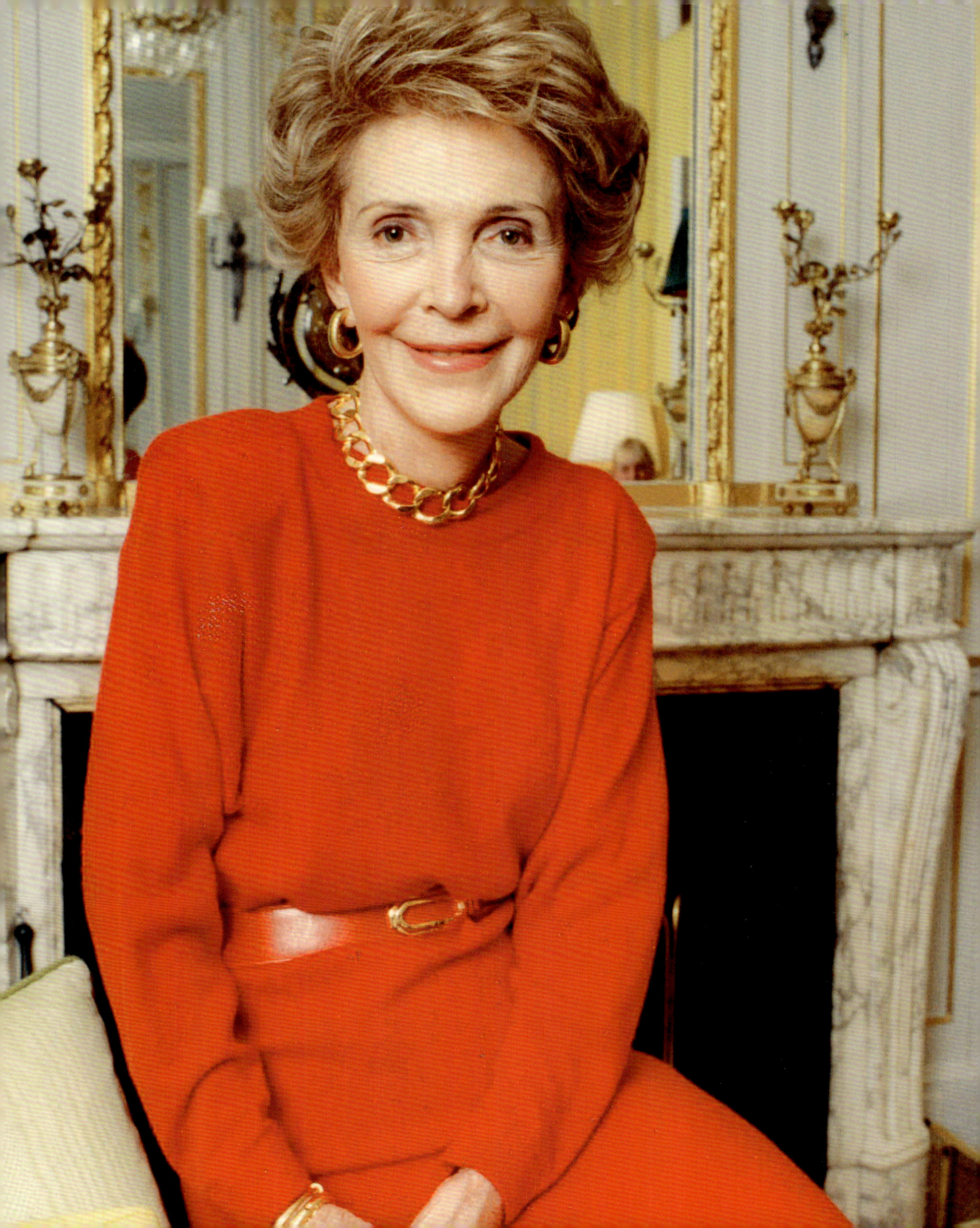

Nancy Reagan's bejewelled Stars and Stripes

Christie's, New York, 21 September 2016

As always at this type of historic sale, it was the most intimate and symbolic objects that sparked the enthusiasm of the buyers – lots with an estimated value of a few hundred, or at best a few thousand dollars, but that recounted a precise moment in the personal life of this couple. The Reagans had played a part in history several times over the past 50 years. After a very honourable career as an actor in Hollywood and with 50 films to his credit – including many Westerns – Ronald had entered politics. His anti-communist stance had anchored him in the Republican camp, even though he came from a family of Democrats. In 1967, he became Governor of California. And in 1980, he had reached the crowning point of his political career – he was elected President of the United States! Resolutely conservative, he remained, after two terms, one of the most popular presidents in American history. This was, perhaps, because it was during his second term as president that the Cold War had ended. Forty years of spying, ideological conflict, and an arms race that had poisoned the lives of everyone on the planet had come to an end. It was Reagan who took the first swing at the wall that had split the city of Berlin in two. On 12 June 1987, in front of the Brandenburg Gate, he appealed to the First Secretary of the Soviet Communist Party, Mikhail Gorbachev: *"Tear down this wall."*

Facing page: *Nancy Reagan (1921-2016), who was America's First Lady from 20 January 1981 until 20 January 1989.* **Previous page:** *Thanks to customers like Elizabeth Taylor, who wore them often, Serpenti jewels from Bulgari quickly became very fashionable in the USA. This gold enamelled Serpenti jewel dates from around 1965. It can be worn either as a necklace or as a belt. American fashion icon Diana Vreeland also had one of these Serpenti necklace/belts. FD Gallery Collection, New York.*

At his side, his wife Nancy, embodied a form of traditional elegance, in a style that was more New Yorker than Hollywood. She too had been an actress, though a little less successful than her husband. They always presented an image of a united couple, who were warm, tender and friendly. The last years of the former president were marked by the ravages of Alzheimer's disease. With great courage, he had announced his diagnosis in November 1994: *"I have recently been told, that I am one of the millions of Americans who will be afflicted with Alzheimer's disease ... At the moment, I just feel fine. I intend to live the remainder of the years God gives me on this Earth doing the things I have always done ... I now begin the journey that will lead me into the sunset of my life."* Nancy stayed with him to the end in 2004, carefully maintaining the warm family atmosphere of their Bel Air residence in Los Angeles.

She survived him by twelve years. And now their furniture, the jewellery of the First Lady, their memories... would be auctioned at Christie's in New York. The profits from the several hundred lots would go to various charities that had been supported by the couple.

From the former President's belongings, a pair of cowboy boots – cut from exceptional leather and never worn – had reached the record price of $199,000. From his wife's possessions, it was over pieces of jewellery that the collectors had fought. The highest price was obtained for a ring: $319,000 for an octagonal ring in the colours of the American flag. The gold jewel, set with rubies, sapphires and diamonds, was estimated at a few thousand dollars. Nancy had worn it for the first time on 4 July, 1986, during the celebrations of the centenary of the Statue of Liberty. Surprisingly, this emblematic ring, which was almost a symbol of the history of the United States, was signed not by an American jeweller, but by an Italian one: Bulgari.

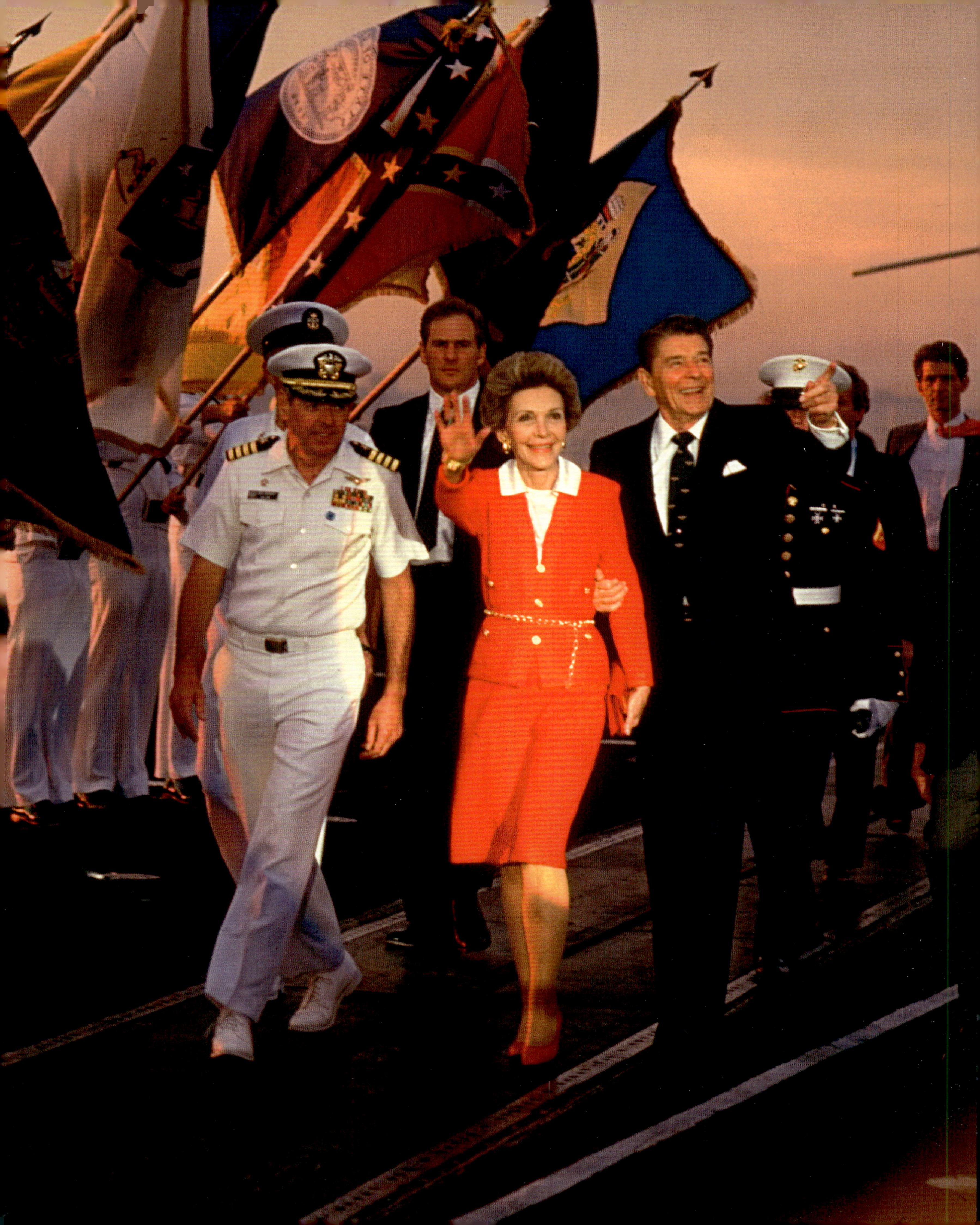

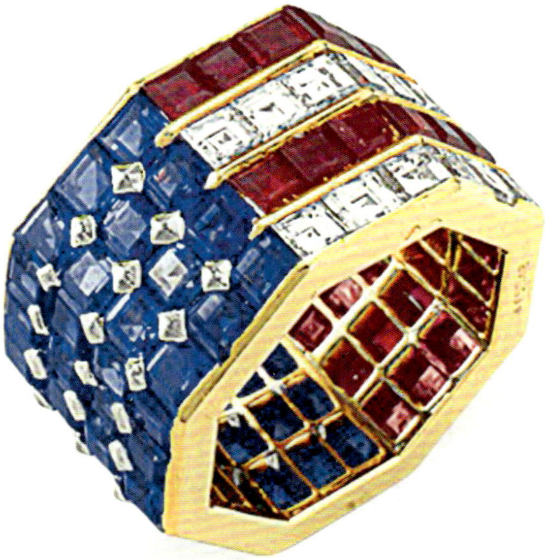

Above: *The ruby, sapphire and diamond ring created by Bulgari for Nancy Reagan.*
Facing page: *Nancy and Ronald Reagan during the celebration of the centenary of the Statue of Liberty.*

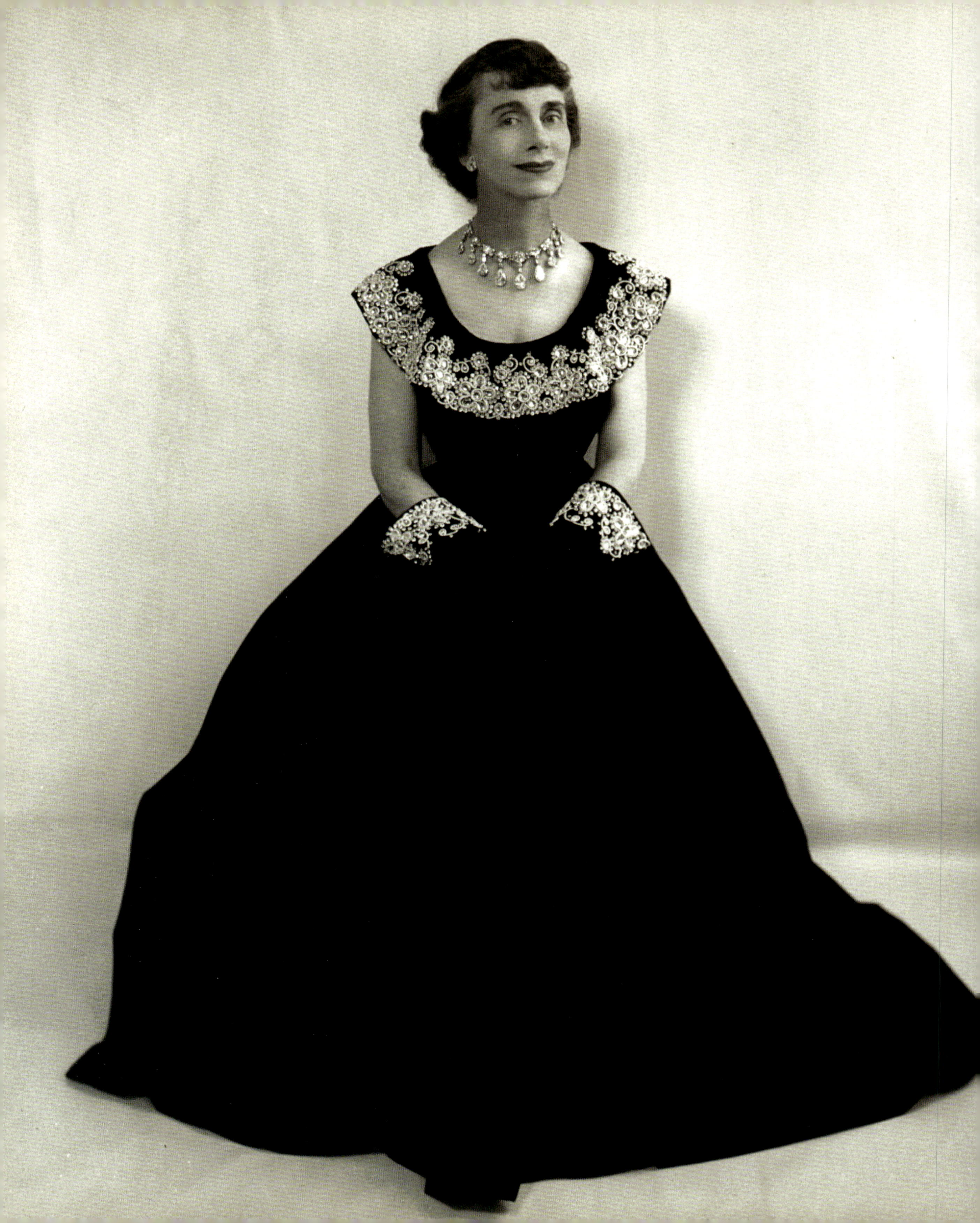

Bulgari's American adventure began in the aftermath of the First World War, when Giorgio Bulgari began to develop *haute joaillerie*. According to Nicola, Giorgio's youngest son, among his first clients were several billionaires: *"My father often told me that he had had American customers since the 1920s. Unfortunately, most of their purchases have been lost in the mists of time. No one was interested in heritage until the 1990s. So many things were simply thrown away, books, drawings ... We have no idea what became of the jewellery that these customers bought from us a century ago. Sometimes we are lucky and one of their descendants brings us a jewel. But I'm sure thousands of these jewels from the past have disappeared. One of the most important was for William Boyce Thompson (1869-1930). He had amassed a considerable fortune by exploiting gold and copper mines in Montana. He first came to Italy aboard his yacht, the* Alder, *in 1927."*[1]

When William Boyce Thompson died in 1930, his only daughter, Margaret inherited an estimated fortune of $85 million, twice the fortune left to another American billionaire and Bulgari client, Barbara Hutton. Wife of a banker, then of a diplomat, Margaret died prematurely in 1956, at the age of 59. She had spent the last ten years of her life in Paris. Her mansion on Rue las Cases in the 7th arrondissement was the last elegant salon in the French capital. In the photos dating from this time, she always appears impeccably elegant and covered with diamonds of imposing size. Alas, it is impossible to determine whether any of these jewels came from Bulgari. In the United States her name is still famous for very practical reasons. A collector of silversmith and goldsmith work she bequeathed more than 1500 pieces of vermeil, or silver-gilt, to the White House. Since 1956, this vermeil collection has been used by all American presidents for the gala dinners they have given in their Washington residence.

One fact is certain, between 1930 and 1939, Giorgio Bulgari made several trips to the United States. It was here that he acquired the two exceptional diamonds – one blue, one pink – that he sold to Count Cini before the war. After the Second World War, Dorothy di Frasso made it easier for Giorgio to return to the USA.

Facing page: *Margaret Boyce Thompson (1901-1956), the only daughter of William Boyce Thompson (1869-1930). Margaret was Bulgari's first American customer.*

According to Bulgari family legend, Giorgio's bank accounts in the United States were frozen during the war as the property of a national of an enemy nation. It was Dorothy's intervention that led to his accounts being released quickly so that Giorgio could resume his business activities of buying stones and selling jewellery. His eagerness to return to New York indicates the importance of the American market at that time.

More evidence of American Bulgari clientele is to be found in the sale catalogue of May Bonfils Stanton's jewels. The auction was organised by Parke-Bernet in New York on 14 November, 1962. Almost forgotten today, Mary Madeline "May" Bonfils Stanton (1883-1962) was, nevertheless, an emblematic character of 20th century American legend. The eldest daughter of one of the most famous journalists of the time, Frederick Gilmer Bonfils and his wife Belle Barton, May was born in 1883 in Troy, Missouri. She was eight when her parents decided to move to Denver, Colorado. In the meantime, her younger sister, Helen, was born. Frederick Gilmer Bonfils was a pioneer of sensationalist journalism, which would bring him much trouble – including being beaten with a whip in the street by a lawyer! Nevertheless, he made a fortune developing the daily newspaper he bought when he arrived in Colorado: The *Denver Post*. Though he himself was unscrupulous in his approach to getting his scoop, he insisted that his two daughters receive a strict Catholic education.

The result was, perhaps, unsurprising. In 1904, having just celebrated her 21st birthday, May eloped with Clyde V. Berryman, who was neither rich nor Catholic. The rift this caused with her family was never resolved. After her father's death in 1933 and her mother's in 1935, May discovered that she had been disinherited in favour of her sister, Helen. Inevitably, the two sisters began a long legal process at the end of which, May recovered a good part of her inheritance. At least she was rich, even if her marriage with Clyde was failing. At the heart of an immense 300-hectare park, east of Denver, she dug an artificial lake and built a replica of the Petit Trianon, Marie-Antoinette's château in Versailles park. May also accumulated jewels, including two huge diamonds, the Idol's Eye, weighing 70 carats, and the Liberator of 39.8 carats. Her emerald necklace was mounted with a series of fabulous stones purchased from the Maharaja of Indore. Her sapphire necklace was also an imposing piece, evidently of Art Deco design. The pendant was made of an oval

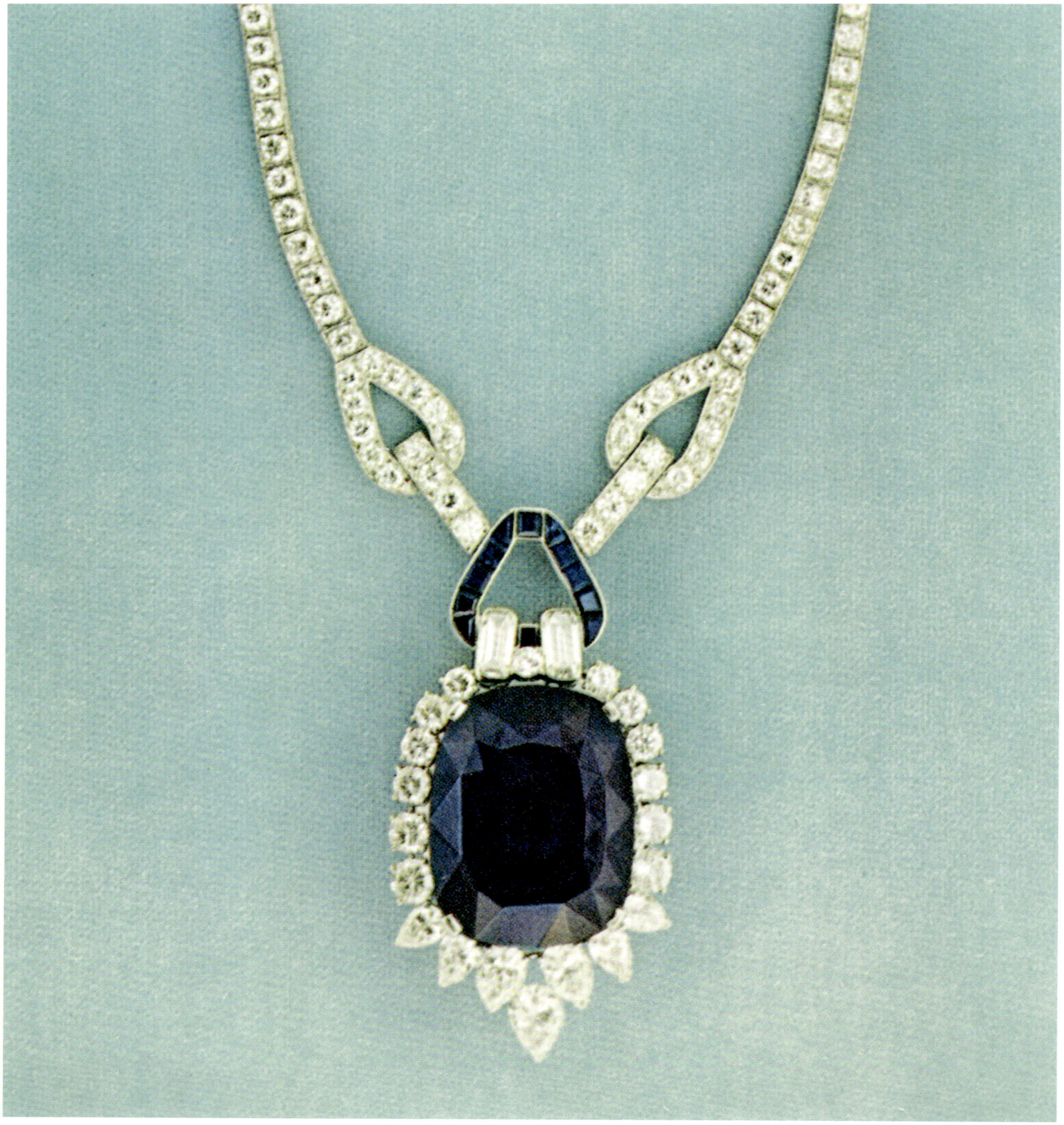

The Bulgari style changed considerably over 40 years.
Above: *This sapphire and diamond necklace was part of May Bonfils Stanton's jewellery collection, which sold at Parke-Bernet in New York in 1962; it was created by Bulgari c.1930 and is typical of the Art Deco style.* **Facing page:** *The diamond and sapphire sautoir bought from Bulgari for, or by, Elizabeth Taylor circa 1969. The central cabochon sapphire weighs 52.72 carats. It was sold at Christie's, New York in December 2011. Bulgari Heritage Collection.*

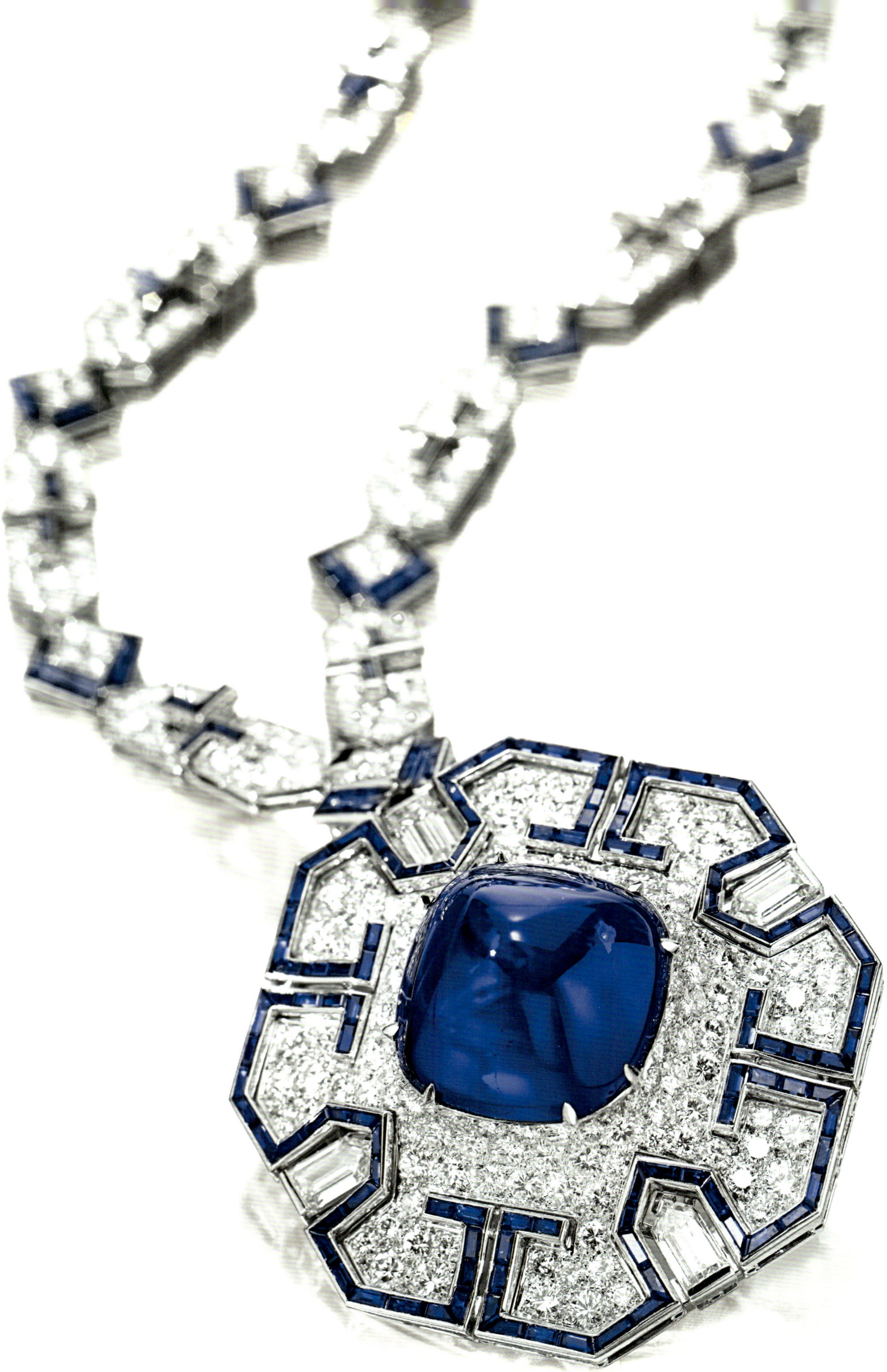

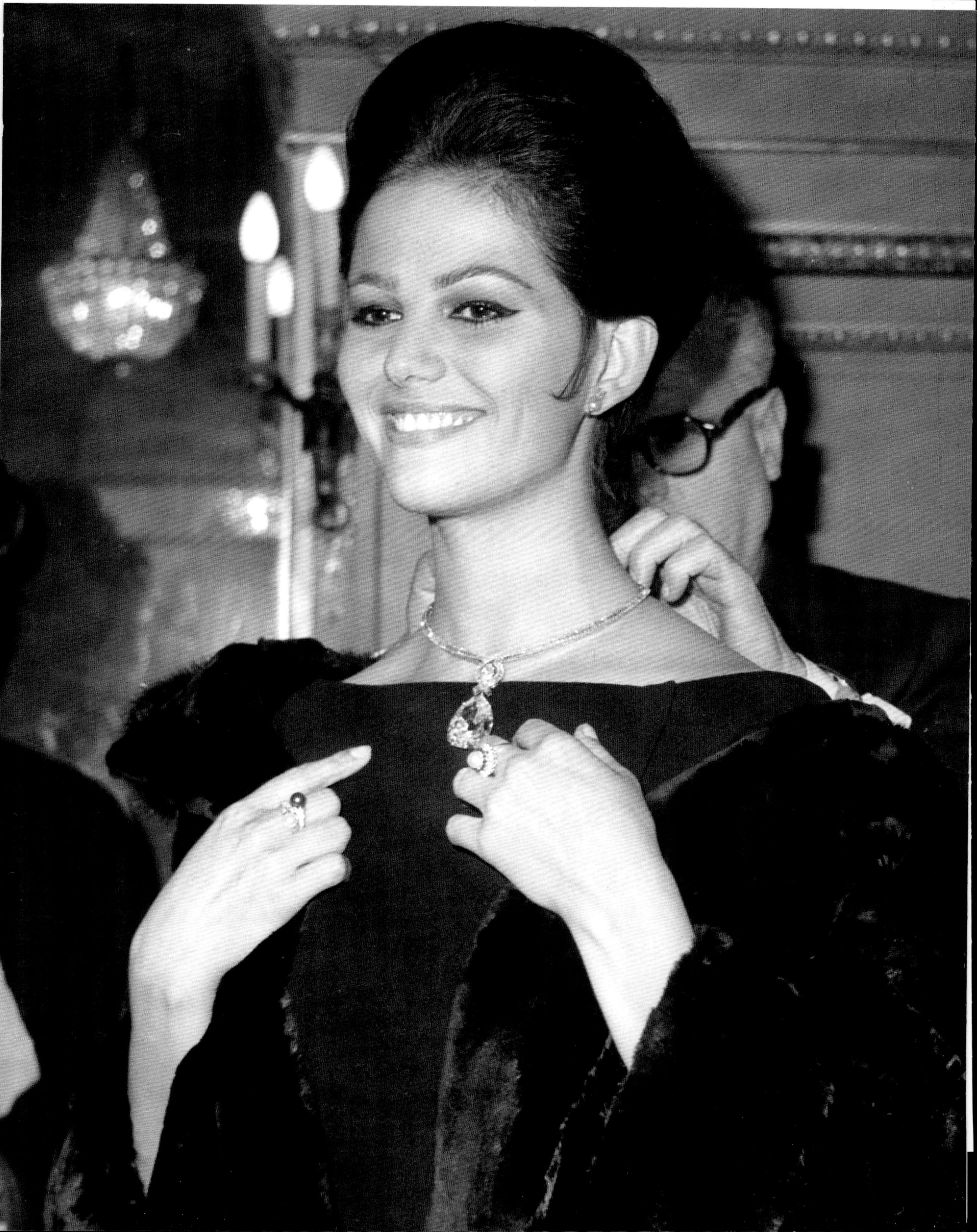

Chapter 11

DIAMONDS OF THE DOLCE VITA

Claudia Cardinale's diamond

In 1962, Claudia Cardinale appeared at a gala at the Italian embassy in Paris wearing a 66-carat pear-shaped diamond mounted on a chain of smaller diamonds by Bulgari. At the time Miss Cardinale was world famous, having starred in the most famous movie ever filmed in Italy: *The Leopard* (*Il Gattopardo*). In 1968 alone she appeared in no fewer than five films. She is known as one the most beautiful women in the world. The pear-shaped diamond was sold a few months later to a collector from Rome.

La Favorite diamond

La Favorite diamond first appeared at the Chicago World's Fair in 1934. It had recently been mined in South Africa and cut into a 50.15-carat VVS-2, D colour gem. The stone is a IIA diamond, a very rare quality of diamond usually found only in some Indian diamonds. In 1934, it was valued at $1million, an outstanding price during those difficult Depression years. From America, it seems it went to France, which is where Paolo Bulgari bought it in 1960. Mounted on a ring by Bulgari, it was sold to an American collector. It was later sold by auction at Christie's, New York.

10 April 2001, Christie's, New York.

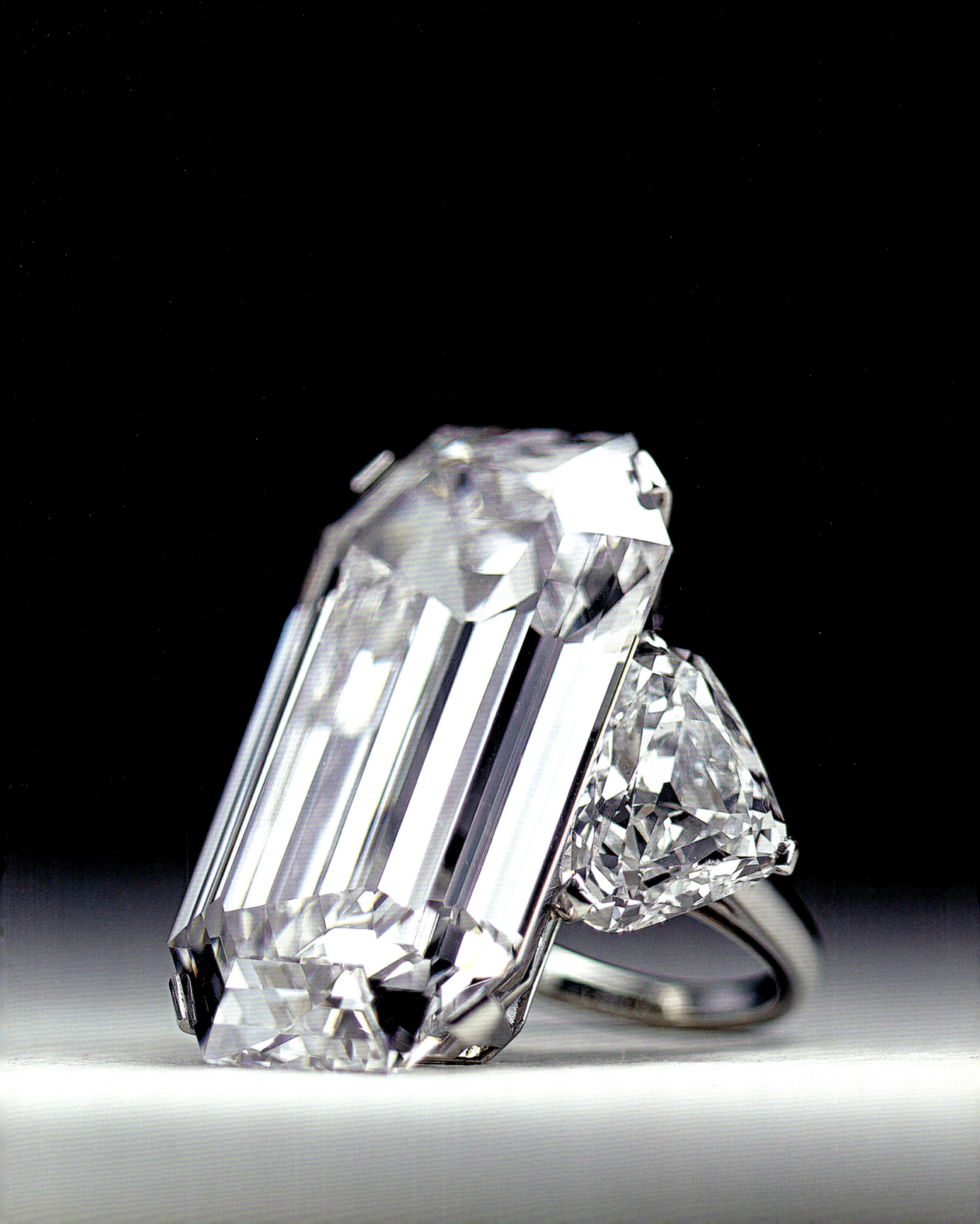

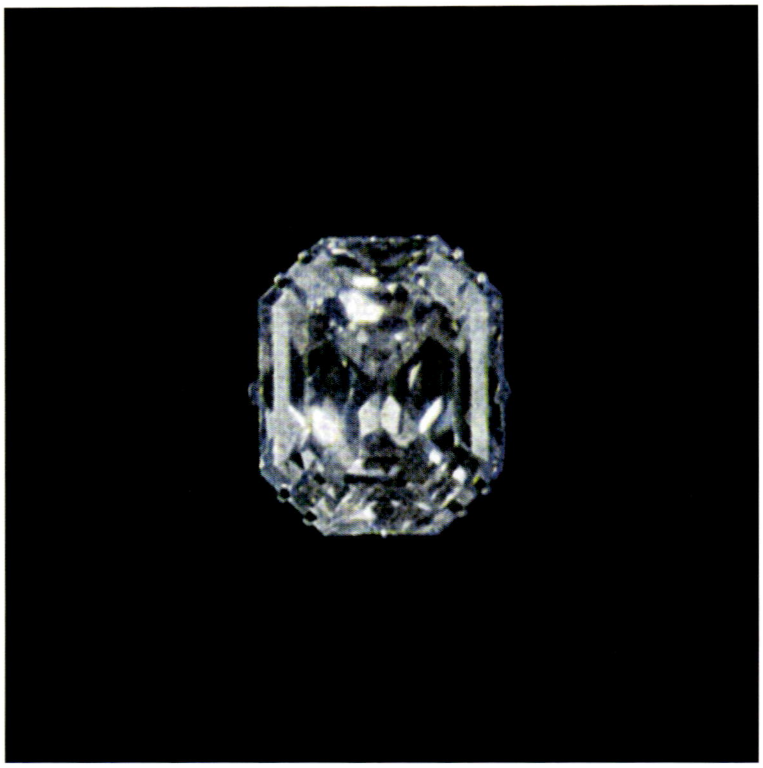

The Nassak diamond

History tells us that from 1500 to 1817, the Nassak diamond was kept as a sacred treasure in the Trimbakeshwar Shiva temple, near the Indian town of Nassak. During one of the Anglo-Maratha wars, at the beginning of the 19th century, this 89-carat blue diamond was handed over to the Marquess of Hastings, the Governor-General of India. It was Hastings who gave the diamond its name. In 1817, the Nassak was sold in London to the famous jeweller, Rundell & Bridge, who had it recut into a smaller 78-carat stone in order to improve its clarity. In 1830 the diamond came into the possession of one of the richest men in Britain, Earl Grosvenor, who the following year became the Marquess of Westminster. He was the owner of a large part of the City of Westminster in the centre of London. At one point, he owned five of the world's biggest diamonds, including the Pasha. In 1927, the diamond left England for America when the 2nd Duke of Westminster (the Marquess's great-great grandson) decided to sell it. There, it was recut again to change its triangular shape into a more classical emerald-cut, reducing it to 43 carats. Bulgari bought it in 1970 in partnership with an American firm from Boston. According to Lord Balfour, one of the world's experts on the history of diamonds, the Nassak was purchased by the King of Saudi Arabia in 1977, along with a large Burmese ruby.

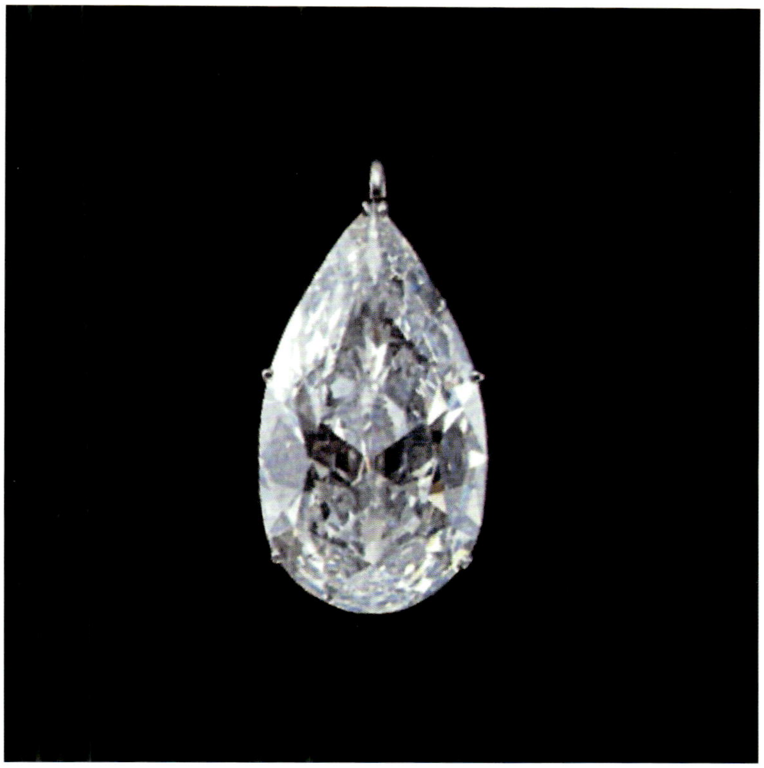

Merle Oberon's diamond

This 17.99-carat diamond is a D-colour, the best colour for diamonds. It was the last lot in the sale of Merle Oberon's personal jewellery at Christie's, New York on 22 April, 1980. By the time of the auction, the diamond was set as a pendant, but it is likely that it was originally set in a ring. Bought from Bulgari in 1949, this diamond is very probably the one given by Giorgio Cini, a few months before his death, to Merle Oberon, the woman he loved and whom he intended to become his wife.

22 April 1980, Christie's New York.

Leonilde Bulgari's diamond Trombino ring

This ring was given to Leonilde Bulgari by her future husband, Giorgio Bulgari in 1932. It was one of the very first "Trombino rings". This type of ring got its name from its shape, which is vaguely reminiscent of a trombone. Its form places the diamond a little bit higher in the setting, while surrounding it with other diamonds in order to focus the maximum light on the central diamond. Leonilde and Giorgio Bulgari had four children: Lia, Gianni, Paolo and Nicola Bulgari.

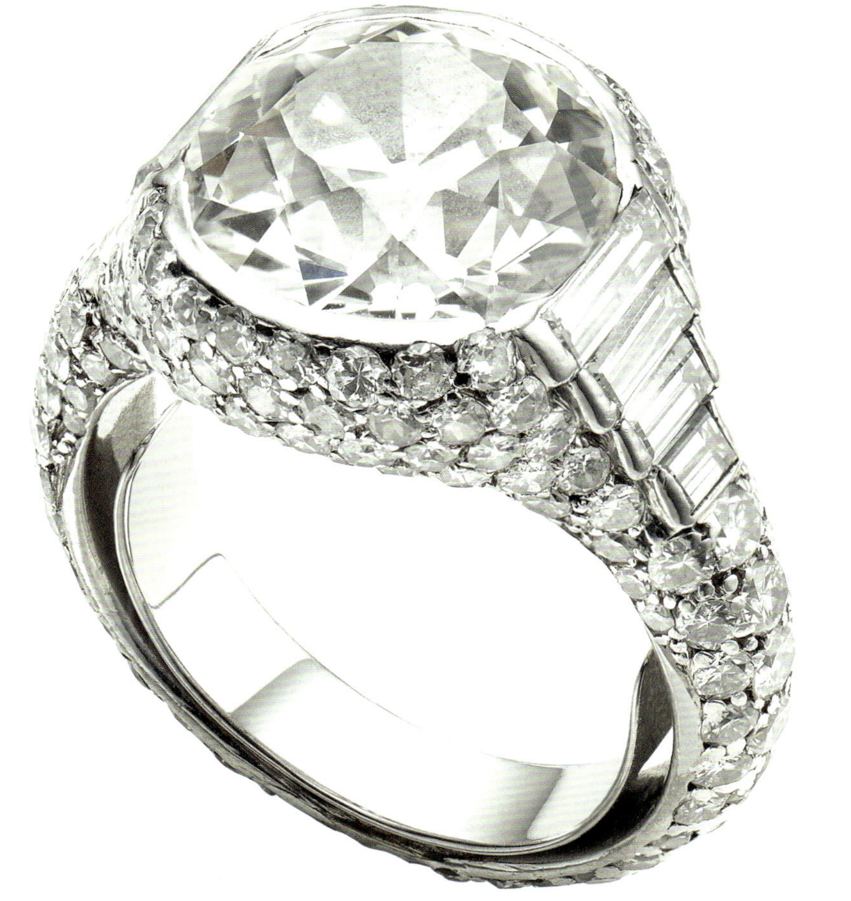

Elizabeth Taylor's yellow diamonds

These two fancy yellow diamonds weigh 15.60 and 15.39 carats. Set on a pair of pendant earrings, they were given to Elizabeth Taylor, by her fourth husband, Eddie Fisher. (Private collection.)

13 December 2012, Christie's New York.

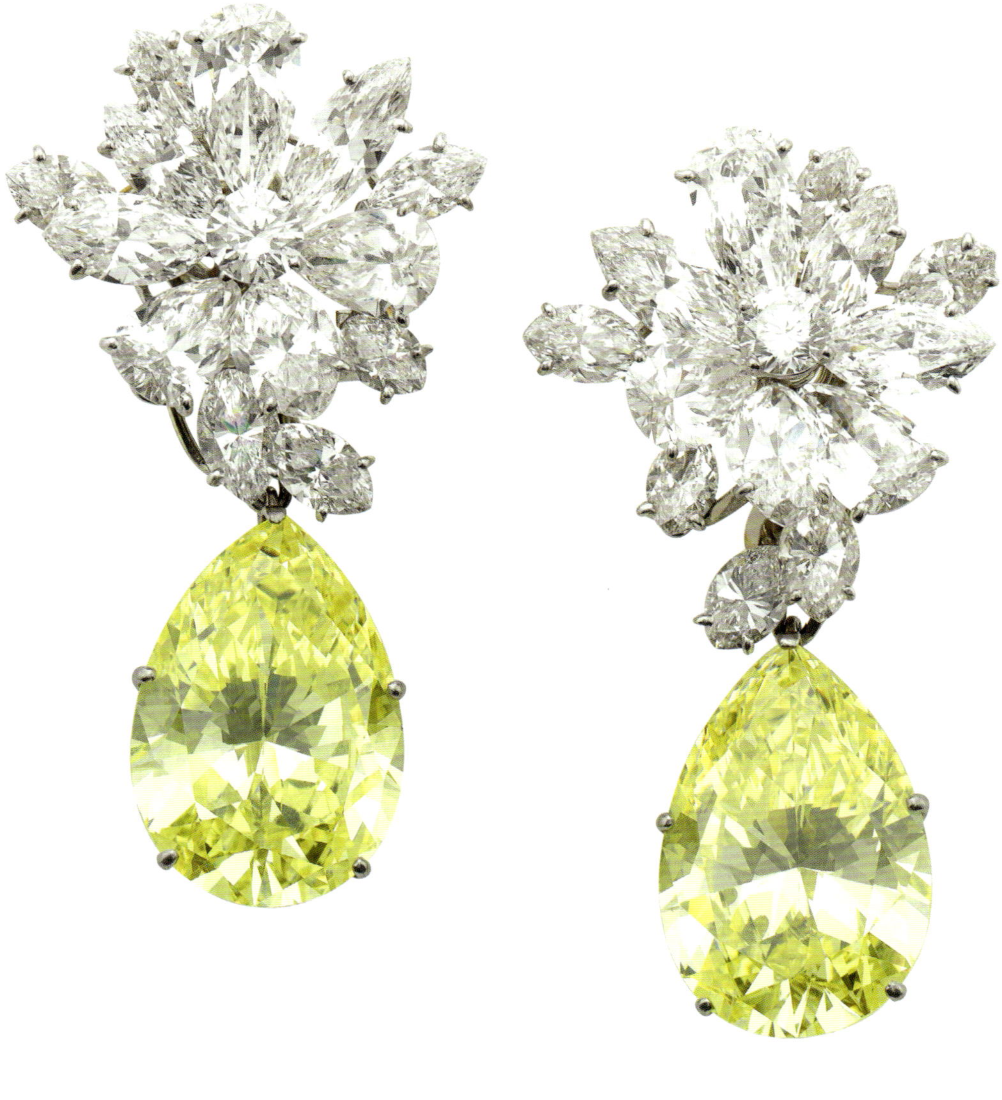

Gina Lollobrigida's diamond

Gina Lollobrigida was a world famous star, appearing in movies in Europe and in America. In 1965, she was photographed in Bulgari's shop in Rome with a 60-carat diamond. Unlike other actresses who would happily pose for this kind of photograph for publicity reasons, Gina Lollobrigida was a serious jewellery collector. Most of her jewels were bought from Bulgari. Among other pieces, she owned two extremely handsome emeralds set as a pair of earrings and two enormous natural pear-shaped pearls. In 1949, her future husband, Dr Milko Skofic gave her a 19.03-carat diamond mounted on a ring. (Private collection.)

14 May 2013, Sotheby's Geneva.

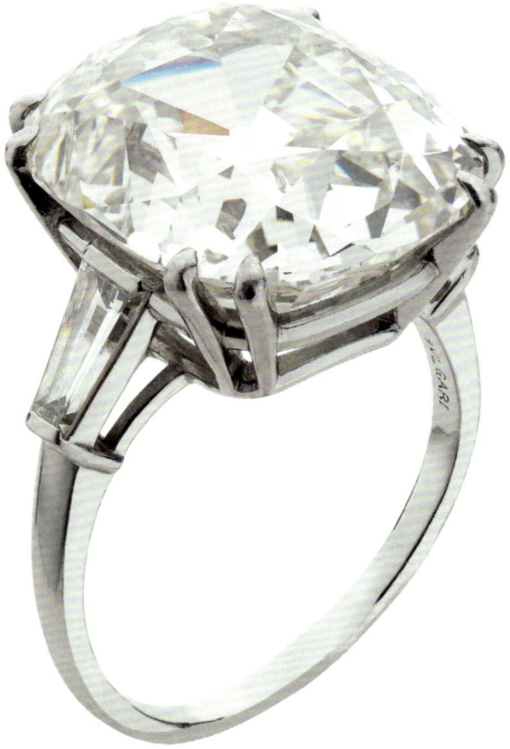

The Rainbow Flower brooch

With a 2.86-carat yellow diamond, a 2.47-carat blue diamond and a 2.09-carat blue-green diamond this brooch – created in 1964 – is certainly one of the rarest ever produced by Bulgari. It is part of a collection of flower jewels created in the 1960s when Giorgio Bulgari purchased the most important collection of coloured diamonds in the world. It belonged to the French diamond dealer Myran Eknayan and Giorgio Bulgari had tried to buy it for years. Finally, and after many years of negotiation, Eknayan agreed to sell his hundreds of coloured diamonds. *"We had to do something with all these diamonds,"* remembers Paolo Bulgari. *"This is why we created the flower jewels."*

9 December 2015, Sotheby's New York.

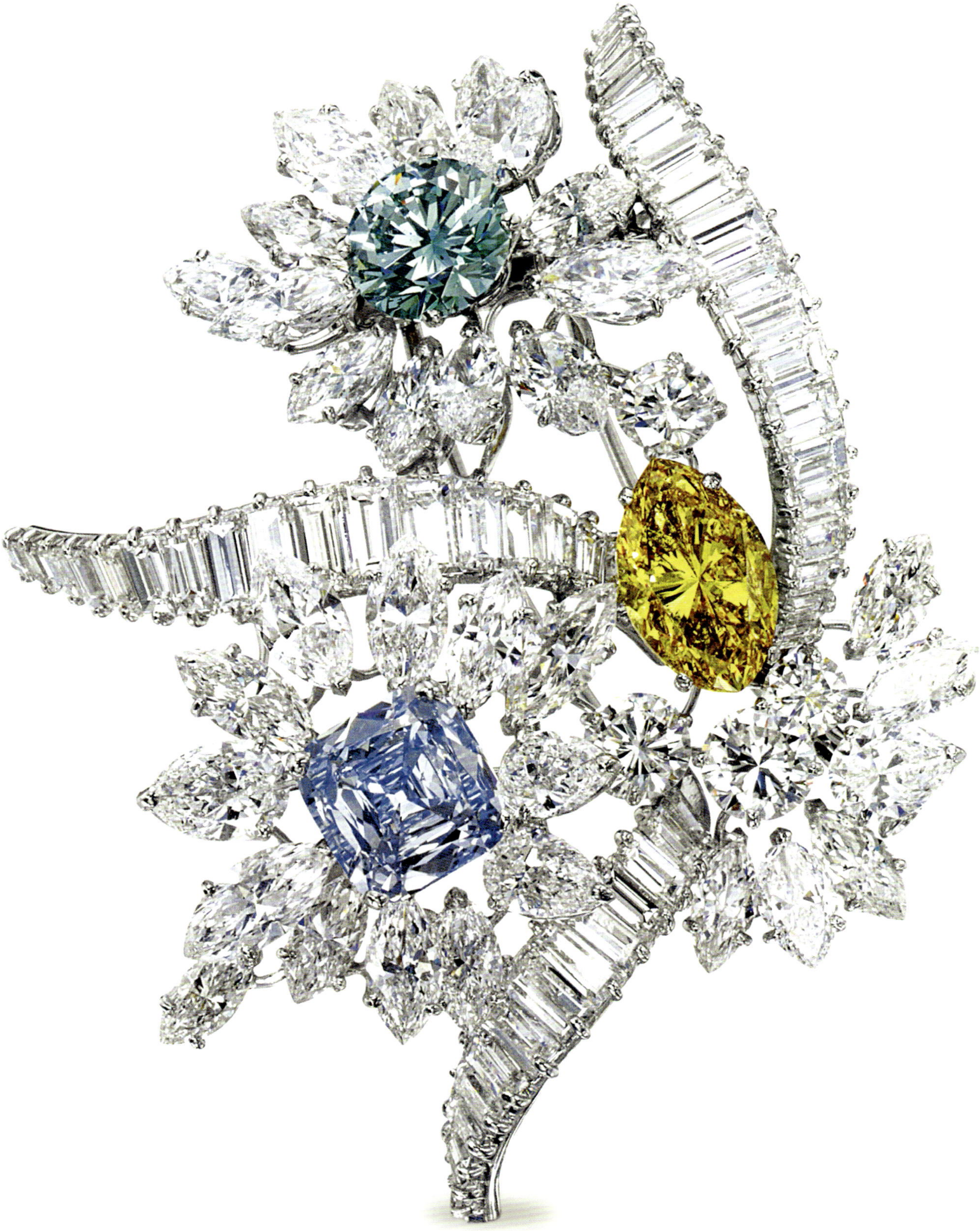

The Pasha diamond

No one knows exactly when this wonderful 40-carat diamond was found. But it seems to be of Indian origin. Its first official records date from the 19th century when it came into the treasure of the Kings of Egypt. The story goes that it was acquired for £28,000, an enormous sum of money at the time, by Ibrahim Pasha (1789-1848), the son of Muhammad Ali, Wali of Egypt. Some say it was sold by Ibrahim Pasha's son, Isma'il Pasha, the Khedive of Egypt in order to finance his exile in Europe after he had lost the crown of Egypt in 1879. Another oral tradition kept in the Egyptian royal family, maintains that the diamond never left the collection of Isma'il Pasha. It was inherited by his second son, Sultan Hussein Kamel, who in turn gave it to his wife, Sultana Melek. At some point, Sultana Melek gave or sold it to her nephew King Farouk. One way or the other, the diamond found its way to King Farouk's collection. And when he was exiled from his country in 1952, he took it with him. Needing to sell some of his treasures in order to fund his flamboyant lifestyle in Rome, he sold the Pasha diamond to Giorgio Bulgari, who in turn sold it to the legendary American heiress, Barbara Hutton (1912-1979). As she did not like the octagonal cut of the Pasha diamond, she had it recut in a perfect brilliant, losing a few carats in the process. The Pasha diamond weighs 38.19 carats, it is a flawless D-colour diamond and arguably one of the most beautiful diamonds in the world. After Barbara Hutton's death it was sold again and is now in a private collection in Italy.

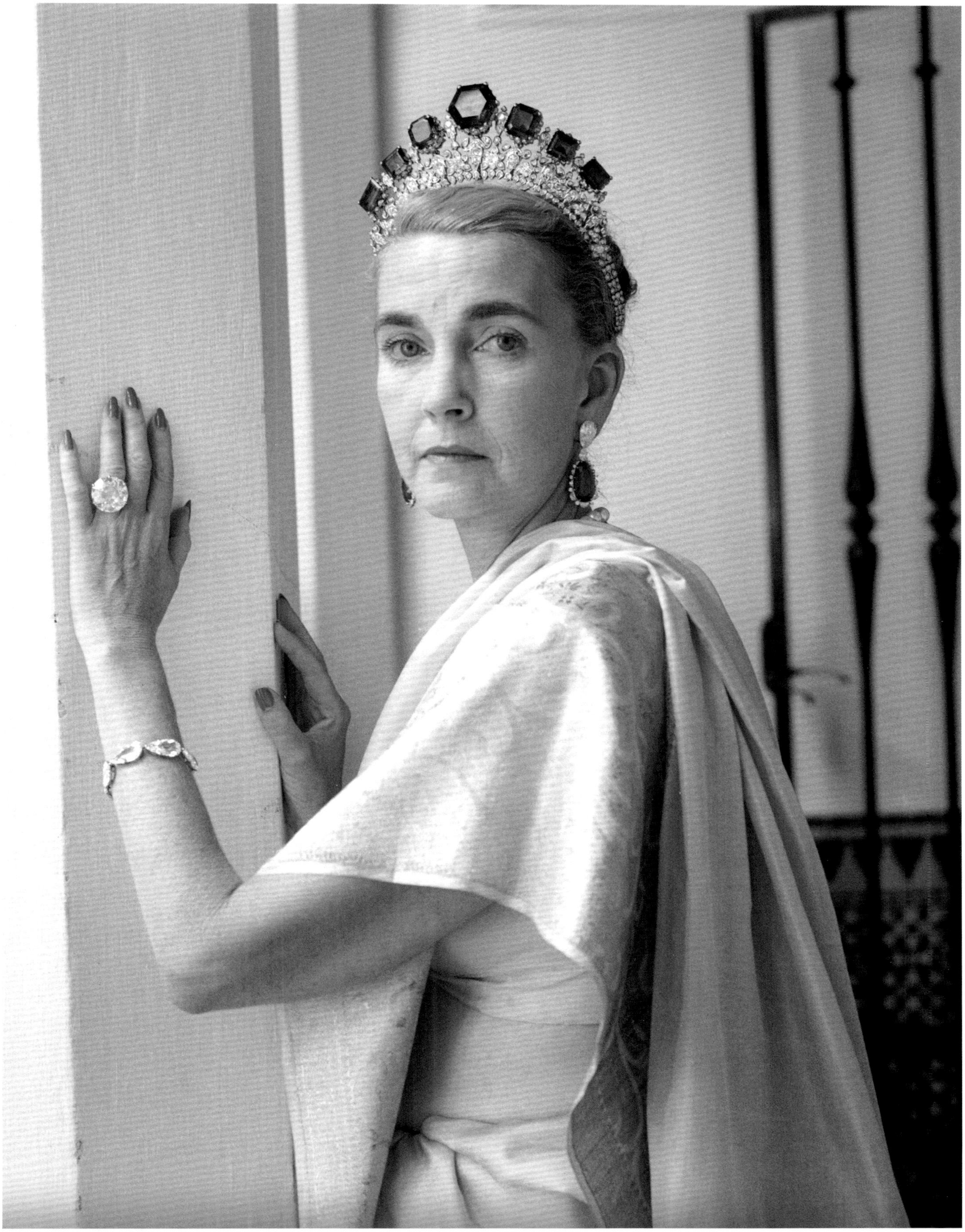

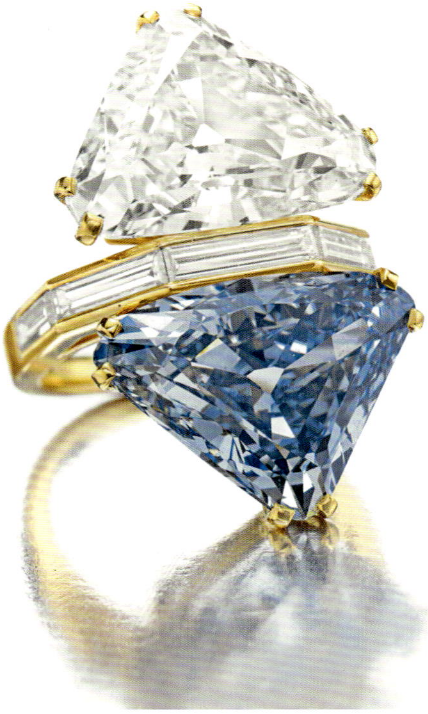

"Toi et Moi" with blue and white diamonds

This diamond ring dates from 1972. It was bought from Bulgari, at Via dei Condotti, by a gentleman who wanted to give his wife an exceptional gift. A few days earlier, she had given birth to their first son. It did not take long for Carlo Tronconi, a salesman at the Bulgari shop, to find something unique for this gentleman: a gold ring with not one, but two large triangular-shaped diamonds. The colourless stone of 9.87 carats and blue diamond of 10.95 carats are set facing each other either side of a belt of baguette diamonds. The jewel's name, "Toi et moi" translates from the French as "You and Me".

20 October 2010, Christie's, New York.

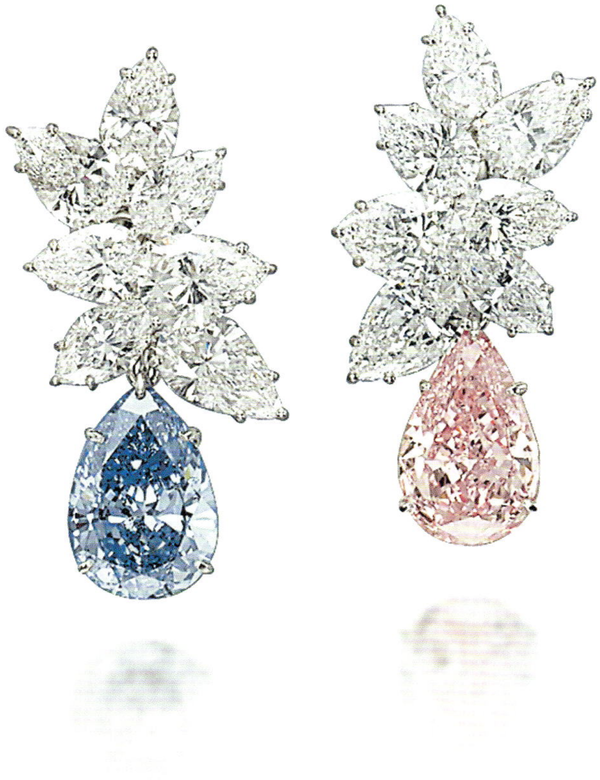

Pink and Blue diamond earrings

These two diamonds are part of Bulgari legend. They were set in earrings in 2007. The pink gem weighed 6.7 carats; the blue, 6.96 carats. A special client order meant that these diamonds had to be set and delivered extremely quickly, so there was no time even to photograph the earrings when they came out of the Bulgari workshop in Rome. The only record was a blurry photograph of the two stones. Fortunately, the earrings came to light seven years later at auction at Christie's in Geneva. They were one of the highlights of the catalogue. Presented in a special showcase they were the stars of the auction.

11th of November 2014, Christie's Geneva.

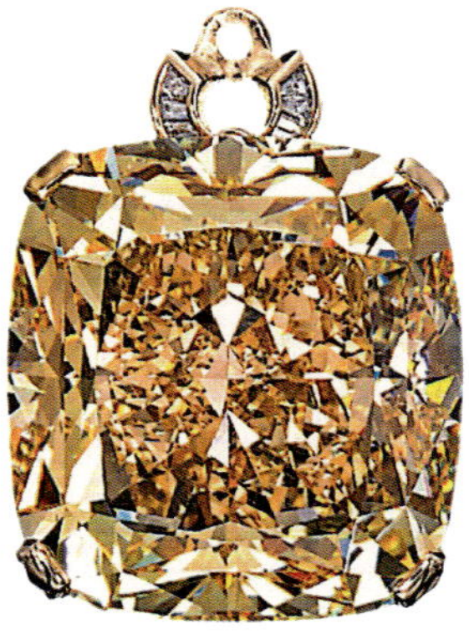

The Mouna diamond

With its 112.53 carats, this fancy yellow diamond is certainly the largest coloured diamond ever sold by Bulgari. It was bought by the famous socialite and business woman, Mouna Ayoub. In order for Mrs Ayoub to wear it, Bulgari created this fabulous diamond necklace with 28 fancy yellow diamonds.

16 November 1998, Christie's Geneva.

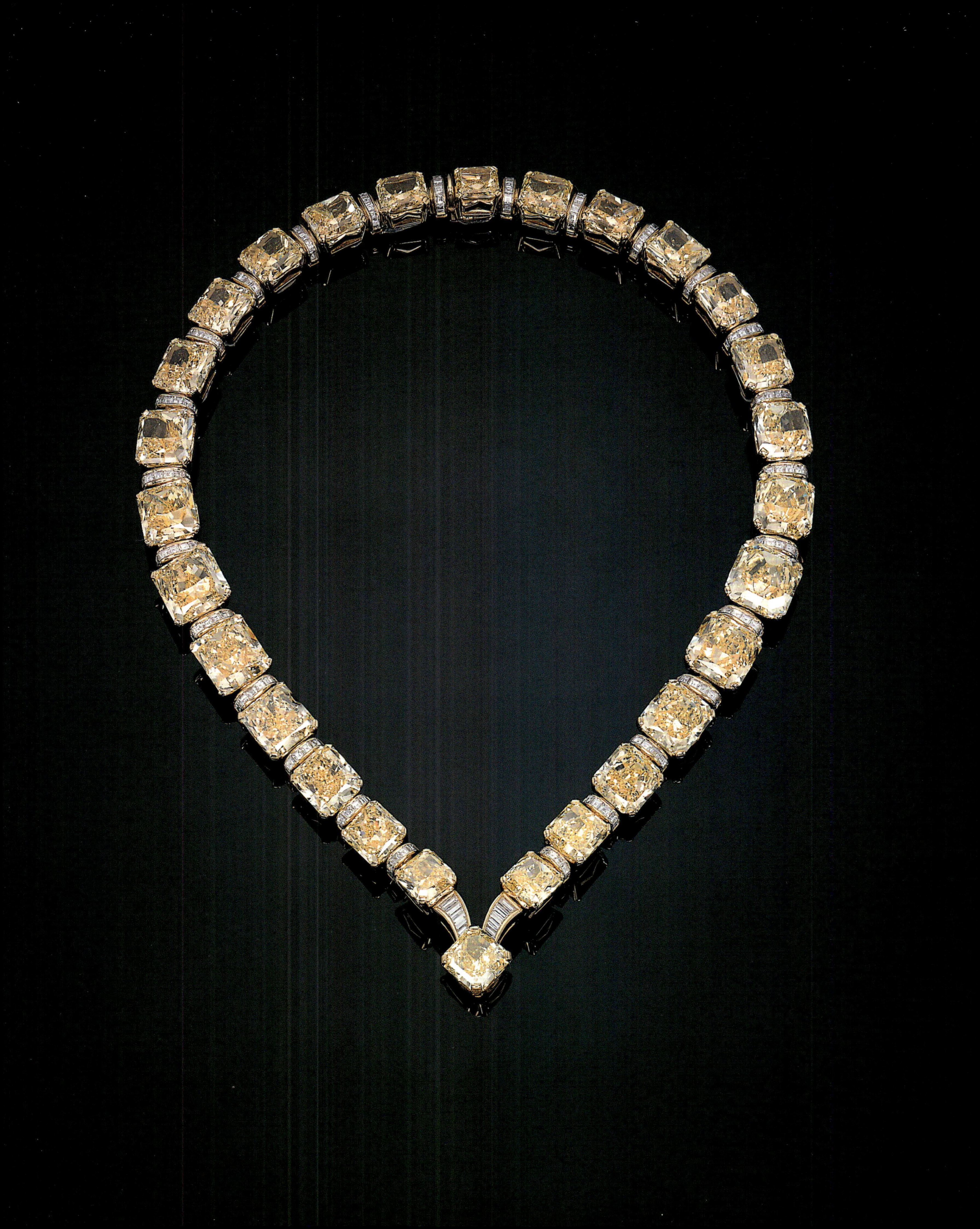

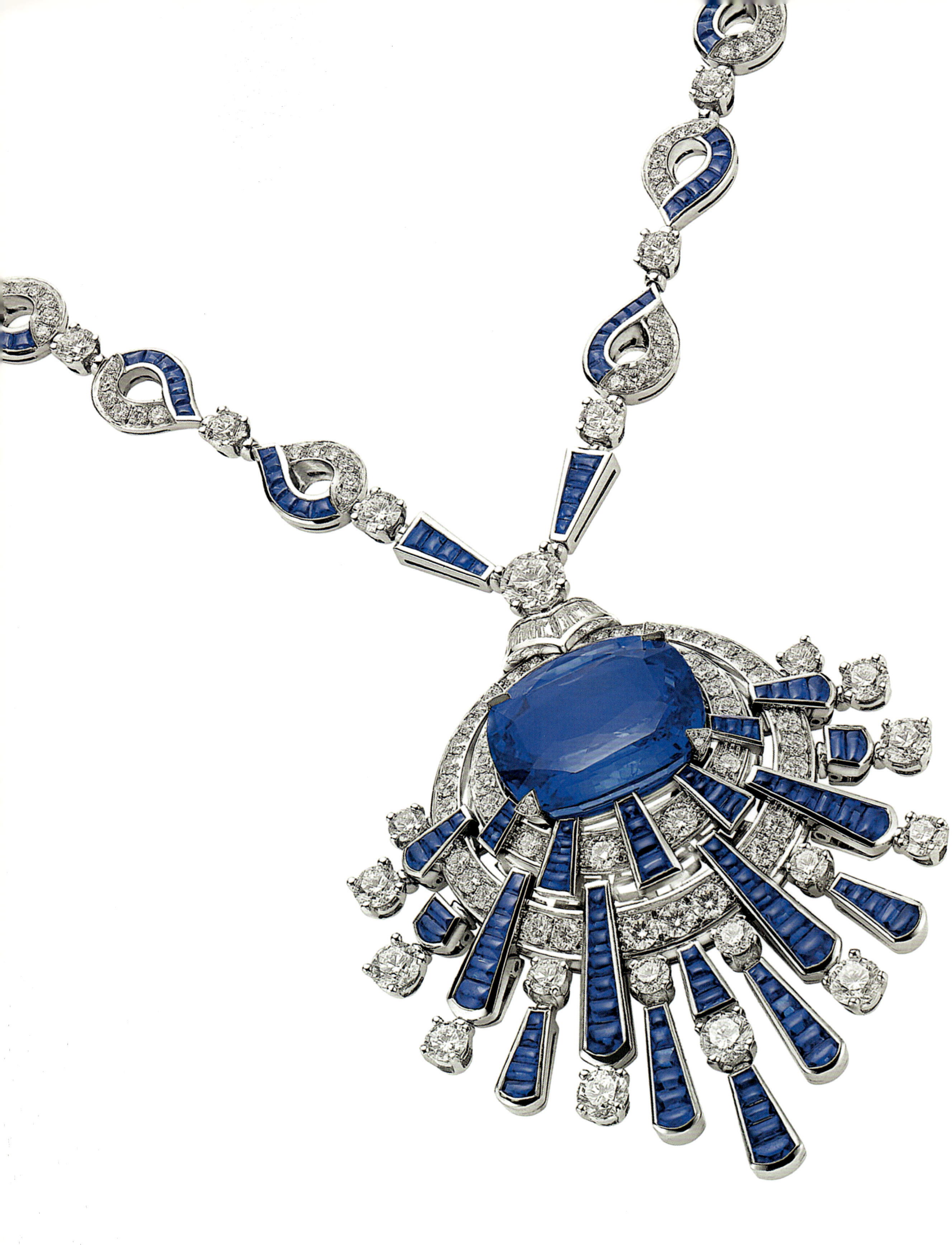

Chapter 12

THE LAND OF SAPPHIRES

BULGARI IN SRI LANKA

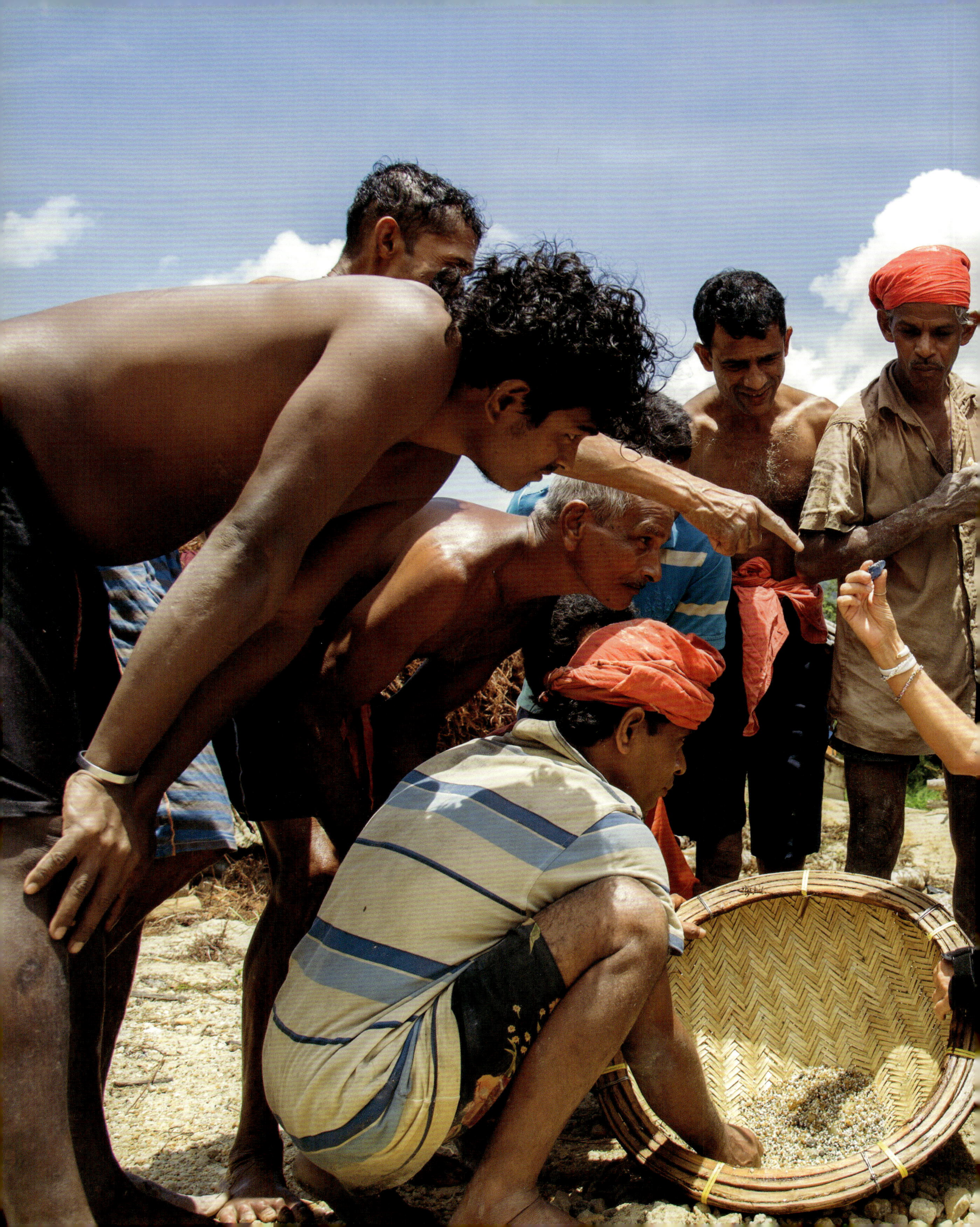

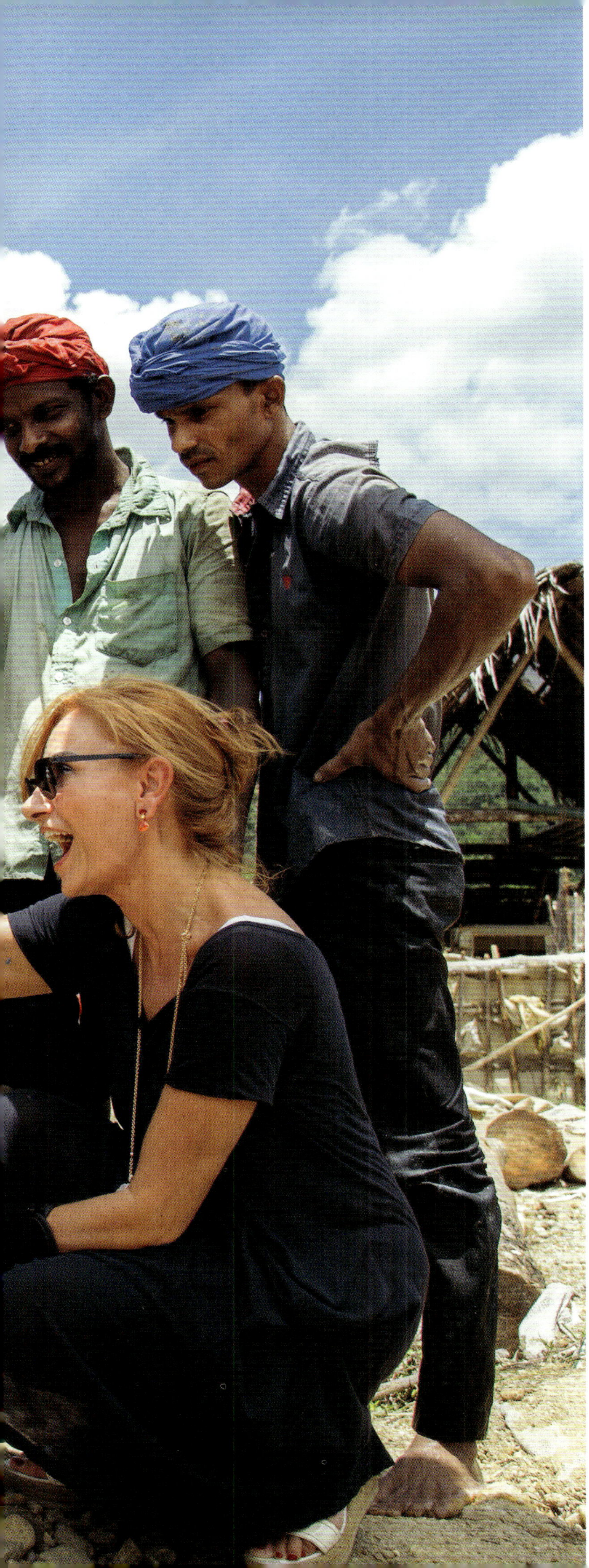

Choosing and buying precious stones is one of Bulgari's best kept secrets. And one place is more important than any: Sri Lanka. Most of the wonderful sapphires mounted on Bulgari jewels originate from this island. Every year Bulgari's Creative Director of High Jewellery, Lucia Silvestri travels to Sri Lanka to select and buy the most beautiful sapphires in the world. Her first stop is usually Colombo, where she meets Rainier Nanayakkara, the most important sapphire dealer in Sri Lanka. She also sometimes goes to Ratnapura where the mines are located. This is a fairytale trip at the very heart of the mysteries that are Bulgari, maybe the most important of all: choosing the very best stones.

This page: *Every year the Bulgari Creative Director, Lucia Silvestri goes to the Ratnapura mines in Sri Lanka to buy sapphires.*
Previous page: *Bulgari necklace from the Festa collection.*

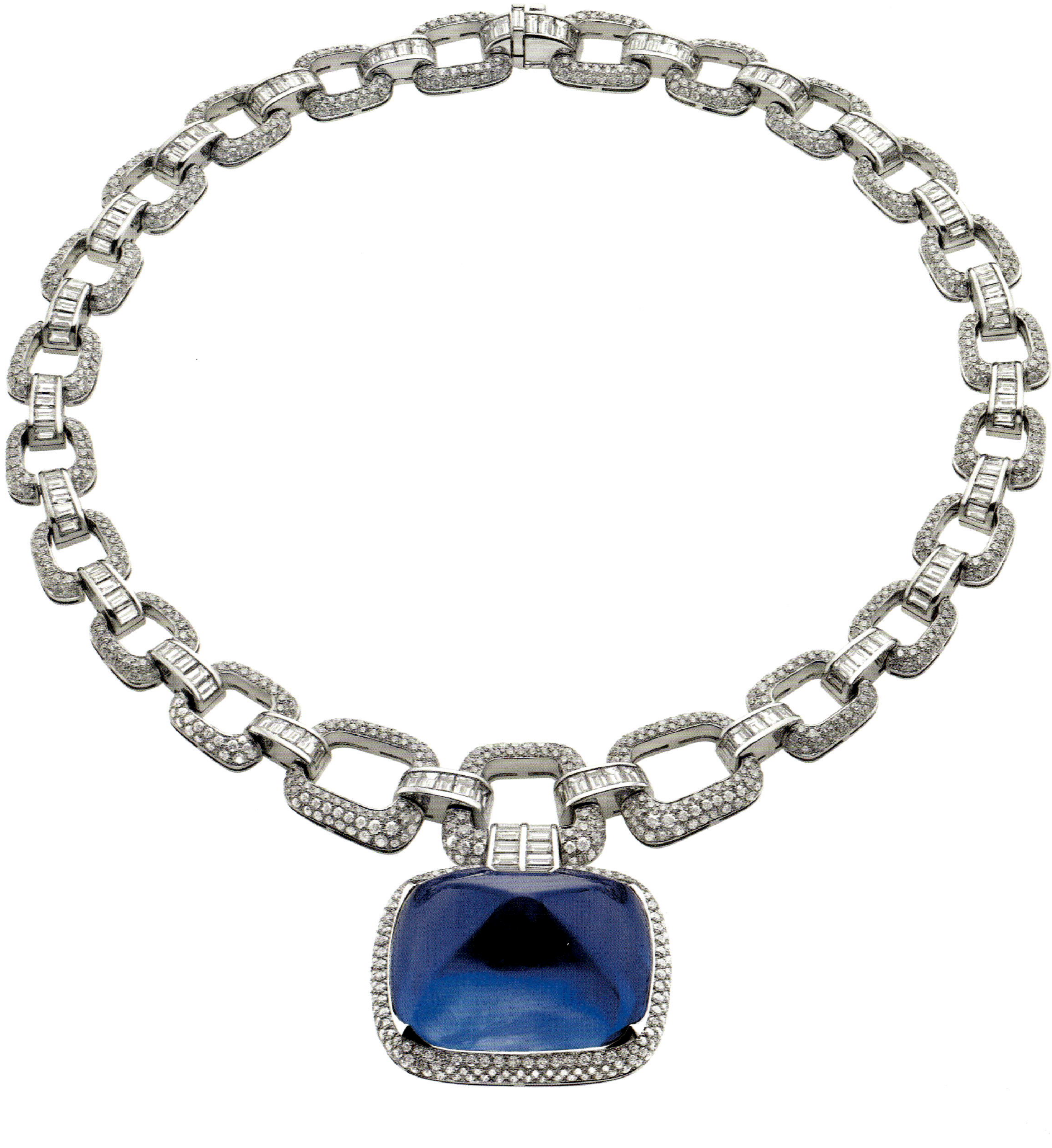

A Treasure Trove of Precious Gems

In a few days time, the first pilgrims will start climbing the sacred mountain. Adam's Peak (Sri Pada) dominates the landscape of the Ratnapura region, which for centuries, has produced some of the most beautiful sapphires in the world. Hindu, Muslim, Buddhist and Christian pilgrims will walk, as they do every year from December to May, to worship the sacred footprint. For some it belongs to Shivah, for others it was left here by Buddha or Adam, the first man of creation. The miners in the Ratnapura region have another belief. For them, the sacred mountain is the sanctuary of the Buddhist god, Saman. He watches over Mother Earth and offers its wealth to her children in the form of precious stones, which have always been found here in huge quantities.

Lucia Silvestri does not contradict that belief. She checks the content of a miner's sieve and observes every single move of these men who constantly dig the soil to extract the natural wonders that Bulgari will set in fabulous pieces of jewellery. Every year she comes to Sri Lanka to buy the stones for her next collection: *"Ninety per cent of the sapphires we use come from here,"* she explains. But even she does not visit the mines often. She usually stays in Colombo and deals with the man known as "The king of Sapphires", Rainier Nanayakkara. This year, at her request, the annual meeting takes place 100 miles from the capital city in the region of the mines, Ratnapura. The name Ratnapura (ratna = precious stones, pura = town) is the byword for sapphires, just like Golconda for diamonds and Mogok in Burma for rubies.

The day begins on the shore of the Kalu Ganga River. Balanced at one end of a raft above the water, a man holds a wooden boat hook several metres in length. His task is to agitate the bed of the river at its deepest point. In front of him five other miners wield long shovels in which they collect the gravel that rises to the surface. Then they lift the shovels into the raft and use their feet to spread the minerals to determine if a sapphire or a spinel has come up to the surface. From the banks of the river, Lucia observes the fascinating work taking place before her eyes. Sri Lanka is her adopted home. *"My first trip here was almost 30 years ago,"* she explains. *"I had met Rainier at a gemstone fair in Tucson, Arizona. We had decided to meet again in Sri Lanka, in the land of sapphires."* For Bulgari, the sapphire is an emblematic stone. The two Bulgari brothers, Paolo and Nicola, are unconditional fans of this stone. It can be blue, yellow, purple and even, in the case of the rarest ones, the Padparadschas, the "lotus flowers" in Sinhalese, a very rare salmon pink.

Let us make one or two things clear about sapphire. The name comes from Greek or Hebrew. It is, in fact, a corundum. Sapphires come in all colours except red; red corundum is ruby. *"It was with sapphires that I began my creative job,"* says Lucia. *"I still remember the pleasure I felt while assembling sapphires of different*

Facing page: *Bulgari necklace from the Festa collection; the principal sapphire weighs 180.98 carats.*

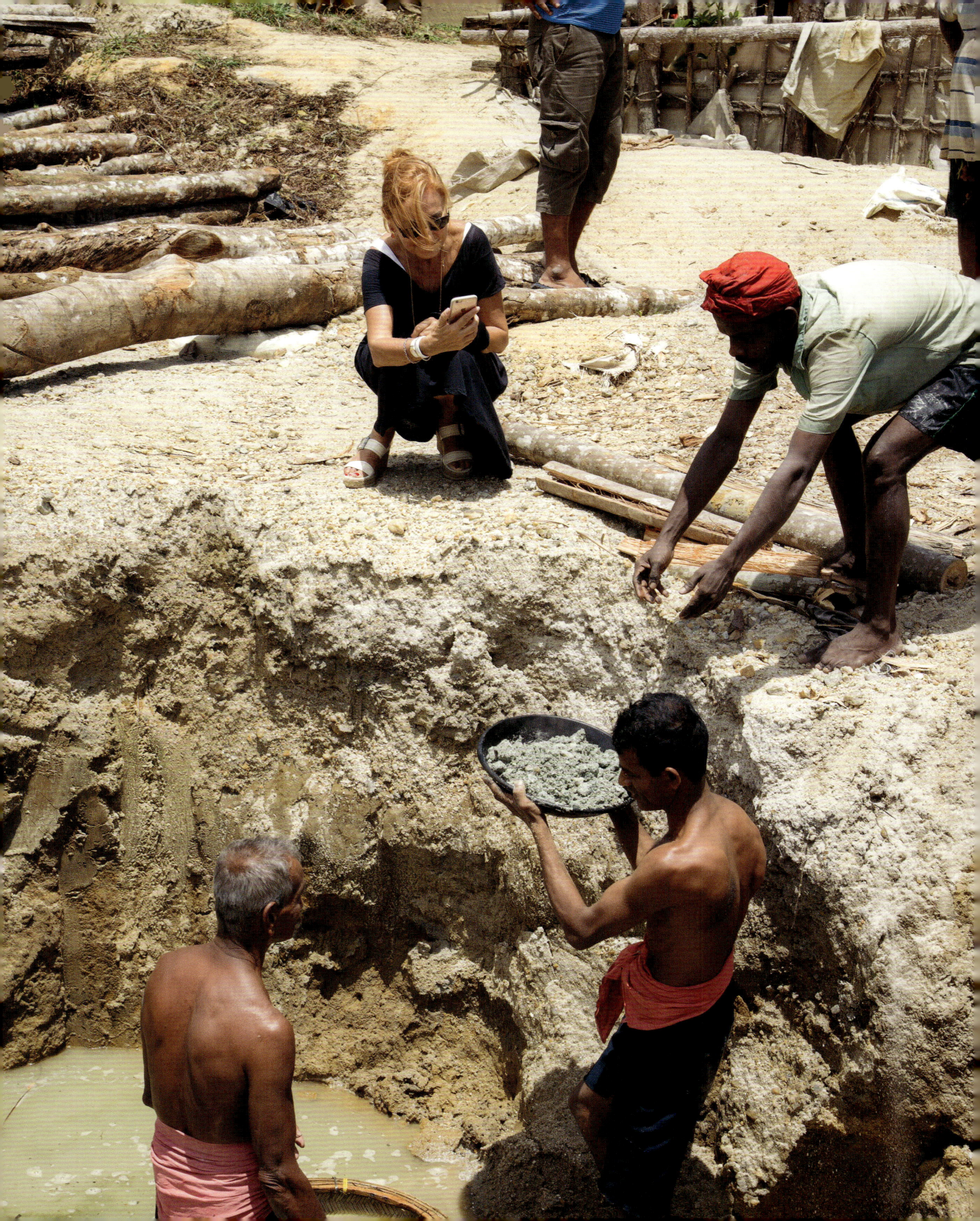

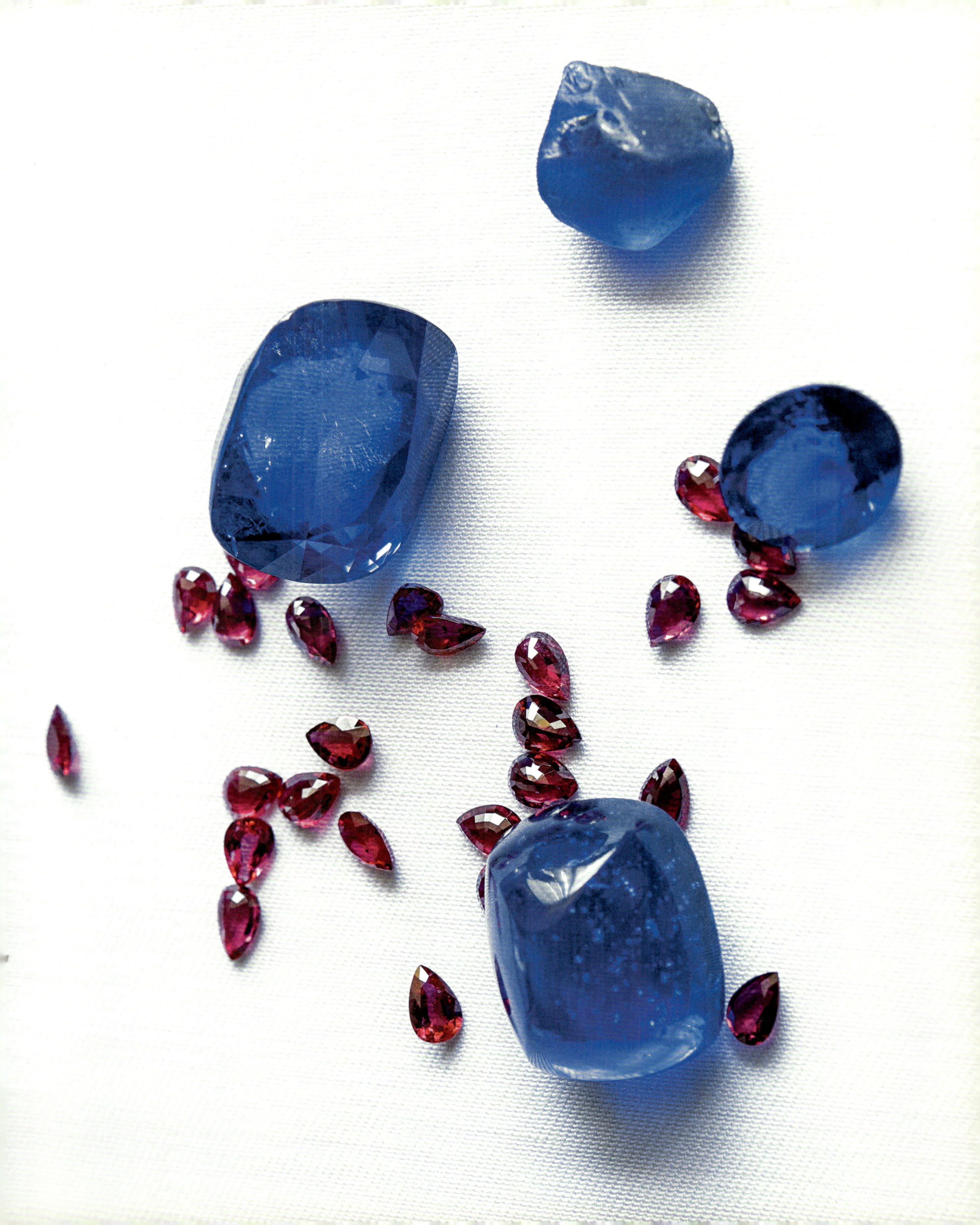

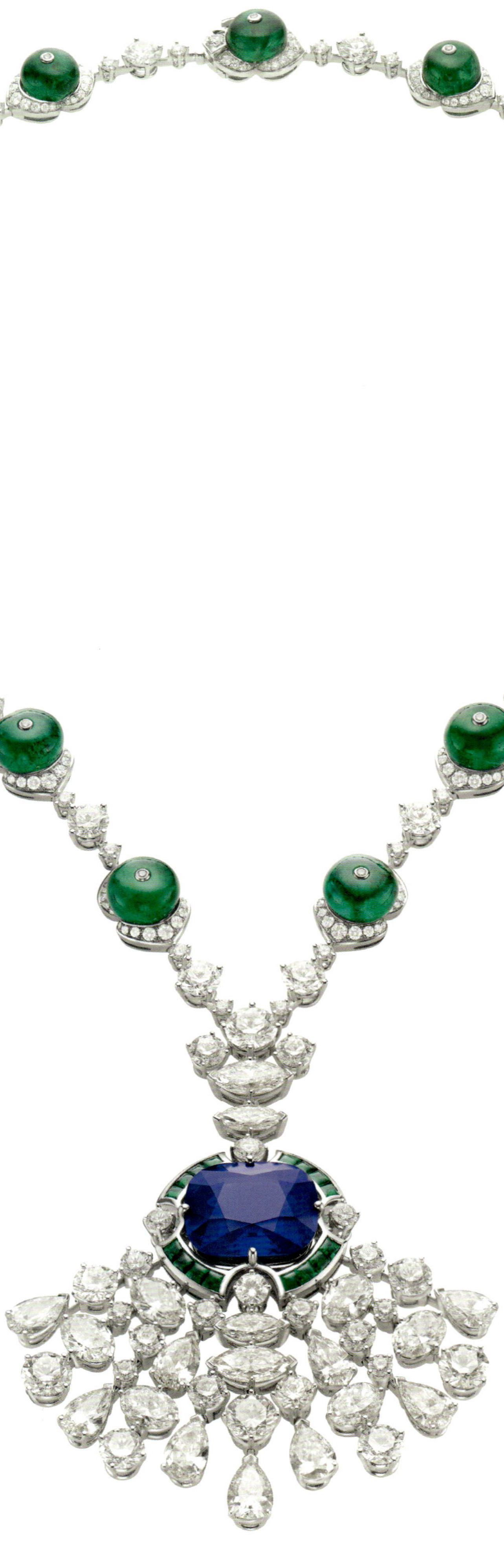

colours in order to harmonise the blues, periwinkles, purples, lilacs, roses, greens and yellows. Coming here to discover the stone at the source has become an annual appointment. I came here several times with Nicola Bulgari. At that time, the miners would come to present their stones wrapped in a piece of white cloth. The news would spread that Mr. Bulgari had come in person and hundreds of miners would gather. We did not know where to look first because there were so many sapphires. Sometimes, coming to Colombo has been a bit frightening, especially during the worst years of the civil war. It was a really dangerous expedition. There had been attacks, crimes and riots in the streets of the capital. And, of course, there was no question of venturing outside of the city. Even the journey from the airport to the hotel was not safe. During the worst two years, I had to give up my expedition."

Of course, sapphires are the main reason for her love of this island, but there is another one: the trees. In this tropical climate, saturated with heat and humidity, they burst from the earth as if they wanted to escape. It only takes a few years for vegetation to cover the most imposing house. And a very orderly garden can return to the wild in a just a few seasons. *"Trees are everywhere here,"* she explains. *"There is an extraordinary diversity that stimulates my imagination. When I see a frangipani or a rubber tree, I imagine flowers of spinels and sapphires. I believe that one of the reasons I love these trees is their common origin with stones. They have the same creative force of nature. If reincarnation existed, I think I would like to be reincarnated as a tree."*

Trees are also one of the major concerns of the Sri Lanka Gem and Jewellery Association. *"Deforestation was a dramatic problem in the 1980s,"* explains Rainier Nanayakkara. *"Thousands of hectares have been destroyed for mining. Today there is a real awareness of the dangers that all this represents. We started to replant 15,000 trees and the rules are strict. When a company begins to exploit, it must pay a deposit. If, at the end of the mine's operating period, the site is not refitted and the wells are not filled, the company will lose the deposit."*

For Rainier and other members of the association, August 2016 was marked by a decisive victory. The Sri Lankan government, through lobbying, explanations and meetings, has become aware of the importance of the ecological cost of mining, which is one of the island's main industries. Indeed, in 2015, jewellery businesses accounted for nearly $1billion in activity, employing 600,000 people, or 8% of the workforce. Sapphires represent a significant part of this turnover. The industry was given a considerable boost in 2010 when Prince William proposed to Catherine Middleton with his mother's engagement ring. Originally chosen by Lady Diana on her engagement to Prince Charles in 1981, the famous ring has 14 diamonds surrounding a stunning 12-carat oval blue sapphire, which of course came from Sri Lanka.

In August 2016, the Sri Lankan Parliament adopted a fundamental law that prohibits all mechanical exploitation. It is no longer possible to ravage entire territories by tearing up trees and blowing up the rock. Now, all mining must be done in accordance with traditional methods. The last mechanical mining licence expired in September 2016. *"This is an extremely important ecological aspect of course, but it is also of vital importance for the preservation of the resource,"* adds Lucia Silvestri. *"In some countries that have allowed massive exploitation, repeated explosions of large volumes of rocks have caused cracks in the subsoil that have repercussions on the minerals. The stones have been fractured and are often of very poor quality."*

As well as from the drainage of the river beds, the other method of mining is of course to dig pits. The work is carried out according to a very sophisticated process. The owner of the land, the director of the mine, and the miners themselves, all get a share from the result of the mining. The distribution follows a subtle formula. Eléonora Rizzuto, who heads Bulgari's Ethical Commission, follows the steps of this meticulous process. *"The coloured stones sector is an essential part of creation for Bulgari. And it was very important for me to come here to understand how it works. It is obvious that the definitive abolition of mechanical exploitation is a fundamental step in the right direction for the trade in precious stones on this island. This measure also has the advantage of keeping the activity in the hands of local populations. Of course, the working conditions of miners seem very harsh, but I think we have to look at them in context. Moreover, if we wish to improve them, it is important to organise our relations with our Sri Lankan contacts in the long term."*

Previous page, left: *In Sri Lanka, the mining of sapphires is carried out according to traditional customs and only by local miners.* **Previous page, right:** *Sapphires and rubies from the stock of Rainier Nanayakkara.* **Facing page:** *Bulgari platinum necklace from the Festa collection, set with diamonds, emeralds, emerald beads and a Kashmir cushion-cut sapphire of 16.51 carats.*

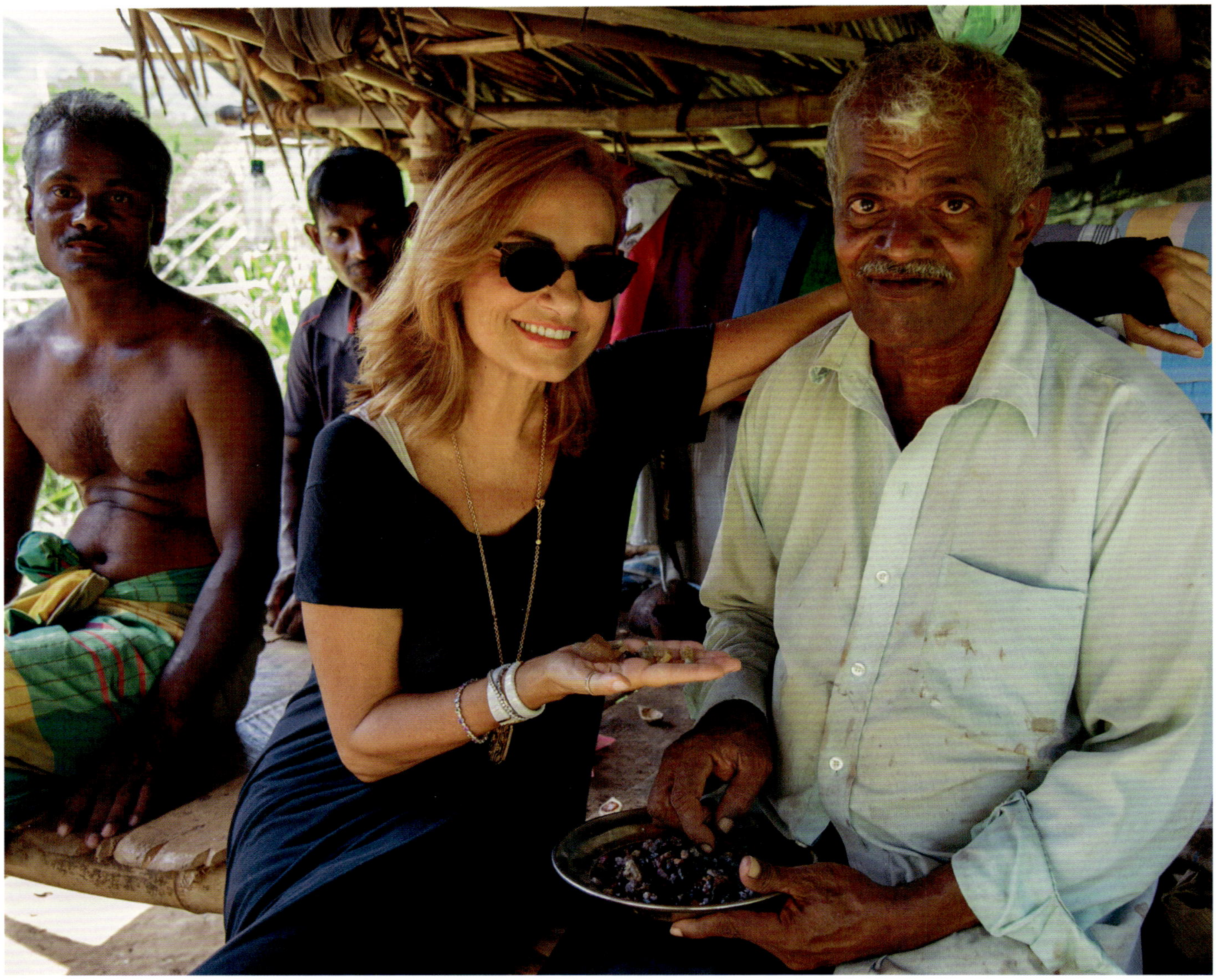

Especially if one keeps in mind the fact that, according to Rainier, *"nearly 80% of the mineral resources are still to be discovered"*. Precious stones are found all over Sri Lanka. And the so-called King of Sapphires evokes another mining region at the centre of the island, in a far wilder area: Elahera, north of the former capital of Kandy. It is there, in the middle of a much denser jungle that one finds the most beautiful sapphires of Sri Lanka. *"They have a colour, a velvety feel, reminiscent of the famous sapphires of Kashmir, the most beautiful in the world. But, in that part of the Island, even elephants are wild. It is not safe at all."*

The most secret part of the annual trip, the selection, and possibly the purchase of the stones for the next collection, takes place in Colombo, in Rainier's safe. The negotiations are long, so lunch has been prepared in one of the rooms of the safe. Dozens of small packages wrapped in pieces of white cloth appear on the table, one after the other – sapphires of all sizes, all different weights and colours. In one cloth there are approximately 200 cabochons weighing between 1 and 3 carats; the hues varying between a very light blue and a light grey. In another, the sapphires tend towards a pink. A third cloth offers different tones of yellow. Each cloth reveals 200 or 300 different cabochons. Finally come the dark blue stones. These sapphires may be destined to be the central stone on a necklace or bracelet. Lucia Silvestri watches, carefully, without making any judgment. She evaluates colour, probably estimates prices. Sometimes she passes a stone to one of her assistants to ask him to weigh it or just to look at it. *"It is the most complicated and interesting part of my*

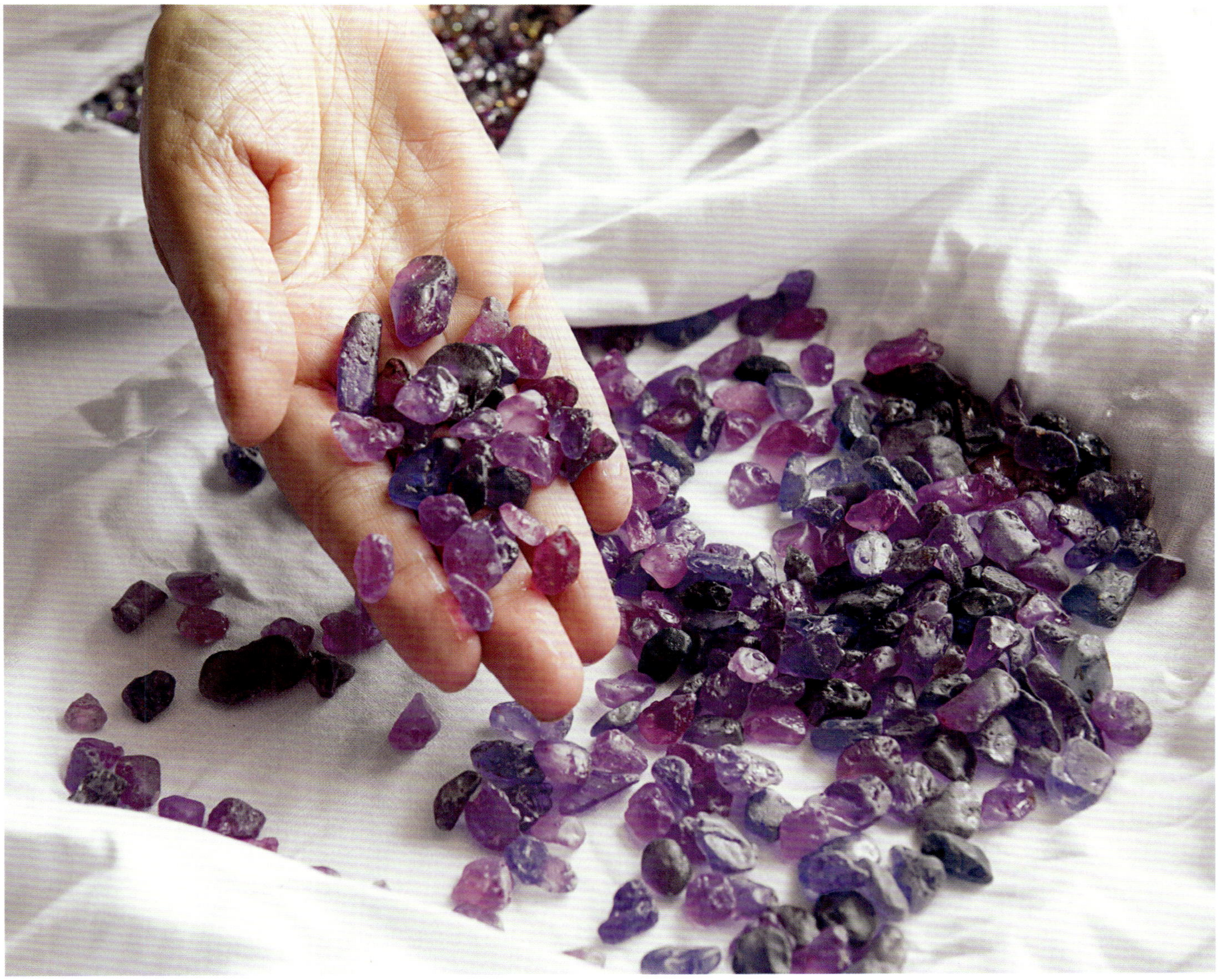

work. I know what I'm looking for. And I have to confront in my head the idea I have for the new collection and the stones that may be able to bring life to my project. I must also retain the idea of a specific financial constraint."

After more than 30 years of working at Bulgari, her eyes are formidable. Paolo Bulgari, who is often called the Lord of the Stones, trusts her completely. *"I came into the house by chance,"* she explains. *"My father was already working at Bulgari. I started working with Gianni Bulgari, then, Paolo. Very quickly, I realised that the thing that interested me was the gemstones. I am absolutely fascinated by them. I like to play with their colours, hold them in my hand, observe them. Paolo Bulgari taught me everything. For several years now, I have been travelling all over the world, to New York, Hong Kong, Jaipur, Colombo ... to choose and buy the stones. On certain, particularly important transactions, I still ask his opinion. He says I am 'his eyes'. When I am in doubt, I call him. He then asks me to grade the stone I am describing, according to its colour, its size, its weight. And we make the decision together."*

Facing page and above: *Lucia Silvestri examining sapphires from the Ratnapura mines.* **Overleaf:** *Raking the river bed is still a very popular method for finding precious stones in Sri Lanka.*

One of these most extraordinary purchases concerns the emerald cabochons of the famous Takti bracelet. It all started in India, in Jaipur. The merchant had spent the day presenting to Lucia the treasures he had amassed since her last visit. Hundreds and hundreds of pearls, rubies, sapphires and emeralds,

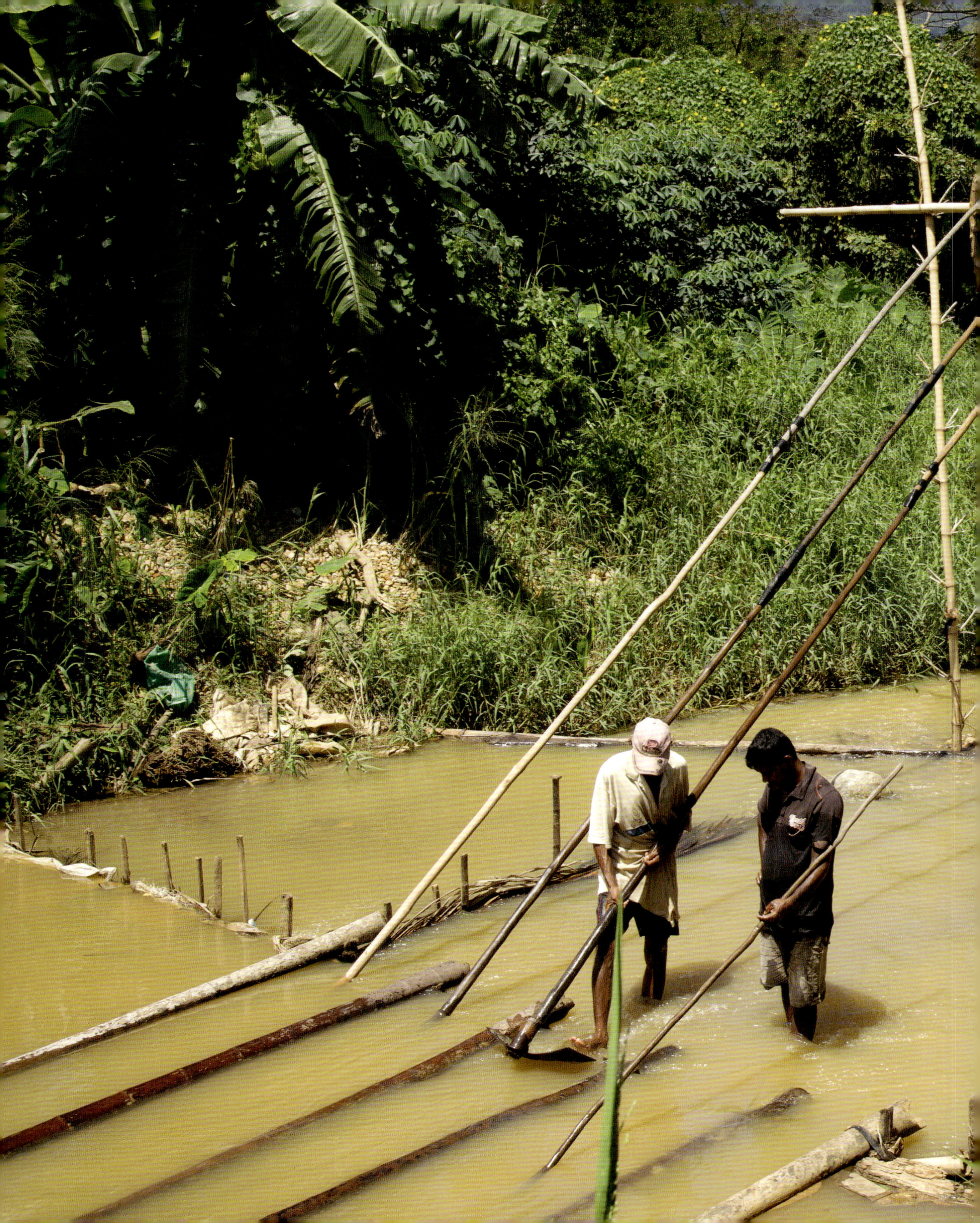

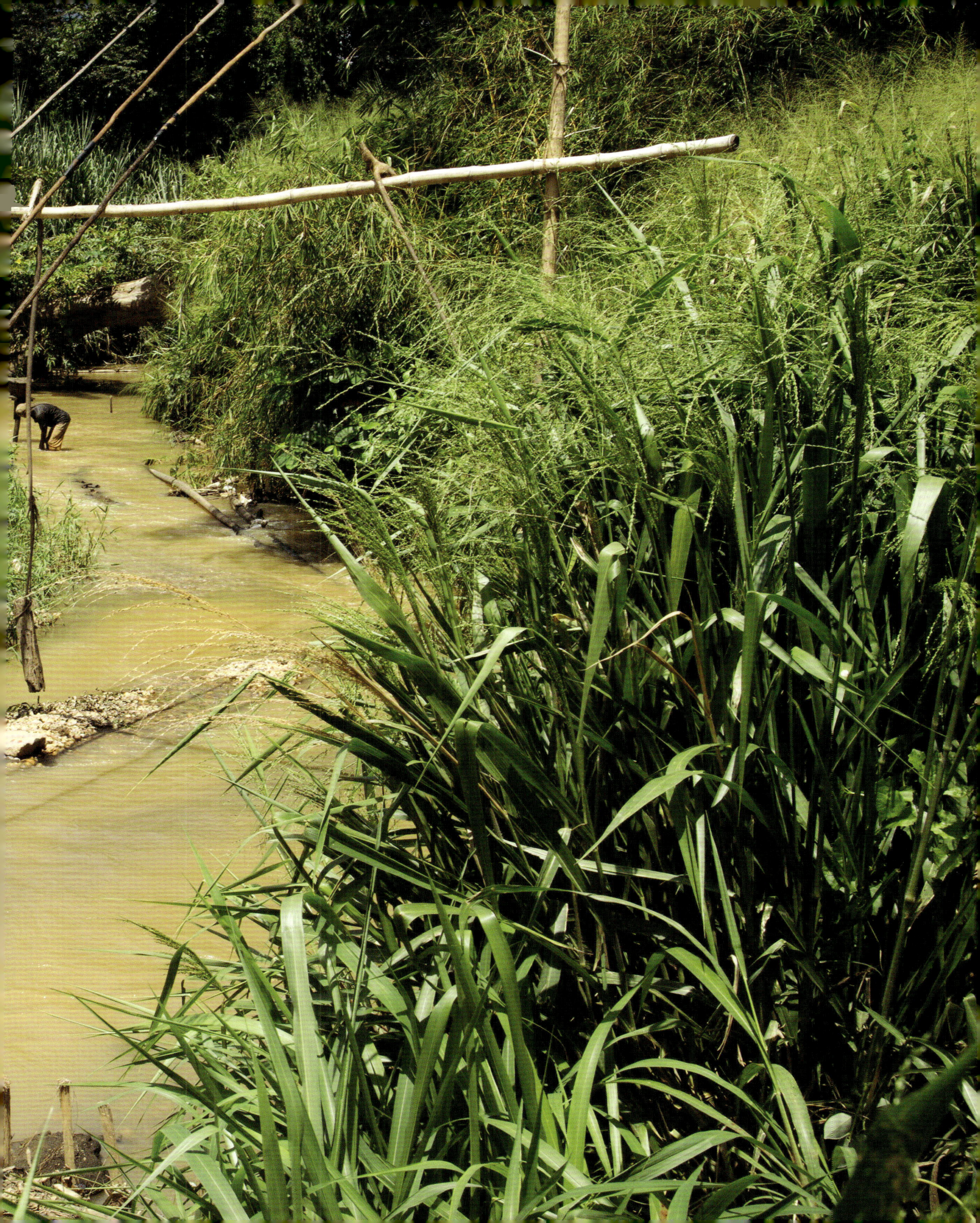

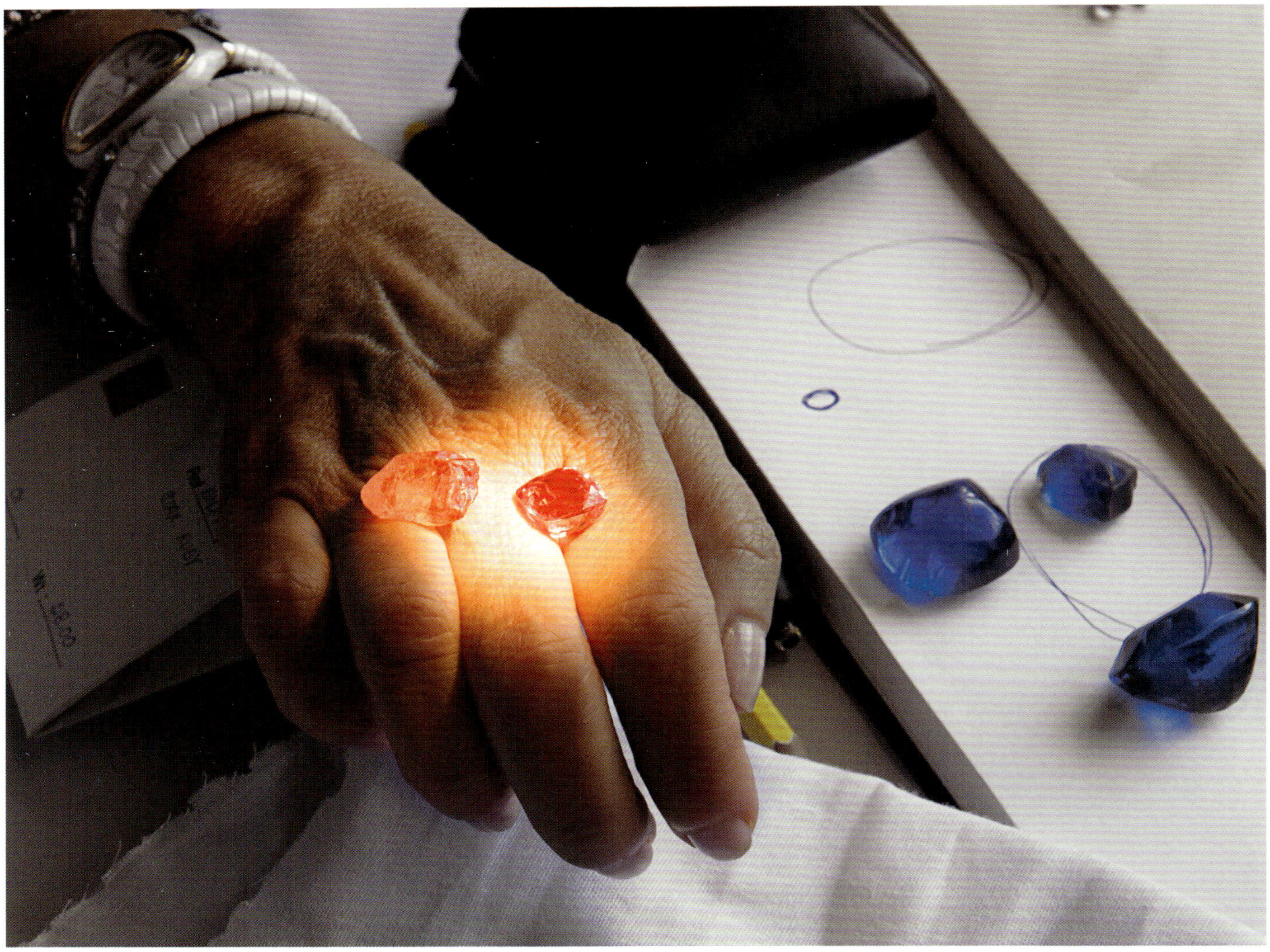

not to mention the fine stones, which were polished at length by the craftsmen of his workshops. *"It is always at the last moment, when I begin to be tired and less attentive that the important stones arrive. It is a sales technique,"* explains Lucia Silvestri. At the end of the day, from a plain velvet case, the merchant brought out large beads of cylindrical emeralds. *"They were pierced in the centre so that they could be threaded on an Indian necklace. They were African stones, recently discovered, but very important. Unfortunately, for the merchant, his emeralds were big and a little dark. There are specific Bulgari colours, codes and criteria and these emeralds did not fit into these criteria. They were far too dark. Almost to amuse myself, I told him, it would be necessary to cut them in two so that the light could enter the stones."*

A year later, Lucia was in New York and the same merchant presented her with a jewel case. Inside were the same emeralds, cut in half. *"It was a huge risk to take. Emeralds are fragile stones. They can burst when they are cut in half. This had been the case for one of these stones, which did not survive. But the result for those that had survived was extraordinary. The dark green of the emeralds had become a spring green, much brighter. That colour was perfect for Bulgari. Still, I called Paolo Bulgari, because this purchase was important. He just said: 'Buy them!' When they arrived in Rome, I was a bit anxious. Mr Bulgari opened the case. He looked at the stones and said simply, 'Brava'. Immediately, he had the idea of a bracelet. He drew the outlines of the piece in five minutes. The workshop made the final drawing. When the jewel was finished after a few months, we were dubious. Some thought it rather big. In fact, it was bought by a very petite woman, in less than five minutes."*

Another exceptional stone, which was discovered in Sri Lanka was a 321-carat cabochon sapphire. The colour was perfect, a beautiful bright blue that made

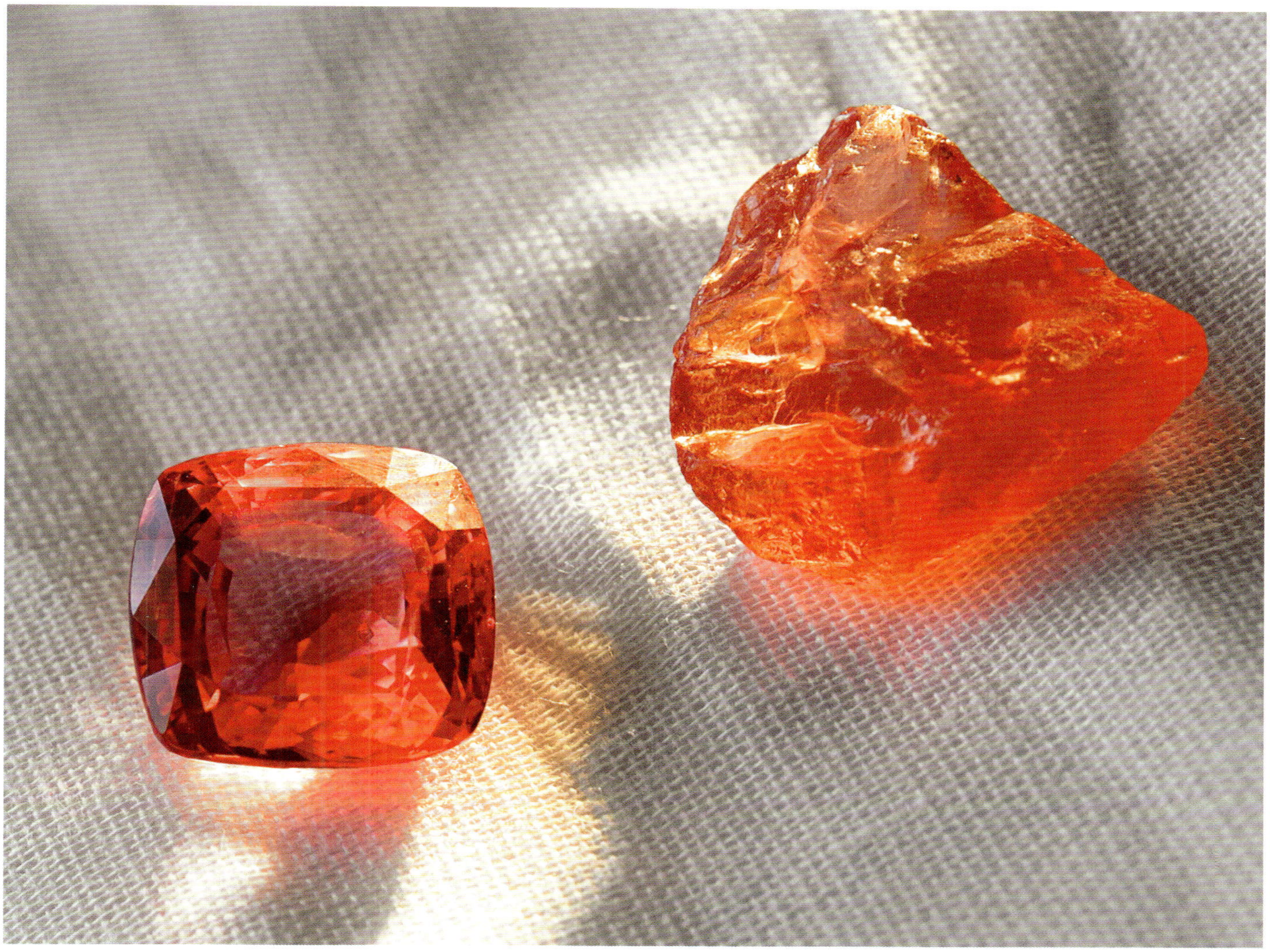

you want to touch it. But what could be done with a stone that big? That was the question. Not to mention that the new collection of fine jewellery was to be presented in just a month, so the designers had no time to prepare several projects to mount this unique sapphire. *"It was Mr. Bulgari who found the solution. He decided to hang the stone from a string of black silk. Without any mount. And again, a customer we know well bought it in under five minutes. She simply said, 'This way I can wear my sapphire anytime'."*

Unfortunately, today Rainier Nanayakkara has no stone weighing several hundred carats to show. But he does have hundreds of beautiful sapphires. Some are presented in pairs. They belong, he says, to his personal collection. He also has a few dozens rubies from Tanzania or Burma. And thousands of spinels of all sizes and colours. Around the table, everyone is waiting for the key moment of the day: the presentation of the exceptional stone, the rarest, the biggest, the blue-est. This time, it will not be "bigger" or "bluer". It will not even be unique, since Rainier has two stones of almost similar weight. From a small white handkerchief, he extracts a cushion-cut sapphire which weighs about 15 carats. Its colour is extraordinary: a flamboyant sunset in a shimmer of orange tones shaded with pink. Here is Lord Padparadscha! The "Lotus Flower". The world's rarest sapphire. Even Lucia Silvestri finds it difficult to hide her admiration for this sublime stone. She has barely had time to admire it, when Rainier opens a second handkerchief. Inside is an uncut sapphire, exactly the same tone as the first. When this second stone is cut, it will create two almost identical

Facing page and above: *Two extraordinary Padparadscha sapphires from Rainier Nanayakkara's stock.*

Padparadscha sapphires. A unique pair, whose value could be worth many millions of pounds.

Perhaps one of the two stones or both will be mounted on a necklace, a bracelet or a pair of earrings imagined by Lucia for Bulgari. Perhaps they will be discreetly sold to a client. Maybe they will stay in Rainier's trunk for a few more years. One thing is certain, he will not sell them easily, as they are unique. There is one detail that needs to be explained about the "King of Sapphires". If you were wondering about the origins of his first name, "Rainier", here is the answer. It has a Princely origin. *"I was born in 1956 and my mother was a huge fan of Grace Kelly, who at that time was the most elegant and beautiful woman in the world. When she married Prince Rainier of Monaco in 1956, the name Rainier became very popular in the whole world, even here in Sri Lanka. And my mother chose it for me."*

Facing page: *Bulgari emerald and diamond necklace from the Festa collection, set with a 53.57-carat Colombian emerald.* **Overleaf, left:** *Famous Bollywood star, Sonam Kapoor wearing a beautiful Bulgari necklace in Florence, 2015.* **Overleaf, right:** *Bulgari emerald and diamond necklace from the Festa collection, set with a cabochon Colombian emerald of 59.11 carats.*

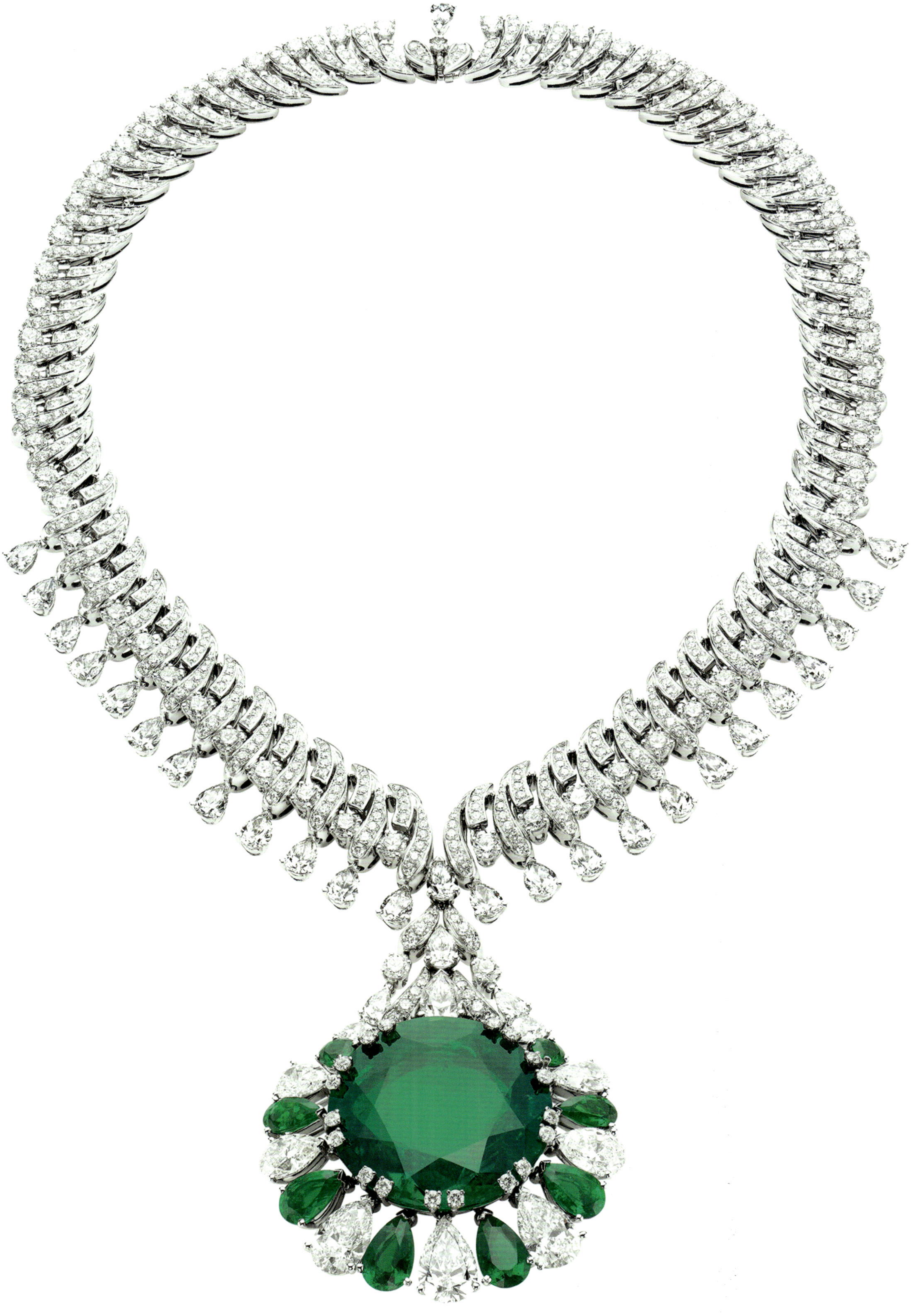

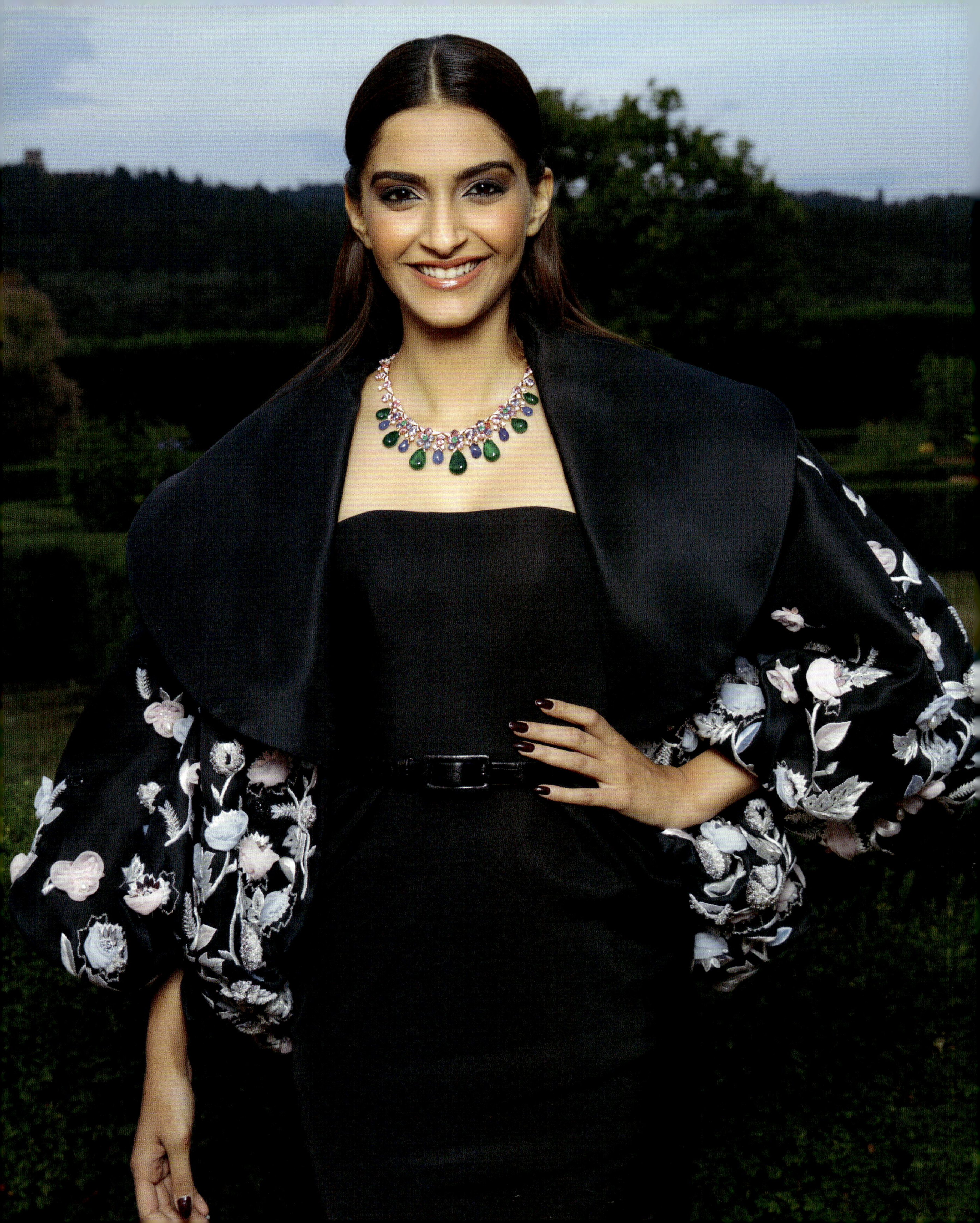

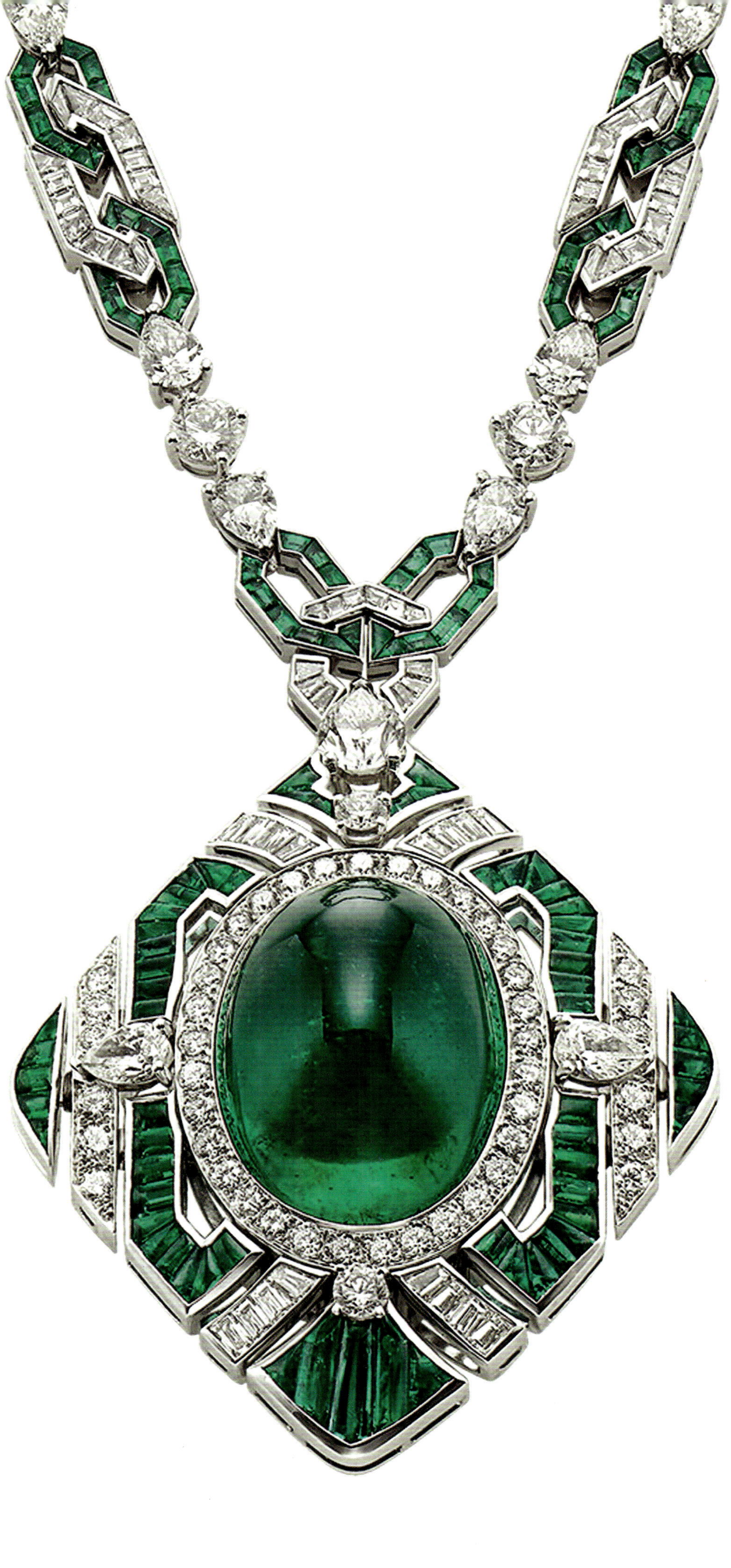

Bulgari Timeline

1823 Birth of Giorgio Boulgaris in the small village of Kalarites, in the region of Ioannina, Greece.

1832 The Constantinople treaty recognises Greece as an independent country, although the Empire region, where Kalarites and Paramythia are located, remains part of the Ottoman Empire.

1857 Birth of Sotirio Boulgaris (son of Giorgio) in Paramythia, another small Greek village, closer to the Ionian Sea.

1861 Rome is officially declared the capital of the new Italian kingdom, but the Italian armies will have to wait until 1871 before they can enter the city and end the Pope's sovereignty in Rome.

1877 Giorgio Boulgaris and his family leave Paramythia to settle in Corfu, part of the Kingdom of Greece.

1878 Giorgio Boulgaris opens a small workshop in Corfu.

1880, October Sotirio Boulgaris leaves Corfu for Naples, where he starts a business in silverware.

1881, 18 February Sotirio moves to Rome after his business in Naples has collapsed. With his associate, Demetrios Kremos, he starts manufacturing and selling small silver jewels. It is around this time that he changes his name from Boulgaris to Bulgari.

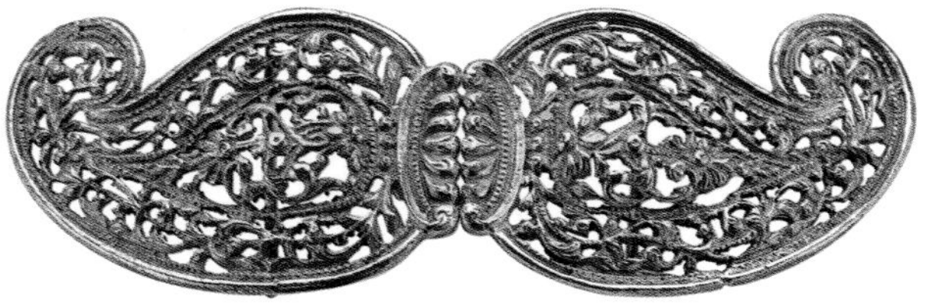

1884 Sotirio Bulgari opens his first shop on Via Sistina in Rome.

1888 Sotirio Bulgari marries Elena Basios

1889 Birth of Costantino Bulgari, first son of Sotirio and Elena Bulgari.

1890 Birth of Giorgio Bulgari, second son of Sotirio and Elena Bulgari. He will be followed by three daughters and a third son.

c.1900 Sotirio Bulgari opens his shop called 'Works of Art' on the Via dei Condotti.

1905 Opening of the Bulgari shop on 10 Via dei Condotti under the name "Old Curiosity shop". At the time, the showcases in the windows contain mainly silverware and precious objects.

1923 Costantino Bulgari marries Laura Gulienetti. They will have three daughters: Anna, Marina, Xenia. Costantino Bulgari will also have a son: Alexis.

1932, 24 November Death of Sotirio. His two sons, Costantino and and Giorgio take over the business. That same year, Giorgio Bulgari marries Leonilde Gulienetti, Laura's sister. They will have four children: Lia, Gianni, Paolo and Nicola.

1934, 9 April Inauguration of the newly refurbished Bulgari shop at number 10 Via dei Condotti, in Rome.

1935 Bulgari creates jewellery pieces included in the "Corbeille de noces" (wedding basket) for Infanta Beatriz of Spain on her marriage to Don Alessandro Torlonia, Prince of Civitella-Cesi, on 14 of February.

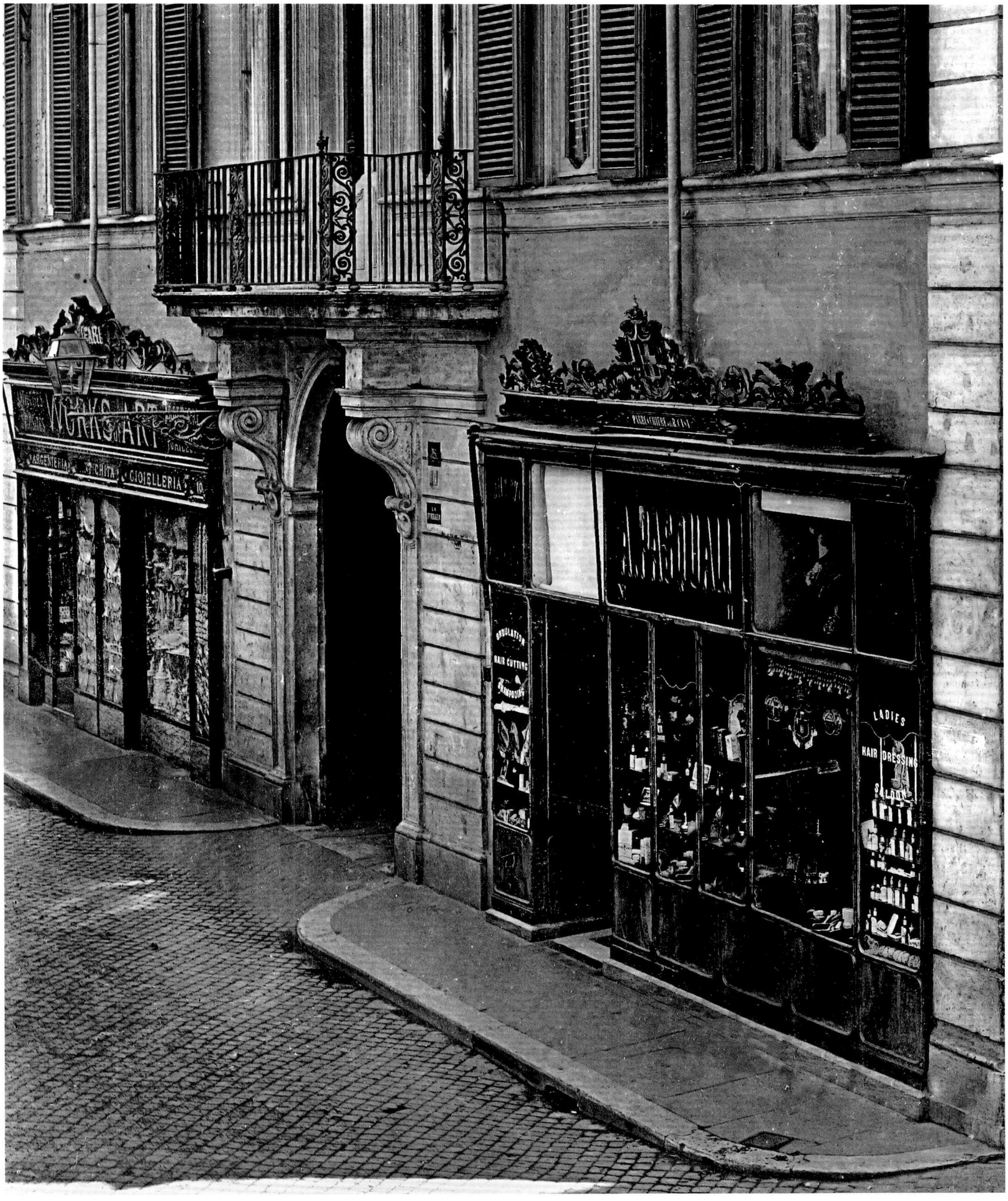

Detail of the Palazzo Lepri on Via dei Condotti, photographed by Romualdo Moscioni (1849–1925), early 1900s. Sotirio Bulgari's shop, 'Works of Art', can be seen on the left of the image. Collodion glass plate, Neg. n. MVF XI.13.1, Vatican Museum Photo Library.

Pages 286 and 288: *Silver buckles by Sotirio Bulgari, c1880. Bulgari Heritage Collection.*

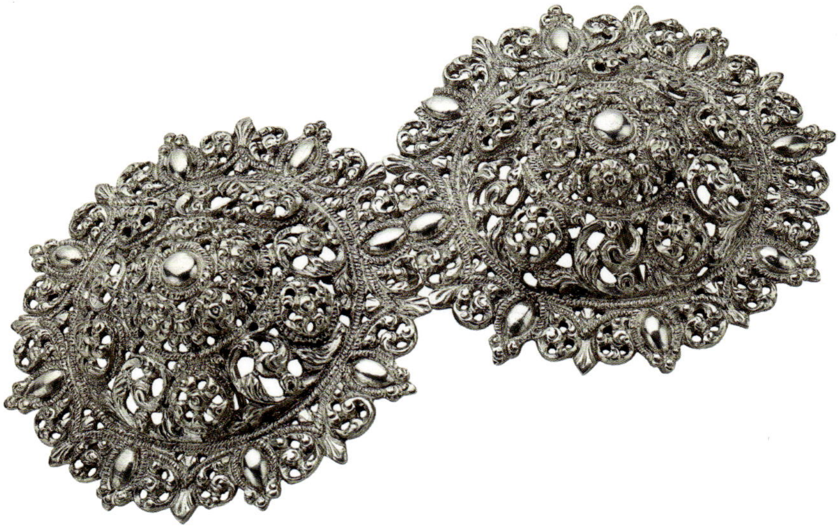

1939 Dorothy di Frasso buys her legendary diamond necklace.

1948 Anna Bulgari starts working at Bulgari with her father Costantino. Her sister, Marina will join them a few years later. Giorgio's three sons, Gianni, Paolo and Nicola will also join the firm in the 1950s and 1960s.

1949, 27 January Tyrone Power marries Linda Christian in Rome.

1951 *Quo Vadis*, the first international movie epic filmed in Cinecittà, starring Deborah Kerr and Robert Taylor, is released. It is a huge success both in America and Europe.

1953, April Clare Boothe Luce, the new American Ambassador to Italy arrives in Naples.

1953, August HM the Shah of Iran and his wife, Queen Soraya, arrive in Rome. Their exile will last just three days.

1954, March King Farouk of Egypt's treasures are sold at auction in Cairo.

1963 *Cleopatra* is released. The film has taken three years to film. During the filming in Rome, Elizabeth Taylor and Richard Burton discover Bulgari.

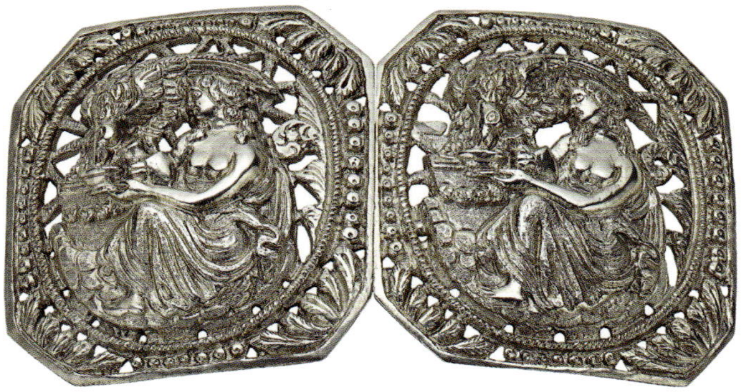

1965, 26 June Princess Olimpia Torlonia marries Paul-Annik Weiller in Rome. The bride wears her mother's Bulgari tiara.

1966 Death of Giorgio Bulgari. His wife Leonilde will survive him by 40 years; passing away in 2004, at the age of 102. Laura Bulgari also dies in 1966.

1973 Death of Costantino Bulgari.

1975 Gianni Bulgari is kidnapped while driving home. He will be freed after a month in captivity on the payment of a ransom.

1976 Marina Bulgari leaves the firm.

1983, 19 November Anna Bulgari and her son Giorgio Calissoni are kidnapped. They will be freed after 35 days of detention and the payment of a huge ransom.

1984 Anna Bulgari leaves the firm. She will remain a consultant on silver until 1990.

1987 Gianni Bulgari leaves the firm.

2011 The LVMH Luxury group acquires Bulgari.

Acknowledgements

Writing this book would not have been possible without Jean Christophe Babin, CEO of Bulgari. I would like to thank him very sincerely for his trust.

Madame Anna Bulgari Calissoni, Monsieur Paolo Bulgari and Monsieur Nicola Bulgari have given me their time and information generously.

I would like to express my admiration for their knowledge.

Princess Olimpia Torlonia (Madame Paul-Annik Weiller) has been very generous and helpful. Without her, much of this book would not have been written. I also want to thank Princess Maria Camilla Pallavicini and her family for allowing us to reproduce within these pages an amazing piece of jewellery.

HRH The Duchess of Castro and her mother, Madame Edoarda Crociani have, as always, been an enormous help; and I thank them very sincerely.

During a memorable lunch, Madame Marisela Federici recreated for me the ambiance of the Bulgari boutique in Rome during the 1970s. It was very kind of her.

Carla Liuni, Lucia Boscaini, Carlotta Sapia, Caterina Riccardi, and all the people at Bulgari – too many to mention here – have been most helpful, and I thank them sincerely.

One lady deserves a special mention here, and that is Monica Brannetti. She has been with me since the very first day I started working on this book. She has been kind, helpful, encouraging, always happy to organise meetings, visits and photographic shoots.

I also want to mention two people who are no longer with Bulgari, but they have supported the book from the beginning: Sabina Belli and Stéphane Gerschel. Thank you to you both.

Talking about beginnings: the whole idea of this book started four years ago during a meeting with Véronique Lépinay from Bulgari France. She is the one who brought me to Rome for the first time, many years ago. Her constant help, ideas and friendship have made all the difference. Thank you so much for everything you have done, Véronique. And I would like to extend my thanks also to Marie-Noëlle Barrere, President of Bulgari France. She has been very understanding about my project, the time I needed to meet people, my special requests. Thank you, Marie-Noëlle.

And, of course, I would also like to send all my love to my "fairy godmother" at Bulgari, the queen of precious stones, Lucia Silvestri.

Thank you for all those special moments in Rome, in Sri Lanka, in Paris, in Venice.

All my friends in the jewellery bussiness have given me time, images and information and they all deserve a very special thank you: Fernando Bustillo and Thomas Tolan at FD Gallery in New York; Sophie Dufresne and Pierre Mothes at Sotheby's Paris. Beverly Bueninck at Christie's Paris. Etudes Beaussant Lefèvre and Gros & Delettrez in Paris.

I would also like to thank Julio Piatti who took most of the wonderful photographs for Chapter 12, and David Atlan, who took the wonderful portrait of Sonam Kapoor, also in Chapter 12.

And of course, a very special thank you to all the people who have helped me working on this book at VM publications, Editions Télémaque and ACC Art Books.

Image Credits

Bulgari: Antonio Barrella, Studio Orizzonte: 5, 8, 23, 26, 27, 34, 35, 40 (2), 43, 46, 50 (2), 51, 53, 57, 64-65, 66, 70, 78-79, 83, 87, 88, 93, 94, 100, 105, 106-107, 129, 130, (2), 131 (2), 162 (2), 163 (2), 164 (2), 165, 170, 173 (2), 175, 179, 181, 182, 184 (2), 187 (2), 198-199, 206-207, 208, 213, 217, 224, 226-227, 243, 251, 253, 255, 264, 268, 272, 281, 283, 286, 288 (2): Gaio Bacci – Roma: 222; Gian Paolo Barbieri: 2; John Bigelow: 237; Monica Brannetti: 239; Bulgari Historical Archive: 11, 12, 25, 31 (2), 62, 72 bottom, 74-75, 77, 117 (bottom), 138-139, 140, 141 (3), 142, 143, 144 (4), 145, 146, 147, 148 (2 sketches), 238

AGE: G. Dagli-Orti/DEA: 15; Keystone Picture USA/ Zumapress: 154-155

AKG Images: Austrian Archives/Imagno: 32; Documenta/ Album: 76; Ullstein Bild: 102; Mondadori Portfolio: 134; Pierluigi Praturion/Reporters Associati & Archivi/ Mondadori Portfolio: 174

David Atlan: 282

Bridgeman Images: Fratelli/Alinari: 20; Arando Bruni/ Alinari: 21

Christie's: 14, 85, 90, 96, 158 (2), 166, 189, 197, 203, 233, 241, 247, 249, 260, 261, 262, 263

Collection Christophe L: 124-125, 183; RnB/Metro Goldwin Mayer/D. R.: 168; RnB © Twentieth Century Fox Films Corporation/MCL Film SA/Walwa Films SA: 178

CPVM: 16, 17, 19 (2), 24, 48-49, 52, 58, 63, 236, 248

Crescenzi Historical Archive: 110

Courtesy of Beaussant Lefèvre: 98-99, 108, 135, 137, 148-149

Courtesy of Gros & Delettrez, Paris: 150, 160

Courtesy of FD Gallery, Tony Falcone Studios: 6, 37, 81, 101, 228, 240, 296

Gamma Rapho: Keystone France: 44, 128, 161, 204; Hervé Gloaguen/Rapho: 242

Getty: Bettmann: 10, 38, 113, 171, 180; George Rinhart/ Corbis Historical: 18; Edward Steichen/Condé Nast Collection: 29, 84; Hank Walter/The Life Picture Collection: 54; Slim Aarons: 68, 112, 114, 117 top; Archivio Cameraphoto/Hulton Archive: 71; Stephane Cardinale/ Corbis: 104; Camerique/Archive Photos: 120; Gordon Parks/The Life Picture Collection: 122; Pictorial Parade/ Archive Photos: 123 right; Fox Photos: 156; Archive Photos: 177; Ray Bellisario/Popperfoto: 185; Earl Leaf/Michael Oachs Archives: 186; Jerry Engel/New York Post Archives © NYP Holdings: 192; Mel Finkelstein/New York Daily News Archive: 196; Diana Walker/The Life Picture Collection: 232; Clifford Coffin/Condé Nast Collection: 234

Hampel Fine Arts Auctions, Munich: 200, 201

Leemage: National Maritime Museum, Greenwich: 39; Photo Re-Pubblic: 72 top left, 72 top right, 82; Farabola: 80, 126; MP Portfolio: 123 left, 132, 176

Madame Paul-Annik Weiller: 210, 214-215, 216, 218 (4), 220-221

The Metropolitan Museum of Art New York, Robert Lehman Collection, 1975: 152, 159

Olycom: Publiphoto: 244

Julio Piatti: 266-267, 270, 271, 274, 275, 276-277, 278, 279

Qatar Museum – National Collection of Qatar: 60-61

Rue des Archives: Everett: 22, 36

Sipa Press: Huffschmitt: 97; AP: 225; Neville Marriner/ Daily Mail/Rex/Shutterstock: 230

Sotheby's: 73, 95, 103, 190, 194 (2), 195, 257; The Cecil Beaton Studio Archive at Sotheby's: 259

Taylor Family Archives: 119

Vatican Museum Photo Library: 287

Index

Page numbers in **bold** refer to images

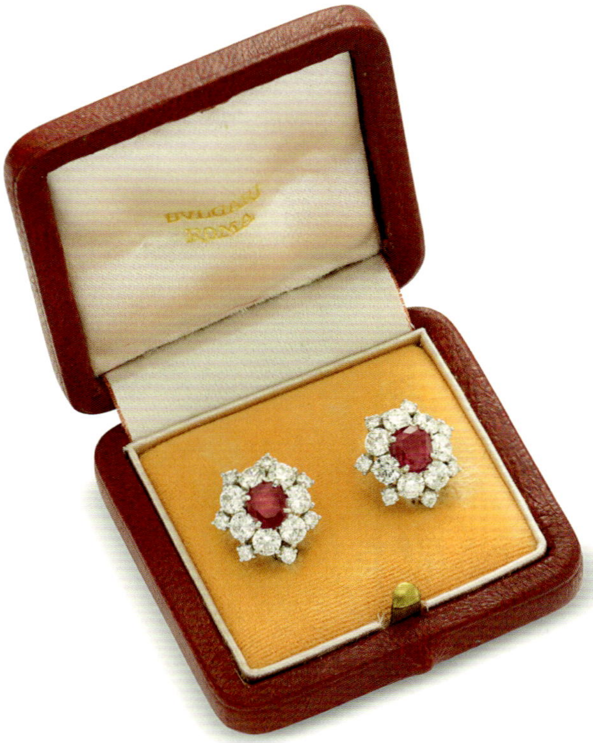